OPERATION 'TORCH'
THE INVASION OF NORTH AFRICA
THEN AND NOW

The Allied invasion of Africa was a most peculiar venture of armed forces into the field of international politics; we were invading a neutral country to create a friend.

GENERAL DWIGHT D. EISENHOWER, 1948

OPERATION 'TORCH'
THE INVASION OF NORTH AFRICA
THEN AND NOW

Jean Paul Pallud

Credits

ISBN: 9 781870 067 966
© *After the Battle* 2019

PUBLISHERS
Battle of Britain International Ltd
The Mews, Hobbs Cross House,
Hobbs Cross, Old Harlow,
Essex CM17 0NN

Telephone: 01279 41 8833.
Fax: 01279 41 9386
E-mail: hq@afterthebattle.com
Website: *www.afterthebattle.com*

PRINTERS
SRP Ltd, Exeter EX2 7LW, UK.

FRONT COVER
American troops landing at the Centre Task Force landing near Oran on the morning of November 8.

PAGES 2-3
Near Arzew, on Z White Beach, engineers are laying steel matting over the sand to provide a firmer foothold for wheeled vehicles.

PAGES 8-9
The 'Riviera' conference in August 1941 between Prime Minister Churchill and President Roosevelt was held on board ships anchored in Placentia Bay, Newfoundland. With the United States still officially at peace, this meeting was only able to discuss possible joint action against Germany sometime in the future, this photo being taken at the conclusion of the Sunday church service held on the after deck of the HMS *Prince of Wales* on August 10. Standing behind them are Admiral Ernest J. King, Commander in Chief, US Atlantic Fleet; General George C. Marshall, Chief-of-Staff of the US Army; General Sir John Dill, Chief of the Imperial General Staff; Admiral Harold R. Stark, US Navy Chief of Naval Operations; and Admiral Sir Dudley Pound, the First Sea Lord.

PAGES 58-59
The assault goes in on Z Beaches near Oran. The forces landing in the Zebra sector — the US 16th, 18th and 26th Regimental Combat Teams, a Combat Command from the 1st Armored Division, and the 1st Ranger Battalion — were the bulk of the Centre Task Force.

PAGES 152-153
The Axis reacted swiftly to the Operation 'Torch' landings and quickly organised a massive reinforcement by air and sea to move troops and supplies to Tunisia. These Fallschirmjägers were pictured in Tunis. By November 25, the Axis forces in Tunisia totalled some 25,000 troops.

PAGES 196-197
Beginning on February 23, Axis forces began pulling back on the Kasserine front but the Allies were slow to react and when they finally advanced at dawn on the 25th contact with the withdrawing Axis forces had been lost. On the 26th Signal Corps photographer George McGray pictured elements of the 2nd Battalion, 16th Infantry, moving down the Kasserine Pass along the road from Tébessa.

East of the Oran bight, near Arzew, unloading was in full swing on one of the Z Beaches during the morning of November 8.

PAGES 254-255
By the afternoon of May 8, the First Army drive to Tunis had split the Axis forces into two. The larger part was east of Tunis where von Arnim attempted to build up a new defence line across the base of the Cap Bon peninsula. Meanwhile the northern group was surrounded by II Corps in the hills east and south of Bizerte where a photographer from the US Signal Corps pictured these German POWs.

FRONT ENDPAPER
On November 10, American troops were pictured disembarking in the Oran sector from British landing craft.

REAR ENDPAPER
The Centre Task Force at Oran experienced the lowest number of landing craft becoming casualties, with only 20 per cent losses, and on November 9, the day after the first landings, *LCM 159* was pictured grounded on the beach at Les Andalouses near Oran. By comparison, at Algiers the Eastern Task Force suffered appalling losses of some 90 per cent and off Morocco the Western Task Force 34 per cent.

REAR COVER
Nick Parrino, Office of War Information photographer, pictured enthusiastic civilians cheering and waving tricolour as the Allies enter Tunis.

ACKNOWLEDGEMENTS
The author is indebted to the following for their invaluable help: Ad'O. Azeddine Afila. Mohammed Riadh Benbouali. Amine Bouattour. Continent 8 Technologies Ltd. Nabila Bouazzaoui. François Denis. Xavier Driencourt, French Ambassador in Algeria. Abdelatif Djerboua. Saidou Ellul. Abdellatif Ettadely. Aziz Lazrak. Majid Majid. Gérard Ménard and Christophe Jean, French Consuls at Oran. Alan Waters. Arif Yelles.

Office of War Information photographer Nick Parrino pictured an enthusiastic crowd waving the French tricolour as the Allies enter Tunis.

Contents

Introduction

Touring the Operation 'Torch' battlefield, at Safi Jean-Paul was thrilled to find the old French coastal battery in such good repair. This is the fire control post where the battery commander, Lieutenant de Vaisseau Jean Laporte, was killed in November 1942.

Operation 'Torch' — the invasion of North Africa — was mainly born out of political considerations when President Roosevelt sent a note to Josef Stalin to announce that a Second Front was to be opened in the West in 1942.

'Torch' was launched against the most unlikely of foes — neutral French North Africa — and far from the strategic realities of the on-going battle in Libya. Norman Gelb in *Desperate Venture, the Story of Operation 'Torch'* (1992) argued that the operation could be questioned as to whether 'it was the right operation, in the right place, at the right time'. However, Vincent P. O'Hara, author of *Torch: North Africa and the Allied Path to Victory* (2015), says that the long series of defeats in Libya and Egypt had sapped the confidence of the British armies and, together with the US Army's lack of combat experience, it required an operation where the Allies could achieve a clear and swift victory. To this end, the 'landings in Morocco and western Algeria do not seem such poor choices'.

Roosevelt had shown an early interest in North African projects and late in 1940, long before America was in the war, he had sent diplomat Robert D. Murphy to French North Africa. Murphy made promising contacts with pro-Allied groupings but the Allied leaders failed to actively engage these groups in the planning of 'Torch', leaving them completely in the dark until a few hours before the landings. This prevented them from organising a major take-over that could have assured that the landings were completely unopposed.

'Torch' was an ambitious and risky endeavour. Despite a shortage of landing craft, the limited training of their crews and beach parties and, more generally, the very limited experience of the Allies in amphibious operations, the initial co-ordinated landings along thousands of miles of coastline, from the Mediterranean shores near Algiers and Oran to the Atlantic coast of Morocco, were successfully accomplished.

Though taken by surprise, the Axis command reacted quickly and moved a large contingent of troops to Tunisia with little Allied interference. This failure caused the Allies to be drawn into a six-month campaign in Tunisia before clearing Axis presence along the southern shore of the Mediterranean.

While the military achievements of 'Torch' were modest, it was a major political success as it helped bring the French back into the war. Within a year, France had a strong corps fighting in Italy and, although political tensions remained, Général de Gaulle had firmly established himself as the leader of all the French forces fighting with the Allies.

At the 'Riviera' Conference in 1941, President Roosevelt had confirmed his support for the Atlantic Charter, and his insistence in including the term 'all peoples' brought the British and French colonial systems into question. In January 1943 at Casablanca, the President made clear what he meant and his encouragement to Sultan Mohammed V gave a major boost to Moroccan aspirations for independence.

Operation 'Torch' has received less attention in literature than other operations. In English, three books — one British and two American — are considered to be the official histories. *History of United States Naval Operations in World War II; Operations in North African Waters, October 1942-June 1943* by Samuel Eliot Morison was published in 1947; *The US Army in World War II, Northwest Africa, Seizing the Initiative in the West* by George F. Howe appeared in 1957, and *The Destruction of The Axis Forces in Africa* by Major-General Ian Playfair followed in 1966.

The French side of the story was told by Jacques Mordal in his book *La Bataille de Casablanca, 8-9-10 Novembre 1942* published in 1952, while the official French reference about Operation 'Torch', *Les Débarquements alliés en Afrique du Nord* authored by René Caroff, was published in 1960. Among the other accounts published later is *An Army at Dawn, The War in North Africa, 1942-1943*, by Rick Atkinson in 2002, which won the Pulitzer Prize for History.

Morison, Howe and Playfair, and all early books in English language, neglected French sources so it follows that their accounts contain factual errors and speculations, Illustrating this general neglect is the epic imagery repeatedly used to depict the daring raid of HMS *Hartland* and HMS *Walney* into the harbour at Oran. The *Walney* was described as being raked by devastating fire from *La Surprise*, misidentified as a destroyer. She was a much smaller and less powerful vessel, and French reports make it clear that she never opened fire on the *Walney* at all. Instead it was the fire from the destroyers *Épervier* and *Tramontane*, together with that of three smaller ships, which sank the *Walney*.

Accounts published prior to 1973 were unable to mention the existence of Ultra — the Allied ability to intercept and decrypt top secret German coded messages. We now know that during the preparatory period and throughout the operation, Ultra kept the Allies informed of German knowledge and intentions. For example, it led the Allies to conclude that the Germans were fully unaware of the coming operation. Ultra also kept the Allies informed of German plans regarding Vichy France and the occupation of the Zone Libre. Ultra then provided information as to the forces being hastily moved to Tunisia and then throughout the six months of battle there.

This book is my second effort to chronicle the Second World War in North Africa. Taking comparison photographs in every corner of Muammar Gaddafi's Libya in 2010 for my earlier volume *The War in the Desert Then and Now* was an interesting experience. However, starting in Tunisia in December 2010, the Arab Spring quickly spread, the governments being overthrown in Egypt, Tunisia, and in Libya where Gaddafi met his end in February 2011. Civil wars broke out in Syria and Iraq and Islamist terrorist attacks multiplied all over the world.

Morocco kept a relatively good record on terrorism, though the country experienced one major attack in 2011. Traveling through this hospitable country in March 2019 was an enjoyable experience. Although security forces were present as the terrorist threat remained, I was still able to take photos anywhere without attracting attention. However, at Mohammédia, I was firmly told that taking photos of a Royal Residence was strictly forbidden (see page 144).

Tunisia suffered two major terrorist attacks in 2015 in which tourists were targetted. Security forces still actively conduct operations in those areas along the borders with Libya and Algeria due to cross-border terrorist activity, and unfortunately the freedom that I had enjoyed while touring Tunisia in 2006 was now no longer possible. In the Kasserine sector for example, the Djebel Chambi and Djebel Semmama that provided the background to so many of the photos of Rommel's enterprise in January and February of 1943 are now no-go areas.

Algeria presented an even greater challenge. The country experienced a harsh internal war against armed Islamist groups for nearly a decade until an amnesty was agreed in 1999 allowing Islamist fighters not guilty of murder or rape to escape all prosecution if they turned themselves in. The remaining active rebel groups were progressively destroyed by army operations over the next few years. However, in 2019 French and British Foreign Offices were still warning that terrorist attacks could target foreigners anywhere in the country and that it was not advisable to travel near the border with Tunisia. I therefore achieved my comparisons with the help of local friends though not without difficulty.

I was pleased to have traced a nice series of photos of the landings on Beer Beach, west of Algiers (see pages 68-70), but in 2016 my photographer experienced major difficulties, including arrest and interrogation, when trying to take photos on this beach. Also attempting to take matching shots from the sea of the landing craft approach to the beach turned out to be a frustrating experience as patrol boats prevented any close approach. It turned out that the whole area — the Club des Pins sector — was now a highly secure state compound with a Presidential residence, and with many villas occupied by the privileged few. The reason why my photographer immediately became suspect was that the Club des Pins was to the population a bitter symbol of the undue benefits obtained by those close to the regime, hence it was a very sensitive area. In massive demonstrations in the spring of 2019, the Algerian people proclaimed their rejection of this regime and their will to see major changes.

Finally, to return to the legacy of Operation 'Torch', after the war General Eisenhower wrote that 'within the African theatre, one of the greatest products of the victory was the progress achieved in the welding of Allied unity and the establishment of a command team that was already showing the effects of a growing confidence and trust among all its members.'

JEAN PAUL PALLUD, 2019

Strategy

On April 9, 1940, Hitler launched invasions of Denmark and Norway followed one month later by attacks on Holland, Belgium, Luxembourg and France. By mid-June, as German troops threatened Paris, the French government pulled out of the capital to the south-west, finally reaching Bordeaux on the 14th. While Maréchal Philippe Pétain formed a new government with those resigned to the defeat, and requested an armistice on June 17, Général Charles de Gaulle, the Under-Secretary of State for National Defence and War in the last government, flew to England and on the 18th launched an appeal over the BBC to continue the fight against Nazi Germany. The armistice with Germany was signed on June 22 (a separate agreement was also reached with Italy) and hostilities ceased three days later. The armistice divided France into two parts: an Occupied Zone which comprised northern France and the length of the Atlantic Coast, while the remaining two-fifths of the country, south of a 'Demarcation Line', would be under the French government established at Vichy.

Meanwhile, the French Navy sailed from the ports in France, away from any German threat, but on July 3, as a statement of British resolve, Prime Minister Winston Churchill directed the Royal Navy to attack the Fleet of his ally anchored at Mers el Kébir in Algeria. The old battleship *Bretagne* was sunk, several ships were damaged and 1,300 French sailors lost their lives. The ill-advised operation irretrievably damaged relations between Britain and France, strengthening the authority of Vichy all over the empire, while badly undermining de Gaulle's effort to recruit French soldiers and sailors to fight with him alongside the British. Following the attack, on July 5 the Vichy government broke off diplomatic relations with the United Kingdom.

On May 10, 1940, the Wehrmacht invaded Belgium and the Low Countries and within five weeks the Blitzkrieg offensive had defeated both the French armies and the British Expeditionary Force. On June 14 the Germans entered Paris, soon marching past the Place de l'Étoile with its striking monument commemorating Napoléon's victories.

On August 7 the British Government recognised de Gaulle as 'Chief of all the Free French, wherever they may be, who may join you to defend the Allied cause'.

However, President Franklyn D. Roosevelt chose instead to cultivate the Vichy regime and Washington quickly granted the government of Maréchal Pétain full diplomatic recognition. American embassy staff relocated to the town of Vichy and the new Ambas-

sador, William D. Leahy, presented his credentials to the French Head of State in January 1941. Remarkably, full American diplomatic representation was to be maintained at Vichy even after Pearl Harbor and the state of war with Germany,

At the end of 1940, when British forces advancing from Egypt defeated the Italians in Libya, and went on to capture Benghazi, there was a distinct possibility of pushing on westwards to

Article 2 of the armistice signed on June 22 provided that 'to assure the interests of the German Reich', German forces would occupy the northern and western parts of France (known in French as the 'Zone Occupée'). Nearly 1,200 kilometres long, the demarcation line ran from the Spanish border at Hendaye to the Swiss frontier near Bellegarde. Out of a total

of 90 departments of France, the Germans occupied 42 entirely, 13 partially, while 35 were not occupied. *Left:* This was the checkpoint set up at the bridge over the Valserine river at Bellegarde, as seen from the 'Zone Occupée'. *Right:* Built in 1908 for a tramway line that ceased to run in 1937, the bridge is still known locally as the Pont du Tram.

join with the French in Tunisia in a French renewal of hostilities against the Axis. However, that opportunity failed to materialise after the Germans sent the Afrikakorps to save the situation in Libya. Nevertheless, the military potential of the French colonies in north-western Africa, either as a friend or foe, remained a major strategic preoccupation for the British Chiefs-of-Staff.

In the summer of 1940, Commander Roscoe H. Hillenkoetter, the US Naval Attaché at Vichy, travelled to French North Africa to assess the situation there. He was surprised to find that the French were still administering their territories as if nothing had happened, with only a few German and Italian members of the Armistice Commission in evidence. He discovered that the French military establishment there was far stronger than he had expected and he was encouraged to see that these officers and men were all confident that they could protect and control their African empire. 'If France is going to fight again anywhere in this war, I believe North Africa will be the place', wrote Hillenkoetter.

His report, together with an assessment of the political and diplomatic situation in Vichy by the Chargé d'Affaires, Robert D. Murphy, was relayed to the State Department whereupon President Roosevelt asked Murphy to come to

The unoccupied part of France was administered by the Vichy government headed by Maréchal Philippe Pétain, the venerated hero of Verdun. Hoping to obtain concessions and a peace treaty, the Vichy administration showed itself increasingly prepared to collaborate with the Germans. The old Maréchal was highly popular, photographed here being greeted in front of his office in the Rue du Parc in Vichy in the spring of 1942.

Most countries, from the USA to the Soviet Union, and including Canada and Australia, granted the Vichy government full diplomatic recognition. The American Embassy relocated to Vichy in the summer of 1940 and a new Ambassador, William D. Leahy, presented his credentials to Pétain at his private residence at the Pavillon Sévigné in January 1941. *Left:* Introduced to the Maréchal on this occasion, the staff at the embassy comprised Lieutenant Commander Roscoe D. Hillenkoetter, the Naval Attaché, (who became the first director of the newly-established CIA in 1947); Major Robert A. Schow, the Military Attaché; Lieutenant Commander Cato D. Glover, Naval Attaché; William C. Trimble, Vice-Consul, and Douglas MacArthur II, (a nephew of General Douglas MacArthur) as the embassy secretary. *Below left:* In May 1942, following the sudden death of his predecessor, the new Japanese Ambassador at Vichy, Takonobu Mitani, visited Pétain to present his credentials.

Above right: The Pavillon Sévigné, located at No. 50 Boulevard du Président Kennedy, is now a private residence.

In June 1940, whilst Pétain and his government were resigned to the defeat and requested an armistice, Général Charles de Gaulle, the Under-Secretary of State for National Defence and War in the previous government, flew to England and on June 18 launched an appeal over the BBC to continue the fight against Nazi Germany. An attack by the Royal Navy on July 3 to cripple the French Fleet at Mers el Kébir when it refused to sail to Britain resulted in the sinking of the old battleship *Bretagne* and damage to five other ships, and the deaths of 1,300 French sailors. The hostile act by an ally caused tremendous resentment in France towards Britain and the Vichy government promptly broke off diplomatic relations with the United Kingdom. Though not particularly minded to support de Gaulle's efforts at first, the British Government recognised him on August 7 as 'Chief of all the Free French, wherever they may be, who may join you to defend the Allied cause'.

Washington to discuss it personally. The President then instructed Murphy to return and make contact with Général Maxime Weygand, Vichy's Governor of North Africa, to ascertain his authority in the region.

Murphy returned to Vichy and gained permission from the French authorities to tour French North Africa. He reached Algiers in mid-December for a three-week fact-finding mission throughout the French colonies while meeting with Général Weygand and senior staff. Later, Murphy would say: 'I was delighted to meet Frenchmen who were strongly anti-Nazi, who were more pro-British than I anticipated, and who acted as if they would really fight for their independence in their African Empire'.

Murphy then returned to Washington where his report was well received by President Roosevelt who immediately sent him back to North Africa to negotiate an economic agreement with Général Weygand. The subsequent agreement dated February 26, 1941 specified that the United States would continue to trade with the French colonies as long as the goods and

The order to attack the French naval squadron in North Africa — given by Churchill in spite of being advised against the plan — badly undermined de Gaulle's effort to recruit French soldiers and sailors to fight with him alongside the British. At the same time, it strengthened the authority of Vichy through the French empire. By mid-August the numbers of Free French — those who decided to follow de Gaulle — still numbered only around 8,000 in both Great Britain and across the world.

Here, Emmanuel d'Astier de la Vigerie, de Gaulle's Commissioner for the Interior, reviews a company of French commandos drawn up in front of Wellington Barracks in London.

The chapel to the barracks took a direct hit from a V1 during the Sunday service on June 18, 1944, killing 63 service personnel and 58 civilians. Today the barracks is home to the Brigade of Guards.

In February 1941, acting under President Roosevelt's direct instructions, the American Chargé d'Affaires Robert Murphy successfully negotiated an economic agreement with Général Maxime Weygand, Vichy's Governor of North Africa. This photo of Général Weygand (left) was taken in Oran during the visit of Général Charles Huntziger (right), Vichy's Secretary of State for War, early in November 1941. The two men were soon to quit the stage, Huntziger being killed on the return trip on November 12 when his aircraft crashed in bad weather in southern France. About the same time, Weygand was dismissed by Vichy following pressure from the Germans and he was subsequently recalled from Algiers.

June and July although the resident consuls were not informed of their true function. Even though they had little training in espionage, the 'food control officers' began their work immediately, acquiring maps, charting fields, measuring coastlines, sounding out French and Arab relations, and recording shipping movements.

In the meantime, though the United States was still neutral, contacts were strengthened with the British government and as early as the summer of 1940 the Navy Department established an office in London to discuss arrangements for co-operation should the United States come into the war. The War Department followed and established a permanent body in London in the spring of 1941.

Between January 29 and March 29, 1941, American, British, and Canadian planners held secret talks in Washington to discuss principles of combined strategy. Though it was already clear that Japan might at any time enter the conflict, the War Department agreed with the British that Germany must be defeated first, a strategy that was subsequently referred to as ABC-1 (American-British-Canadian 1), the code-name of the conference.

From August 9-12, President Roosevelt and Prime Minister Churchill secretly met for their first wartime conference, code-named 'Riviera', held on board ships anchored in Placentia Bay, Newfoundland. There they drafted the Atlantic Charter that was issued as a joint declaration on August 14 even although the United States would not officially enter the war until four months later.

services remained out of Axis hands. To monitor this, 'food control officers' were to be posted in Algeria, Morocco, and Tunisia to supervise all shipments. Weygand and the Vichy administration knew quite well that these men would spy not only on the German and Italian officials of the Armistice Commission, but also on the French themselves, but that was not a concern. Weygand made large concessions to let the American consular staffs work undisturbed with unchecked liberty of movements and free use of diplomatic bags without inspection.

Following this success, in the spring of 1941 Murphy was officially assigned as American Consul to Algeria to supervise the work of the 'food control officers'. As the officers staffing the existing seven American consulates in French North Africa were not trained to perform intelligence duties, the State Department hastily recruited 12 new Vice-Consuls for this particular duty. The men selected came from a variety of occupations, two were bankers who had lived in Paris; one was a lawyer; another an advertising executive, two were librarians and one an anthropologist from Harvard University; Ridgway B. Knight was a wine merchant, and John H. Boyd was a Coca Cola branch manager in Marseille. They were soon becoming known as the '12 disciples' or '12 apostles'.

Having been hastily schooled in basic French culture and politics, they took up their duties in Algeria and Morocco in

In the spring of 1941, Murphy was assigned as American Consul to Algeria, his remit being to search for a French leader who could secure the co-operation of the French armed forces in North Africa to the Allies. Général Alphonse Juin (right), commander of ground forces in North Africa, was one of those approached but with no success. This photo was taken later in 1942, after the French armed forces in North Africa had sided with the Allies. Murphy is wearing the Distinguished Service Medal that had just been awarded to him for his tireless efforts in the pre-preparations for Operation 'Torch'.

In August 1941, President Roosevelt and Prime Minister Churchill met in secret to discuss their respective aims for the war and to outline a post-war international system. Code-named 'Riviera', the meeting was held on board ships anchored in Placentia Bay, Newfoundland. *Left:* Destroyer USS *McDougal* went alongside HMS *Prince of Wales* to transfer the

President to the battleship for a meeting with the Prime Minister. *Right:* Later, Churchill came aboard USS *Augusta* to meet with Roosevelt. Admiral Ernest J. King is saluting just to Churchill's right. Behind, on the gangway, is Admiral Sir Dudley Pound, the First Sea Lord, and Field-Marshal Sir John Dill, Chief of the Imperial General Staff.

Roosevelt's great post-war design was to put an end to all colonial empires — French, Dutch, Portuguese and British — but this raised a fundamental difference of opinion. This conflict is recalled by the President's son Elliott, a captain in the US Army Air Force, who was present at the 'Riviera' conference together with his brother Franklin Junior, an Ensign in the US Navy. In his book, *As He Saw It*, published in 1946, he gives a remarkable inside view of the brutal exchanges between the British Prime Minister and his father. Elliott describes a neck-reddening Churchill crouching forward: 'England does not propose for a moment to lose its favoured position among the British Dominions. The trade that has made England great shall continue, and under these conditions prescribed by England's Ministers.' Roosevelt did not budge, insisting: 'I can't believe that we can fight a war against fascist slavery, and at the same time not work to free people all over the world from a backward colonial policy.' *Above:* On the first day of the conference, August 9, the President stood for official photos on the deck of the USS *Augusta*, supported by his son Elliott. With them, from left to right, Ensign Franklin D. Roosevelt Jr; Sir Alexander Cadogan, Under Secretary of State for Foreign Affairs; Captain John R. Beardall, US Navy; and Prime Minister Churchill. This photo was taken just after Churchill handed the President a personal letter from King George VI.

On the other hand, Churchill's primary goal 'to get the Americans into the war', was not achieved but the 'Joint Declaration by the President and the Prime Minister' that was drafted clearly affirmed the sense of solidarity between the United States and Great Britain. Soon to be known as the 'Atlantic Charter' the document included eight 'common principles' that the United States and Great Britain would be committed to supporting in the post-war world. Both countries agreed not to seek territorial expansion; to seek the liberalisation of international trade; to establish freedom of the seas, and international labour, economic, and welfare standards. And both countries were committed to supporting the restoration of self-governments for all countries that had been occupied during the war and allowing all peoples to choose their own form of government. The Prime Minister was alarmed by the third principle that covered the rights of all peoples to choose their own government, and he tried to have this re-written so that it only applied to the occupied nations. However, Roosevelt demanded the inclusion of the term 'all peoples' meaning that the clause was universal, including all colonial peoples. Churchill had to give way and when he forwarded the text to his Cabinet on August 11, he warned them that would it be imprudent to raise unnecessary difficulties. The Cabinet followed the Prime Minister's recommendation and approved the Charter. Another point which Roosevelt insisted upon was the affirmation by the British Government that it was not involved in any secret treaties, particularly ones concerning territorial questions such as those concluded by the Allies during the First World War. The British asked for an interpretation of this clause in order to allow the Soviet Union to continue to control the Baltic states. Also, the desired Polish annexation of Danzig, East Prussia and parts of German Silesia would be impossible if national self-determination was taken into account. Roosevelt died in April 1945 and neither his successor, Harry S. Truman, nor Churchill cared much with the self-determination principle of the Charter.

The Prime Minister and the British Chiefs-of-Staff came to Washington on June 18, 1942, for another decisive war conference code-named 'Argonaut'. *Left:* Dressed in his 'siren suit', Churchill is pictured on the lawn of the White House together with Harry Hopkins, Roosevelt's Commerce Secretary and close adviser, and Harry's daughter Diana. With them is Commander Charles Thompson, ADC to the Prime Minister, not forgetting Roosevelt's dog Fala. *Right:* The Jacqueline Kennedy Garden now occupies this area just south of the East Colonnade.

The Charter detailed the goals and aims of the Allied powers concerning the war and the post-war world.

Despite the Japanese attack on Pearl Harbor on December 7 which resulted in an immediate declaration of war, the 'Germany first' strategy was reaffirmed at the 'Arcadia' Conference that brought together the top British and American military leaders in Washington. Meeting from December 22, 1941 to January 14, 1942, Churchill brought to the conference his own strategic analysis for 1942 and 1943 containing strong arguments for giving the liberation of French North

Africa the highest priority in the Atlantic area. President Roosevelt showed marked interest in the project.

The Conference established the Combined Chiefs-of-Staff, to formulate and execute policies and plans concerning the conduct of the war, the allocation of supplies and the requirements for transportation. To provide opposite numbers to the British Chiefs-of-Staff, the US Joint Chiefs-of-Staff came into being, and by mid-1942 the Combined Chiefs-of-Staff consisted of General Sir Alan Brooke, Chief of the Imperial General Staff; Admiral Sir Dudley Pound, First Sea

Lord; Air Chief Marshal Sir Charles Portal, Chief of the Air Staff; and Lieutenant-General Sir Hastings Ismay representing the Prime Minister. For the United States the C-in-Cs were General George C. Marshall, Chief-of-Staff of the Army; Admiral Ernest J. King, Commander-in-Chief of the US Fleet; Lieutenant General Henry H. Arnold, Commanding General of the Air Force; and Admiral William D. Leahy as Chief-of-Staff to President Roosevelt. (Formerly ambassador at Vichy, Leahy had just been recalled to Washington, leaving S. Pinkney Tuck as American Chargé in France.)

Another meeting of the main members of the Combined Chiefs-of-Staff was held in the US Public Health Service Building in Washington. The British representatives on the left are an unidentified commander, Rear-Admiral Wilfrid Patterson, Field-Marshal Sir John Dill, Brigadier Vivian Dykes, Lieutenant-General Sir Gordon Macready, Air Marshal Douglas Evill. The Americans include Vice Admiral Frederick J. Horne, Admiral Ernest J. King, Admiral William D. Leahy, Brigadier General John R. Deane, General George C. Marshall, Lieutenant General Joseph T. McNarney, and an unidentified lieutenant colonel.

On July 31, 1942, President Roosevelt approved the appointment of General Dwight D. Eisenhower as Allied Supreme Commander for Operation 'Torch' but formal confirmation was awaited from the Prime Minister. When this was received on August 6, the Combined Chiefs-of-Staff announced that Eisenhower was to be Commander-in-Chief, Allied Expeditionary Force although, for security reasons, he soon altered the title to Commander-in-Chief, Allied Force. This photo was taken on the eve of the operation just after Eisenhower arrived in Gibraltar with his staff on November 5 to man his advanced headquarters which had been prepared within the Rock.

Pressed by President Roosevelt who wanted immediate action for US troops to stiffen American morale, the War Department turned its attention to plans for assaulting occupied Europe. In April 1942, General Marshall proposed an outline plan for a cross-Channel attack committing 48 divisions in landings that would take place in the Pas-de-Calais. The earliest possible date for the attack was set at April 1943 providing the overseas movement of the troops and the organisation of the forces began at once.

In the second week of April, Marshall and Harry L. Hopkins, the President's adviser, came to London to discuss strategy and Marshall presented his project for a cross-Channel attack in 1943. The proposal was agreed, and code-names already in use within British planning organisation were assigned. The cross-Channel operation was coded Operation 'Roundup' while 'Sledgehammer' was an emergency plan that would take place late in 1942 should it be absolutely necessary to act to prevent a collapse of Soviet resistance. American participation was defined and plans were drawn for the build up of American forces in Great Britain to over one million men. This build-up operation was code-named 'Bolero'.

At the end of May, Vyacheslav Molotov, the Soviet Foreign Minister, paid a visit to London and Washington. He insisted on the necessity to open a second

The original plan to have a Deputy Commander-in-Chief from the British side was dropped on British initiative in favour of a US officer to retain the American character of the expedition in case General Eisenhower was prevented from exercising his command through disability. Major General Mark W. Clark was therefore appointed Deputy Commander-in-Chief, Allied Force, and took charge of the detailed planning. This photo was taken on the airfield at Gibraltar on November 5 but remarkably, the original captions to the series of photographs taken that day of Clark and Eisenhower were all given the wrong month: October instead of November.

The offices of the British Aluminium Company in Norfolk House in St James's Square, London, were taken over for the main Allied Force Headquarters (AFHQ), and the basic planning for Operation 'Torch' took place there. Eisenhower had an office not far away at 20 Grosvenor Square, and he only came to Norfolk House for conferences (which were held in the company boardroom) in case his appearance might attract the attention of German agents. His deputy, General Clark, was in charge at Norfolk House and he would go to see Eisenhower at Grosvenor Square several times a day. *Left:* This photo of Eisenhower leaving Norfolk House was taken later in 1944 when the building was used again for Operation 'Overlord'. *Right:* Though the interior of the building was totally gutted in 1977, a preservation order ensured that the façade remained unchanged.

front in 1942 on a scale large enough to compel the Germans to withdraw 40 divisions from the Eastern Front. Churchill and Marshall were deliberately vague, replying that a second front was already in preparation but Roosevelt went further and in a note sent to Stalin through Molotov, he announced that this second front was to take place in 1942. Pressure from the Russians added to Roosevelt's impatience, and in a note sent to Marshall on May 6 he pointed out that 'the necessity of the case calls for action in 1942, not 1943'.

The Prime Minister and the British Chiefs-of-Staff arrived in Washington on June 18 at a time when British military fortunes were at their lowest ebb. Tobruk was beleaguered by the Afrikakorps and the news of the surrender of the British garrison arrived in the middle of a meeting at the White House on June 21.

While agreeing that the Allies should act offensively in 1942, the British outlined their conclusions that with the forces available, a cross-Channel operation in 1942 was unfeasible. In their view, the only favourable location for action against Germany in 1942 was North Africa. The meeting ended on a compromise: while reaffirming the priority of 'Bolero', it was agreed that if Operation 'Sledgehammer' proved unlikely to succeed, an alternative should be prepared and the best option in that case was Operation 'Gymnast', a landing in North Africa.

Marshall was annoyed with Roosevelt's surrender to the British. He knew that if the Allies turned to North Africa, the build-up of American forces in Great Britain would slow down and a cross-Channel attack might in consequence prove impossible in 1943.

On July 6, a meeting of the British Chiefs-of-Staff agreed that 'Sledgehammer' had no reasonable chance of success for the time being. Reporting their decision to their American counterparts, the British recommended proceeding with the planning of 'Gymnast'. Marshall reacted strongly and decided to play some politics himself. With Admiral King, who may or may not have seen through Marshall's ploy, he proposed to President Roosevelt that the United States now turn their main effort to the Pacific against Japan.

The President firmly rejected this proposal and instead sent Marshall and King to London, together with Hopkins, to come to a final agreement with the British over strategy for 1942. Their instructions were to urge for action somewhere in 1942, and more particularly to press for 'Sledgehammer'. If convinced that such an operation could not be mounted with any reasonable chance of success, they were to proceed with the consideration of other projects, either in North Africa or the Middle East.

At the first meeting held on July 20, the Americans pushed for 'Sledgehammer' to be launched at the Cotentin in France but over the following three days they were

On the third anniversary of D-Day, a plaque was unveiled to commemorate the use of the building by General Eisenhower, both for 'Torch' in 1942 and 'Overlord' two years later. The plaque shows the insignias of both the Allied Force Headquarters (AFHQ) of 1942 and the Supreme Headquarters Allied Expeditionary Force (SHAEF) of 1944.

Admiral Sir Andrew Cunningham was appointed Allied Naval Commander for the operation. This picture of him with a jubilant Eisenhower was taken on the deck of HMS *Nelson* in the Algiers harbour after the success of the operation.

argued down, point by point. On July 23, the President sent supplementary instructions to his Combined Chiefs directing them to arrive at an agreement on an operation that could be launched in 1942. Among the possibilities listed, the occupation of French North Africa was given top priority. On July 25, the Combined Chiefs reached a compromise, the American members agreeing to accept the invasion of French North Africa on condition that a final decision be postponed to mid-September. If it then appeared likely that the Russians could actively resist German military power in the spring of 1943, Operation 'Roundup' would retain its priority over any other undertaking. If the Russians then seemed about to collapse, the invasion of North Africa would be mounted in time for landings before December 1. The Combined Chiefs-of-Staff named the prospective North African project Operation 'Torch'.

Knowing that the President would not accept the conditional nature of the decision, Hopkins immediately cabled Washington, urging Roosevelt to intervene to avoid 'procrastinations and delays'. The President made up his mind at once and, disregarding the conditional nature of the Combined Chiefs' decision, immediately summoned Henry L. Stimson, the Secretary of War, and the Joint Chiefs to the White House. He read them, without discussion, his decision to go ahead with the North African operation. To Marshall, King and Hopkins in London, he cabled: 'Tell Prime Minister I am delighted that decision is made'.

When Marshall returned from London, apparently he still had the belief that the final decision to mount the North African invasion was to be reached on September 15 as agreed by the Combined Chiefs. However, during a special conference of representatives of the Joint Chiefs at the White House, the President pointed 'that he, as Com-

mander-in-Chief, had made the decision that Torch should be undertaken at the earliest possible date. He considered that this operation was now our principal objective, and the assembling of means to carry it out should take precedence over other operations.'

General Dwight D. Eisenhower, who had been appointed in June as Com-

manding General, European Theatre of Operations, was directed to get Operation 'Torch' under way immediately. At the expense of the staffs working on 'Roundup' which then came to a standstill, a 'Torch' planning committee was created.

Appreciating the anti-British feeling in France following the ill-advised attack by the Royal Navy on the French Fleet at Mers el Kébir in July 1940, Roosevelt cabled his reservations to Churchill on August 30: 'I am reasonably sure a simultaneous landing by British and Americans would result in full resistance by all French in Africa, whereas an initial landing without British ground forces offers a real chance that there would be no French resistance or only a token resistance.' Thereafter, as far as possible, the planning for Operation 'Torch' took on an outward appearance of being an American operation.

Major General Mark W. Clark was appointed as the Deputy Commander with Operation 'Torch' headquarters located in Norfolk House on St James's Square, London. Eisenhower was also working from his office situated at 20 Grosvenor Square.

The preparations for 'Torch' soon diverted considerable resources from 'Bolero' which seriously affected the build-up in the United Kingdom. Marshall's fears were soon to prove to be well founded for the commitment to Operation 'Torch' actually made a cross-Channel operation impossible in 1943.

The troops destined for North Africa began to be assembled in late September. This picture shows ships being loaded with guns, armoured equipment, and vehicles on Merseyside. On October 17 the Centre and Eastern Task Forces began to concentrate in the River Clyde in Scotland.

Operation 'Torch'

On August 14, General Eisenhower was appointed Allied Commander-in-Chief for Operation 'Torch' with Admiral Sir Andrew Cunningham as Allied Naval Commander Expeditionary Force. The outline plan was approved by the American and British Chiefs-of-Staff at the end of September, orders being issued on October 8. They provided for two landings in the Mediterranean at a number of beaches on either side of Algiers and Oran, and one on the Atlantic coast of Morocco. About 70,000 assault troops were to be used to capture the three ports. The landing at Algiers was to be made by a mixed British and American force, while the Oran and Casablanca landings were to be executed solely by American troops.

After establishing initial objectives, which included the port and neighbouring airfields, the Oran and Morocco forces were to join hands to form the US Fifth Army, ready to meet a possible German attack from Spain. The forces at Algiers were quickly to become the British First Army and start to push eastwards to capture the airfield at Djidjelli and the port of Bougie, and ultimately to advance into Tunisia.

Everything depended upon whether or not the French resisted and plans were made flexible to meet anything from full-scale opposition to token defence or even positive co-operation. Although each condition called for stores and equipment to be loaded in the transports in a different way, the ships had to be loaded to meet full-scale opposition and this could not be changed once the convoy had sailed.

All the troops for the Algiers and Oran operations were to sail from the United Kingdom, the Royal Navy being responsible for their transport and for all naval operations within the Mediterranean. The Eastern Task Force, supporting the Algiers landings, was commanded by Vice-Admiral Sir Harold Burrough while Commodore Thomas Troubridge commanded the Centre Task Force for the Oran landings.

The troops for Morocco were to sail direct from America, the US Navy being responsible for their transport and for all naval operations off the coast west of Morocco. This Western Task Force was commanded by Rear Admiral Henry Kent Hewitt.

The War Department appointed Major General George S. Patton to command the Western Task Force. A preliminary plan to capture Casablanca was devised and Patton then flew to London to map out co-ordination. However, in conformity with a provisional outline plan then being submitted to the Combined Chiefs-of-Staff by General Eisenhower, when Patton returned to Washington on August 20 he carried with him a directive to prepare an attack instead against Oran. That was promptly superseded by another directive from the War Department and it was not until September 5 that the objective of the Western Task Force firmly established.

As the assault fleet set sail for Gibraltar, a Royal Navy photographer, Lieutenant Reginald Coote on board HMS *Bulolo*, pictured Vice-Admiral Sir Harold Burrough, the commander of the Eastern Naval Task Force that was due to land forces at Algiers.

D-Day was set as November 8, with the three amphibious landings at Algiers, Oran and Casablanca to begin in the pre-dawn hours with no moonlight. With more than 700 miles separating Casablanca and Algiers, the sunrise at these beaches would vary from 6.18 a.m. (GMT) at Algiers, 6.31 a.m. at Oran and 6.55 a.m. at Casablanca. Consequently, H-Hour was flexible with each task force commander being left free to land at any time after 1 a.m. in order to secure the most favourable conditions, rather than be forced to meet a precise overall schedule. The Eastern and Centre Naval Task Forces chose to come ashore at 1 a.m. while the Western Task Force planned from 4 a.m.

The Central Task Force, supporting the Oran landings, was commanded by Commodore Thomas Troubridge. This picture was taken later in June 1944 when he commanded the naval force for the invasion of Elba island in the Mediterranean (see *After the Battle* No. 173).

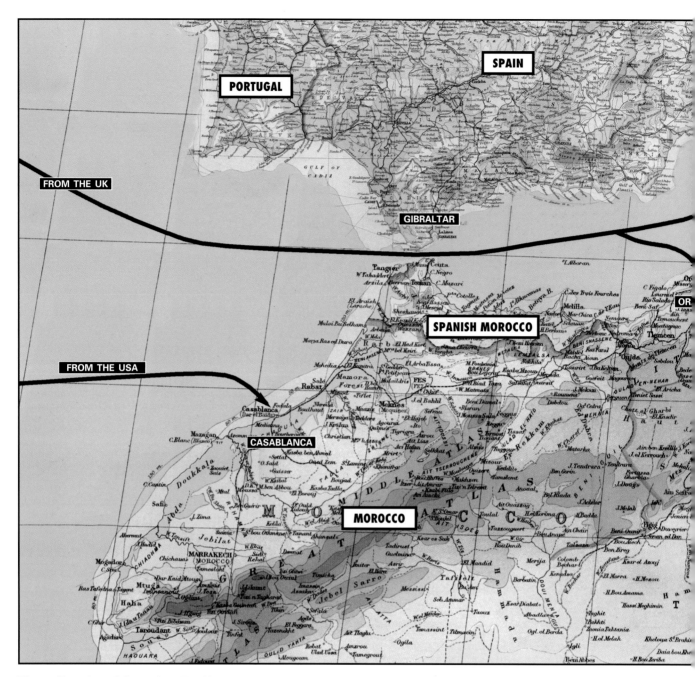

PORTUGAL

SPAIN

FROM THE UK

GIBRALTAR

OR

SPANISH MOROCCO

FROM THE USA

CASABLANCA

MOROCCO

The outline plan of Operation 'Torch' was approved by the American and British Chiefs-of-Staff and orders were issued on October 8, 1942. They provided for two landings in the Mediterranean at a number of beaches near Algiers and Oran, and one on the Atlantic coast of Morocco. With the operation due to be launched before December, this left a very short time to organise a logistically complex operation covering multiple landings over 600 miles apart. Unlike the much larger operation in 1944 to land on the Normandy coast of France, a distance across the Channel of less than 100 miles from Britain, the invasion of French North Africa was a far more difficult proposition with the invasion troops having to travel partly from assembly points in Scotland and also from ports 6,000 miles away in the United States. With almost no experience at this stage of the war with amphibious landings, it was a huge and risky undertaking.

Compared to the operations of the Eastern and Centre Task Forces in the relatively quiet Mediterranean which has no tide, the operations of the Western Task Force on the Atlantic coast of Morocco would face a much more difficult situation. On that shore, high surf and swell was to be expected, and the tide was a major factor to take into account as was the timing of the touch-down to ensure that landing craft in the first wave could be unloaded and retracted before becoming stranded.

When the date of November 8 was chosen for D-Day, Admiral Hewitt

checked and found that high tide would be some time after 1 a.m (at 1.21 a.m. at Casablanca for example), hence it would be ebbing when the first waves of landing craft reached the beaches at 4 a.m. With the risk that his craft could become stranded, he recommended that the operation be deferred one week so that he could land with the tide rising at 4 a.m. The proposal was discussed at higher US Navy levels but rejected, partly because the moonlight on the later date would make surprise less likely and also due to the reduced likelihood of good weather.

EASTERN (ALGIERS) TASK FORCE

The Eastern Task Force was charged, in the first place, with seizing Algiers and the airfields at Blida and Maison Blanche. The American/British assault force consisted of the US 39th and 168th Regimental Combat Teams, the 11th and 36th British Brigade Groups, and the 1st and 6th Commandos. The force was to be transported from the United Kingdom in 15 LSI (Infantry Landing Ships), including four US Combat Loaders, two landing ship carriers (derrick hoisting), and 16 cargo ships. To give the impression that the whole

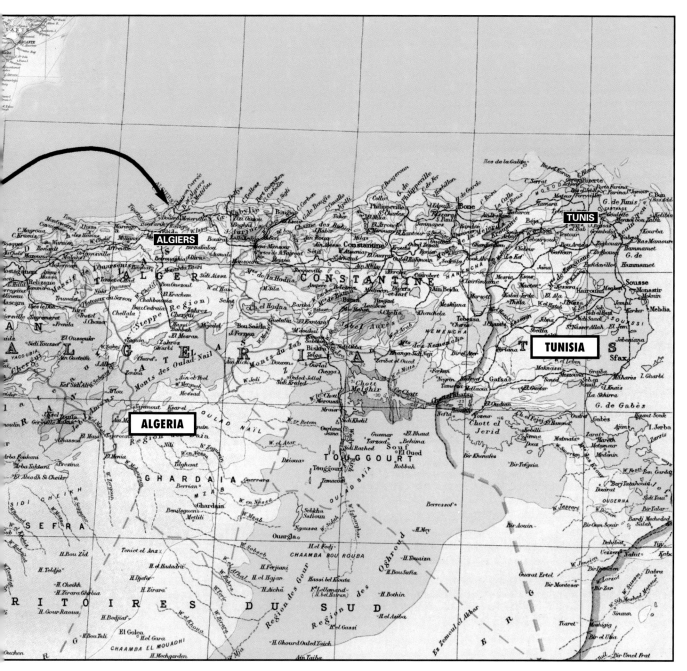

ALGIERS

TUNIS

ALGERIA

TUNISIA

Invading French North Africa was also a journey into the unknown as it was by no means certain that the force would be welcomed as liberators. To secure the co-operation of the French armed forces and authorities was one vital aspect of the 'Torch' operational plan and from early 1941 the US diplomat Robert D. Murphy was assigned as American Consul to Algeria with the mission to establish contacts with Frenchmen willing to co-operate with the Allies. It was only in October 1942, one month before the planned invasion, that he was given permission to warn his contacts of the planned operation. He was still forbidden however to tell them how soon the operations were to commence. The Deputy Commander, General Mark Clark, was secretly landed by submarine at the very last minute to meet with Murphy's contacts (see Operation 'Flagpole' on page 46). It was far too late for the pro-Allied French organisations to muster their forces and turn them into action.

enterprise was American, the Eastern Task Force was to be commanded by Major General Charles W. Ryder of the US Army.

After Algiers had capitulated, the British First Army was to be created at which point Ryder was then to hand over to British Lieutenant-General Kenneth Anderson, the designated army commander, who was then to control the operations to seize Tunisia. The shift of command at Algiers was clarified in a conference held between Generals Clark, Anderson, and Ryder which took place on September 8.

CENTRE (ORAN) TASK FORCE

The Centre Task Force, under the command of US Major General Lloyd R. Fredendall had as his first task the capture of Oran and the nearby airfields at Tafaraoui and La Sénia. His force was composed of the US 16th, 18th and 26th Regimental Combat Teams, a Combat Command from the 1st Armored Division with 180 tanks, and the 1st Ranger Battalion. It would be transported from the United Kingdom using 15 LSI, one landing ship carrier (derrick hoisting), three tank landing ships (converted from shallow-draft oilers used on Lake Maracaibo) and 28 cargo ships.

WESTERN (MOROCCO) TASK FORCE

The Western Task Force, commanded by Major General Patton, comprised five Regimental Combat Teams and one Armored Combat Team of two battalions with 250 tanks. The force was to be shipped direct from the United States aboard 29 assault transports, 23 of them troop transports (AP) and six cargo transports (AK).

The mission of the Western Task Force was to secure the port at Casablanca and its airfield and, in conjunction with the Centre Task Force at Oran, establish and maintain communications between Casablanca and Oran.

It was to build up land and air striking forces capable of securing Spanish Morocco should that action become necessary.

The Royal Navy and the US Navy had the hugely complex task of escorting the various convoys to their destinations, protecting them from any intervention by hostile surface ships and submarines, and giving direct fire support to the assaulting forces. Also, aircraft carriers had to give initial air support until landing grounds had been captured and air forces established ashore. Within three days of the landing, 160 fighters were to fly in from Gibraltar to captured airfields in the Oran sector, 160 fighters to Casablanca and 90 to Algiers.

Responsibility for air support for the landings was divided between the Eastern Air Command under Air Marshal Sir William Welsh, who was to look after the assault on Algiers, and the Western Air Command under Major General James H. Doolittle who was responsible for Oran and Casablanca.

As an underlying objective of the whole 'Torch' operation was to speedily create conditions that would bring the French back into the war on the side of the Allies, a directive covering the treatment of the French armed forces during initial contact was drafted on October 5. It stated that no offensive action was to be taken against them by the Allies unless in response to definite hostile action. The directive laid down three general principles: (1) the French must be permitted to take the first hostile action; (2) a hostile act by an isolated unit should not necessarily be interpreted as indication that all units in that area had hostile intent, and (3) once resistance in any particular area ceased, Allied forces were to abandon hostilities unless the French resumed their opposition.

Written material was carefully prepared in furtherance of these political and propaganda aims. It included a set of formal communications, prepared partly in London and partly in Washington, from the President of the United

Providing air power for the Western Task Force destined for Morocco was a challenge as by the end of 1942 the US Navy was woefully short of carriers. The Japanese had sunk the *Lexington*, *Yorktown*, *Wasp* and *Hornet*, and damaged the *Saratoga* and *Enterprise*, and none of the new *Essex* class had yet been commissioned. The only large carrier available in the Atlantic Fleet was the *Ranger*, a relatively small ship then deemed too slow for use with the Pacific Fleet's carrier task forces. Consequently, the new *Sangamon* class of four escort carriers, converted from tankers, was thrown into 'Torch' even though they had carried out less than half of the normal training period. Although these carriers were smaller and slower than the fleet carriers, and carried fewer planes, their inclusion was a positive advantage for they provided an enormous oil supply with plenty of spare fuel for other ships. To increase the number of fighters available over Morocco, the *Ranger* left her torpedo-bomber squadron VT-41 behind to make room for VF-9 with 27 Wildcats. *Above:* At the Norfolk Navy Yard, a TBF Avenger torpedo bomber is being hoisted aboard USS *Santee*, one of the escort carriers, just before she departed for Africa.

So as not to attract undesired attention, the Western Naval Task Force which was sailing direct from the United States, assembled in different ports. The main part of the fleet assembled at the Norfolk Navy Yard, Virginia, this picture *(left)* being taken on October 10. Moored near the entrance to Dry Dock 3 (which appears to be occupied by an unidentified Royal Navy warship), is the fleet oiler, the USS *Tallulah*, AO 50, although she was not assigned to 'Torch'. *Right:* The same stretch of the southern branch of the Elizabeth River with the USS *George Washington*, CVN 73, aircraft carrier berthed at Pier 4. Dry Dock 3 is just off to the left.

The Western Naval Task Force was commanded by Rear Admiral Henry Kent Hewitt, seen here sharing a light moment on board USS *Augusta* with General George S. Patton, the Western Task Force commander. (This photo also appears to have an incorrect date because the wartime caption states it was taken on December 4 whereas Patton left the ship to go ashore on November 9.)

States to the rulers and chiefs of government of Portugal, Spain, Vichy France, Morocco, Algeria, and Tunisia. Proclamations were formulated, both in French and in Arabic, to be issued in the name of the President or of the Commander-in-Chief. Propaganda leaflets were also prepared for dropping from aircraft. Radio technicians and broadcasting teams were sent from the United States to the UK to accompany the Centre Task Force. Other field units were organised to produce and distribute leaflets and to work with local newspapers.

In the hope that resistance to the landings might be minimised through action by pro-Allied Frenchmen in the armed services or civil administration, Murphy and his 'apostles' were to enrol suitable individuals. At the same time, British and American agents were also operating secret intelligence and special operations in French North Africa. Instructions were given to them on October 14 regarding programmes of sabotage and subversive activity near the main objectives of each of the task forces depending on the reaction of the French. These programmes involved either destructive sabotage or close control over communications and transportation, neutralisation of coast defences, immobilisation of ships and submarines in port, sending up signal flares and supplying guides for the Allies, and other such activity.

However, Eisenhower was concerned that 'subversive activities, propaganda, and political warfare had to be carefully and completely co-ordinated with military plans if they were to avoid being not only inappropriate but also a positive menace'. In furtherance of this aim, Murphy was empowered to control or modify all the secret operations, and even direct them in Algeria and Tunisia should that become necessary. After the Allies had landed he was to become a member of Eisenhower's staff.

The Air Group assigned to support Operation 'Torch' was commanded by Rear Admiral Ernest D. McWhorter, photographed here on the bridge of the *Ranger* on November 1 with his Chief-of-Staff, Captain John J. Ballentine. The escort carrier *Sangamon* was to support operations of the Northern Attack Group, while the *Ranger* and the escort carrier *Suwannee* were to support the Centre Attack Group, and the *Santee* the Southern Attack Group.

The Assault Forces Embark

On board the carrier *Victorious*, Royal Navy photographer, Lieutenant Leslie Priest, pictured Seafires parked on the flight deck. The *Duke of York*, *Rodney* and *Formidable* are visible in the background.

With its airfield, dockyard, storage and communication facilities, and the sheltered anchorage in the adjacent Bay of Algeciras, Gibraltar became the pivotal point of preparation of Operation 'Torch', and the first of six advance convoys (code-named KX) left from the United Kingdom for Gibraltar on October 2. These comprised tankers, ammunition ships, colliers, tugs and all the various auxiliaries needed to service the warships and assault forces that were to follow.

Aircraft to be assembled at Gibraltar were among the cargo brought in.

Meanwhile, following a carefully prepared programme, equipment, supplies and vehicles poured into the ports and loaded aboard ships. From late September, the troop units boarded the assault vessels in Liverpool and Glasgow. On October 17, the Centre and Eastern Task Forces began to assemble in the Clyde. Destroyers carried out practice bombardments on the Arran island

range and communication exercises were practiced with the forward observation officers due to land with the assault troops. On the night of October 20/21 Exercise 'Flaxman' was carried out in the Loch Fyne area to exercise landing officers, landing craft crew and beach parties. However, as it was vital to take care of the landing craft, which could not be replaced if damaged, the exercise was carried out on a much reduced scale.

BRITISH ASSAULT CONVOYS

Convoy	Composition	Speed	Sailing date	Departure port	Date due Gibraltar	
KMS(A) 1 KMS(O) 1	47 ships 18 escort	8 knots	October 22	Loch Ewe and Clyde	November 5 and 6	Included 39 transports; Algiers and Oran sections divided west of Gibraltar
KMS.2	52 ships 14 escort	7 knots	October 25	Loch Ewe and Clyde	November 10	Included 46 transports
KMF(A) 1 KMF(O) 1	39 ships 12 escort	11.5 knots	October 26	Clyde	November 6	Included two HQ ships and 32 LSIs; Algiers and Oran sections divide west of Gibraltar
KMF 2	18 ships 8 escort	13 knots	November 1	Clyde	November 10	Included 13 personnel ships for Algiers and Oran

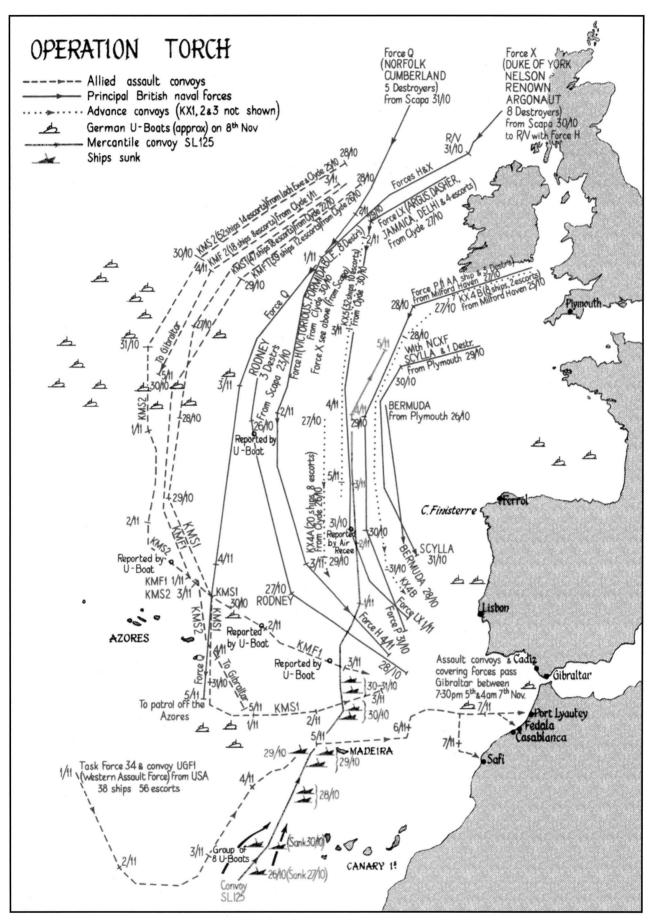

OPERATION TORCH

- – – – ► Allied assault convoys
- ――――► Principal British naval forces
- ·······► Advance convoys (KX1,2&3 not shown)
- ⚓ German U-Boats (approx) on 8th Nov
- ―――― Mercantile convoy SL.125
- Ships sunk

Force Q (NORFOLK CUMBERLAND 5 Destroyers) from Scapa 31/10

Force X (DUKE OF YORK NELSON RENOWN ARGONAUT 8 Destroyers) from Scapa 30/10 to R/V with Force H

R/V 31/10

Forces H&X

28/10

28/10

KMS 2 (52 ships 14 escorts) from Loch Ewe & Clyde 25/10
KMF 2 (18 ships 8 escorts) from Clyde 1/11
KMS (47 ships 18 escorts) from Clyde 22/10
KMF 1 (39 ships 12 escorts) from Clyde 26/10

Force LX (ARGUS, DASHER) JAMAICA, DELHI & 4 escorts, from Clyde 27/10

2/11

1/11

Force H (VICTORIOUS, FORMIDABLE, 8 Destrs) from Clyde 30/10
Force X (32 ships 10 escorts) from Clyde 30/10
Force X see above (from Scapa)

Force P (1 AA ship & 5 Destrs) from Milford Haven 27/10
KX 4 B (8 ships, 2 escorts) from Milford Haven 25/10

27/10

28/10

5/11

28/10 With NCXF SCYLLA & 1 Destr. from Plymouth 29/10

30/10

BERMUDA from Plymouth 26/10

Plymouth

RODNEY 3 Destrs 23/10
From Scapa 30/10

2/11

Reported by U-Boat

27/10

4/11

4/11

29/10

C. Finisterre

Ferrol

31/10

To Gibraltar

31/10

5/11

30/10

28/10

KMS2

1/11

KX 4 A (20 ships, 8 escorts) From Clyde 29/10
KX 5 (32 ships, 8 escorts) from Clyde

31/10 Reported by Air Recee

2/11

29/10

30/10

SCYLLA 31/10

BERMUDA 28/10

KX4B

Lisbon

2/11

Reported by U-Boat

KMS1 KMF1

KMF1 1/11
KMS2 3/11

KMS1 30/10

RODNEY 27/10

Reported by U-Boat

31/10

KX4B

Force LX 1/11

Force P 3/11

AZORES

KMS2

KMS1

Reported by U-Boat

Force Q

KMF1

Reported by U-Boat

3/11

28/10

Force H 4/11

Assault convoys & covering forces pass Gibraltar between 7·30pm 5th & 4am 7th Nov.

Cadiz

Gibraltar

To Gibraltar

31/10

To patrol off the Azores

5/11 KMS1

1/11

2/11

5/11

30-31/10
3/11

30/10

6/11+

7/11

7/11+

Port Lyautey

Fedala
Casablanca

29/10

MADEIRA

29/10

Safi

Task Force 34 & convoy UGF1 (Western Assault Force) from USA 38 ships 56 escorts

1/11

4/11

28/10

2/11

3/11 Group of 8 U-Boats

(Sank 30/10)

26/10 (Sank 27/10)

CANARY IS.

Convoy SL.125

Movements of the advance and assault convoys and naval forces of Operation 'Torch'. The slow convoys from Great Britain sailed down the meridian of 18 degrees West, so keeping within range of shore-based air patrols, but the faster convoys were routed further out in the Atlantic at 26 degrees West. Being out of range of air cover from British bases for a large part of their journey, protection was provided by carriers: HMS *Biter* sailing with KMF 1 and the HMS *Avenger* with KMS 1.

MARITIME FORCES ENGAGED, ALGIERS AND ORAN

	Eastern Naval Task Force Algiers Vice-Admiral Harold Burrough	Centre Naval Task Force Oran Commodore Thomas Troubridge	Force H Covering force Vice-Admiral Neuville Syfret
HQ Ships	*Bulolo*	*Largs*	
Landing Ships Infantry	11	15	
Combat Loaders	4		
Landing Ships Tank		3	
Transport and other ships	18	29	
Special operations	*Broke*	*Walney*	
	Malcom	*Hartland*	
Battleships		*Rodney* *	*Duke of York*
			Renown
Aircraft Carriers	*Argus*	*Furious* *	*Victorious*
			Formidable
Escort Carriers	*Avenger*	*Biter*	
		Dasher	
Cruisers	*Sheffield*	*Aurora*	*Argonaut*
	Scylla	*Jamaica*	*Sirius*
	Charybdis		
	Bermuda *		
Monitors	*Roberts*		
AA Ships	*Pozarica*	*Alynbank*	
	Palomares	*Delhi*	
	Tynwald		
Destroyers	11	13	17
Sloops	3	2	
Corvettes	4	6	1
Submarines	*P45 Unrivalled*	*P54 Unshaken*	
	P48	*N59 Ursula*	
	P221 Shakespeare		
Minesweepers	7	8	
Motor Launches	8	10	
Auxiliaries and supports	8	8	6

* Detached from Force H

The American combat loaders (assault transports) included in the Eastern Naval Task Force comprised three troops transports (AP) and one cargo ship (AK). Operations by special forces in order to prevent scuttling of ships and destruction of the port facilities were planned for Algiers (Operation 'Terminal') and Oran (Operation 'Reservist'). In addition to the beacon submarines appearing in this table, the Royal Navy deployed four submarines off Toulon to counter the French fleet stationed there in case it ventured out to attack the assault force. These were the *Seraph, Sibyl, Unseen* and *P-222* from November 7, replaced on November 14 by *Splendid, Unshaken, Tribune* and *Sturgeon*. However, when it became clear that the French were not going to interfere, the four submarines were withdrawn. The 'auxiliaries and supports' listed in this table comprises trawlers and tankers. *Right:* An assault convoy sailing 200 miles off Cape Saint Vincent, Portugal, en route to North Africa. This photo was taken from *Monarch of Bermuda,* one of the five troopships carrying the force due to land at the Y Sector near Oran.

Two slow convoys carrying vehicles, tanks, equipment and stores were assembled. KMS 1 comprised 45 cargo vessels with 18 escorting warships, and KMS 2 included 52 transports and 14 escort ships. They sailed on October 22 and 25 respectively, on a timetable that would permit them to be overtaken by the two fast convoys that were to follow. Comprising the combat-loaded transports of the Eastern and Centre Task Forces, convoy KMF 1 (39 vessels with 12 escorting warships) set sail on October 26, and convoy KMF 2 (18 transports and 8 escorts) departed on November 1. On approaching Gibraltar, the convoys were to divide into those destined for Algiers (KMS A and KMF A) and for Oran (KMS O and KMF O).

Commanding this consolidated armada was Vice-Admiral Burrough on board the specially designed command ship HMS *Bulolo*. With him were Major General Ryder and British Major-General Vyvyan Evelegh, and RAF Air Commodore George Lawson. Second in command in another headquarters command ship, HMS *Largs*, was Commodore Troubridge with Major General Fredendall and US Colonel Lauris Norstad (Assistant Commander, US Twelfth Air Force).

Admiral Cunningham, the overall naval commander, sailed from Plymouth in the cruiser HMS *Scylla* at the end of October, arriving in Gibraltar on November 1. General Eisenhower reached Gibraltar by air on November 5.

In the United Sates, the convoys due to carry the Western Task Force for the Morocco landings were considered too large to be sent from any single port without attracting undesired attention, so it was therefore assembled at sea after a series of departures of small groups of ships departing at various times and places, ostensibly for different destinations.

First to leave were five submarines, then the first section of the transports and warships sailed from Hampton Roads, Virginia, on October 23, allegedly heading

A Martlet fighter — the American-built Grumman F4F known as a Wildcat in the US Navy — on the flight deck of the *Formidable*. She also embarked a squadron of Seafires as did the *Victorious*. Although these were modern vessels, the lifts were too small to accommodate the Seafires as they lacked the ability to fold their wings. Consequently, the aircraft had to be parked on the flight deck (see page 24). (The older *Furious* and *Argus* had larger elevators so could transfer the Seafires to the hangars below.)

FLEET AIR ARM, AIRCRAFT EMBARKED

Force H				**Eastern Naval Task Group — Algiers**			
HMS *Formidable*	885 Squadron	6	Seafire IIC	HMS *Argus*	880 Squadron	18	Seafire IIC
	888 Squadron	12	Martlet II/IV	HMS *Avenger*	802 Squadron	9	Sea Hurricane IIC
	893 Squadron	12	Martlet IV		883 Squadron	6	Sea Hurricane IIC
	820 Squadron	12	Albacore				
				Centre Naval Task Group — Oran			
HMS *Victorious*	884 Squadron	6	Seafire IIC	HMS *Furious*	801 Squadron	12	Seafire IIC
	882 Squadron	18	Martlet IV		807 Squadron	12	Seafire IIC
	817 Squadron	9	Albacore		822 Squadron	8	Albacore
	832 Squadron	9	Albacore			1	Fulmar
	809 Squadron	6	Fulmar	HMS *Biter*	800 Squadron	15	Sea Hurricane IIB/IIC
				HMS *Dasher*	804 Squadron	6	Sea Hurricane IIC
					891 Squadron	6	Sea Hurricane IIB

Biter and *Avenger* each had one flight of 833 Squadron embarked on board, both with three Swordfishes, but these were disembarked at Gibraltar for A/S patrols from there

for the waters off Bermuda where manoeuvers were going on. Next morning, the second half of the troop transports with screening warships, including the cruiser USS *Augusta* with Admiral Hewitt and General Patton aboard, left Hampton Roads and took a north-easterly course as though bound for the United Kingdom. On October 27, the covering group sailed from Casco Bay, Maine, in time to take its place at the front of the formation, while the transports and warships, which had left Hampton Roads in two sections (see above), were joining up.

The armada comprised a strong force of four carriers, the fleet carrier USS *Ranger* and three escort carriers. To increase the number of fighters available, the *Ranger* left her torpedo-bomber squadron VT-41 behind to make room for VF-9 with 27 Wildcats. That gave the force a total of some 105 fighters. In addition, a fifth carrier, USS *Chenango*, ferried 76 P-40 War-hawk fighters of the 33rd Fighter Group that were to be launched on D-Day to operate from the airfield at Port-Lyautey after its capture by the assault force. A second batch of 35 P-40s ferried on board HMS *Archer* was to be delivered some days after the first one.

On October 24, the Western Naval Task Force assault transports, with screening warships, left the Norfolk Navy Yard on a north-easterly course as if they were bound for the United Kingdom. Admiral Royal E. Ingersoll, Commander-in-Chief, Atlantic Fleet, watched them depart from Hampton Roads.

The US Navy's numerical designation for the Western Naval Task Force was Task Force 34. In addition to the three main parts, the Northern, Center and Southern Attack Groups, it comprised a Covering Group (TG 34.1) of battleships, cruisers and destroyers, and an Air Group (TG 34.2) with two aircraft carriers. When complete, the task force covered an area roughly 20 by 30 miles, including the outer screen. This photograph taken from a Dauntless shows just a fraction of the Western Naval Task Force with the battleship *Texas* and cruiser *Augusta* in the distance.

A destroyer belonging to the Air Group Screen passes astern of the *Ranger*. Wildcat fighters are ranged on the carrier's deck.

The assault convoy UGF 1, totalling 38 transports and its escort of 56 ships including aircraft carriers, battleships and cruisers was designated Task Force 34. It sailed eastwards in formation, refuelling en route, maintaining radio silence and avoiding contact with other ships as much as possible. For the troops, the three-week voyage was a huge discomfort as the men were jammed into every available place on the transports, were fed in seemingly endless lines, and suffered repeated seasickness. They were brought up on deck for periods of exercise and also engaged in detailed study briefings not touched upon during training.

The assault wave was followed by supply and reinforcement convoys organised in three successive forces — Task Force 38, Task Force 37 and Task Force 39.

The huge convoys of the British and American naval forces, each spread out over 30 or 40 square miles of sea, offered magnificent targets for the U-Boats. It was estimated that if the Germans got wind of the Allied movements, 50 U-Boats could be deployed against them by the end of October, and another 25 by November 6. However, good fortune attended the passages for though there were some reports from U-Boats and Focke-Wulf FW 200 aircraft operating on the Atlantic trade routes, the Germans failed to deduce that anything unusual was afoot. A number of U-Boats that might have intercepted the armada drew away to attack a small convoy from Sierra Leone that was passing east and north of the invasion fleet bound for the United Kingdom.

On board USS *Augusta*, Rear Admiral Hewitt (left) observes the invasion convoy steaming toward its destination. With him is Rear Admiral John L. Hall, the commander of the Sea Frontier Forces, Western Task Force, which was to protect the Moroccan harbours once they were secured.

MARITIME FORCES ENGAGED, MOROCCO

Western Naval Task Force
Rear Admiral H. Kent Hewitt

	TG 34.10 Southern Atttack Group — Safi Rear Admiral Lyal Davidson	TG 34.9 Center Attack Group — Fédala Captain Robert Emmet	TG 34.8 Northern Attack Group — Port-Lyautey Rear Admiral Monroe Kelly	TG 34.1 Covering Group Rear Admiral Robert C. Giffen
Assault transports, troops	5	12	6	
Assault transports, cargo	1	3	2	
Special operations	*Bernadou* *Cole*		*Dallas* *Contessa*	
Battleships	*New York*		*Texas*	*Massachusetts*
Aircraft Carriers		*Ranger*		
Escort Carriers	*Santee*	*Suwannee*	*Sangamon* *Chenango*	
Cruisers	*Philadelphia*	*Augusta* *Brooklyn* *Cleveland*	*Savannah*	*Wichita* *Tuscaloosa*
Destroyers	8	15	8	4
Submarines	*SS 220 Barb*	*SS 253 Gunnel*	*SS 235 Shad*	
Minescraft	3	6	2	
Auxiliaries and supports	3	1	3	1

Unlike standard troopships that relied on a quay or tenders to unload, the assault transports — AP and AK — carried their own fleet of landing craft. Here, the special operations included a surprise landing in Safi harbour by two destroyer-transports (APDs), while at Port-Lyautey the APD *Dallas* was to proceed up the Sebou river to land a detachment of men near the airfield. The *Contessa*, a chartered fruit carrier, was then to follow up to deliver fuel and ammunition to the airfield for the aircraft due to be based there. In addition to the beacon submarines appearing in this table, the US Navy despatched *SS 233 Herring* to operate offensive reconnaissance off Casablanca, and *SS 231 Blackfish* to do the same off Dakar. The line 'auxiliaries and supports' of the table comprises tankers (AO) and tugs (AT), and the *Barnegat*, a seaplane tender with TG 34.8.

From November 4 the weather deteriorated severely, confirming forecasts of adverse conditions at the time and place set for the landings.

On November 4, some 300 and 400 miles west of Gibraltar, both the slow convoy KMS 1 and the fast convoy KMF 1 spilt into their separate Algiers and Oran sections. Preceded by the screen of warships of the Royal Navy's Force H, the Algiers section crossed the Strait of Gibraltar and entered the Mediterranean during the night of November 5/6. The Oran section of KMS 1 convoy followed during daylight the following day and the Oran section of KMF 1 passed through the strait during the night of November 6/7. Once inside the Mediterranean, the separate sections consolidated into the Eastern and Centre Naval Task Forces, the process being further complicated by the refuelling of some ships in Gibraltar harbour and others from tankers a sea.

Continued on its easterly course throughout daylight on November 7, the Eastern Naval Task Force suffered the first casualty of Operation 'Torch' when early in the morning the transport *Thomas Stone* (*AP-59*) was torpedoed by *U-205*. The torpedo hit the ship's port side, aft, blowing a hole in her bottom; breaking her propeller shaft; and bending her propeller and her rudder to starboard. The convoy continued on, leaving *Thomas Stone* behind, adrift some

En route to Morocco aboard USS *Augusta*, General Patton checks the progress of the convoy on a chart of the Atlantic Ocean.

Gun crews manning their weapons on the after-deck of an unidentified assault transport carrier which is en route to Morocco.

The armament includes two 20mm AA guns, one .5-inch Browning and a Lewis machine gun.

150 miles from Algiers, guarded by the corvette HMS *Spey*. Then in the afternoon a force of Junkers Ju 88s attacked Force H off Algiers, a near miss inflicting light damage to destroyer HMS *Panther* forcing her to return to Gibraltar.

At 6 p.m., as darkness was falling, the Eastern Naval Task Force turned south and an hour later divided into two columns heading for their rendezvous with their beacon submarines. The transports for the eastern landings, with their

escorts, headed for *Unrivalled*, lying north-east of Cap Matifou, while the other two groups formed a double column and continued together to a point north-west of Cap Sidi Ferruch. There at around 9.30 p.m. they separated, one

It was surprising to find cork insulation fitted to the bulkheads of the *Augusta*. While at sea, members of the crew stripped it off as a fire prevention measure.

Sailors get a few hours sleep topsides aboard a transport — a photo taken on November 7, the night before the invasion began.

section seeking submarine *P48* north of Cap Sidi Ferruch and the other *Shakespeare* north of Castiglione. (Admiral Burrough and General Ryder on HMS *Bulolo* were with the Centre Group nearest Cap Sidi Ferruch.)

Meanwhile, 200 miles to the west, the Centre Naval Task Force prepared to deploy. At 6.15 p.m. two columns turned south, one comprising Group I for the western landing and Group II for the centre landing, heading for a rendezvous with their beacon submarine *Unshaken* north-east of Cap Figalo. The second group, comprising a sizeable part (Groups III and IV) of the eastern landing force, headed south-eastwards for the rendezvous with their submarine, *Ursula*, off Cap Carbon. The rest of the task force maintained an eastward course until 7.50 p.m. when Group V swung away, also seeking a rendezvous with *Ursula*. Then at 0.45 a.m. the last vessels of Groups VI and VII, also turned south.

After an uneventful crossing of the Atlantic, the Western Task Force arrived precisely on time off the coast of Morocco. The Southern Attack Group,

While on board the aircraft carrier *Santee* en route to North Africa, a former *Life* photographer Horace Bristol, now a lieutenant in the US Navy, pictured crewmen exercising on the flight deck.

Testing machine guns of Wildcat fighters aboard the *Ranger*. The new F4F-4 version of the Wildcat had six .50-calibre machine guns instead of the four fitted to the earlier F4F-3. This change was not so popular with American pilots because, with the same amount of ammunition spread over two additional guns, the firing time decreased from 34 seconds to less than 20 seconds. The three aircraft in the front belong to VF-9 and those behind to VF-41.

A SBD-3 Dauntless from the *Ranger* carries out an anti-submarine patrol over the convoy while en route to North Africa. There was great concern about air-ground recognition — or rather the possible lack of it — on this first big Allied operation. To reduce the risks of friendly fire incidents by British and American gunners unfamiliar with each others aircraft, an instruction had been issued on September 25 to add a yellow circle (of unspecified thickness) to the national insignia on each side of the fuselage and on both lower wing surfaces. This Dauntless clearly shows the new ID markings for 'Torch'. The 41-S-7 identifies its squadron, the letter of the mission, and individual aircraft number, hence the seventh machine of Squadron VS-41. In the US Navy squadron designation system introduced in 1922, the first letter signified the type of equipment flown with 'V' standing for fixed-wing aircraft; 'VF' for Fighting Squadron; 'VS' Scouting Squadron; 'VGF' Escort Fighting Squadron, and 'VGS' Escort Scouting Squadron. The letter of mission, also known as class letter, followed indicating the primary mission of the unit, but it was soon realised that this was too much information as it was unwise to tell the enemy the squadron number and mission so this procedure was discarded in the spring of 1942. From then on, the remaining aircraft number painted on the aircraft grew in size. Since this memorandum was concerned with air-ground recognition, no mention was made of the insignia on the upper wing surfaces.

This Dauntless radioman-gunner is test-firing his twin .30 machine guns into the sea while the aircraft was purposely parked on the side of the carrier's flight deck. Two other sailors were observing, with one apparently protecting his hearing by holding his fingers in his ears. The Dauntless was also fitted with two .50 machine guns firing forwards under the engine cowling. Having a long range, able to carry a potent bomb-load and with convincing defensive armament, good manoeuvrability and great diving characteristics and ruggedness, the Dauntless remained the US Navy's main carrier-borne scout plane and dive-bomber from mid-1940 through to the middle of 1944. The Dauntless gained fame as the bomber that delivered the fatal blows to the Japanese carriers at the Battle of Midway in June 1942.

Another photo by Lieutenant Bristol of Dauntless bombers and Wildcat fighters on the *Santee*'s flight deck, several displaying the yellow markings specific to Operation 'Torch'. Of interest are the distance and target information temporarily marked on the carrier's flight deck. Some published sources state that this photo was taken on *Sangamon* but the camouflage pattern on her island definitely identifies the ship as *Santee*.

commanded by Rear Admiral Lyal A. Davidson, split from the main formation at daybreak on November 7 and headed toward Safi. The task force kept on eastwards and at 3 p.m. the main part of the force — the Centre Attack Group under Admiral Hewitt — swung slightly southeast, separating into three groups to approach the Fédala-Casablanca area.

The Northern Attack Group, under command of Rear Admiral Monroe Kelly, continued eastwards on a course toward Port-Lyautey. All forces remained as far offshore as possible until nightfall, the transports reaching the debarkation area at midnight.

Hastily converted from tankers, the four escort carriers of the *Sangamon* class were smaller and slower than the fleet carriers and they could operate only about 30 planes compared to some 75 for the *Ranger*. Following the contemporary US Navy practice for oilers, the four ships were all named after rivers and they retained these names following their conversions to carriers. All told, air group of the Western Naval Task Force comprised 172 planes, the *Ranger* and the three escort carriers being equipped with 27 Avenger torpedo bombers (TBF), 36 Dauntless dive-bombers (SBD) and 109 Wildcat fighters (F4F-4).

WESTERN NAVAL TASK FORCE, AIRCRAFT EMBARKED

Northern Attack Group — Port Lyautey

CVE 26 *Sangamon*	VGF-26	12	F4F-4 Wildcat
	VGS-26	9	TBF-1 Avenger
		9	SBD-3 Dauntless

Centre Attack Group — Fédala and Casablanca

CV 4 *Ranger*	VF-9	27	F4F-4 Wildcat
	VF-41	27	F4F-4 Wildcat
	VS-41	18	SBD-3 Dauntless
	Air Group 9	1	TBF-1 Avenger
CVE 27 *Suwannee*	VGF-27	11	F4F-4 Wildcat
	VGF-28	12	F4F-4 Wildcat
	VGF-30	6	F4F-4 Wildcat
	VGS-27	9	TBF-1 Avenger

Southern Attack Group — Safi

CVE 29 *Santee*	VGF-29	14	F4F-4 Wildcat
	VGS-29	8	TBF-1 Avenger
		9	SBD-3 Dauntless

Ferry carriers

CVE 28 *Chenango*	33d Fighter Group (USAAF)	76	P-40F Warhawk
HMS *Archer*	33d Fighter Group (USAAF)	35	P-40F Warhawk

The *Chenango*, one of the four escort aircraft carriers available for the operation, was detailed to ferry to Morocco 76 P-40F Warhawk fighters of the 33rd Fighter Group. The planes were to be launched on D-Day to land and operate from the airfield at Port-Lyautey after its capture by the assault force. The Army pilots had been given brief training at Philadelphia in carrier launches but the Navy had serious misgivings about the aircraft's ability to withstand the strain of the catapult and the pilot's ability to handle such a launch from the carrier. *Above left:* At Norfolk Navy Yard the P-40s were hoisted on board the *Chenango* moored along Pier 7. *Above right:* This shot of the P-40F fighters lined up on board *Chenango* was taken on October 15. *Right:* The carrier's hanger deck was also jam-packed with P-40s, although these aircraft are still without the additional yellow identification which were being added during the voyage.

In this shot there are 62 aircraft on the flight deck of the *Chenango* leaving quite a small area to catapult them forward.

(Sources disagree as to the precise number of aircraft embarked on Operation 'Torch'.)

Gibraltar, situated at the mouth of the Mediterranean, became the key of Operation 'Torch'. It had been ceded to the British Crown by the King of Spain in the Treaty of Utrecht in 1713 and had assumed the status of Crown Colony in 1830. The opening of the Suez Canal in 1869 increased Gibraltar's strategic value to the Royal Navy and the Admiralty dockyard with its 440-acre harbour was constructed on land reclaimed from the sea in 1895-1905. On the landward side, a 1,450-metre-strip of the isthmus between the British and Spanish lines was stated in the treaty to be neutral ground, based on the maximum range of 18th century cannons. However, the British gradually began utilising their half of the zone, initially as a camping ground with the addition of barrack huts and rifle ranges.

Then in 1908 the British government decided to erect a fence along their edge of the neutral territory, and by 1914 North Front (as the whole area from the Rock to the frontier fence was called) had been accepted as a British possession with a racecourse being added by the Gibraltar Jockey Club. In 1931 a local aircraft company was given permission to use the centre of the course as a landing ground. Over the following years the simple grass field was progressively developed, being called 'an emergency airfield' to try to placate the objections from Spain. It was not until September 1939 that the RAF arrived, initially operating flying boats from the harbour, but now at war, the need for an efficient operational airfield was a matter of urgency.

The strip across the isthmus permitted a take-off run of only 1,000 yards and in October 1941 instructions were given by the Air Ministry to extend it to 1,550 yards. The 570-yard extension into the Bay of Algeciras would require 400,000 cubic yards of fill giving a freeboard of just over six feet. Although it was anticipated that Spain would object, labour and plant were brought in from Britain plus help from America now in the war and needing a staging airfield for the US Air Ferry Service. Work on the new runway now began in earnest, rock being blasted from the north-eastern face of the Rock and dug from tunnels at a phenomenal rate of tonnage. By April 1942 it had reached 1,150 yards and by the time that Gibraltar was taken over for Operation 'Torch', it was just under 1,550 yards. (For a detailed account of the building of Gibraltar airfield, see *After the Battle* No. 21.)

No. 202 Squadron arrived in September 1939, operating flying boats from the harbour to patrol the approaches to the Mediterranean and to monitor German ships trapped in ports in southern Spain and Spanish Morocco at the outbreak of hostilities. The squadron flew the Saro London flying boat until April 1941 when it began to receive its first Catalinas. No. 233 Squadron on anti-submarine duties was the first to operate from the tricky short runway with its Hudsons, a detachment operating from Gibraltar from December 1941, the rest of the unit gradually following. The Hudson was operating at its limits on the runway then only 950 yards long and the accident rate remained high for some time. When this shot of a Hudson of No. 233 Squadron preparing for take-off was taken in August 1942, the runway operational length was 1,150 yards. Another flying boat squadron, No. 210, moved to Gibraltar with its Catalinas in October 1942, followed in November by another anti-submarine squadron, No. 179, flying Wellingtons (by then the operational length of the runway was 1,550 yards), and in December it was joined by another Hudson squadron, No. 48.

The North African operation brought the airfield to breaking point. In this amazing photo taken at Christmas 1942, P-38s Lightnings are crammed with Wellingtons, Hudsons, Liberators, Mosquitos, Spitfires, Hurricanes, B-25 Mitchells and B-26 Marauders. A Swordfish, Argus, Halifax, Walrus and even an Auster can also be identified.

From mid-October Gibraltar became the centre of preparations for Operation 'Torch'. A delivery of 116 Spitfires and 13 Hurricanes arrived on October 28, followed by a further shipment a few days later. The Special Erection Party worked frantically to assemble, test-fly and cannon-test all the aircraft in time for the commencement of the invasion. AFPU photographer Lieutenant George Dallison pictured newly assembled Spitfires, mainly Mark Vs, parked at North Front.

The Allied Air Force was grouped in two commands. The Royal Air Force units under Air Marshal Sir William L. Welsh of the Eastern Air Command were to support the Algiers assault force, while the Western Air Command, formed from the new US Twelfth Air Force under Major General James H. Doolittle, would support the Oran and Morocco assault forces. The plan was to have over 400 aircraft ready at Gibraltar to fly to North Africa within three days of the landings, 160 to operate from captured airfields near Casablanca, 160 to Oran and 90 to Algiers. One of the American fighter squadrons was the 14th Fighter Group that moved its P-38s to Gibraltar in the last days of October. This photo taken on November 10 shows Lieutenant Leo M. Yates of the 48th Fighter Squadron just after he arrived in his P-38. The 14th Fighter Group moved to North Africa on November 14, based at Tafaraoui, near Oran. (Lieutenant Yates, from Ogdon, Utah, was later killed in action near Medenine on January 23, 1943. His name is now inscribed on the Memorial to the Missing at the American Cemetery in Carthage, Tunisia.)

On the eve of Operation 'Torch', Gibraltar's harbour was packed with oilers, tugs, refuelling warships, and many other craft. Such an extraordinary accumulation of ships and aircraft did not pass unobserved by the Axis observers in adjacent Spain but if the Germans were aware of a threat, somehow they seemed not recognise its import, the OKW warning for example on October 17 that an attack might be imminent at Dakar, as well as inside the Mediterranean.

Not a perfect comparison but this barbary macaque, the symbol of Gibraltar, offers such a nice shot!

In late 1941, Admiral Darlan, the overall Commander-in-Chief of the Vichy armed forces, confided to the US Ambassador, Admiral Leahy, that he might be willing to lead his countrymen to join the Allies. However, the admiral's conduct left some doubts as to whether he was motivated more by ambition than patriotism. This photo was taken in December 1942 in Algiers just after Darlan awarded the Croix de Guerre to the captains of three submarines that sailed their boats out of the trapped Toulon base to avoid capture by the Germans.

Friend or Foe?

The Armistice signed with the Axis powers in June 1940, allowed for the retention of a small French army, the Armée de l'Armistice (Army of the Armistice). The Axis soon ruled out the strength and armaments of this army, limiting it to some 100,000 men in France, stationed in the unoccupied zone of the country, with stronger forces in the colonial empire overseas to keep internal order and to defend the territories. The terms of the Armistice also practically deprived the 'Armistice army' of tanks, armoured vehicles, heavy artillery, anti-tank and anti-aircraft guns, and reduced the amount of transport available to virtually nothing. Reduced in accordance with the terms of the Armistice, the armed forces in the French North African territories of Morocco, Algeria and Tunisia had 140,000 men under arms in 1942.

One vital aspect of the 'Torch' operational plan was to secure the co-operation of the French armed forces in North Africa and, to this end, it was important to find a leader who could rally them in a renewed war against the Axis powers. He had to be a man able to persuade the officers of the armed forces to set aside their orders from Vichy for reasons of higher patriotism and seize the opportunity to begin the liberation of France.

While the United States maintained cordial relations with the Vichy government, that person could not be Général de Gaulle for Roosevelt and his administration showed strong and persistent antipathy to the leader of the Free French. Also, on the French side, the attitude still prevailed among government servants, both civil and military, of obedience to the chain of command, and many of those who desired to re-enter the war against Germany wished to be led by those whom they recognised as their legitimate ruler: Maréchal Pétain and his government. Many even regarded de Gaulle, who escaped to England in June 1940 to be able to keep on fighting, as a traitor.

Amiral François Darlan, next in succession to Marshal Pétain, and Commander-in-Chief of all the French armed forces, had already confided to the US Ambassador, Admiral Leahy, late in 1941 that he might be ready to disassociate himself from the policy of collaboration and lead his countrymen to the side of the Allies if he were supported by sufficient American aircraft, tanks, and effective troops. His conduct left doubts however as to whether he was motivated more by ambition or by patriotism. If he were appraised of Allied intentions, would he assist or would he betray the project?

Général Weygand, with whom Murphy had already negotiated an economic agreement, had since been recalled from Algiers, being dismissed by Vichy in November 1941 following pressure from the Germans. Général Charles Noguès, Resident General of Morocco, had shown marked zeal in 1940 in organising and

The other choice was Général Giraud who was now living in Lyon in unoccupied France after having escaped from the camp at Koenigstein in April 1942. In December 1942, French Army photographer Marcel Viard pictured the general visiting the offices of the Chantiers de la Jeunesse (the Vichy youth organisation) in Algiers and saluting Colonel Alphonse Van Hecke, the chief of the organisation there.

Left: Général Charles Noguès, the Resident General of Morocco, was another possibility. This picture was taken late in 1941 in Rabat when Noguès assisted to a traditional exhibition of horsemanship in company with Général Charles Huntziger, Vichy's Secretary of State for War. With them is the son of the Sultan of Morocco, Prince Moulay el-Hassan, the future King Hassan II. However, Robert Murphy, Roosevelt's man on the spot, reported that he doubted that Noguès would break with Marshal Pétain's authority. *Right:* The attitude of Général Charles Mast, the commander of the Division d'Alger, was the complete opposite. He immediately agreed to assist the Allies, and he soon became one of Murphy's most important contacts in North Africa. This photo of the general with de Gaulle was taken in Tunisia in 1943, after the successful ending of the campaign.

preparing for eventual resumption of hostilities against the Axis by the French Army, but by 1942 he appeared to Murphy to have become dispirited by the long delay. Despite his antagonism toward the Germans, and their cordial distrust of him, would assume the burden of breaking with Marshal Pétain's authority?

So the burning question was, could the Allies find an eminent person outside the Vichy establishment able to win over the higher civil and military leadership in French North Africa; a high-ranking officer who would accept the role for reasons of higher patriotism?

Following a recommendation from his pro-Allied contacts in Algiers, Murphy then turned to Général Henri Giraud. Then in his early 'sixties, Giraud had achieved considerable distinction in a career which involved many years of service in Morocco; combat, capture, and escape in both World Wars; instruction for three years at L'École Supérieure de Guerre in Paris, and four-star rank as commander of the 7ème Armée in 1940. Also, his escape from the Koenigstein prison in Saxony through Switzerland to unoccupied France in April 1942 had attracted wide attention.

Although he had undertaken to support Marshal Pétain's authority and had been permitted to retire to Lyon, Giraud still nurtured a secret desire to bring about a successful return to arms. Although his residence was kept under surveillance, he still managed to maintain relations with French patriots in Algiers, and through them he was in contact with others in the major centres of French North Africa as well as with demobilised officers in France. His principal representative in Algiers was Général Charles Mast, commander of the Division d'Alger, and in Morocco, Général Émile Béthouart, commander of the Division de Casablanca. Giraud had communicated with the Allies through his friends in Algiers and via the US Military Attaché at Bern in Switzerland.

Two other commanders who were ready to countermand the authority of Vichy was Général Émile Béthouart, the commander of the Division de Casablanca, and Général Joseph de Goislard de Monsabert, the commander of the Blida sector at Algiers. *Above:* This photo of Béthouart (left) was taken in Norway in April 1940. *Right:* After 'Torch', Général de Monsabert went on to command the 3ème Division d'Infanterie Algérienne.

The small army permitted to France by the armistice treaty of June 1940 comprised around 140,000 men stationed in the North African territories of Morocco, Algeria and Tunisia. This patrol was pictured in May 1942 at a 'marabout' — a tomb of a venerated saint.

Murphy flew back to Washington early in September. He presented his appraisal and reported that a reputable military group in Algiers recommended that the Allies accept Général Giraud as a French leader. Having received detailed instructions, and to avoid drawing attention, Murphy then flew to London disguised under the fictitious name and rank of 'Lieutenant Colonel McGowan' to discus his findings with Eisenhower. The General outlined the extent of the projected landings and Murphy confirmed that these closely approximated what the French in North Africa had estimated would be necessary. He also indicated the civilian and military co-operation that could be expected. However, it was accepted that, because of insufficient ships and escorts, it would be impracticable to meet Giraud's wish for simultaneous assistance to the French Army in southern France during the invasion of North Africa.

Also debated was the tricky problem of how long an interval should elapse between notification being given to the French before the actual Allied landings took place, to enable them to muster their forces and turn them into action, against the risk of losing surprise.

Another difficult point was that of the inter-Allied command wherever Allied troops would fight beside French troops on French soil. Giraud and his supporters were eager that he must appear before the French as a free national leader, not as the appointee of the Allies, and they expected in consequence that he should be the Allied Commander-in-Chief in French North Africa. His position, as he wrote to a fellow countryman, was clear: 'We don't want the Americans to free us; we want them to help us free ourselves, which is not quite the same'. Eisenhower took the position (that was later to be asserted to Giraud), that the French forces must first be rearmed by the Allies — and be in sufficient strength to defend north-west Africa — before the Allies could consider permitting them to exercise supreme command there. He said that French forces could remain under French command, but would have to co-operate fully with an Allied supreme commander.

Just after Murphy returned to Algiers, he was approached by a representative of Amiral Darlan who revealed that he was now considering getting involved providing he was given guarantees of ample American aid to offset French deficiencies in military equipment. However, Général Mast made clear to Murphy that Giraud

Training with a Hotchkiss machine-gun in southern Tunisia although this photograph was actually taken early in 1943, by which time the French army was fighting side by side with the Allies.

would prefer to act apart from Darlan, confident that he alone could rally the French Army in North Africa. Nevertheless, Murphy suggested to Washington that they should encourage a co-operative relationship between Giraud and Darlan.

Considering these new developments, both London and Washington agreed that Giraud should be recognised as Governor-General of all French North Africa, responsible for all civil and military affairs, and as such should receive Allied support and protection.

Eisenhower had then in mind the early activation of the US Fifth Army under Major General Clark and the elevation of Giraud to be the Deputy Commander-in-Chief. The British Chiefs-of-Staff, however, pointed out that the Governor-General (Giraud) would already have enough to do and could not properly also serve as the Allied Deputy Commander-in-Chief, so that the latter position would be available only to Darlan.

With Giraud's willingness to co-operate with the Allies now assured, Murphy explained that he was finally given permission to give his pro-Allied contacts 'positive assurances of American support'. However, he was forbidden to tell them how soon the military operations were to commence.

Not realising that that the Allies were withholding so much information from him, and thinking the pro-Allied associates in North Africa still had time for organisation, Mast asked Murphy to meet senior American military officers to discuss the coming operation. (Mast knew that Murphy was uninitiated when it came to military matters.) Murphy wrote later: 'This was a possibility I had discussed with Eisenhower in London, and after an interchange of messages, the General asked me to arrange a secret meeting somewhere along the Mediterranean coast to which the Americans could come in a submarine.'

THE PRO-ALLIED ASSOCIATES

Pre-emptive action by pro-Allied officers and civilians to neutralise possible opposition to the landings were of particular importance in Algiers, the seat of government for all French North Africa, with the civil and military administrations centred there. The key men of the pro-Allied organisation in Algiers were Général Mast, commanding the Division d'Alger; Lieutenant-Colonel Germain Jousse who commanded the town garrison; Général Joseph de Goislard de Monsabert commanding the Blida sector; and Colonel Alphonse Van Hecke, the chief of the Chantiers de la Jeunesse, the Vichy youth organisation in Algeria.

There were also civilian groups totalling several hundred men belonging to several different organisations. An important one was the Jewish resistance group created late in 1940 to oppose the persecution imposed on them by the Vichy regime and another was the 'Committee of Five' of right-wing patriots and monarchists eager to resume the war against Germany. Neither the British nor the Americans

The terms of the Armistice deprived the Vichy army of any modern weapons like tanks and armoured vehicles, heavy artillery, anti-tank and anti-aircraft guns. Lacking signal equipment, the men of the 67ème Régiment d'Artillerie d'Afrique are having to use hand signals to communicate during this gunnery training exercise in the Aurès in eastern Algeria in June 1942.

This 75mm mountain gun dating from 1928 is another example of the sorry state that the French army in North Africa found itself.

Facing a massive build-up of German arms in the late 1930s, and desperate for modern aircraft, the French Air Force purchased American aircraft of various types like the Curtiss H-75 fighters and the Glenn-Martin 167F and Douglas DB-7 twin-engine bombers. *Above:* The Glenn-Martin 167F had a crew of three in two separate compartments. The bombardier sat in the nose below the pilot while the gunner was in a twin-machine gun turret in a rear compartment so the photo *(right)* showing five men boarding the bomber would appear to have been staged. All the serviceable Glenn-Martin bombers in North Africa were based in Morocco, the Aéronavale (Fleet Air Arm) having ten at Port-Lyautey.

delivered any sizeable number of firearms to them however and only a small quantity of old rifles were obtained from the French military.

Plans were based upon Général Mast's ability to issue orders to units of the Division d'Alger to facilitate speedy Allied advance to Algiers and the Blida aerodrome from the vicinity of Cap Sidi Ferruch. Algiers itself was to be neutralised by occupation of the many key positions by teams of civilians masquerading (with the complicity of Lieutenant-Colonel Jousse) as regular 'Volontaires de Place' in the town's system of civilian defence. A number of officers and NCOs were to take part as leaders of these groups. With the complicity of Commissaire André Achiary who was dedicated to the cause, they could expect the connivance of the police. The Villa des Oliviers, the official residence of Général Alphonse Juin, Commander-in-Chief of the Army, in Algiers, would be cordoned off and

Right: **Dewoitine 520 fighters were based in Morocco (39 at Casablanca and 26 at Port-Lyautey); in Algeria (50 near Algiers and 20 at Oran), and a further 26 in Tunisia. Armament was a 20mm cannon firing through the propeller hub and four machine guns in the wings.**

Général Louis Koeltz, commanding the 19ème Région Militaire, was also to be taken into protective custody.

Should the Allies manage to take over Algiers within a few hours of landing, it was believed that they could do so almost without firing a shot, and thus confront the civil and military leaders with a fait accompli. All could then rally to Général Giraud.

Plans were equally ambitious at Oran although Général Robert Boissau, commander of the Division d'Oran, was not part of the pro-Allied preparations. It was his Chief-of-Staff, Colonel Paul Tostain, who had made plans for combined action by the military with a sizeable group of civilian patriots who had been organised from March 1941 by Roger Carcasonne. Units of the 2ème Régiment de Zouaves were to seize control of the two main military installations and to furnish arms for use by the civilians to seize communications centres and arrest Axis armistice commissioners. Guides were to be furnished for the invading troops and destruction of the port was to be forestalled by civilian teams. Général Boissau was either to be persuaded to support the unresisted occupation of Oran or held in custody until the operation had been completed.

However, when Colonel Tostain went to Algiers to meet Général Mast on November 6, he admitted that he could not bring himself to agree to such insubordination and made it clear he would not take part. Consequently, the American Vice-Consul in Oran, Ridgway B. Knight, radioed a warning to Gibraltar that the plans for Oran were falling apart and that the Centre Task Force must expect a hostile reception. While the civilian teams could be relied on, the arrangements for Army officers to join in must be abandoned.

In Morocco, arrangements for sabotage, seizure of key points, and capture of leading Vichyists and German Control Commissioners had been prepared

Article 5 of the Armistice directed that 'all the aircraft still in possession of the French armed forces are to be disarmed and secured under German control'. However, in September 1940, a strong British and Free French naval force attempted to seize Dakar in French West Africa but the Vichy forces did not back down and the attackers withdrew. This attempt, following the attack at Mers el Kébir in July, convinced the Germans that the Vichy forces needed some air defence, sparing the surviving squadrons from planned non-existence. This Bloch 152 fighter was pictured in March 1942 in Lyon.

for some time by French civilian groups co-ordinated by Vice-Consul David W. King. However, in early November, these plans had to be set aside as Murphy said control of all these actions was being transferred to Général Béthouart, the commanding general of the Division de Casablanca, acting for the organisation headed by Général Mast. Béthouart's plan was to seize temporary control at Rabat by a military coup, then to order the garrisons along the coast to remain in their barracks while the landings were taking place, and to hold potential reinforcements at their interior bases.

To avoid confusion with British aircraft the Germans ordered that the Vichy aircraft must be identified by special markings of horizontal red and yellow stripes on the fuselage and tailplane. The French national markings — roundel on the fuselage and tricolour on the fin — were retained. In Morocco, the Vichy air force had 40 Curtiss H-75 fighters although not all were operational for the lack of spare parts made it very difficult to maintain the aircraft.

Operation 'Flagpole'

Following the reception of Murphy's cable requesting the immediate dispatch of a top-secret, high-level group to meet with Général Mast in North Africa, a conference was held in Norfolk House on October 16. Present with Eisenhower were his deputy, General Clark; Brigadier General Lyman L. Lemnitzer, the head of the Allied planning section for Operation 'Torch'; Colonel Archelaus L. Hamblen, the staff expert on shipping and supply; Colonel Julius C. Holmes, the head of civil affairs branch for Operation 'Torch'; and Captain Jerauld Wright, US Navy liaison officer with the Royal Navy.

Eisenhower told them about Murphy's urgent request and said that he wanted Clark to go as his personal representative together with all of them. As he spoke French, Holmes would serve as the interpreter and Wright would be the liaison officer with the French Navy, with the objective of convincing the French to have their fleet presently anchored in Toulon join the Allied cause. The date set for the rendezvous was October 21, and the code-name for the secret mission was Operation 'Flagpole'.

Clark's instructions drafted in Washington covered various aspects of the projected relationship. He was to declare that selection of a French commander for French forces was 'a matter to be handled by the French themselves' with parallel guarantee that the Americans would not interfere with French civil government. To dispel any fears of a future British hold on French colonial territory, Clark was also to emphasise the American control of the operation. Finally, Clark was authorised to indicate that an overall French commander in North Africa might eventually be possible but that in the interim, the Americans would equip French troops engaged in fighting the Axis powers.

An urgent meeting was then arranged in London, Churchill being summoned from Chequers where the Prime Minister was spending the weekend. Clark recorded that 'when Eisenhower and I arrived at No. 10 Downing Street there was about dazzling an array of Britain's diplomatic, military, and naval brain as I had yet seen. The Prime Minister, without knowing exactly what was on our minds, was as enthusiastic as a boy with a new electric train.

'We discussed the implications of the trip at some length with Attlee, Mountbatten, Sir Dudley Pound, and Sir Alan Brooke. Anthony Eden chimed in on the political phase. What Ike wanted was a specific British opinion as to how much I could tell the French about Operation 'Torch'. We knew that Giraud would want an important position in the command, and I offered, if it would help matters, to step down as Deputy Commander to Ike in favour of Giraud. That was rejected. At the end we told Churchill,

The decision to send a party of high-ranking Allied officers to North Africa (Operation 'Flagpole') for secret negotiations with Vichy-French officers was taken on October 17, quite late as it was only three weeks before the landings were due to take place.

The date for the meeting had been set for the 21st, so the party had to leave in a hurry and Major General Carl Spaatz, commanding the US Eighth Air Force, was ordered to provide his best two B-17 pilots to fly the eight high-ranking officers to Gibraltar. He chose Major Paul Tibbets (later to gain fame as the pilot of the *Enola Gay* which dropped the atomic bomb on Hiroshima in August 1945) and Major Wayne Connors, both from the 97th Bomb Group. Taking off from Polebook on the 19th, General Clark and four members of the party were flown by Tibbets in B-17 41-24444 *The Red Gremlin*, while Connors flew Brigadier General Lyman L. Lemnitzer, head of the Allied Force Plans section and Clark's deputy on the mission, and the rest of the party in 41-24377 *Boomerang. The Red Gremlin* was the first B-17 ever to land on Gibraltar's restricted airstrip. *Above:* A perfect comparison on Gibraltar airfield today.

happy as a detective-story fan, the more fantastic details of our plans for this secret rendezvous on which the fate of thousands of British, American, and French soldiers and sailors might hang.

'Escorting me to the door, Churchill emphasised Britain's entirely co-operative spirit. We would have the submarine, destroyer, amphibious planes, and facilities at Gibraltar which we needed.'

For the assignment, Clark replaced his insignia with that of a lieutenant colonel and the party made for the Eighth Air Force base at Polebrook to be flown to Gibraltar. Their departure, delayed by bad weather, finally got underway in two B-17s early on October 19, Clark in the *Red Gremlin*, Lemnitzer in *Boomerang*.

Clark: 'Even before we had identified Gibraltar, Spitfires were shooting up to look us over. Lemnitzer's plane went in first, and we were all relieved to see the big bomber make a safe landing on Gibraltar's limited strip. One of the pilots had already climbed out of my plane when the British rushed up and motioned to everybody to stay inside. They explained that the Gibraltar field was always under full observation by German agents in Spain. The arrival of two B-17s — the first sent there — would give the Nazis enough to think about without their spotting high officers aboard. The British suggested that we leave off our coats and hats. A big car with drawn curtains pulled up as close as possible to the plane; we jumped swiftly into it, to be whisked off to the Governor's house.'

In Algiers, when informed of the proposed meeting, Mast asked Jean Queyrat, the man of the pro-Allied organisation in charge of the Ténès—Cherchell sector west of Algiers, to find a suitable place for a landing. Queyrat turned to his friend Jacques Tessier who lived in an isolated farmhouse on the bluff overlooking the beach at Messelmoun, 70 miles west of Algiers.

Meanwhile, Murphy directed Ridgway Knight, the 'apostle' posted at Oran, to come to Algiers to manage the logistics of the operation; he was the only completely bilingual member on the Vice-Consul's staff and Murphy wanted him to act as a second interpreter. Knight and John Boyd, another of the 'apostles', worked all of October 19 to prepare for the meeting so that all parties would secretly reach the farmhouse in the early morning of the 20th. Everyone was ordered to travel by private car or bicycle, avoiding attention, and to leave at different times.

THE SEA PARTY

Clark conferred briefly with Lieutenant-General Noel Mason-MacFarlane, the Gibraltar Governor, and officers of the Royal Navy, including Captain Barney Fawkes, the commander of British submarine fleet in the Mediterranean. The party was then taken down to the submarine tender HMS *Maidstone* where they had a quick meal in Fawkes's cabin. The HMS *Seraph*, captained by Lieutenant Norman Jewell, was moored alongside.

Although this photo was taken later when the headquarters staff for Operation 'Torch' arrived in Gibraltar, this shot of Clark hiding from view under the wing of a B-17 is a good illustration of the security measures that were in place when he flew in on October 19.

Clark: 'I had never been aboard a submarine before. I soon realised that they were not made for a six-foot-two man. All the time I was in *P219* I had to bend over and watch my head. The officers' quarters, which the submarine crew had hospitably given up to their passengers, was only a cubby-hole alongside the middle catwalk. The submarine crew, almost all youngsters, welcomed us aboard. All they knew was that they were going on a crazy mission with some Americans.'

In addition to the American party, *Seraph* embarked four Folbots — small collapsible, wood-framed canvas canoes — and three British officers of the Special Boat Service (SBS) to handle them and help the five American officers ashore: Captain Godfrey B. Courtney, Captain Ronald P. Livingstone, and Lieutenant James P. Foot.

HMS *Seraph* (P219) was the S-class submarine assigned to take the 'Flagpole' party to Algeria. This photo of her captain, Lieutenant Norman Jewell, on the bridge was taken in January 1943 as she entered Holy Loch in Scotland. The wartime caption explained that the *Seraph* had just completed 'three highly important secret missions' in the Mediterranean, one being Mark Clark's secret trip. (The following year, the *Seraph* under Captain Jewell carried out Operation 'Mincemeat' when a corps carrying false plans was released into the water off Spain in April to mislead the Germans as to future Allied intentions — see *After the Battle* Nos 54 and 94).

The submarine slipped anchor at 2200 hours on October 19 and proceeded due eastwards. The escort returned to Gibraltar in the early hours on the 20th and HMS *Seraph* went on her way uneventfully. That evening, when it was completely dark, Jewell stopped engines to carry out a rehearsal for launching and retrieving the boats, and to test the radio set and the R/G infra-red signalling gear. (This equipment sent a beam of invisible infra-red light from an Aldis-type lamp, the signal being visible only when the beam was intercepted on a little receiver, that, when looking through monocular eyepiece would show the beam as a green spot on a small screen; R/G standing for Red/Green.)

Clark: 'The sea was choppy. Holmes and Captain Livingstone launched their boat first, after practising stepping into the frail and very tipsy craft on the dry deck. They paddled noiselessly away, and from a distance of several hundred yards tried out the infra-red signal-light with which we had been supplied. This light cannot be seen by the naked eye, but with a proper sort of glass it becomes a useful signal-light. The light worked perfectly. Holmes and Livingstone returned to the submarine, with Lemnitzer and Lieutenant Foot trying the next trip. The General got pretty wet, but they did it all right, and Colonel Hamblen and Captain Wright in their turn as well. Captain Courtney was my small-boat pilot, and we tried it last. He was the expert on these boats, and was in charge of instructing all of us. With small-boat exercises complete, the submarine was quickly under way again.'

At 0410 on October 21 *Seraph* arrived off Messelmoun and spotted the lone farmhouse overlooking the beach. The property was illuminated in accordance with instructions but it was now too late to risk a landing before daylight so the *Seraph* stayed submerged keeping observation through the periscope as two trawlers began fishing right in front of the beach.

The 'Flagpole' party was to get ashore from *Seraph* by means of four Folbots, collapsible canoes of the type seen here being used by commandos during an exercise in Scotland in 1941. The three British officers from the Special Boat Service who were assigned to handle them were commanded by Captain Godfrey 'Gruff' Courtney. (It was his brother, Captain Roger Courtney, known as 'Jumbo', who had successfully pioneered the use of the Folbot, triggering kayak raiding and the creation of the SBS.)

In the afternoon orders were received from North Atlantic Station, Gibraltar, that 'your parties were originally expected night October 20th-21st up to 0500 GMT. If not contacted then, you would be expected on night 22nd-23rd.'

THE LAND PARTY

The villa was a typical French colonial red-roofed, white stone house built round a courtyard, with the main highway to Algiers 50 yards away. Jacques Tessier had sent all his Arab servants away, and to secure the sector Queyrat had called in Lieutenant Georges Le Nen who commanded the auxiliary native gendarmes (the Douairs) on this sector of the coastline.

The French delegation was to comprise Général Mast and four officers: Lieutenant-Colonel Germain Jousse (Army), Capitaine de Frégate Pierre Barjot (Navy), Commandant Louis Dartois (Aviation) and Colonel Alphonse Van Hecke, the chief of the Chantiers de la Jeunesse in Algeria. There were also three civilian members of the resistance groups in Algiers, Henri d'Astier de la Vigerie, Jean Rigault, and Bernard Karsenty.

On the 20th Murphy and Knight drove west from Algiers in Knight's official grey Studebaker coupé and stopped at Chenoua Plage, a beach resort some distance east of Messelmoun. They sat down at a café and

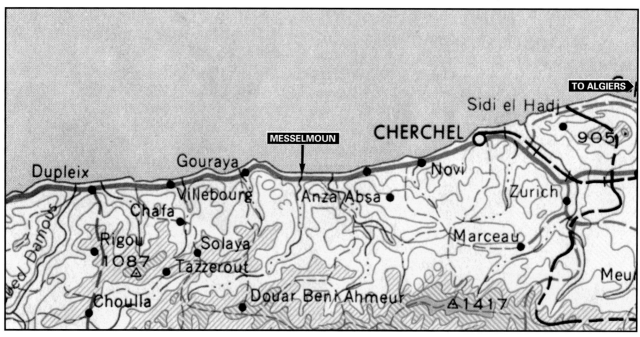

enjoyed themselves with two bottles of wine, referring loudly to the ladies who would soon join them. They reached the Messelmoun villa in the evening and spent the night here only to realise by dawn that something had gone wrong. French delegates started to arrive to whom Murphy had to apologise and sent them back home before he and Knight returned to Algiers.

On the 21st, Murphy got message that *Seraph* had arrived and that the meeting was to be held that night. He rushed to visit Mast and the other trusted conspirators to alert them and then drove to Messelmoun with Knight.

HMS *Seraph* closed the shore on the evening of the 21st, but, seeing no lights, she turned about and surfaced out to sea to charge her batteries.

Queyrat, d'Astier de la Vigerie, and Lieutenant-Colonel Jousse arrived first by bicycle at around 2230. At 2315, Tessier switched on the signal light in a window on the first floor which was immediately spotted by the *Seraph*.

At 2350, the crew of *Seraph* commenced to slip the Folbots into the sea. In the first one were Colonel Holmes and Captain Livingstone of the SBS; in the second, General Lemnitzer and Lieutenant Foot, SBS; in the third Captain Wright and Colonel Hamblen; and in the fourth General Clark and Captain Courtney of the SBS.

The first three Folbots launched successfully and formed up ready to proceed in line ahead but Courtney's boat was swept under the foreplanes and capsized. Fortunately, General Clark was still on deck; later he wrote that 'the stalwart Commando was absolutely devastated at this accident at such a crucial moment'.

Folbot No. 3 was recalled and Clark took Hamblen's place with the R/T set until the fourth boat was righted. Once tested in the water, it proceeded ashore with Captain Courtney and Colonel Hamblen. The submarine now put out to sea to complete the charging of its batteries while remaining within radio contact.

Clark: 'We approached the beach in V formation, Holmes and Livingstone ahead. My boat and the others waited

On the night of October 21/22, the 'Flagpole' party landed on this beach at Messelmoun. The house where the secret conference took place still stands on top of the bluff, just off to the right.

about 200 yards offshore until, through the darkness over the feathery surf, we saw the letter 'K' flashed by a torch — the signal that the first boat had got ashore and all was well. We followed, coming pretty dry through a quite moderate surf.'

Meanwhile in the villa Murphy and the French party were anxiously waiting while Knight who had drawn the first watch stood behind a bush at the edge of the beach. Lieutenant Le Nen: 'D'Astier reported seeing the submarine some distance off shore and we all rushed down to the beach. We peered to the sea in the darkness for some time but nothing could be seen. And suddenly a kayak was there, only four metres away. We made the agreed coded signal with a torch light and the kayak came in. Quickly, three more kayaks landed. Our joy was immense.'

By 0125 all four boats were on shore safely and ten minutes later the party radioed to the submarine, reporting their safe arrival and stated that they

would be ready to return at 2100. They all climbed up the stony path over the bluff and entered the house. (Le Nen was clear that Murphy and the French party were already down on the beach for some time before the kayaks landed but in his book *Calculated Risk* Clark states that they climbed up the bluff before meeting Murphy and his French associates. Le Nen reported that Murphy gave a hug to Clark, 'a spontaneous and emotional gesture', but Clark only reported Murphy greeting them with a sober 'Welcome to North Africa'.)

Général Mast was not due to arrive before 0500 next morning and the American party, exhausted after having been submerged for 16 hours in the discomfort of the submarine narrow quarters, put their heads down in the upstairs bedrooms.

While Le Nen had his second, Aspirant Michel, patrolling the coastal road, he himself regularly telephoned his posts at Cherchell and Gouraya to check if anything had been noticed.

In 1950 a memorial commemorating the historic meeting of October 1942 was inaugurated near the villa (see page 54). *Left:* A French newsreel crew covered the event and they asked Jacques Tessier, the son-in-law of the owner who

made the house available for the secret talks and who was present in October 1942, to point out the significant locations, starting here with the landing beach. *Right:* The same beach today, looking westwards.

Left: **Looking up at the villa in 1950 from the beach where the American party came ashore.** *Right:* **Today the house is a ruin** **and is no longer visible from the beach although the terrace wall still remains.**

CONFERENCE

Van Hecke arrived by car about 5 a.m. together with his Number two, Capitaine George Lindsay-Watson. He was soon followed by Mast, dressed in civvies, who spoke little English and simply said, 'Welcome to my country'. The French changed from civilian clothes into their uniforms and, after a breakfast had been served, the first conference began with Generals Clark, Lemnitzer, and Mast, Lieutenant-Colonel Jousse, and Murphy. Général Mast was then told that the Allies had decided to send a large American force to North Africa, supported in the air and on the sea by British units.

Murphy later wrote that 'the meeting at Cherchell was one of the oddest conferences of the war, because the French participants in those staff talks were ignorant of the essential details of the Allied plans. Both Clark and I were under instructions to avoid giving the French conferees specific information about the timing of the expedition or the exact locations selected for troop landings. So these discussions inevitably misled our French associates, who assumed they had months in which to prepare for African D-Day, whereas we Americans knew they had only sixteen days. In fact, the first slow convoys of the expedition already were starting from the United States as we talked.'

Tessier then showed the cameraman another significant spot. As the submarine waited off shore, this was the first-floor window facing the sea from where a signal light was shone at exactly 23.15 p.m. on October 21, 1942.

Clark recalled that 'remembering my instructions not to reveal the facts of the impending operation, I was in a difficult position. Mast asked how big an American effort could be made. I tried to keep a poker face while saying that half a million Allied troops could come in, and I said that we could put 2,000 planes in the air, as well as plenty of the US Navy.'

Jacques Tessier said that he was standing here on the terrace when he spotted the *Seraph* some distance offshore.

Tessier then indicated the trap-door to the cellar where Clark and the other four American officers and two of the SBS men had to hide.

Mast advised the Americans to prepare for the swiftest possible movement into Tunisia to counter-balance the Axis capacity to quickly send in reinforcements from Italy. He also urged the necessity of establishing a bridgehead in southern France by simultaneous aid to French forces waiting there.

The discussion then shifted to the role to be played by Général Giraud. It was agreed, first, that he should receive from the Allies a letter setting forth their intentions and, second, that if Giraud consented to come to North Africa, he should be brought out by an American submarine. A draft letter was then prepared which was to be subject to approval by General Eisenhower. It covered the restoration of France to its 1939 boundaries; an acceptance of France as an ally; the assumption of the supreme command in North Africa by the French 'at the appropriate time' following the landings, and the rearming of French troops.

At noon, the group sat down for lunch but Général Mast and Colonel van Hecke had to leave to return to Algiers to prepare their commands for an imminent visit by Darlan.

The second meeting covered detailed discussions on the various phases of the operational plans. The French came with voluminous written information covering detailed positions and strengths of troops and naval units, and where supplies of petrol and ammunition were stored. They also provided details of those areas controlled by friendly commanders like at Casablanca, Meknès, and Constantine, and of those commands that would prove hostile like the Division d'Oran. Information was listed about airports: where resistance would be strong, and where airborne troops could land safely. Clark commented that all this intelligence 'later turned out to be accurate in every respect' and Eisenhower's planners would say that 'the completeness and terrific value of the material was astounding'.

So far, the gathering did not appear to have aroused any suspicion and at the villa everyone relaxed. At 6 p.m., however, while patrolling the road east of the house, Michel suddenly came across the car of the chief of the

Cherchell police who directed him to follow him to Gouraya. Reaching the Gendarmerie there, Michel saw several Gendarmes and custom officials already gathered. The chief of the police explained that they had been tipped of some smuggling activities at Messelmoun and that they were preparing to mount a raid on the premises.

Michel explained that the reason for all this activity at the villa was that the American consul in Algiers happened to be there, having a little party with friends at the Tessier house. He also reported that Lieutenant Le Nen had already gone to the house to inquire. (Who tipped the police is unclear. One possible explanation is that one of Tessier's servants, surprised to be given time off so suddenly, spoke about at a local café and someone, thinking all this might well be smuggler activities, went to the police to report, hoping to collect the rewards for information.)

At 6.30 p.m., Le Nen called the Gendarmerie at Gouraya to check and Michel himself answered: 'Lieutenant,

there is a police alert!' The tone was casual not to warn the Gendarmes all around him but it was a pressing warning. Le Nen rushed to the conference room and tell them of the alert. Suddenly, as Knight later witnessed, 'it was sheer pandemonium'. The French swiftly gathered together their papers and maps, changed into civilian clothes and took off in the direction of Algiers. Meanwhile Tessier led the Americans and two of the SBS men (the third was hiding in the bush near the beach with the radio set to liaise with the submarine) to a trap-door in the patio and they dropped down to the cellar.

'We had our musette bags with us,' wrote Clark, 'stuffed with the incriminating French documents, which, if found upon us, would make it pretty difficult.'

From then on, only Tessier, Le Nen, Murphy and Knight remained in the house having agreed to pose as somewhat inebriated members of a raucous social gathering, talking loudly and clanking bottles in the living room to

There are several entrances visible today which lead to the old cellars but most have been filled in with rubble so it is difficult to determine which is the correct opening.

In April 1957, a French Army photographer Jacques Bouchenoire took a series of photos at Messelmoun. The villa had been set on fire by fellaghas (armed anti-colonial militants) the previous spring and he found the building completely gutted. The spot where the American party came ashore was some distance off to the right.

mislead any unwanted visitors. They anxiously waited from news from Michel, or for the arrival of the police, while the five American officers and the two SBS men were holding their breath in the wine cellar. As Clark later described it, he even had to give Captain Courtney a piece of chewing-gum from his own mouth to stop him from coughing and give away their hiding-place.

Though Clark claimed in his post-war memoirs that the French police actually visited the house while they were in the cellar, a detailed account written by Lieutenant Le Nen (which gives a precise hour-by-hour description of the events) makes it clear that in actual fact the police swallowed the story of the American consul having a party there and no one came to check.

At about 1930 Le Nen went out to check the road. With no sign of anything abnormal, he then went down to the beach. The sea was becoming rough so he returned to report that they should not delay any longer. At 2000 they opened the trap-door and urged the party to leave.

The Folbots were recovered from the room where they had been hidden and everybody proceeded down to the beach. Surf was heavy and sizeable breakers could be seen rolling just off shore. The Folbots were camouflaged in the scrub and sentries posted while the party waited out of sight.

At 2102 Captain Livingstone sent a radio message to HMS *Seraph* to come in as close as possible and at 2110 the SBS operating the R/G infra-red receiver picked-up the submarine's signal beam.

General Clark and Captain Livingstone embarked first but, as reported by Captain Courtney of the SBS, 'they nearly got through but were capsized by a large wave'. Clark: 'The waves looked impossible, but we had to make a try

during the full darkness or risk ruining the whole mission. I knew that I was going to be soaked, so I stripped to shorts and shirt. It was cold paddling about in the water. We tried one spot, and were immediately overturned by a wave. I had put my money-belt — containing several hundred dollars in gold — in my rolled-up trousers, not wishing to be pulled down by the gold in a turbulent surf and heavy undertow. My trousers and the money were lost at that time. This attempt convinced us that a launching was impossible in those circumstances.'

At 2149 the SBS team sent a radio message to the submarine stating that they could not leave yet and that she must await a further message. The boats were concealed and the SBS posted as sentries while the rest returned to the house.

It was now about 2200 and the surf was still very heavy. The Americans wanted a fishing-boat to be hired or bought to take the party out to the submarine but the French pointed out that in the current situation, with the security forces all poised to deter smuggling, trying to buy a fishing boat in the dead of night was the recipe for disaster.

Michel, who had first returned to the villa at 2130 before returning to Cherchell to survey the situation, finally came back at 2300 with good news: the story of the American consul having a party had been accepted and the police would not intervene before morning.

At 0400 the party returned to the beach to check the state of the sea. At 0438 the SBS sent a message to the *Seraph* to come in as close as possible, and they soon picked-up the R/G infra-red beam from the submarine that was in position five cables (about 3,000 feet) from the shore. There was still a nasty swell and breakers were still rolling in, so Clark was hesitating, still talking about finding a fishing-boat.

After another half an hour had passed, and with daylight approaching, at 0500 Clark finally decided to risk it. All the heavy gear was discarded and two members of the shore party waded through the surf to steady each boat. The first with Clark and Captain Wright got off successfully but the following boat with General Lemnitzer and Lieutenant Foot capsized. It was righted and sent on its way followed by the third boat of Colonel Hamblen and Captain Courtney. The last boat with Colonel Holmes and Captain Livingstone first overturned before being righted and sent off successfully. Le Nen remembered how Murphy gave a hug to each of the launching party, all soaked to the skin, wet and cold, after each successful launch.

Clark: 'We passed the first breaker all right, and I heaved a sigh of relief. Just then the second loomed up ahead, gleaming just a little in the starlight and appearing about a hundred feet

Looking from the beach with the terrace wall and the crumbling remains of the ruined villa crowning the bluff.

Left: **While Bouchenoire was taking his photos, a local man approached him to announce that he had been charged with guarding the estate after Tessier had left following the fellagha attack in 1956. It turned out that the man was Belkacem Tayebi who had previously worked at the farm as stable lad. He then indicated a room that might have been the one where the main** meetings had been held in 1942. *Right:* **After the independence of Algeria in 1962, the villa became a squat for homeless families for several decades until the Algerian authorities finally decided to safeguard the building. In 2006, the squatters were relocated and what remained of the villa was cleared of all post-war makeshift constructions.**

high. We managed it, however, and were in the clear after we had passed the second breaker. Our musette bags and brief-cases, loaded with the secret papers, were soaked, as were the papers I had stored inside my borrowed sweater. We seemed to be paddling for hours without seeing anything before we spotted the loom of the *Seraph* in the blackness.' (Once again, Clark embellished his tale for in the Mediterranean, even the strongest breakers might reach a maximum of ten feet, not one hundred!)

The Americans and the SBS party boarded *Seraph* wet through and exhausted. Clark said that he heard somewhere about the British Navy having a rum ration even on submarines but Jewell said that it was only for use in case of emergencies. When Clark replied that this was an emergency Jewell explained that an order to issue rum had to be signed by 'an officer of sufficient rank', which Clark immediately signed for a double rum ration to all!

Clark was worried that the wreckage of one of the Folbots left behind might be washed up on the beach or, even worse, the bag containing the letters that Murphy had given Holmes to deliver in England might come ashore. Much against Jewell's judgement, Clark ordered the submarine to surface in the afternoon long enough for a radio message to be sent to Gibraltar: 'Request you will notify McGowan [code-name for Murphy] that letters he handed Julius [Holmes] were lost when his canoe broke up. They were in a weighted musette bag which may have fallen out. Canoe may float inshore. Search of beach should be commenced immediately.'

At first light, Murphy, Knight, Tessier and Le Nen carried out a careful inspection of the beach to pick up everything left, jackets, trousers and weapons etc. They loaded the uniforms and weapons in the trunk of the Studebaker and Murphy and Knight drove back to Algiers. Le Nen then went to the police in Cherchell to confirm the story of the noisy party. The explanation was believed and all enquiries were dropped.

Some days later a trawler recovered a purse full of golden coins, binoculars, and a sizeable batch of documents and maps. Having seen a submarine off shore, 'all black and silent' some nights before, the captain knew the documents would mean trouble so he weighted them with ballast and dumped them back in the sea. The valuables were shared out amongst the crew but one of them proved too talkative and the police soon made enquiries. Fortunately, nothing compromising was found and the coins were deemed a legitimate discovery at sea. Those retained as souvenirs by Paul Di Maïo were four coins of 10 and 20 Canadian dollars dated 1912.

Later in the morning Mast and the 'Committee of Five' were informed of the successful ending of the operation. In the meantime, *Seraph* proceeded west to Gibraltar, radioing on the morning of October 24 that: 'Consider weather condition ideal for transfer to Sunderland. Request you will have Sunderland rendezvous as soon as practicable.' A Catalina was then

Tayebi also claimed that he was there in 1942 and he pointed out where he saw the submarine.

The original wall of the villa's terrace still survives on top of the bluff.

53

despatched from Gibraltar and at 3.20 p.m. all passengers were reported to have been transferred aboard the aircraft. Reaching Gibraltar, a message was sent to London reporting the successful outcome and early on October 25 the party returned to England in the two B-17s.

Clark: 'On arrival after a rough, cold trip I went directly to Telegraph Cottage, Ike's country place, where he and Bedell Smith were waiting for me. I gave them a complete account of the affair. Ike was delighted, and phoned the Prime Minister to tell him that I was back. Churchill asked us both for supper that night. I was too tired to accept.'

The Western Task Force, coming directly from the USA, was by then already on its way and the other task forces were about to sail yet the French were still unaware that the operation was so far advanced.

Afraid that the French had been left with not enough time to implement the measures agreed, Murphy wanted to inform Mast and other trusted conspirators but on October 27 Eisenhower cabled him to wait eight more days: 'You are authorised to notify Kingpin or Flagpole on November 4th of the assault date (November 8).'

Consequently, Murphy waited until November 4 to warn Mast that the attack would take place four days later. The immediate response was irritation and dismay for Mast, rightly surmising that this fundamental information had been withheld from him at the Cherchell staff conference, realised that the brief period remaining would jeopardise successful operations by the pro-Allied French organisations in Morocco, Oran, and Algiers. His insistence upon a delay of at least three weeks, to permit them to make adequate preparations, which Murphy transmitted sympathetically to General Eisenhower, was rejected in Washington and London as out of the question. All that remained was for Mast to hurry preparations as best possible.

By the time Bouchenoire took this photo of the memorial plaque in April 1957 it showed bullet holes from a clash between fellaghas and a patrol from the 22ème Regiment d'Infanterie on the night of July 31/August 1, 1956. Its wording began with the statement 'Here began the road to liberation' followed by a list of the participants. In the left-hand column were the members of the Allied party: General Clark, General Lemnitzer, Colonel Hamblen, Colonel Holmes and Captain Wright; the three SBS men, Captain Livingstone, Captain Courtney and Lieutenant Foot (mis-spelled Foote), and Murphy and Knight. Though none of the participants at the meeting ever mentioned them being present, the names of John H. Boyd and Gordon H. Browne appeared at the end of the list, possibly because of their role in its preparation. The French participants were given in the right-hand column: Général Mast, Capitaine de Frégate Barjot, Lieutenant-Colonel Jousse, Colonel Van Hecke (mis-spelled Van Eycke), Capitaine Lindsay-Watson, Tessier, Lieutenant Le Nen, Aspirant Michel, Karsenty, Rigault, Queyrat, D'Astier de la Vigerie, and Commandant Dartois.

Left: By then, the historic villa (seen in the background) had already been destroyed by fire. Right: The original plaque was smashed after the independence in 1962. When a replacement was made in 2006, only bits of the original could be found, and the new wording appears fragmented and jumbled.

On November 6 — two days before the 'Torch' landings — Général Giraud escaped from Vichy France to join Allied HQ at Gibraltar, embarking in a fishing boat at La Fossette, some 40 kilometres east of Toulon, to make for HMS *Seraph* waiting just off the bay.

lord, USAAF, boarded the submarine which arrived in position 50 miles off Toulon on October 30. There she lay for four days, awaiting news of the rendezvous. Orders finally arrived at 2100 on November 4 to proceed immediately to position 15 miles off Île du Levant and await instructions.

At 0200 on the 5th the submarine received message that 'Kingpin' and three others would embark from La Fossette, one miles east of Lavandou, at 2300 on November 5. Recognition signal was to be 'S' on blinker, answered from the submarine by dimmed blue light.

During the morning of the 5th the submarine made a brief periscope reconnaissance of the rendezvous from about 2,000 yards from shore, studying terrain, skyline and local activity, and then returned to seaward. At 1900 *Seraph* headed in toward rendezvous, now on the surface but carefully trimmed down to awash condition. She rounded the northern point of the Île du Levant, about three miles off, and then headed direct for Lavandou. At 2020 a small boat was sighted so the submarine

GÉNÉRAL GIRAUD AT GIBRALTAR

At the very last minute Général Giraud, code-named 'Kingpin', was finally given the three central features of Allied policy in informal letters dated November 2: (1) France would be fully restored to her pre-war boundaries and sovereign independence; (2) purely French national matters would be left for determination by the French without American interference; (3) the government of the United States regards the French nation as an ally and will deal with it as such.

Giraud had the documents in hands when he was summoned to leave his retreat. For him, the decision was not an easy one for the Allies required him to advance the date for rallying the French by several months. It also meant that simultaneous military action in southern France, which he considered vital to effective liberation of all France, had been abandoned. Nevertheless, he decided to co-operate.

It was now top priority to extract Giraud from southern France and take him to Gibraltar. To maintain the American character of the operation, it had been intended to pick him up with a US submarine but none were within easy reach so instead HMS *Seraph* was put under US command with Captain Jerauld Wright of the US Navy in charge.

Late on October 27, Captain Wright and Lieutenant Colonel Bradford Gay-

Operation 'Flagpole' failed to achieve its primary goal which was to persuade the French authorities in North Africa to simply welcome the Allied invading forces. The cause of this failure was that the meeting was laid on much too late, leaving no time for the pro-Allied French military and civilian authorities to take widescale measures. A decidedly positive result however was the large amount of accurate military information given to the American delegation by the French.

Today a memorial marks the spot from where he departed.

This picture of Robert Murphy in company with Generals Eisenhower and Clark and Amiral Darlan was taken in Algiers on November 13.

On November 5, General Eisenhower and his key staff flew from the United Kingdom to Gibraltar to the advanced command post. The original caption of this photo taken that day states that Eisenhower was 'confident of success' in discussing plan with Lieutenant Commander Harry C. Butcher, his naval aide.

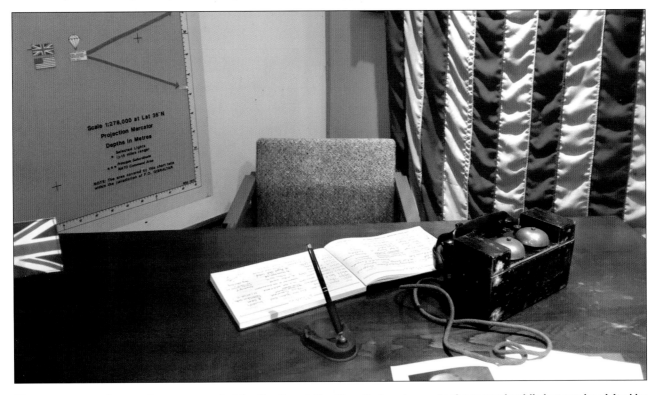

The reconstructed room is now occupied by Continent 8 Technologies Ltd which kindly provided this nice comparison. The site is not open to the general public but can be visited by special arrangement.

submerged but it proved impossible to fix its position through periscope. At 2300 *Seraph* fully surfaced and took bearings that placed her about 1,500 yards south-south-east La Fossette Point. Sea conditions were poor with waves rolling in from north-east and still no signal could be seen from the beach.

At 0015 on the 6th a garbled message was flashed in French which was interpreted to mean 'wait one hour'. *Seraph* closed to within 1,000 yards of the point of rendezvous and at 0115 the first flash of 'S' was finally picked up from beach.

At 0140, guided by the blue light from the submarine, a fishing boat came alongside with four passengers: Général Giraud, Capitaine André Beaufre, Lieutenant de Vaisseau Hubert Viret and Aspirant Bernard Giraud, the son of the general.

The *Seraph* retired on the surface at maximum speed on one engine, charging batteries on the other, but when a message was received from Gibraltar indicating that a plane would take off in the early hours of the 7th, it was then discovered that all the submarine's radio transmitters were out of commission, so no reply could be sent.

With the radio still unserviceable, Captain Wright decided to sail on the surface during daylight to try to spot the aircraft, and at 11.30 a.m. a Catalina was sighted on northern horizon, heading south-east. Fortunately, the submarine was spotted and the pilot made a perfect landing in spite of the choppy sea.

Passengers and baggage were brought on deck and Folbots were about to be launched when an unidentified aircraft appeared on horizon. Everyone and everything was cleared down below (except the Folbots) with the *Seraph* preparing to crash dive but the plane, still unidentified, circled area for about 20 minutes before disappearing to the north.

The crew now redoubled their efforts to transfer the passengers to the Catalina, one at a time in the Folbots, but the sea was rough, washing over forward casing. Even so, Giraud, aged 67, did masterful job boarding the Folbot in one go without falling overboard. In about 40 minutes, all six passengers — the four French and the two American officers — and their baggage were successfully transferred to the Catalina. The take-off was bumpy and the party arrived Gibraltar at 3.20 p.m. on November 7.

Gibraltar was honeycombed with tunnels — the 16,000-strong garrison of the Rock could be housed with enough food and water to last them for 16 months — and Eisenhower's command centre was located in Admiralty Tunnel deep within the Rock. This photo shows WRENS manning the cypher office in November 1942.

On the 8th, in another hectic operation, the *Sibyl* picked up seven persons of Giraud's entourage, including Mrs Beaufre, off Cros-de-Cagnes, just west of Nice, and took them to Algiers on November 11.

Conferring with Eisenhower, Giraud was briefed on the Operation 'Torch', which was now just hours away, only to find out that the question of the inter-Allied command had not been agreed as he had understood. When he decided to come, he firmly believed that he held President Roosevelt's acceptance of his explicit requirement that he be the inter-Allied supreme commander wherever Allied troops fought beside French troops on French soil. At some point in his negotiations with the Allies, if not through Murphy, a memorandum listing the four conditions governing his acceptance was returned with 'OK. Roosevelt' written in the lower left corner. The memorandum has survived in his handwriting but the authenticity of this document cannot be established.

To succeed in the plan — to swiftly rally the French armed forces in a renewed war against the Axis powers — Giraud knew he must appear before the French as a free national leader, not as the appointee of the Allies, and with resolute persistence, he refused to accept the secondary role which the Allies had planned for him: that of Commander-in-Chief of French forces only.

Although the matter became the subject of a prolonged discussion, extending beyond the time when the transports had begun to disembark troops, Giraud realised that he had been dealt a fait accompli. With Operation 'Torch' now underway, the pro-Allied French in Algiers, in ignorance of Giraud's whereabouts and status, were obliged to proceed without his support. On November 8, after the landings had been announced and President Roosevelt had sent a message of profound friendship with France, Général Giraud broadcast an appeal for support for the Allies.

With General Eisenhower at Gibraltar were his deputy, General Clark, his naval Commander-in-Chief, Admiral Cunningham, his air officer, Air Commodore Arthur Sanders, the two air force commanders, Major General Doolittle and Air Marshal Welsh, the commanding general of the force which would push eastward from Algeria into Tunisia, General Anderson, and others. The conditions in the tunnels were reported as being very unpleasant as humidity was up to 98 per cent, causing condensation and damp throughout. Eisenhower later wrote: 'At Gibraltar our headquarters were established in the most dismal setting we occupied during the war. The eternal darkness of the tunnels was here and there partially pierced by feeble electric bulbs. Damp, cold air in block-long passages was heavy with a stagnation that did not noticeably respond to the clattering efforts of electric fans. Through the arched ceilings came a constant drip, drip, drip of surface water that faithfully but drearily ticked off the seconds.' *Left:* In 1998, the Gibraltar-American Council and the Government of Gibraltar commemorated the anniversary of Operation 'Torch' with this bronze plaque at the American War Memorial.

THE LANDINGS

The Eastern Task Force: Algiers

The Eastern Naval Task Force comprised 11 Landing Ships Infantry, four US Combat Loaders and 18 Transports.

Algiers was the most important objective of Operation 'Torch'. First, it was the seat of government for all French North Africa with the civil and military administrations centred there, hence an objective of major importance when the underlying purpose of the whole operation was to promote conditions that would bring the French back into the war on the side of the Allies. The headquarters of the Commander-in-Chief of all the French armed force in North Africa, Général Juin, and that of the Governor General of Algeria, Yves Châtel, were both located in Algiers, as were the headquarters of the 19ème Région Militaire of Général Koeltz, and Général Mast's Division d'Alger.

Also, Algiers was the nearest city to Tunisia where it was planned that the Allies would fight the final battles and win the North African campaign. Then Algiers offered a large harbour, sizeable railway terminal, two airfields, and ample facilities for housing the Allied Force Headquarters when that was moved from London.

Algiers lies on the western shore of a large bay that extends for about 12 miles between Pointe Pescade on a broad headland in the west and Cap Matifou, a sharper promontory at the eastern end.

The naval commander of the Eastern Task Force was Vice-Admiral Sir Harold Burrough (pictured left in this photo) with US Major General Charles W. Ryder (right) who was in charge of the combined land operations. With them in this shot taken on board the headquarters ship HMS *Bulolo* off Algiers are Major-General Vyvyan Evelegh, commanding the British 78th Division and the RAF liaison officer, Air Commodore George Lawson.

Including the 36th Infantry Brigade Group of over 7,100 men which was initially held offshore as a reserve for either A or B Sectors, the total strength of the Eastern Assault Force was over 33,300 officers and men, mostly British, including the Royal Navy personnel in the landing craft and beach parties.

Royal Navy photographer Lieutenant Leonard Pelman aboard *Marnix van Sint Aldegonde* pictured Brigadier Edward Cass, the brigade commander, carrying out a last inspection of troops of the 11th Infantry Brigade Group. The force that was to assault the A Sector, west of Algiers, totalled some 7,200 men.

Of the ground troops at Algiers, 7,000 men of the Division d'Alger were believed to be stationed in the immediate vicinity of the town, 4,500 being based to the west of it and 3,500 to the east. However, as a result of the conditions imposed by the armistice with the Axis powers in 1940, these units of the 'armistice army' were below strength and were badly lacking modern weapons and equipment, including transport. Potential supporting ground units were based in the west near Orléansville as well as to the east at Sétif.

The two aerodromes at Algiers were Maison Blanche, ten miles to the east and Blida, 20 miles to the south-west. Forty-seven Dewoitine 520 fighters and six Potez 63.11 reconnaissance aircraft were based at the former airfield with 26 Douglas DB-7 and two Lioré et Olivier 451 bombers at Blida.

A dozen coastal batteries commanded the harbour and all sea approaches for several miles on both sides of the bay, the main ones being in the old fort at Cap Sidi Ferruch, ten

miles west of Algiers. Another lay near Pointe Pescade, five miles from the harbour, and the Batterie du Lazaret on Cap Matifou was some 20 miles to the east.

When choosing the landing sectors, the planners for the operation found that the best beaches to land near Algiers were those on the eastern shore of the bay. However, these all lay within range of the coastal gun batteries so it was decided instead to use three other landing sectors: two to the west of the bay, designated A and B, and one further to the east designated C.

Using Beer and Charlie is not surprising as they were part of the British inter-service phonetic alphabet in use since 1921, but Apples (plural) was an oddity in 1942, being last used in the Army code alphabet back in 1918.

Apples and Beer Sectors lay west of Algiers where two pairs of landing beaches were chosen on either side of Cap Sidi Ferruch. Apples Sector was sub-divided into Green and White Beaches near Castiglione, and Beer Sector's Green and White Beaches lay

just east of Cap Sidi Ferruch. Closer Algiers, on the rugged shore on both sides of Pointe Pescade, four sections of Red Beach were designated in coves and small bays.

Off to the east of Algiers bay, Charlie Sector, comprising four beaches, lay on the eastern side of Cap Matifou. C Green Beach, measuring some 800 yards, was sited halfway between the villages of Jean Bart and Aïn Taya, while C Blue Beach of similar length lay directly in front of Aïn Taya. Red Beach, sub-divided into Red 1 and Red 2, stretched from the hamlet of Surcouf, east of Aïn Taya, to the marshy mouth of the Réghaïa river. The latter two beaches were all smooth sand and of a fairly easy grade but C Blue and Green led to a low escarpment with limited exits. Once this had been surmounted and a ridge had been crossed, the Mitidja flatland stretched toward the south-west and offered easy access to Algiers from the east and south.

Reminiscent of the Zeebrugge raid of 1918 (although Admiral Cunningham made it clear that they were not planned

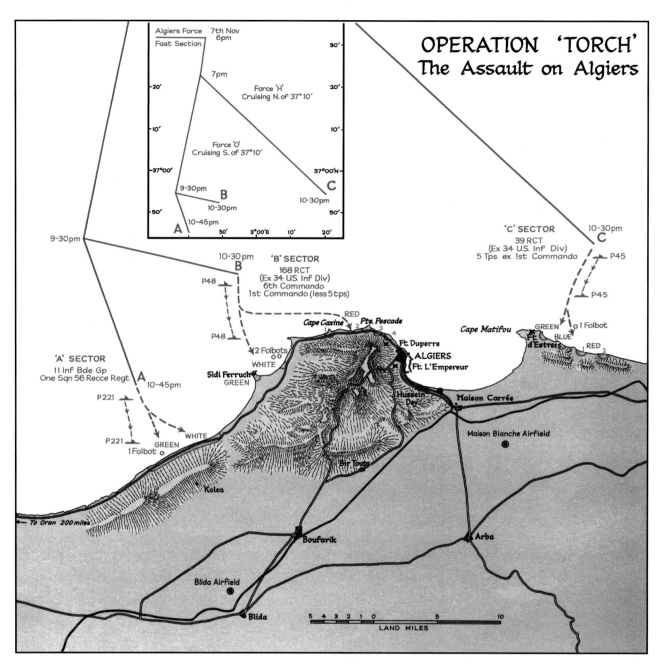

OPERATION 'TORCH'
The Assault on Algiers

The landing at Algiers. The dashed lines show the landing operations as intended, the inset the tracks from 6 p.m. on November 7. The landing group for A Sector comprised three LSIs and four transports; the group for B Sector was made up of seven LSIs and ten transports, while C Sector had three Combat Loaders, one LSI, and one transport.

as imitations) in the hope of preventing the scuttling of vessels and sabotage of the dock facilities, Operation 'Terminal' provided for a direct attack right into the harbour by two destroyers, HMS *Broke* and HMS *Malcolm*. The operation was difficult in its timing, the correct moment depending on the degree of resistance encountered. The assault group included 650 Americans from the 135th Infantry Regiment and 74 Royal Navy personnel to board and seize ships in the harbour.

Naval forces sailing off shore were to furnish support to protect the transport areas and landing beaches from seaborne interference, and, in the initial phases preceding the capture of airfields, to provide support with carrier-borne aircraft. Forward observation officers were to move inland with each landing team — one for A Sector, four

with B Sector, and two for C Sector — keeping in touch by radio with the fire-support ship assigned to each sector. If shelling was required that was heavier than that which could be provided from a destroyer, it could be requested from one of four cruisers, HMS *Sheffield*, HMS *Scylla*, HMS *Charybdis* and HMS *Bermuda*. In the case of calls for gun-fire from the cruisers, a safety margin of 2,000 yards between the target and the nearest Allied troops was deemed necessary.

The naval air support would come from the carriers HMS *Argus* and HMS *Avenger* sailing some distance off shore, the aircraft dive-bombing, spotting, or smoke-laying, as requested. Once the Maison Blanche airfield had been captured, RAF fighter squadrons would fly in from Gibraltar and thereafter take over air defence of the airfield, the port,

and the convoys as well as reconnaissance and close support missions.

H-Hour for the Eastern Task Force was set at 0100 GMT. There would be no moonlight and sunrise at Algiers would come at 6.18 a.m. Also, being in the Mediterranean, there would be no tide to take into consideration.

The assault force for A Sector was the British 11th Infantry Brigade Group under Brigadier Edward E. E. Cass, a force totalling some 7,200 men. The anti-aircraft vessel *Pozarica*, the sloops *Enchantress* and *Stork*, and the corvettes *Convolvulus* and *Marigold* were assigned as escorts, and the destroyer *Bramham* was available for fire-support.

The Group's initial mission was to seize control of two key bridges on the coastal road east of A White Beach and to establish southern flank protection for B Sector. Then, from the vicinity of Bir Touta and the elevations of Dovera, the force was to be ready to move into Algiers or south-west to Blida to support an attack on the airfield there.

The assault force designated for B Sector was the US 168th Combat Team commanded by Colonel John W. O'Daniel. It comprised 4,355 Americans and 1,065 British troops, to which part of the 1st Commando and all of the 6th Commando (British and American) were attached. The *Palomares* was to furnish anti-aircraft protection while the monitor *Roberts* and the destroyers *Blyskavica* and *Wilton* were designated for fire-support.

The mixed force was directed to move from B Green Beach to seize the fort at Sidi Ferruch; from B White Beach it was to gain control of a warning device on the projection of Rass Acrata, and from the separate sections of B Red Beach to capture similar installations on Cap Caxine and to occupy the battery at Fort Duperré. Meanwhile other elements were to push inland through Cheragas to the heights of La Bouzaréa, almost 1,500 feet above sea level, and thence down into Algiers where key points in the town and the port were earmarked for swift capture.

East of Algiers, the assault landings at C Sector were to be made by the US 39th Combat Team, some 5,700 strong, with the addition of 310 men (two-thirds British and one third American) of the 1st Commando, all under the command of Colonel Benjamin F. Caffey. The anti-aircraft ship *Tynwald* and the fire-support destroyers *Cowdray* and *Zetland* were the principal escort vessels. The mission of the 39th Combat Team was to capture the airfield at Maison Blanche, the towns of Maison Carrée and Hussein Dey, and close Algiers from the south-east.

The British 36th Infantry Brigade Group of over 7,100 men was held offshore in eight troop and cargo transports as a reserve for either A or B Sectors. The total strength of the landing force in this sector was over 33,300 officers and men, mostly British, including Royal Navy personnel in the landing craft and beach parties.

The British Admiralty furnished the units of the Eastern Naval Task Force with 17 transports, including four US combat-loaders, 16 mechanical transport ships, and some 50 escorts (not including Force H). The Naval Commander for the Eastern Task Force was Vice-Admiral Sir Harold Burrough, and the landing force commander, Major General Charles W. Ryder. Both were on the headquarters ship HMS *Bulolo* with the centre group off Cap Sidi Ferruch.

In case the French ordered out their fleet at Toulon to attack the assault force, the Royal Navy deployed four submarines to stop them. On November 7-8, the *Seraph*, *Sibyl*, *Unseen* and *P-222*, were sent from Gibraltar to patrol off Toulon, being replaced on November 14 by *Splendid*, *Unshaken*, *Tribune* and *Sturgeon*. However, all were soon withdrawn when it became clear that the French were not going to interfere.

About a third of the Eastern Assault Force was made up of American soldiers (note the US flag patch on the uniforms). A Signal Corps photographer pictured these GIs climbing down into the assault craft from their transport.

Unfortunately, we failed to trace exactly where these two photos were taken as the original captions only state it was 'somewhere off the North African coast'. No doubt the photographer was more concerned with the task at hand. This man is armed with the Browning Automatic Rifle.

Général Juin, the Commander-in-Chief of the French armed force in North Africa, at his residence in May 1942.

The Pro-Allied Patriots Turn to Action

At 10 p.m. on November 7, as the assault armada was approaching the shore, Murphy held a final meeting with Général Mast and other leaders of the patriot movement before they dispersed to their various tasks, and shortly before midnight the BBC broadcast in French the agreed message that Operation 'Torch' landings were beginning: 'Allo, Robert. Franklyn arrivé'.

Half an hour after midnight, the pro-Allied patriots began executing their long-prepared plans, and small organised parties — about 400 men in total — occupied the major centres from which opposition to the landings might otherwise have been directed. One vital task was to block the telephone system and many of the principal authorities — other than those whose loyalty could be guaranteed — were placed under house arrest. This included Général Juin. At the police headquarters and outlying stations, the pro-Allied patriots soon gained control, locking up Vichy officials. They took possession of the radio station and prepared to broadcast an appeal by Général Giraud.

These steps were taken without much difficulty for they appeared as if part of the authentic defence scheme in place for the defence of Algiers. This laid down that in an emergency, civilians should relieve military guards for more active tasks. Each group of patriots presented an order signed by Général Mast that such an emergency existed. All groups discharged their tasks effectively and by 1.30 a.m. on D-Day the pro-Allied French were in control of Algiers.

Meanwhile, guides were sent to the anticipated points of landing to expedite the arrival of Allied troops to take over control of the city.

West of Algiers, right in between B Green and B White Beaches, Colonel Louis Baril, another of the pro-Allied insurrectionists, took over the fort and the coastal batteries at Sidi Ferruch with one of his companies.

At the Blida airfield south of Algiers, Général de Monsabert moved in at 2 a.m. with a platoon of his troops. With him was Jacques Lemaigre-Dubreuil, a member of the 'Committee of Five', ready to meet Général Giraud who was due to land at daybreak. At first the airfield commander, Colonel Charles Montrelay, greeted the announcement of the Allied landings with enthusiasm but a phone call from the Air Force HQ in Algiers (via the one secure phone line to the airfield which had not been cut) soon ordered him to oppose the American invasion by force. De Monsabert tried to explain the situation by suggesting that Général Mast's orders had not yet been transmitted to Air Force HQ but he knew that Vichy Air Minister, Général Jean Bergeret, was in Algiers and was obviously acting to block the rebel take-over.

Left: Shortly after midnight on November 7, Robert Murphy came to see Général Juin at his residence in Algiers. he had some difficulty getting in to see the general as he was challenged by the guard of pro-Allied French patriots who had now taken charge of security. Right: The Villa des Oliviers is now the residence of the French Ambassador in Algeria, and it was thanks to Xavier Driencourt, the current Ambassador, that we were able to achieve this nice comparison in 2017.

The pro-Allied patriots took great risks before the landings in trying to prevent useless bloodshed and on November 8, 1943 their efforts were officially recognised. At a ceremony held in the yard of the Palais d'Été on Rue Franklin Roosevelt in Algiers, Général Giraud awarded some of them with the Croix de Guerre. L-R: Lieutenant-Colonel Jousse, Colonel van Hecke, Jacques Lemaigre-Dubreuil, Capitaine Lindsay-Watson, Capitaine Dimarie, Henri d'Astier de la Vigerie, Jean Queyrat, Raphaël Aboulker, Aspirant Belegt, Bernard Karsenty, Sous-Lieutenant Libine and André Achiary.

Montrelay finally chose to comply with the orders and he directed the airfield gates be closed and his staff to stay on the alert while de Monsabert's men took up combat positions in trenches around the airfield. As Lemaigre-Dubreuil spoke to him about the imminent arrival of the aircraft bringing in Général Giraud, Montrelay pointed out that his orders were now to fire on any aircraft attempting to land. In the end, he agreed not to fire on any plane that bore the markings of Giraud's aircraft. Nevertheless, for several hours a hostile confrontation existed at the airfield between the aviators holding the place and de Monsabert's soldiers surrounding it.

Meanwhile, in Algiers, Murphy went to see Général Juin at his residence, the Villa des Oliviers, shortly after midnight but just before the pro-Allied patriots went into action. He had some difficulty in convincing the guards — 'tall Senegalese soldiers' — to let him in and then to persuade a servant to wake up the general. Juin soon appeared 'tousled and sleepy' but the news that the Americans were about to land quickly brought him to his senses.

In order to impress Juin, Murphy multiplied the size of the operation (though making no mention of its British component), and to reassure the Frenchman he explained that the operation was an answer to an invitation to co-operate in the liberation of France. A surprised Juin asked who delivered this invitation to which Murphy replied: Général Giraud.

Juin said that he would follow willingly 'if matters were entirely in my hands' but he pointed out that as Darlan was in Algiers, there was no doubt that the admiral would immediately overrule any orders he may give. (Darlan had arrived with his wife to visit their son, Alain, who was suffering from a serious illness in hospital.)

Juin then telephoned Darlan who was staying in the residence of Amiral Raymond Fenard, the Navy commander in Algiers, and told him that Murphy had an urgent message to deliver. Twenty minutes later Darlan arrived at the Villa des Oliviers together with Fenard to be advised of the current situation. It was now 2 a.m.

After getting over his initial irritation, Darlan paced the floor while Murphy tried to convince him of the 'unique opportunity to strike an effective blow now for the liberation of France'. After arguing for half an hour, Darlan finally said he would only co-operate if Pétain authorised him to do so. A message was drafted for transmitting to Vichy outlining the situation with a request from Darlan asking for a free hand to deal with it. The signal would have to be sent from the radio room at Admiralty headquarters down in Algiers but the men got no further than their front door when they were halted in their tracks by a party of young patriots who had come to take over the villa. Their commander, Aspirant Bernard Pauphilet, calmly told the admirals and the general that they were under house arrest and that no one was allowed to leave save for representatives from the American Consulate. Vice-Consul Kenneth Pendar was then sent for while Murphy remained at the villa with Darlan and Juin.

Meanwhile the authorities in Algiers were recovering from their surprise and gradually re-establishing their control. At 6.30 a.m. the young patriots surrounding the Villa des Oliviers were swiftly expelled by a party of Gardes Mobiles. Leaving Murphy under house arrest at the villa with Amiral Fenard, Darlan and Juin immediately departed for Fort L'Empereur, the military headquarters in Algiers, where Juin set about regaining control of the town. Général Mast was immediately relieved of his command and Général Koeltz, by then freed from arrest, put Mast's deputy, Général Jean Roubertie, in command instead.

By 7 a.m., with the absence of any sign of American troops, the operation was obviously running late. Also, as Giraud had still not arrived, the insurrectionists decided to broadcast an appeal on the radio, Raphaël Aboulker delivering the message as if he was the general.

During the morning, the insurrectionists progressively lost control of all the positions that they had been holding in Algiers. Some succeeded in escaping but others were arrested and two were killed: Lieutenant Jean Dreyfus and Capitaine Alfred Pillafort. Murphy commented that 'our friends had done more than had been asked of them, controlling the town for hours beyond the time appointed for their relief'.

Debarkation Begins

Late on November 7, within minutes of the scheduled times, the three groups of the assault fleet made contact with their beacon submarines which were on station indicating the way to the beach. Each group was now six or seven miles offshore, and two miles to seaward of its submarine: *Shakespeare (P221)* off A Sector, *P48* off B Sector and *Unrivalled (P45)* off C Sector.

The sea was slight, the sky clear with a moderate north-westerly breeze. Visibility was good, the moon was new, and lights could be seen burning along the coast.

Beginning at 10.45 p.m. landing craft were lowered and loaded, and at 11.50 p.m. they set out for the beaches led by motor-launches. The main assault began touching down from 1 a.m. as planned in all three sectors but from this point, in the interests of clarity, it is necessary to follow the activities of each force in turn until the conclusion of their primary missions.

Thank to Mast's orders to the Division d'Alger to assist the landings accepting the Allies as friends, French resistance was initially weak. However, when he was relieved of command in the morning, his orders were cancelled and Général Roubertie instructed instead to resist the invasion. As a result, French troops began to contest the advance toward Algiers.

The assault force destined for A Sector was the British 11th Infantry Brigade Group, some 7,200 men strong. Lieutenant Pelman pictured *LCM 594* carrying stores and light guns to the Apples beaches.

Another shot by Lieutenant Pelman shows landing craft *LCM 73* about to touch down on Apples White with troopships *Karanja* (left) and *Viceroy of India* (right) in the background. *LCM 73* was actually lowered from the *Marnix van Sint Aldegonde*, a Dutch passenger liner and the third of the three troopships transporting the 11th Infantry Brigade Group. (LCM stood for Landing Craft Mechanised.) *LCM 594* (top of this page) was a Mark 3 version and *LCM 73* a Mark 1, the first British small landing craft designed to land light armoured vehicles. It could be used for unloading carriers, a tractor plus Bofors gun, or any combination of lorries and anti-tanks guns direct onto the beach.

As the swell was moderate, disembarkation from the three troopships off the Apples Sector proceeded with little difficulty. The landing craft carrying assault troops of the 1st Battalion of the East Surrey Regiment, 5th Battalion of the Northamptonshire Regiment, and 2nd Battalion of the Lancashire Fusiliers began reaching beaches about 1 a.m. All 235 boat-loads came ashore without mishap and the force promptly set off for its inland missions. Headquarters of the 11th Infantry Brigade landed at 2.30 a.m. on Apples White. Before daylight, the troops secured the bridges and took Castiglione, Koléa, and Zéralda. Those French troops encountered at Koléa barracks declared that they had been instructed not to resist. *Above:* Later in the morning, Lieutenant Pelman pictured troops making their way off the beach after landing. *Right:* However, the loose sand did not make it easy and men struggled to move the equipment off the beach.

Then and now on Apples White, three quarters of a century later.

APPLES SECTOR

In A Sector the operation proceeded smoothly as the assault waves — the 1st Battalion of the East Surrey Regiment, the 5th Battalion of the Northamptonshire Regiment, and the 2nd Battalion of the Lancashire Fusiliers — touched down at the appointed time. On A Green Beach the first flight reached the shore exactly at H-Hour, but heavy surf resulted in some delays on A White Beach where the first flight landed eight minutes later.

The force met no opposition and it continued on its inland missions. Before daylight, the troops had taken Castiglione and at Zéralda, troops seized the radio station. At Koléa the French units at the local barracks said that they had been instructed not to resist. Group headquarters had got ashore on A White Beach at 2.30 a.m. and the rest of the 11th Infantry Brigade Group had completed its landing shortly before noon.

During the morning of November 8, another Royal Navy photographer, Lieutenant John Hampton, took a wonderful series of photographs of the landing operations. *Left:* His first shots were taken from the landing craft on its way to the beach.

Right: Unfortunately, an era of heightened security has led to this sector of the coast now being patrolled by the Algerian Navy to prevent vessels approaching the shore; hence our comparison had to be taken some distance out to sea.

BEER SECTOR

Things did not go so smoothly at B Sector where the westerly current caused ships to drift. In the resulting confusion, the 168th R.C.T. bound for B White Beach was set ashore west of Sidi Ferruch and as far west as A White Beach.

Landing near their objectives on B Green Beach, five troops of the 1st Commando pushed on to capture Fort de Sidi Ferruch although there was no resistance given by the garrison, and Colonel Baril came from Koléa to formally surrender the fort to Lieutenant-Colonel Thomas Trevor.

The 6th Commando did not fare so well. Because of difficulty in assembling their landing craft and then some losing touch with their escorting motor launches, the 6th Commando landed late, the first elements touching down two hours behind schedule and the last more than five hours late. Consequently, it was broad daylight before Fort Duperré was encircled at 8.15 a.m. This garrison resisted capture, and it was only after an attack had been carried out by nine Albacores of the Fleet Air Arm that the ground assault was successful, the fort finally surrendering early in the afternoon. A prospective naval bombardment was hurriedly cancelled.

The troops had an unopposed landing, with no opposition whatsoever, and civilians soon came wandering along the beach amongst the military struggling to bring their equipment ashore. The wartime captioning for this series is poor, simply stating that the photos were taken in the Algiers area without indicating the particular sector.

The procedure designed to guide the landing craft to their assigned landing spot totally miscarried for the Beer beaches. The motor launch detailed to embark the pilot for Beer White from the beacon submarine failed to find her and eventually she set out for the beach without him. This resulted in the troops destined for Beer White being guided instead for a landfall in the Apples Sector, six miles to the west! The pilot for Beer White finally embarked in the nearest landing craft that proved to be one belonging to a flight bound for Beer Green. The only craft to beach at Beer White before dawn were three LCPs destined for Beer Green. Total confusion reigned during the morning with components of each battalion being scattered along 15 miles of coast. The 1st Battalion, 168th Infantry, for example, had half its strength landed at Beer Green and the remainder, including the commanding officer, Lieutenant Colonel Edward J. Doyle, at points south-west of Cap Sidi Ferruch on the wrong side of that headland, and as far south-west as the Apples Beaches.

Above: According to Hampton's dope sheet notes, this British naval officer was talking to natives 'with the aid of a dictionary'. He wears the badge of Combined Operations — an eagle over a sub-machine gun over an anchor — that suggests that he is from a scattered party of either the 1st or the 6th Commando. With no information as to where these photographs were taken, it was a real challenge to trace the location, but the fact that houses had been built right backing the beach was a valuable clue. Checking old maps and recent aerial views finally brought the author to focus on the beach at the Club des Pins — Beer White Beach as it was in November 1942. There he was thrilled to find that three of the houses visible in the wartime photos were still standing. *Left:* While many of the photographs were taken in front of the building that the author initially called House 'A', the photo top of this page shows Houses 'B' and 'C'.

Left: British and American soldiers and sailors struggling to extricate equipment like this 40mm Bofors from the beach. Out to sea lies an impressive armada of supply ships and other vessels.

The naval assault force off the B Sector comprised five troopships — *Keren, Winchester Castle, Otranto, Sobieski,* and *Awatea* — and ten cargo vessels. *Right:* Beer White today.

The bluff where the houses stood offered a perfect grand-stand to observe what was going on all along the beach and dozens of local people arrived to watch the extraordinary scene that was unfolding in front of them. Meanwhile, as GIs doled out cigarettes, they tried to find out exactly where they were.

Having cleared access with the local authorities, Riadh Benbouali was able to reach the far side of author's House 'A' which is now surrounded by a high wall separating it from the beach. A truly remarkable then and now!

East of Algiers, the assault force landing on C Sector was the US 39th Combat Team, some 5,700 strong, with the addition of 310 men (two-thirds British and one third American) of the 1st Commando.

CHARLIE SECTOR

Some confusion also occurred with the landings in C Sector resulting in troops that were due to touch down on Red Beach landing instead on Blue Beach, and part of the 1st Commando that were due to attack the battery on Cap Matifou were two hours late. From 2 a.m., this particular battery swept the sea with searchlights and lit up *Zetland* although neither side opened fire and the destroyer turned away, making smoke.

At 3.40 *Zetland* was again picked up by a searchlight from Batterie du Lazaret. The battery opened fire at the destroyers which replied, dousing the searchlight and forcing the battery to cease firing.

Both Batterie de Lazaret and the adjacent Fort d'Estrées declined to surrender and proved too strong to be taken by the available force, so naval gun-fire had to be called in to break the

The landings at C Sector were also marred by confusion and delay. The landing craft of the first flight destined for Charlie Red all followed the one to Charlie Blue instead of their beach.

Left: This shot shows how the Charlie Beaches were generally backed by a steep bluff with no good exits for vehicles. *Right:* Adel took this nice comparison at Aïn Taya.

71

British photographer, Sergeant Charles Bowman, was on Charlie Green on November 9, ready to picture troops of the 39th Infantry Regiment coming ashore. This was the only beach in C Sector with easy access to the interior so wheeled vehicles and service units were soon redirected to land on this beach.

deadlock. The Commandos pulled back to allow a safety zone, and from 2.30 p.m. the cruiser *Bermuda* and a flight of Albacore dive-bombers from the carrier *Formidable* pounded the area for more than an hour. The Commandos then renewed their assault on the Lazaret battery and some 50 French marines surrendered about 5 p.m. The Commandos then went on to attack Fort d'Estrées but without success and the attempt was broken off at 8 p.m.

A nice comparison at Surcouf by Nacer. The promontory in the far background is Cap Matifou.

The landing party disembarked and the various teams quickly departed on their respective missions. Within a short time, they had taken possession of the mole itself, the electric power station, and the petroleum tank farm, and began slowly extending along the street paralleling the shore and northward to the seaplane base. At 9.20 a.m. *Broke* suddenly came under fire from an unseen weapon, probably a howitzer, which scored several hits. This made a quick withdrawal essential. The ship's siren sounded the recall signal and around 60 men near the ship were able to hurry aboard. However, the commander of the American party, Lieutenant Colonel Edwin T. Swenson, whose force could not have reached *Broke* in time, ordered his men to keep their positions. At 9.40 a.m., the destroyer limped out into the bay, being hit repeatedly. HMS *Zetland* soon took her under tow, taking aboard all her passengers, but the damage was such that *Broke* sank the next day.

Colonel Swenson's party, some 250 strong, held their ground for some time but then ammunition began to run low. When several French armoured cars appeared, Swenson surrendered his group shortly after midday.

Having pictured American troops transferring from HMS *Sheffield* to HMS *Malcolm*, Royal Navy photographer, Lieutenant Reginald Coote, pictured the *Malcolm* moving away before HMS *Broke* came alongside the *Sheffield* to take on more troops. The plan for Operation 'Terminal' called for the *Broke* to pierce the boom barrier, enter the southern basin, and discharge troops and naval boarding parties onto the Quai de Dieppe. The *Malcolm* was to follow on a similar course 15 minutes later and make for the Grand Môle.

OPERATION 'TERMINAL'

At 1.31 a.m., Admiral Burrough released the destroyers HMS *Broke* and HMS *Malcolm* to make the frontal attack on Algiers harbour. The plan called for *Broke* to pierce the boom barrier, enter the southern basin and discharge troops and naval boarding parties on the Quai de Dieppe. *Malcolm* was to follow on a similar course 15 minutes later and make for the Grand Môle.

As the vessels neared their objective, the lights in the town suddenly went out and searchlights swept across the bay at the approaching ships. Shelling followed at once, particularly from the Batterie des Arcades on the crest of a knoll about 300 feet high directly south of the port. In the glare and tumult, both ships twice missed the harbour entrance and then circled for a third attempt. At this juncture, just after 4 a.m., *Malcolm* was badly hit and caught fire so had to withdraw, effectivly removing half of the 'Terminal' force.

The *Broke* proceeded in for the third time, receiving greater fire from the shore batteries, she missed the entry again and turned back to sea. At her fourth attempt to enter the harbour, *Broke* approached at speed, finally smashing through the boom barrier. However, the quay at which it had planned to land was filled with ships, so she berthed instead along the Môle Louis Billiard.

As the two ships approached at 2.20 a.m. searchlights swept across the bay and the shore batteries opened fire. The two ships missed the harbour entrance twice and had to circle for a new attempt [1]. Badly hit, the *Malcolm* had to withdraw [2]. The *Broke* manoeuvred for another try and finally crashed through the boom [3]. She then berthed against the Quai de Falaise at the extremity of Môle Louis Billiard [4].

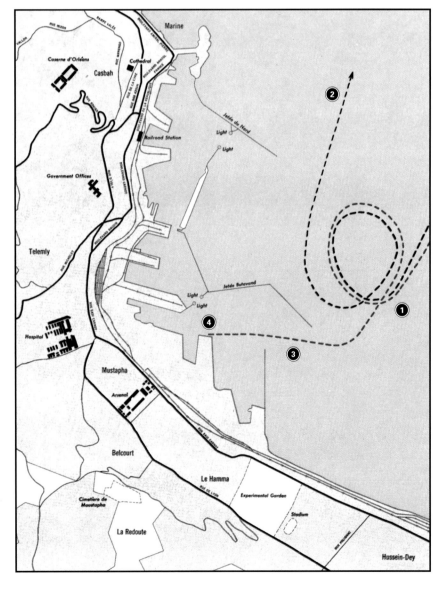

TAKING THE AIRFIELDS

Général Mast had gone to the vicinity of Sector B's Green Beach, where he supervised the voluntary surrender of Fort de Sidi Ferruch. He met Lieutenant-Colonel Trevor about 4 a.m. and implored him to immediately push to the aerodrome at Blida. He explained that de Monsabert was holding the airfield as Général Giraud was expected to land any moment but the situation might well deteriorate if de Monsabert was not quickly reinforced by Allied troops. He said that he had lorries requisitioned from Koléa ready and waiting to transport a detachment the 15 miles to the objective. Despite the fact that it necessitated a departure from his orders, Trevor agreed to undertake the mission and at 4.15 a.m. three Commando troops started out for Blida.

At the airfield, since daybreak a standing patrol of four Martlet fighters from the aircraft carrier *Victorious* had been circling overhead, strafing a bomber and another aircraft as they started to take off. At 8 a.m. another four-aircraft patrol replaced them and within 30 minutes white flags appeared. On authorisation from his commander, the patrol leader, Lieutenant Barry Nation, then landed and taxied up to the hangars. There he was given a written message from de Monsabert that the airfield was now at the disposal of Allied forces. Nation remained alone in this awkward situation for about an hour until the Commandos arrived.

About 8.30 a.m., Lieutenant Barry Nation, leading the flight of Martlets patrolling over the airfield at Blida, radioed seeing white flags being waved. He was instructed to land and report back. Once on the ground he met with Général de Monsabert commanding the small pro-Allied force there.

When commando troops arrived about an hour later, Lieutenant Nation took off and flew back to the carrier. No photos were taken of Nation's aircraft on the ground at **Blida but this shot of a Fleet Air Arm Martlet pictured later in December at the airfield at La Sénia is included as a convenient stand in.**

The Maison Blanche airfield (the 'White House'), a primary objective for the Eastern Task Force, was occupied from 8.30 a.m. on November 8. The first group of B-17 heavy bombers operated from the airfield from November 13, soon joined by a group of P-38s and another of B-26s. This photo was taken in 1944 when the airfield was a major trans-shipment hub for the US Army Air Force. Today it is Algeria's premier airport.

On reaching the airfield Trevor found a confused situation with de Monsabert holding part of it but with the air force commander, Colonel Montrelay, still not willing to agree to uncontested occupation in view of contrary orders from Algiers. Trevor deployed his men near the main gate and waited there for reinforcements before provoking hostile action.

The capture of Maison Blanche airfield was entrusted to the 1st Battalion of the 39th Infantry, moving from C Sector. An advance party set off and marched the ten miles to the airfield, arriving there at approximately 6.15 a.m. A few French tanks were encountered as the battalion neared the airfield but they put up only a token resistance before withdrawing as the American troops occupied the airfield. Negotiations for its surrender were completed by 8.30 a.m.

However, by then visibility was poor with thick fog so the first RAF squadron, No. 43, was not able to land

The Hurricanes from No. 43 Squadron were the first Allied aircraft to land at the aerodrome, touching down from 10.35 a.m. with the Spitfires of No. 81 Squadron following two hours later. Squadron Leader Ronald Berry (third from left in this photograph), was the commanding officer of the latter squadron and was pictured with some of his pilots on the first day of the operation.

its 18 Hurricanes until 10.35 a.m. The Spitfires of No. 81 Squadron followed two hours later. The main problem in using Maison Blanche was the lack of fuel and maintenance facilities, but sufficient petrol was found to get some of the aircraft aloft over Algiers and Cap Matifou before sunset.

Consequently, almost all air support and defensive patrols over the landing beaches and the harbour continued to be furnished on D-Day by naval aircraft from the carriers. At dusk 15 Ju 88s attacked shipping in C Sector seriously damaging the destroyer HMS *Cowdray* and the transport USS *Leedstown* off Cape Matifou. Another US transport received minor damage. (The *Leedstown* sank the following day after being torpedoed by *U-331*.)

Officers of the 39th Infantry Regiment inspected a Heinkel He 111 found in one of the hangars on November 10. Bearing the civilian registration D-ACLQ the plane had been used for liaison duties with the German Armistice Commission operating in Algiers.

Negotiations

What looks like a nice action photo was most probably staged as this shot was taken well after the situation was cleared in Algiers. It was in the Hôtel d'Angleterre on the left that the Italian Armistice Commission was based.

Following the plan, the American Chargé d'Affaires in Vichy, S. Pinkney Tuck, arrived to see Maréchal Pétain at his office just before 9 a.m. on November 8 to deliver the President's official message. Declaring that he was an 'old friend of France', Roosevelt recalled how the Axis powers had plundered the country of its savings, industry and transport, and looted the nation's farms and factories 'all for the benefit of a Nazi Reich and Fascist Italy'. He insisted that the USA was not looking to take over French territory in North Africa and called for co-operation by the French authorities there 'in repelling Axis threats'. A radio message along the same vein was broadcast.

Having received word of the landing of troops in North Africa, Pétain had already prepared a reply that he handed to Tuck. Beginning with 'it is with stupor and sadness that I learned tonight of the aggression of your troops against North Africa', it made it clear that he had issued orders to resist this attack upon the French empire. At the conclusion of the interview, when Tuck rose to leave, Pétain showed the greatest amiability and good spirits. The Chargé d'Affaires cabled the response to Washington and later in the day he was informed that Vichy had broken off diplomatic relations with the United States. Tuck then left France and the

Swiss Ambassador, Walter Stucki, took over US interests at Vichy.

During the afternoon, Darlan in Algiers asked Murphy to establish contact with the commander of the assault

force who was reported to him as being 'on a beach about ten miles west of Algiers'. The French provided a chauffeur and a car showing both a French and a white flag and Murphy was driven

However, the hotel is no longer standing as Islamist terrorists exploded a vehicle packed with explosive outside on September 4, 1996, killing 12 persons with over 20 injured. The explosion damaged the building to such an extent that it had to be demolished in 2001.

Left: **A French cine cameraman filmed the scene outside the hotel as GIs waited for the Italians to emerge to take them prisoner.** *Right:* **The corner of Boulevard Mustapha Ben Boulaid (then Boulevard Bugeaud) with Rue Colonel Haouas (originally Rue des Généraux Morris) was a desolate empty spot when Abdelatif Djerboua took this comparison for us in 2017.**

to White Beach in B Sector where he met Major General Ryder sometime after 4 p.m. They returned to Algiers to confer with Darlan and Juin at Fort L'Empereur. It was soon agreed that a cease-fire should be declared in Algiers and the neighbourhood, and that Allied forces should occupy the town at 7 p.m.

The terms of the cease-fire were that French troops would return to their barracks, retaining their arms and colours. The Americans would occupy key points in the city and rely on the aid of French police to maintain order. Detailed armistice terms would be the subject of further discussion at a meeting to be held the following morning. While these informal arrangements were being put into effect, General Ryder returned to HMS *Bulolo* and reported back to Gibraltar, recommending that he be permitted to arrange an armistice on the basis of the terms prepared during the planning in the event of merely token resistance from the French. Another conference was held at 8 p.m. to prepare the way for general negotiations with General Clark as soon as he arrived. That evening, as agreed, American troops entered Algiers.

During the night, a heavy swell halted all unloading on the beaches and at dawn on the 9th, Darlan having consented to the use of Algiers harbour, Admiral Burrough ordered all his shipping into the bay. HMS *Bulolo* soon entered the harbour and berthed alongside.

NOVEMBER 9

Général Giraud finally arrived by air early on the 9th but the French leaders in Algiers gave him a very cold welcome. Realising that his usefulness had been vastly overestimated, for the time being Giraud decided to go into virtual retreat. General Clark landed at Maison Blanche during the afternoon in the midst of a German bombing raid. When he was updated by Murphy on the current situation, he stressed that 'We've got to put Giraud back into this business right away!'

That evening Lieutenant-General Kenneth Anderson arrived by air at Blida and was transferred to the *Bulolo* where he assumed command of the Eastern Task Force for the drive eastwards on Tunis. Giraud passed the night of November 9-10 with compatriots near Algiers and conferred with adherents who revealed how completely their plan had failed. In Algiers, Général Mast and his associates were still being held in seclusion by the French authorities as were Général Béthouart and many others in Morocco.

Under the watchful eyes of American soldiers, the Italian team finally appeared carrying an impressive amount of luggage.

NOVEMBER 10

On the morning of November 10, General Clark and Murphy met Amiral Darlan and his associates at the Hôtel Saint-Georges. Clark made clear that he was not going to wait for a decision by the Vichy cabinet that was due to meet that afternoon. Clark told Darlan he must act at once and issue a cease-fire order for all French North Africa, or he would be taken into custody and held incommunicado. The Americans would then arrange matters with other French leaders.

Shortly before noon Darlan agreed and he drafted and signed in Pétain's name directives to the chiefs of armed forces in North Africa requiring them to break off all hostilities and to observe complete neutrality. The orders were sent out by radio and also transmitted by courier planes. (We will see later how the commanders at Oran had already yielded when the order reached them, and how they were put into effect in Morocco just in time to save Casablanca from attack.)

At first Pétain approved the agreement but Prime Minister Pierre Laval was en route to Munich to see Hitler when he learned of it. He promptly telephoned the Maréchal to persuade him to withdraw his agreement. Pétain then disavowed Darlan's action but, at the Amiral's own suggestion, the Allies put him under arrest before he could issue counter orders of annulment.

Axis aircraft and submarines were now closing in on the concentration of shipping off the North African coast and on November 10, while an Italian aircraft torpedoed the sloop HMS *Ibis* and sunk her ten miles north of Algiers, U-Boats torpedoed and sunk the destroyer HMS *Martin* (*U-431*) and the collier *Garlinge* (*U-81*).

On November 11, the troopships *Viceroy of India* and *Nieuw Zeeland* had been sailed independently for Gibraltar as soon as they were empty. *Viceroy of India* was torpedoed some 35 miles north-west of Oran by *U-407*. The destroyer HMS *Boadicea* took her in tow for a while but she soon sank. The *Nieuw Zeeland* was torpedoed by *U-380* south-east of Gibraltar.

The Italians were loaded into lorries in front of the hotel to be taken to the harbour. In the background is the Aletti Hotel.

Now named the Safir, the hotel is still in business in the centre of Algiers.

At first, both the German and Italian armistice commissions had their offices in the Hotel Aletti. Following the attack on a convoy by the Royal Navy, the Germans held the Italians responsible for the incursion. As a result of the dispute that followed, the Italian delegation left the Aletti to move into the Angleterre. *Left:* Another still from the French cine film shows the population jeering the departure of the transport carrying the Italian party to the docks. *Right:* The present day scene in front of the Hotel Safir, at the junction of Boulevard Mustapha Ben Boulaid (left) and Rue Asselah Hocine (right).

Left: **These British motorcyclists are probably seeking directions from the locals.** *Right:* **Abdelatif took this nice comparison for us from the top of Rampe Magenta. In the background** is the tower of the lift that links the Square Port-Saïd (Square Aristide Briant in 1942) with the railway station and inner harbour down below.

NOVEMBER 11

In the early hours of November 11, the Germans and Italians launched Operation 'Anton' and started to enter the unoccupied zone of France. A total of more than ten German divisions, two of which were armoured, swept across southern France while six Italian divisions marched into eastern France. Pétain and his military advisers had long discussed the possibility of a German invasion of the unoccupied zone and accepted that there was no possible way for the small Vichy army to resist an Axis take-over. French outposts were accordingly ordered not to try to oppose the invading forces. However, Pétain did make a broadcast during the day, angrily reproaching the Germans and Italians for violating the terms of the armistice.

After four days of deliberation, on November 13 Clark and Darlan reached an agreement as to the terms for French collaboration with the Allies. Darlan was to be High Commissioner and Commander-in-Chief of Naval Forces; Général Giraud, Commander-in-Chief of Ground and Air Forces; Général Juin, Commander of the Eastern Sector; Général Noguès, Commander of the Western Sector and Resident General of French Morocco, with Châtel the Governor General of Algeria. This picture was taken the same day when Eisenhower made a quick visit to Algiers from Gibraltar. He is seen with Clark, Darlan and Robert Murphy.

In Toulon, the Axis forces stopped in front of the perimeter surrounding the naval base, and the French fleet there remained under close surveillance, the object of covetous attention from both Allied and Axis leaders.

At a conference on November 11, Clark sought to get an assurance from the French to resist the Axis occupation of ports and aerodromes in Tunisia, and to get Amiral Darlan to order Amiral Jean de Laborde at Toulon to bring the fleet over to the Allied side. At first Amiral Darlan professed to be powerless as a result of Pétain's instruction the previous day but he then received a message by a personal cypher, held only by himself and Amiral Gabriel Auphan, the Minister of Marine, that the disavowal had been made under pressure and was contrary to the Maréchal's actual wishes.

Darlan thereupon ordered Général Juin to direct the ground and air forces in Tunisia to resist the Axis. Officially, however, under strong German pressure exerted through Pierre Laval, Vichy confirmed the disavowal of Darlan's armistice and announced the transfer of all authority in North Africa to Général Noguès in Morocco.

Darlan repeatedly appealed to Toulon for the fleet to sail over to the Allies but de Laborde maintained his strict obedience to Vichy that made it impossible for the fleet to move. At Vichy, Amiral Auphan supported Darlan's efforts to have the Fleet sailed over to the Allied side but he finally had to resign on November 15.

NOVEMBER 12-13

On November 13, after almost four days of deliberation, General Clark, with Robert Murphy's assistance, had conceived a workable solution for French collaboration with the Allies.

On the morning of November 7, the *Thomas Stone* (AP-59) bound for C Sector east of Algiers was torpedoed although the question is still being debated as to who was responsible: was the torpedo fired by the *U-205* or dropped from a He 111 torpedo-bomber of II./Kampfgeschwader 26. The explosion blew a hole below the water-line, broke her propeller shaft, and bent the rudder to starboard. The convoy had to continue leaving the *Thomas Stone* adrift some 150 miles from Algiers, guarded by the corvette HMS *Spey*. Major Walter M. Oakes, the commanding officer of the 2nd Battalion, 39th Infantry, who was on board the *Thomas Stone,* persuaded Captain Olten R. Bennehof to use all but two of the small landing craft on board to take the bulk of his unit to Algiers in time to join in its capture. At dusk, Oakes and over 700 men set out for Algiers in 24 boats under the protection of the *Spey*. However, the motors of the small craft soon proved unequal to the task, causing a succession of breakdowns during the night. At daybreak a rising easterly breeze soon made clear that it would be impossible for the flotilla to reach Algiers that day, so abandoning the boats, which were eventually scuttled, the men crowded aboard the corvette and continued to Algiers, arriving late that evening. Meanwhile two destroyers, HMS *Wishart* and HMS *Velox*, joined by a tug, HMS *St. Day*, on the morning of the 8th, began towing the *Thomas Stone* and finally managed to bring her into Algiers harbour on November 11. She was tied up to a quay to discharge the remaining troops and equipment on board but then had to be moved to the outer harbour to make room for incoming ships. She was hit during an air raid on the night of November 24/25; then on the 25th a high wind and heavy swell caused the ship to drag anchors and drive her hard aground. The battered hulk was later scrapped.

On the first day of the invasion, Darlan agreed to let the Allies use Algiers harbour so Admiral Burrough ordered all his shipping into the bay at dawn on November 9. This shot of reinforcement transports unloading at Algiers was taken on November 24.

Responsibilities were assigned as follows: Darlan, High Commissioner and Commander in Chief of Naval Forces; Giraud, Commander-in-Chief of Ground and Air Forces; Juin, Commander of the Eastern Sector; Noguès, Commander of the Western Sector and Resident General of French Morocco; Châtel, Governor General of Algeria. Save for Giraud, just a few days previously all these men were senior members of the Vichy administration.

Part of the agreement was due to the fact that two major points were solved. First Général Noguès had renounced Pétain's assignment to him of supreme authority in French North Africa and had advised the Maréchal that it should remain with Darlan, and second that Général Giraud be accepted by the others despite his standing as a discredited officer.

Also, as a consequence of a message from Pétain received via the navy's secret channel that Darlan's leadership had his approval, the agreement was put into force by the military commanders and civilian authorities with much greater peace of mind. However, none of those officers who had been relieved of command for having sided with the Allies right from the beginning — Généraux Mast, Béthouart, de Monsabert, Colonels Jousse and Baril, and many others — were given back their commands. They were ostracised, even Giraud tending to distance himself from them, and the procedures engaged on November 9 to strip them of French nationality were left in place.

At Algiers, the Eastern Task Force first established headquarters in the Villa Sésini that had served as the German consulate since 1927. On November 12, a Signal Corps photographer pictured the American guard in front of the entrance.

This agreement coincided with the arrival in Algiers of General Eisenhower, who, accompanied by Admiral Cunningham, was paying his first visit to North Africa to appraise himself of General Clark's progress in the political negotiations as well as receive briefings on the military situation. Eisenhower expressed his satisfaction with what had been achieved.

The Villa Sésini acquired a terrible notoriety during the War of Algerian Independence when the French army established a centre there for the interrogation of suspects, torture being the rule. In 2016, the Algerian Cultural Ministry classified the house as an historic place to be preserved.

Centre Task Force: Oran

Off Z Sector, Royal Navy photographer Lieutenant Francis Hudson pictured American troops on the deck of the *Reina del Pacifico* before landing.

Oran lies on the southern shore of a wide bay between Cap Falcon in the west and Pointe de l'Aiguille in the east. Two headlands projecting into the bight sub-divide it into three bays with Oran in the centre between Mers el Kébir and Pointe Canastel. About 20 miles east of the city, on the eastern side of a wide and hilly promontory, the small port of Arzew nestles on the western shore of another wide gulf.

The Oran defence sector was commanded by Contre-Amiral André Rioult with Général Robert Boissau's Division d'Oran under his command. The force in the area was 15,000-strong and could be reinforced from inland barracks within a few days. Here, too, these units of the 'armistice army' were below strength and were badly lacking modern weapons and equipment, and transport.

The sea approaches to Oran and Arzew were protected by 13 coastal batteries armed with 50 guns. The most important were those on Djebel Santon, west of Mers el Kébir, mounting four 190mm weapons and a concentration of anti-aircraft artillery. Pointe Canastel, north-east of Oran, had three 235mm guns, and Fort du Nord at the western edge of the Golfe d'Arzew another four guns of 105mm.

Another shot by Hudson of GIs embarking in Royal Navy LCAs from a doorway in the side of the *Reina del Pacifico*.

Over 50 aircraft were based at the airfields at La Sénia and Tafaraoui — 26 Dewoitine 520 fighters, 26 Lioré et Olivier 451 bombers and 11 Bloch 174 and 175 reconnaissance aircraft — with 13 Latécoère 298 seaplanes at Arzew. Several naval vessels could be expected to be moored at the large naval station at Mers el Kébir and in the harbour at Oran.

THE PLAN

The plan for seizing Oran by the Centre Task Force involved a double envelopment by troops landing simultaneously at beaches located in bays beyond the one on which Oran lay. The planners selected three zones of attack, two to the west of the Oran bight and one east of it. All told, there was more than 50 miles between the easternmost and westernmost landing points. From west to east the landing sectors were designated X-Ray, Yorker and Zebra.

X-Ray, the westernmost beach-head, comprised two beaches on the bay of Bou Zedjar. In the north-east, X White Beach lay adjacent to the village. X Green was just to the south-west, separated by a jutting rocky headland. Both sections of X Beach measured about 30 yards to high dunes and, in the case of Green Beach, to a single exit up a steep slope over deep, soft sand.

The assault force for X Beaches was Task Force Green which consisted of a contingent from Combat Command B of the 1st Armored Division, under the command of Colonel Paul M. Robinett. Twenty light tanks and various other vehicles of the task force were loaded on the *Bachaquero*, a tank landing ship built from a shallow-draft oiler formerly used on Lake Maracaibo. Through openings in the bows, light tanks could move over pontoon bridges to shallow water, cross the beaches, shed their waterproofing equipment, and press on inland. (The Sherman tanks were too large for this ship so more than half of CCB's armour was aboard transports for unloading at the harbour at Arzew in a second phase of the operation.)

Once ashore, Task Force Green was to move inland to capture the airfield at Lourmel and then push on eastwards, south of a salt lake, to join with the other section of CCB advancing from Z Red Beach and then capture the airfields at Tafaraoui and La Sénia.

About midway between X Sector and Oran, the Yorker beach-head lay on the south-western part of a wide bay west of Cap Falcon. Inland from the beachhead lay the Plaine des Andalouses, a level cultivated area between the coast and the slopes of Djebel Murdjadjo, a great hill mass dominating the western approach to Oran.

The Y Sector assault force was the 26th Regimental Combat Team under Brigadier General Theodore Roosevelt, the assistant commander of the 1st Infantry Division, and Colonel Alexander N. Stark, commanding officer of the 26th Infantry. Once ashore, the 26th RCT was to secure Djebel Murdjadjo and then enter Oran from the west.

East of the Oran bight, the three beaches of the Zebra Sector extended

The assault goes in on Z Beaches. Lieutenant Hudson joined the troops on board the LCA.

Nice shot from a LCM approaching the X Beaches at Bou Zedjar on the morning of November 8 with X White in the left, adjacent to the village, and X Green in the right.

LCM 102 about to touch down on X White right in the village of Bou Zedjar.

more than three miles from near Arzew to an eastern limit beyond the village of Saint-Leu. The approaches were generally good, the gradient easy and the sand fairly firm, although the exits were limited to breaks in a low, rocky cliff. Also, the beaches were all exposed to wind and surf and well within range of artillery fire from the heights above Arzew.

The forces landing on Z Beaches — the bulk of the Oran attacking forces — were the 16th and 18th Regimental Combat Teams plus a Ranger force in two sections, attached to the 1st Infantry Division, all three under command of Major General Terry Allen, and Task Force Red of Combat Command B, 1st Armored Division, commanded by Brigadier General Lunsford E. Oliver. The light tanks of CCB were to be brought to the beach by the *Misoa* and *Tasajera*, two other tank landing ships of the makeshift Maracaibo type.

On the western wing, the 1st Ranger Battalion (Lieutenant Colonel William O. Darby) landing between Arzew and Cap Carbon, was to send parties up the heights to the south-east to take the coastal battery there and then advance into Arzew harbour.

The 18th Regimental Combat Team (Colonel Frank U. Greer) landing on Z Green Beach was to capture the coastal defences and Arzew and then advance on Oran from the east. The 16th Regimental Combat Team (Colonel Henry B. Cheadle) was to secure the beachhead at Z White and Z Red Beaches ready for the armoured Task Force Red of CCB to land on Z Red. The 16th RCT was then to take part in the attack on Oran.

All units landing on the Z Sector beaches were under Major General Allen 'for purpose of coordination and control', but Brigadier General Oliver retained responsibility for the tactical employment of his Combat Command B.

While the infantry units from the Z Sector were to encircle Oran from the east and block the approach of reinforcements from the interior, an armoured column from CCB was to thrust inland before daylight to capture the airfields at Tafaraoui and La Sénia, and to approach Oran from the south.

To quickly gain control of these airfields, an airborne force from the United Kingdom was scheduled to drop before daylight south of Oran while the armoured columns advanced from the beaches. As soon as an airfield had been secured, land-based aircraft of the Twelfth Air Force were to be flown in from Gibraltar.

Like at Algiers, a small anti-sabotage naval operation, code-named 'Reservist', was to make a direct assault on Oran harbour to try to prevent destruction of the port facilities.

The Centre Task Force had a total strength of 37,000 American and 3,600 British troops, including Royal Navy personnel in the landing craft and beach parties.

The British Admiralty furnished the Centre Naval Task Force with 19 combat transport ships, including three tank carriers, 28 mechanical transport ships and 55 escort vessels. In addition to the battleship *Rodney* and the aircraft carrier *Furious* detached from Force H, this force comprised two escort aircraft carriers, *Biter* and *Dasher*; the cruisers *Aurora* and *Jamaica*; two anti-aircraft

SEIZURE OF ORAN

AXIS OF ALLIED ADVANCE, DATE INDICATED
FRENCH COUNTERATTACKS
CENTER OF FRENCH RESISTANCE

MAJOR FRENCH COAST DEFENSE BATTERIES
① FORT DU SANTON   ④ POINTE CANASTEL
② FERME COMBIER   ⑤ FORT DU NORD
③ FERME STE MARIE   ⑥ FORT DE LA POINTE

ELEVATIONS IN METERS

0   100   200   400 AND ABOVE

0   5   10 MILES

0   5   10 KILOMETERS

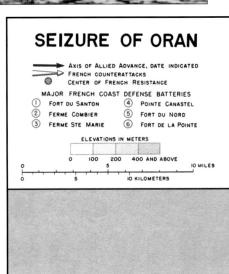

ships, *Alynbank* and *Delhi*; 13 destroyers, two sloops and six corvettes.

The assault was to be controlled from the Headquarters Ship *Largs* carrying Commodore Troubridge and Major General Fredendall. With them was Leland L. Rounds, the American Vice-Consul in Oran, who had recently been brought out to furnish liaison with friendly French elements ashore and to provide political intelligence to General Fredendall.

Two destroyers were assigned for fire support off Mersa bou Zedjar (X Beaches). The cruiser *Aurora* and one destroyer had the same role off Les Andalouses (Y Beaches), and the cruiser *Jamaica* and three destroyers were positioned at the Golfe d'Arzew (Z Beaches). Further out to sea were the battleship HMS *Rodney* and three destroyers. All naval gun-fire was to be withheld until it became certain that surprise had been lost. Forward observation officers were to move inland with the separate elements of the landing force to direct naval gun-fire on appropriate targets.

From first light on D-Day, bombers and fighters from the three aircraft carriers sailing between 20 and 30 miles offshore were to neutralise the French airfields and clear the air of hostile aircraft.

Above: **The photographer has just jumped down from the LCA on the left to take this shot of** *LCM 102* **being moored before unloading.** *Below:* **The seizure of Oran, November 8-10. The landing group for X Sector comprised three LSIs, one LST and four transports; the landing group for Y Sector three LSIs and two transports; the landing group for Z Sector nine LSIs, two LSTs, one LSG and 22 transports.**

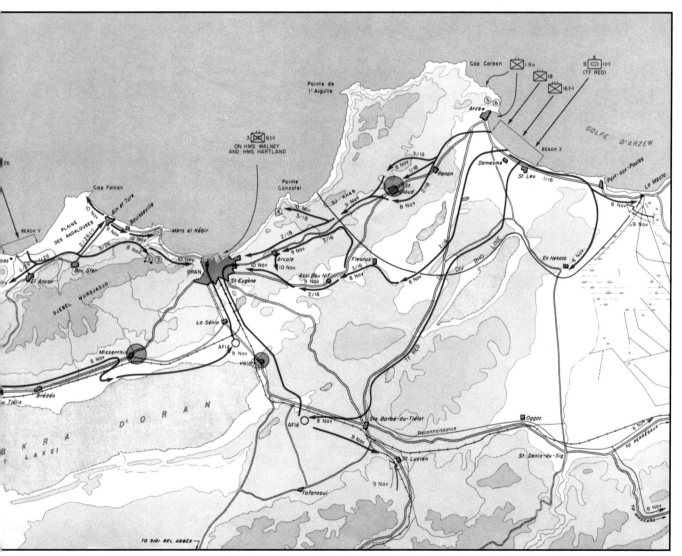

Left: **The first shore party to land, 200 officers and men of the 591st Engineer Boat Regiment, was now controlling the** landing operation. *Right:* **Bou Zedjar then and now . . . a nice comparison by Mohammed.**

DEBARKATION BEGINS

At 9.30 p.m. on November 7, sailing southwards, the assault groups met their beacon submarines marking the assault beaches. HMS *Unshaken (P54)* was on station north of Cap Figalo to guide Forces X and Y, and HMS *Ursula (N59)* north of Cap Carbon for Force Z. After releasing motor launches to pick up the lead-in officers from the submarines, the transport groups for each beach, preceded by minesweepers, headed for positions where the landing craft were scheduled to assemble. It was now some time before midnight.

As the landing craft were lowered and loaded, and then proceeded to their prescribed assembly area, Admiral Troubridge on *Largs* (which stood less than a thousand yards on the beam of the anchored column of transports), reported that no sound was heard and not even the flash of a torch was observed.

Like the Eastern Task Force at Algiers, H-Hour at Oran was set at 1 a.m. with sunrise due at 6.31 a.m. Also, there was no moon and no tide.

The simultaneous landings by the several elements of the Centre Task Force are now described in sequence from west to east.

As the exit from X White was difficult, it was planned to land only stores and personnel on this beach. The main force was to land on X Green via the tank landing ship, the *Bachaquero*. This shot of X White was taken from the rocky headland, the boats being mainly LCMs, some Mark 1s and some Mark 3s.

All these photographs were taken later in the morning when following up waves were landing but unfortunately none show X Green where the *Bachaquero* beached. According to the plan she started unloading at 4 a.m. and backed off at 8.15 a.m. after the 20 light tanks and all equipment on board had been brought ashore. *Left:* ***LCA 254*, crewed by British sailors, has just landed on X White.** *Right:* **Local civilians were soon hired to help unload stores and equipment.**

The assault force for Y Beaches consisted of the 26th Regimental Combat Team under Brigadier General Theodore Roosevelt, the assistant commander of the 1st Infantry Division, and Colonel Alexander N. Stark, commanding officer of the 26th Infantry. The landing of troops and unloading of stores proceeded well though a sandbar off the beach made things difficult for the LCMs conveying heavy vehicles as many grounded causing damage to propellers and rudders.

TOUCH-DOWN

To the west, as the transport ships of Force X drew near to the point for initial release of the landing craft, a French convoy of five ships bound for Oran then appeared with lights burning, being led by a trawler. One of the ships was stopped and boarded but the others made off to the east until they sighted the ships of Force Y off Les Andalouses where the cruiser *Aurora* engaged them. They then reversed course, came across the fleet for X Beaches and then ran ashore off Cap Figalo while trawler made off. This interference held up the minesweepers of Force X, so disrupting the planned timetable, but the landing craft finally got underway at midnight.

In spite of these mishaps, the landings on X White proceeded more or less as scheduled but an unexpected current then caused the second wave for X Green to reach land before the first.

In the centre, off the Y Sector near Les Andalouses, as the cruiser *Aurora* engaged the French convoy that was interfering, the transports began lowering their boats from 11.20 p.m. The debarkation took much longer than planned as the heavily-laden men

Left: **The Signal Corps photographer then took this shot of Lieutenant Russell disembarking from the same *LCA 287*. He landed with his Speed Graphic camera at the ready, though his first priority appeared to be smoking a cigarette.** *Right:* **Les Andalouses beach as it is today, with the small Île Plane in the far distance.**

Above: **A GMC CCKW pulls a 105mm howitzer ashore from *LCM 567*.** *Right:* **The comparison at Les Andalouses.**

struggled down the scrambling nets in dark. An unexpected sandbar, parallel to the shore, then proved a major disruption. While the smaller craft were able to clear it, the first three LCM from the *Glengyle* arriving in the third

Below: **Three landing craft — *LCA 243*, *LCM 159* and *LCP (R) 838* — lie abandoned on the beach. Compared to the appalling losses suffered by the Eastern Task Force with 94 per cent of the landing craft becoming casualties, the Centre Task Force at Oran did much better, suffering only 20 per cent losses. (Off Morocco, in the much more exposed waters of the Atlantic, the Western Task Force experienced 34 per cent losses of landing craft.)**

This 'Deuce and a Half' is towing a 105mm howitzer along the beach at Les Andalouses. Other photos taken along Y Beach show that engineers laid down lengths of steel matting to stabilise the sand.

wave at 1.45 a.m. grounded on it. Under the impression that they had reached the beach, and failing to realise that the water between the sandbar and the beach was up to five feet deep, the crew disembarked. Those Jeeps and guns which started forward just rolled straight under the water, the submerged equipment having to be salvaged later. Nevertheless, the delay has no consequence as there was absolutely no resistance.

East of Oran, the landings on the three Z Beaches were carried out without difficulty. The Rangers landed punctually and Fort de la Pointe and Arzew harbour were soon in their hands. However, due to minor problems during the initial debarkation and also the five-mile approach in formation by landing craft, some of the assault

Left: Ready for action, this Bofors has been dug in on a mound overlooking the beach to provide anti-aircraft protection. (In the US Army, the ubiquitous Bofors was known as the 40mm Automatic Gun M1.) *Right:* A perfect comparison taken by Muszka on the Y Beach of 1942, with the Cap Lindlès in background.

The force landing on the Z Beaches comprised the 16th and 18th Regimental Combat Teams (plus a Ranger force), and Task Force Red of Combat Command B, 1st Armored Division. Combat Team 16, comprising 5,608 officers and men under Colonel Henry B. Cheadle, landed on Z White and Z Red from 1 a.m., while Combat Team 18, 7,092 strong, under Colonel Frank U. Greer, began landing on Z Green at 1.20 a.m. Although motor launches led the landing craft to the beaches, some became lost and came ashore at scattered points along the beach which made reorganisation difficult. The Rangers landed as planned in the vicinity of Arzew.

waves did not touch down on schedule. Combat Team 16 on Z White in the centre landed at 1 a.m.; Combat Team 18 began landing on the western sector, Z Green, at 1.20 a.m.; and Z Red in the east, to be used by Task Force Red, CCB, was reported ready to receive the armoured force by 3.30 a.m.

By 7 a.m. unloading at all beaches was in full swing. On Z Red, the two tank carrier ships, *Misoa* and *Tasajera*, beached around 4 a.m. and began unloading via their pontoon bridges at 6 a.m. The light tanks and vehicles were all ashore by 8 a.m. The leading assault force of Task Force Red under Lieu-

tenant Colonel John K. Waters consisting of the 1st Battalion, 1st Armored Regiment (less Company C); Company E, 6th Armored Infantry; one platoon of Company B, 701st Tank Destroyer Battalion and a platoon reconnaissance party, all moved out at 8.20 a.m., soon followed by another column.

Left: This shot of Rangers landing near Cap Carbon was actually taken when they were practicing training landings in December 1942. *Right:* A nice comparison with Cap Carbon in background.

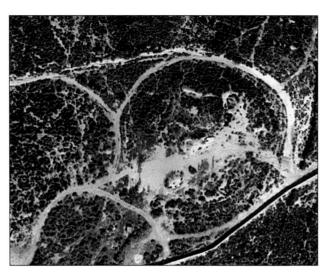

Under Lieutenant Colonel William O. Darby, the 1st Ranger Battalion was split into two detachments. The first, consisting of two companies, assaulted the harbour, the town and Fort de la Pointe. Darby himself led the other group of four companies to capture the four 105mm guns of Fort du Nord sited on top of a hill north or Arzew. Climbing the cliffs in the dark with heavy combat loads was slow work and the Rangers were behind schedule by the time that they reached the battery. In spite of sporadic fire heard in the town down below where Company B were in action, there was no sign of an alert. Darby ordered Company D to set up mortars at the foot of the last ravine and left Company G with them in

reserve. The two assault companies finally reached the barbed wire that surrounded the battery when they received some fire from the high ground. This was a signal for Company D to open fire and volleys of mortar shells hammered the French emplacements. In a perfect co-ordinated attack with the mortar barrage, the Rangers then rushed the guns. *Left:* A somewhat posed shot of Rangers in possession of the battery fire control bunker. *Right:* Although the battery itself is now abandoned, the hill is still within a restricted military area and access to it is forbidden. This aerial view shows the fire control bunker and the first of the four emplacements in the bottom left-hand corner.

The firing of green flares at 4 a.m. was the signal to the assault fleet offshore that the battery had been neutralised. Another

posed shot of Corporal Robert Bevin of Estherville, Iowa, and Corporal Earl Drost from Dubuque, Iowa, covering the gun position.

Lieutenant Hudson took this photo of a party of GIs leaving Z Beach. It was perfect for the front page of newspapers back home but the US Army press censor obviously disliked the cigarette in the hand of the flag-holder, so annotated the original print: 'Remove cigarette'!

Things were not so easy at X Green where the *Bachaquero* bringing the western component of the armoured command, including 20 light tanks and various other vehicles, touched down at seven feet. She actually came to a stop more than a hundred yards offshore and the pontoon bridge, which was only in place after three hours of frantic work, still did not quite reach dry land. Nevertheless, the light tanks successfully negotiated the shallow water and all were ashore before 8.15 a.m. They cleared the beach and started towards Lourmel at about 9 a.m.

Above: Unloading was in full swing on Z White Beach during the morning of November 8. In this picture engineers are laying steel matting over the sand to provide a firmer foothold for wheeled vehicles although it is difficult to see if it was the American bar-and-rod system or British Sommerfeld tracking. The former comprised 12-foot-wide panels designed to be handled easily by two men. Each three feet long, these panels were laid transversely and then tied together solidly. Sommerfeld tracking was 10 feet wide and constructed of steel rods spaced eight inches apart and held in place by a hexagonal wire mesh. It was supplied in rolls 25 yards long that could be easily transported. *Right:* In the 1970s a large refinery was built at Arzew to process oil piped up from the Sahara. Mario took this photograph in 2012 when the plant was being enlarged.

Lieutenant Hudson pictured French and French colonial prisoners being kept under guard near Saint-Leu, just inland from Z Red Beach. He noted in his dope sheet that they were captured 'by troops of Combat Command B'.

Above: A nice shot of Signal Corps photographer Tech/3 Norman W. Harrington at work at Z Beach taken by his team-mate, Private Ned Modica. Their experience there was later recounted in a chapter by war correspondent Ernie Pyle in *Here Is Your War*. 'As soon as they reached shallow water they tumbled out of the barge and landed waist-deep in the Mediterranean. Holding their cameras high over their heads, they waded ashore. After dumping their bags and extra film, they waded back, and began grinding away at the hordes of soldiers landing. They worked for fifteen minutes waist-deep in the water and then ran up and down the beach getting shot of the troops dashing ashore. They filmed their first blood when they found some navy medical men tending a wounded French soldier lying on the beach.' (Harrington continued covering the war in North Africa, Sicily, Italy and Western Europe, ending it at Berchtesgaden in 1945.)

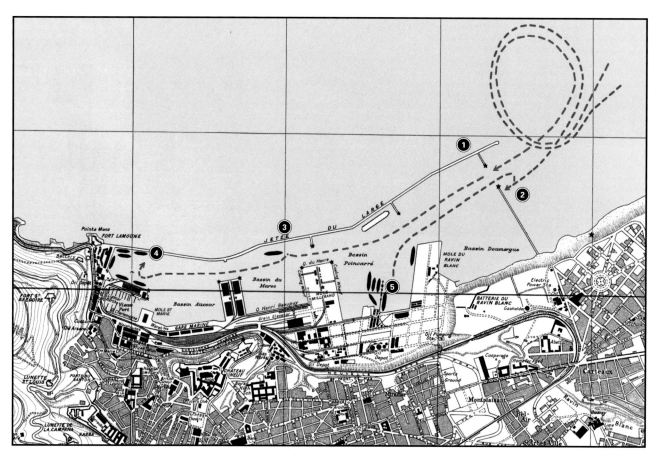

OPERATION 'RESERVIST'

Although they approved the inclusion of an anti-sabotage unit in the Oran operation the Americans soon expressed sharp dissent with the British plan for executing the project. Their objections were mainly based on the timing of the operation, that was to enter the harbour at H plus two hours. Rear Admiral Andrew C. Bennett, Commander, Advance Group, Amphibious Force, Atlantic Fleet in the United Kingdom, gave his considered opinion in a letter to General Eisenhower of October 17: 'An entry into the port by these cutters, with additional objective of seizing batteries fully manned, prior to the capitulation of the town by the military authorities, or at least before our Army is about to enter the town, is suicidal, and will probably result in defeating the purpose of the party . . . If determined resistance is met from the French Navy, which seems to be the general opinion, it is believed that this small force will be wiped out before the Army can enter the city, if they go in at H plus two.'

Pointing that the proper time for the cutters to enter the harbour was when the French command in Oran would consider that the port cannot be held for longer, he insisted that this hour would strike considerably later than H plus 2. He also insisted that its determination, on which the success or failure of the mission would depend, should be made on the spot rather than in an operation plan.

Admiral Bennett also protested orally and in writing to Admiral Cunningham but unfortunately, all his protests were in vain.

Operation 'Reservist' was the code-name for the attempt by HMS *Walney* and *Hartland* to force Oran harbour. On her second approach, the *Walney* broke through the boom [1] at 3.15 a.m. Some 600 yards behind, *Hartland* hit the breakwater [2] at 3.25 a.m., backed off and followed her through. Manoeuvring into the port, the *Walney* encountered the aviso *La Surprise* which had cast off as soon as the alarm was raised. The two ships passed within yards but neither opened fire. Approaching the western end of the harbour, the *Walney* was suddenly illuminated by a searchlight. She immediately opened fire, which was returned by the *Épervier*. The *Tramontane* and three smaller ships joined the action. Her deck swept by gun-fire and her engines wrecked, the *Walney* was soon a blazing hulk. She finally exploded and sank [4] at 7.30 a.m. In the meantime, as she swung round the Môle du Ravin Blanc, *Hartland* came under fire from the *Typhon*. Ablaze and out of control, she was abandoned at 4.10 a.m. [5], finally sinking 10.25 a.m.

HMS *Hartland* pictured sinking during the morning of November 8.

It has been said that the operation to capture the harbours at Algiers and Oran was modelled on the Zeebrugge raid of 1918 but in his report of March 1943, Admiral Cunningham makes it clear that the direct assaults on the harbours 'were in no sense planned as imitations of Zeebrugge'. Released after the surrender of the French garrison on November 10, Captain Peters was flown back to England on the 13th but unfortunately the Sunderland in which he was travelling, crashed in Plymouth Sound in thick fog. The pilot held on to Peters for an hour and a half in the water but he had expired by the time rescue arrived. Captain Peters received the posthumous award of the Victoria Cross. *Above:* Later in November, a Royal Navy photographer, Lieutenant Claude Parnall, pictured the wreck of HMS *Walney* lying on her side in the Bassin Gueydon.

Two small ex-US coastguard cutters, renamed HMS *Hartland* and HMS *Walney* and manned by the Royal Navy, and two British motor launches, *ML-480* and *ML-483*, were designated to carry the anti-sabotage unit into Oran. The Royal Navy, in view of the aggression at Mers el Kébir in July 1940, entertained no illusions about its popularity with the French sailors and the Operation Plan Centre Task Force, October 14, granted *Hartland* and *Walney* permission 'to wear the largest size American Ensigns they could carry', in addition to their own White Ensigns.

The landing party of some 480 men was predominantly American drawn from the 6th Armored Infantry regiment. Canoes were carried on the for use by special teams in boarding ships to prevent them being scuttled in the entrance or alongside the wharves. In charge of the operation, and mainly responsible for its planning was Captain Frederic Peters, a retired Royal Navy officer who had volunteered for this undertaking.

Given discretion over the timing of the operation, Commodore Troubridge gave the order to go ahead at 2.45 a.m. By that time, the harbour defences had been thoroughly aroused and Admiral Cunningham later admitted: 'The moment chosen could hardly have been less fortunate, since the French alarm to arms was in its first full flush of Gallic fervour and they had not yet been intimidated by bombing or bombardment.'

The approach began shortly before 3 a.m., just as air-raid sirens were heard ashore. HMS *Walney*, leading, missed the entrance on her first approach, and as she maneuvered for another try, a

shore searchlight picked her up. The battery on the mole nearest the entrance and several machine guns immediately opened fire. Both cutters and motor launches commenced putting up a smoke screen, but the offshore wind blew it away. On the second approach, searchlights picked up the ships when they were about half a mile from the harbour entrance, and they were immediately brought under heavy fire from guns and machine guns ashore. In the confusion, *ML-483*

crashed into the *Walney*, but the cutter gained on the turn for the second approach and broke through the boom at 3.15 a.m. and forged into the harbour.

Following about six hundred yards behind the *Walney*, the *Hartland* hit the breakwater just to the left of the entrance but she backed off and followed through. Manoeuvring into the port, the *Walney* encountered the aviso *La Surprise* (a large colonial patrol boat) coming toward her but the French ship mistook the cutter for a friendly trawler returning to port and neither opened fire. The *Walney* reached the end of the port where the destroyers *Épervier* and *Tramontane* were moored at which point a searchlight revealed her. She immediately opened up at the *Épervier* which quickly returned fire, soon joined by the destroyer *Tramontane*, the patrol boat *La Bônoise* and two minesweepers, the *Pigeon* and *L'Ajacienne*. The French fire wrecked the *Walney*'s engines and she soon drifted helplessly while suffering a devastating barrage from the port side and dead ahead. Now a blazing hulk, she drifted round the harbour out of control until about 7.30 a.m. when she rolled over and sank. The survivors, including Captain Peters, were taken prisoner.

Having already been heavily hit, the *Hartland* entered the port and swung round the end of the Môle du Ravin Blanc in an attempt to unload the troops near its base. This course took her past the *Typhon* at her moorings beside the mole and point-blank fire from the destroyer set the *Hartland* ablaze. Now totally out of control, she lay in the centre of the harbour on fire from stem to stern. Those who were still alive left the ship by one way or another shortly after 4 a.m. It was daylight before she blew up.

The operation ended in failure with over 300 killed and 250 wounded. The survivors were taken prisoner although they were released when the French garrison surrendered on November 10.

The harbour is now a secure area to which we were refused access. However, this shot snapped from the Maritime Station is a fair comparison with Santa Cruz hill in the background, topped by its fort and a chapel.

A column from Task Force Red arrived at Tafaraoui just before midday on November 8 and it quickly secured the airfield.

This shot of American and French troops raising the Stars and Stripes and French Tricolour was taken ten days later.

FAILURE OF THE AIRBORNE OPERATION

The 39 C-47s of the 60th Troop Carrier Group bringing the Paratroop Task Force — the 2nd Battalion of the US 509th Parachute Infantry Regiment under Colonel William C. Bentley — took off late from St Eval and Predannack in Cornwall and assembled over the south-west tip of England. Rain, fog, faulty radio communication, and defective running lights interfered with the maintenance of formation, and when the aircraft climbed through clouds to 10,000 feet to surmount Spain's northern mountains, they became completely dispersed. To make matters worse, the homing signal sent from the ship off Oran was broadcast on a frequency other than that expected by the transports so was never received.

Six aircraft veered far to the west of Oran, one landed at Gibraltar, two in French Morocco and three in Spanish Morocco. A seventh C-47 released its parachutists while over Spanish Morocco with the result that 61 paratroopers were interned by the Spanish.

Of the 32 C-47s that finally arrived about 6 a.m. at various points along the Algerian coast, all were low on fuel, and on Colonel Bentley's order, one group of 12 aircraft dropped their parachutists south-east of Lourmel. From there they marched eastwards to reach Tafaraoui the next day.

One of the C-47s continued over Tafaraoui airfield where it received anti-aircraft fire, causing it to turn away while radioing a warning. All but four of the C-47s then begun touching down at the western end of the Sebkra d'Oran from 8.30 a.m. There they established a defensive position and were soon reinforced by a platoon of light tanks from Task Force Green.

After his C-47 had released its paratroopers, Colonel Bentley continued flying over Tafaraoui and La Sénia where he observed evidence of hostile forces. As he could not rejoin the main group at the western end of the salt flat, instead he was forced to divert to the eastern end. Two other C-47s then landed near him, one still carrying paratroopers but all, including the crew, were soon captured by French civilian police.

By the afternoon of D-Day, with Tafaraoui aerodrome in Allied hands, an attempt was made to assemble the airworthy C-47s at the western end of the Sebkra d'Oran but French fighters

A column from Task Force Green reached La Sénia soon after sunrise on the 9th and by 10 a.m. the airfield was reported in Allied hands. This ruined Dewoitine 520 was found destroyed in a bombed-out hangar.

from La Sénia shot down seven of them. Meanwhile artillery began shelling the airfield, damaging more C-47s that had just arrived. It will be several days before all the 60th Troop Carrier Group airplanes, crewmen, and passengers were accounted for, and only 14 of the 39 original aircraft will be available for use. Of the 556 paratroopers that embarked, only about 300 could be assembled at Maison Blanche airfield on November 15.

In spite of the failure of the airborne plan, measures to silence the French airfields continued as planned. At first light, eight Albacores from 822 Squadron took off from *Furious* and flew to La Sénia with a fighter escort of six Sea Hurricanes from each of the two auxiliary carriers (800 and 804 Squadrons). They were greeted by anti-aircraft fire but the Albacores were still able to bomb the empty hangars on the north-western side of the airfield. Dewoitine 520 fighters then intervened, shooting down four of the Albacores, including the squadron commander, Lieutenant John Nares, while five of the French fighters were claimed shot down by the escort in the ensuing dogfight.

About the same time, seven Seafires from 807 Squadron on HMS *Furious* delivered a strike at Tafaraoui airfield in low-level strafing runs against parked aircraft and anti-aircraft batteries. Pilots of 800 and 804 Squadrons failed to find their mother ships (*Dasher* and *Biter*) after the raid and nine were forced to land at various points ashore when their

Brigadier General Theodore Roosevelt Jr, the eldest son of President Theodore Roosevelt, commanded the assault force for Y Sector. Here he was photographed inspecting landing operations near Les Andalouses beach on the morning of November 8.

fuel ran out. A second flight of five Sea Hurricanes from the 800 Squadron was launched at 9.30 a.m. to conduct patrols over the Arzew sector. They headed back to *Biter* after two hours of uneventful patrolling and all but one were ordered to land instead on *Dasher* and remain on her as all of 804 Squadron had failed to return from the original mission.

On November 9, the 16th and 18th Regimental Combat Teams pushed westwards from the Z Sector but the 18th RCT was soon halted at Saint-Cloud by French resistance. General Allen directed the regiment to contain the town while pushing on westwards.

D-DAY OPERATIONS

After the clash with the *Walney*, *La Surprise* left the harbour and sailed to intercept the invasion force off Les Andalouses, but the two destroyers covering Y Sector quickly turned their guns on her and she was sent to the bottom at 7.30 a.m. Three destroyers sailed from 5 a.m. to interfere with the landings but the heavy guns of the *Aurora* soon disabled the *Tramontane* which had to beach herself under the cliffs at Cap de l'Aiguille. The *Tornade* fired off six torpedoes in the direction of the cruisers before being heavily hit and sunk by 8.25 a.m. The *Typhon* was also badly damaged but managed to return to Oran by 8 a.m.

Three French submarines also tried to attack the armada but two of them, the *Actéon* and the *Argonaute*, were soon sunk, the former by *Westcott*, the latter by *Westcott* and *Achates*. The third, the *Fresnel*, was depth-charged but she survived to escape to Toulon.

At first light a field battery behind Arzew opened up on the ships off the Z Beaches, hitting a large transport, the *Reina del Pacifico*. Then, shortly before 9 a.m., the coastal battery at Fort du Santon above Mers el Kébir opened fire and soon scored a hit on the *Llangibby Castle*. Bombardment from *Rodney* temporarily silenced the battery but did not knock it out and at 10.50 a.m. the shelling resumed, driving the *Monarch of Bermuda* out of range after scoring a hit.

Pushing swiftly inland from Z Beaches, Water's force arrived at Tafaraoui just after 11 a.m. and quickly secured the airfield along with 300 prisoners. Shortly after midday it was declared ready to receive aircraft and the first Spitfires of the 31st Fighter Group of the Twelfth Air Force began arriving at 4.30 p.m. from Gibraltar. Four Dewoitine 520 fighters from GC III/3 flying from La Sénia then suddenly appeared overhead and strafed C-47s on the airfield. They also surprised the 309th Fighter Squadron as they were landing, shooting down Lieutenant Joe Byrd. The last flight of four Spitfires then turned on the Dewoitines, shooting down three of them.

Later two Lioré et Olivier 451 bombers from GB I/11 flying from La Sénia with six Dewoitine 520s as escort raided the airfield at Tafaraouni but with little success although Seafires from the *Furious* intercepted the French aircraft as they landed back at La Sénia, destroying one of them as it was taxiing.

By nightfall on November 8, the forces on the eastern flank had advanced to the planned beach-head line except in the area of Saint-Cloud where the French had halted the 18th RCT, 12 miles from Oran. To the left of the 18th RCT, the 16th RCT was now approaching Hassi bou Nif, seven miles from Oran. To the south, the main body of Task Force Red had joined with Water's force at Tafaraoui and was preparing a detachment to push north-westwards to the airfield at La Sénia early next morning.

On the western flank, the 26th RCT had moved steadily forward from the Y Sector beaches and captured Bou Sfer

By daybreak on November 10, Oran was completely enveloped by American forces closing in for concentric attack, these elements of the 16th RCT being pictured at Hassi Bou Nif. The railway line was later moved some distance to the south and the old railway station has been demolished.

and Ain el Turk and was scheduled to attack next the coastal battery on Cap Falcon and to push past Djebel Santon. To the south Task Force Green from the X Sector beaches was firmly established in possession of Lourmel airstrip and was also on its way to La Sénia to attack that airfield at dawn.

NOVEMBER 9

After scores of craft had been damaged by the increasing roughness of the surf, further beach landings were suspended, both along the Golfe d'Arzew in Z Sector and at Les Andalouses in Y Sector. The cove near Mersa bou Zedjar in X Sector remained usable, if hampered by the swell. Fortunately, the harbour at Arzew could now be used.

Early in the morning, those French aircraft still airworthy, both fighters and bombers, started to take off from La Sénia to reach the safety of bases in Morocco and Tunisia.

Two destroyers, the *Épervier* and the *Typhon*, tried to escape from Oran in the morning but finding their way barred by the cruisers *Aurora* and *Jamaica*, after a sharp engagement in which the *Typhon* succeeded in approaching within range of the *Aurora* and firing two torpedoes, though without result, they were forced to turn back. The badly damaged *Épervier*

This shot of a battle group readying for the push into Oran is a good illustration of how the US Army was still in the process of re-equipping in late 1942. Two of the officers are still wearing boots and two soldiers have the old M1917 helmet.

Two columns from the Combat Command B entered Oran shortly after 10.15 a.m. on November 10; this is Avenue d'Arcole, then and now. The author traced the location at the eastern entrance to the town. Possibly those troops are elements sent by Colonel Waters to join with the leaders of the 1st Infantry Division advancing from the east.

beached herself under Cap de l'Aiguille while *Typhon* succeeded in gaining the harbour only to be scuttled across the entrance.

On the Allied side, the corvette *Gardenia* was sunk off Oran in a collision with the minesweeping trawler *Fluellen*.

In the east, the 18th RCT was still blocked at Saint-Cloud and the attack launched during the morning soon bogged down in the face of heavy fire. Before launching another attack, plans were made to shell the town with massed artillery but when Major General Allen was informed of this he rushed to the regiment's forward command post to check with Colonel Greer. Bearing in mind that Allied policy was to reduce to a minimum all destruction of civilian life and property, he directed that the proposed bombardment be suspended and that there be no further shelling of Saint-Cloud. With General Fredendall's concurrence, he ordered instead that the town be contained with one battalion while the main body of the 18th RCT move on westward immediately after nightfall to participate in an attack on Oran. During the night, the advance reached a line abreast the 16th RCT, some five miles from Oran.

While a column under Lieutenant Colonel John Todd went straight to Général Boissau's headquarters in the Château Neuf, and to the harbour beyond it, another under Lieutenant Colonel William B. Kern drove to Fort Saint-Philippe at the western side of the town. There they released over 500 Allied prisoners who were being held there.

Général Boissau accepted the terms of a provisional armistice, and a cease-fire order was issued at 12.15 a.m. *Left:* No doubt still stunned from the naval bombardment, nevertheless the townspeople lost no time in crowding onto the streets. *Right:* This was then Avenue d'Arzew but since renamed Rue Larbi Ben M'hidi after a latter-day Algerian patriot.

French and American officers stand together to salute the raising of the flags on November 26. L-R: Préfet Louis Boujard, General Fredendall and Général Boissau.

In the morning on the eastern flank of the beach-head, a counter-attack developed from a French force in battalion strength which had forded La Macta river and crossed a swamp during the night. It attacked the rear of 1st Battalion of the 16th Infantry causing great confusion, the naval gun-fire officer with the American force reporting the situation as 'horrible'. Three Albacore bombers from 822 Squadron on *Furious* intervened some time after midday in an attempt to silence the French artillery while naval gun-fire support was being prepared. Meanwhile, a small armoured force of medium tanks from Task Force Red was sent to La Macta to help but in the end the 1st Battalion was able to drive the French away by themselves.

Early in the afternoon, a French armoured force was reported assembling near Saint-Lucien, seven miles east of Tafaraoui airfield, and Company B of the 1st Armored Regiment and a platoon of tank destroyers was prepared to counter it. The French force was totally outmatched and was quickly driven off leaving behind 14 disabled obsolete R-35 tanks.

Inland, moving from the west along the northern bank of the salt lake, a column from Task Force Green, comprising a few light tanks and self-propelled guns, reached the southern perimeter of La Sénia aerodrome soon after sunrise. Resistance by the garrison was minor, some of the defenders quickly departing towards Oran, and by 10 a.m. the airfield was reported in Allied hands, all the remaining French aircraft having been flown to airfields in Morocco. Nevertheless, the airfield still came under attack from 75mm guns emplaced near Valmy so in the afternoon a detachment was sent to deal with them. They returned that night after having destroyed three guns.

THE FINAL ATTACK

By daybreak on November 10, Oran was completely enveloped by American forces closing in for concentric attack. At 8 a.m. a general assault was launched in which the *Rodney*, *Aurora* and *Jamaica* joined in bombarding the batteries at Fort Du Santon and Pointe Canastel while Spitfires from the 31st Fighter Group operating from Tafaraoui provided air support.

While the coastal guns were being neutralised by naval gun-fire, Task Force Green assembled a 'flying column' under Lieutenant Colonel John Todd with two and a half companies of light tanks, one company of armoured infantry and a tank destroyer section. Moving out at 9 a.m. from La Sénia, the column pushed northward aiming for the centre of the city and the adjacent port,

A little later, Colonel Waters started out from the airfield at Tafaraoui with a section of Company B along a parallel road less than a mile to the east of Todd's column. Shortly after 10.15 a.m. the two columns entered a city silent except for some odd sniping. Public buildings had been barricaded but not the streets.

Todd's column went straight to Général Boissau's headquarters in the Château Neuf and to the harbour beyond it to prevent further destruction of the port facilities. Another column drove to Camp Saint-Philippe and released the 500-odd Allied prisoners being held there.

Meanwhile Colonel Waters sent one section to move further through the city while another turned eastward toward the area about to be attacked by the 1st Infantry Division. Colonel Waters also brought General Fredendall into Oran in his tank.

Général Boissau accepted the terms of a provisional armistice and a cease-fire order was issued at 12.15 a.m. Fifteen minutes later, Contre-Amiral Rioult and Général Boissau met General Fredendall and others, including a representative of Commodore Troubridge, to negotiate the terms of capitulation. It was agreed that the French tricolour could continue to fly but with a white flag beneath it, and that French forces were to be confined to quarters but retain their arms. Meanwhile American troops were to occupy key positions and harbours, airfields, and other facilities were to be made freely available.

At Saint-Cloud, the garrison repulsed all attacks by the 1st Battalion in the morning and the town was still in French hands when the garrison received Général Boissau's orders to surrender. With the end of the fighting at Saint-Cloud, organised resistance in the Oran area came to an end.

Oran was to be an American-operated supply base and Rear Admiral Andrew C. Bennett was tasked to operate the major port of Oran and three

Another name change intended to expunge any memories of the French colonial era. Place de la Bastille is now Place du Maghreb, the square being completely rejuvenated in 2016.

The harbour at Arzew was undamaged and readily usable so this M5 light tank could be landed directly on to the quay.

The port now supports a fleet of small fishing boats working the local waters.

A nice view of the Arzew harbour packed with Allied shipping although this photo was taken in the spring of 1943 as American troops assembled for the invasion of Sicily.

Since the war, the construction of a large oil refinery, and alterations to the harbour, have completely obliterated the landing beaches in this sector.

minor ports nearby. He came with a complement of 850 officers and men of the US Army, US Navy and US Marine Corps. Though the ports at Arzew and Mers el Kébir were already usable, as was the outer part of Oran's harbour, the entrance of the latter was blocked and the inner port cluttered with scuttled vessels. However, after examination, the situation was not so bad as it first appeared. The French authorities willingly placed all available tugs, salvage equipment, lighters and local pilots, at the disposal of Admiral Bennett, and the harbour was quickly brought into partial use, ready for the first follow-up convoy which was due on November 13.

Meanwhile the Twelfth Air Force developed the airfields at Tafaraoui and La Sénia for the maintenance and efficient control of air operations.

At 9.45 a.m. on November 11, Headquarters, Centre Task Force, was transferred from HMS *Largs* to the Grand Hôtel in Oran.

With the city now in Allied hands, the Centre Task Force prepared to establish contact with the Western Task Force through the Taza gap, and with the Eastern Task Force in the vicinity of Orléansville.

U-Boats were now seeking rich pickings off the North African coast and in the afternoon of November 12, *U-593* torpedoed the ammunition ship *Browning* off Oran. The burning vessel was soon abandoned by her crew and she later exploded and sank. On the 13th, *U-431* torpedoed the Dutch destroyer *Isaac Sweers* some distance north-west of Algiers. She was part of Force H and had been detached on the 12th to cover two oilers when she was struck by two torpedoes on the starboard side. The burning ship soon sank with heavy loss of life. The same day, *U-81* sunk the freighter *Maron* some distance north of Oran.

On November 14, the Centre Naval Task Force ceased to exist. When it was plain that no interference by the Italian Fleet was likely, Admiral Syfret took most of his Force H ships back to Gibraltar. They arrived on November 15, and the *Duke of York* and *Victorious* promptly returned to the Home Fleet to which they properly belonged.

The Western Task Force: Morocco

The Western Naval Task Force, Task Force 34, in action. Flags flying on the battleship *Massachusetts* on November 8.

The mission of the Western Task Force was to secure the port at Casablanca and adjacent airfields and to establish and maintain communications with the Centre Task Force at Oran. It was also to build up land and air striking forces capable of securing Spanish Morocco if that action should become necessary.

French ground forces in Morocco were estimated to number between 55,000 to 60,000 troops, organised into four divisions stationed near the coast, along the border of Spanish Morocco, and at inland stations such as Marrakech, Meknès, and Fez. Like all the units of the 'armistice army', these forces were, well below strength and lacking modern weaponry and transport. There were a few armoured vehicles, partly vintage Renault FTs from the era of the First World War, and some more recent Renault R-35s.

Naval forces manned coastal defence guns and a sizeable naval force — the light cruiser *Primauguet*, several destroyers and 11 submarines — were based in Casablanca harbour.

The partly completed battleship *Jean Bart* was also moored beside one of the quays in the harbour. In June 1940 she had been in a fitting-out basin at Saint-Nazaire when the Germans approached the port. Although she was far from complete, with only half the propulsion

The two-star flag on the *Massachusetts* (nicknamed 'Big Mamie') was that of Rear Admiral Robert C. Giffen, commander of the Covering Group (TG 34.1). The commander of the Western Naval Task Force, Rear Admiral Hewitt, was sailing on the *Augusta* with Major General George S. Patton, the commander of the land operations, seen in this photograph (centre) with Rear Admiral John L. Hall, Admiral Hewitt Chief-of-Staff, and Major General Geoffrey Keyes, Patton's deputy.

machinery installed and only one of the two main 380mm turrets fitted, in the early hours of June 19, almost within sight of the German vanguards, she was removed from the dock with the help of tugs. She succeeded in reaching Casablanca under her own steam on the 22nd and had remained there ever since. Facilities to complete her there were lacking so the two 90mm and the three 37mm AA mountings that had been quickly fitted the day before she left Saint-Nazaire were removed to be used to defend the harbour.

The front-line aircraft in Morocco comprised 86 Curtiss H-75 and Dewoitine 520 fighters, 65 Lioré et Olivier 451, Douglas DB-7 and Glenn-Martin 167F bombers, plus some 26 reconnaissance aircraft. They were based for the most part at Casablanca, Port-Lyautey and Rabat.

The American planning staff believed the Casablanca sector to be strongly defended so a direct frontal assault was ruled out. Instead it was decided to attack the city from the rear by forces landing close enough to reach it before effective resistance could be organised. As it was planned to use armour, the attack forces would require a port to unload since landing craft able to land medium tanks on a beach were not then available. Also, an airfield had to be captured quickly so that land-based aircraft could support the landing.

In trying to find a suitable port there were few choices. All the ports near Casablanca were small, shallow, and inadequate. Safi, the most likely possibility of three ports along the coastal roads to the southwest, was 140 miles from Casablanca. The other two, Agadir and Mogador, were more than 200 miles away. In August, General Pat-

In spite of its size and a voyage of about 4,500 miles, the Western Naval Task Force adhered to the scheduled timetable with remarkable accuracy. These officers were pictured on November 5 discussing forthcoming landing operations at Safi (see page 111) although unfortunately the caption fails to identify either the individuals or the ship. The Southern Group arrived at its planned position off Safi at 2345 hours on November 7; the Centre Attack Group was off Fédala at 2353 hours, and the Northern Attack Group made Port-Lyautey by 2400 hours.

ton had come to London with a sketch plan to illustrate that he wanted the main weight of the attack to be delivered well south of Casablanca with landings at Safi, Agadir and Mogador. This proposal was changed early in September when the attack was shifted northwards, with the main landing coming ashore at Fédala, 18 miles north-east of Casablanca, and the armour being unloaded at Safi. As to the airfields, Cazes on the south-western edge of Casablanca was considered too well defended so the one at Salé, five miles north-east of Rabat, was initially preferred.

These two ships were part of the Centre Naval Task Force: the light cruiser *Brooklyn*, part of the fire support group, with the aircraft carrier *Suwannee* of the air support group (TG 34.2). Built as a tanker, she was converted into a Sangamon-class escort carrier.

On board USS *Ranger*, armourers prepare for the coming operation by arming a SBD-3 Dauntless with a 1,000lb bomb.

Together with the *Suwannee*, the *Ranger* was to provide air support for Sub-Task Force Brushwood landing at Fédala.

However, there was serious concern that fighting near Rabat, where the Sultan of Morocco resided, might bring serious repercussions among the Moslem population throughout the Mediterranean. Accordingly, the airfield at Port-Lyautey, 78 miles north-east of Casablanca, was substituted for Rabat-Salé as the third objective of the Western Task Force.

The battleships and cruisers carried spotter seaplanes to direct the accuracy of the naval bombardment. During Operation 'Torch', 29 SOC-3 Seagulls were carried by the task force, the *Massachusetts* being equipped with Vought OS2U Kingfisher floatplanes. This Seagull was about to be launched from the cruiser *Philadelphia* off Safi.

The final outline plan was ready for distribution on October 16. It confirmed that the main assault would take place at Fédala, with two simultaneous landings near Port-Lyautey and Safi. Subsequently, the Fédala force was to attack Casablanca from the east, reinforced by armour from the Safi force. Other elements of that force were to prevent the French garrison at Marrakech from reinforcing the defenders at Casablanca. Landing at Mehdia, the Port-Lyautey force was expected first to seize the airfield just north of the town in time for its use not later than noon on D-Day as a base for P-40 aircraft ferried in by the USS *Chenango*, and next to capture and occupy the airfield at Rabat-Salé while protecting the northern flank of the entire operation.

On the day chosen for the assault — November 8 — the condition of the sea on the Moroccan coast was far from ideal. High tide would come at 1.20 a.m. at Fédala with low tide at 7.25 a.m. meaning that it would be ebbing at 4 a.m. when the first wave of landing craft touched down. This meant that there was a risk that the craft might become stranded before they could be unloaded and taken back to sea. Admiral Hewitt tried to have the operation deferred by one week to be

In the early hours of November 8, in the ready-room of USS *Ranger*. Pilots scheduled to take off before dawn wear dark goggles to adjust their eyes to darkness.

The USS *Santee* provided air support for Sub-Task Force Blackstone landing at Safi on the southern wing. Lieutenant Horace Bristol photographed this F4F-4 Wildcat of VGF-29 taking off on a photo-reconnaissance mission. (In the complicated identity structure of American air units, 'VGF' stands for Auxiliary Fighter Squadron, a designator that became 'VF' in 1943.)

On board Augusta at 6.13 a.m. on D-Day, Admiral Hewitt radioed 'Play Ball', the order directing general offensive action, to Captain Robert R. Emmet who was in tactical command of the Centre Attack Group. At 6.17 a.m. the captain of every ship in the Center Attack Group heard Captain Emmet's familiar voice over radio telephone giving the long-anticipated 'Play Ball' command. Early that morning French fighters attempted to stop a Kingfisher from the *Massachusetts* spotting the fall of shot for it, the caption to this photo stating that the anti-aircraft fire was to 'chase four French fighters away from a spotting plane'. Those aircraft were French Curtiss H-75s from GC II/5 led by Sergent René Lavie, and they finally managed to force Lieutenant Thomas A. Dougherty in the King-fisher to ditch just east of Casablanca.

able to land on a rising tide but his appeal was rejected. With no moon, and sunrise coming at 6.55 a.m., H-Hour for the Western Task Force was set at 4 a.m.

The Western Naval Task Force was organised in three attack groups with one covering group. The whole formation comprised 34 transport ships and many support and auxiliary vessels, guarded by a strong escort of three battleships, the *Massachusetts*, *Texas* and *New York*, seven cruisers, five aircraft carriers (including the *Chenango* ferrying the P-40s) and 35 destroyers.

Beginning on D+2, and growing by daily flights from Gibraltar, the outline air plan for the Western Air Command provided for 160 short-range fighters, 13 observation aircraft, and 15 light bombers to be operating in the Casablanca area by D+6. As soon as the French Air Force in western Morocco ceased to be a threat, 80 of these fighters were to be shifted to the Oran area.

In accordance with the directive of October 5, two signals were to govern the American response to the onset of any fighting by the French: 'Batter Up' and 'Play Ball'. The former would indicate a local encounter, the latter being an order directing general American offensive action. Any unit about to return French fire could signal 'Batter Up', while task group commanders would have discretionary authority to signal 'Play Ball'.

Lieutenant Malcolm T. Wordell (right), the Squadron Executive Officer of Fighter Squadron VF-41 equipped with Wildcats on board the *Ranger*, joined his pilots in a last minute singalong in company with Lieutenant Jacob W. Onstott on the left. Later that morning Wordell led the squadron on its first mission only to be shot down near Casablanca. He crash-landed in a pasture and was taken prisoner. After being held in a bug-infested stall at the Anfa hippodrome, he was released on November 11 after the French forces surrendered. In the book *Wildcats over Casablanca* that he wrote in 1943 with Lieutenant Edwin N. Seiler, another Wildcat pilot of VF-41, Wordell made clear how extremely chagrined he was: 'Imagine being shot down on the first hop of the first day in the first engagement. Too many firsts!'.

THE PRO-ALLIED FRENCH GO INTO ACTION

As the assault fleets were in the process of closing the coast, Général Béthouart, the leader of the pro-Allied organisation in Morocco, drove to Rabat to take the first critical steps in his projected military coup. At 2 a.m. he had a letter delivered to Général Noguès explaining that Général Giraud, aided by American troops, was taking command over all French North Africa. It also explained that Giraud had designated Général Béthouart both to take command in Morocco and to assist the American expedition about to land there. Général Noguès was told that orders were being issued to all Moroccan garrisons and airfields not to oppose the landings. He was asked either to issue confirming orders or, if he preferred, to absent himself until he could simply accept a fait accompli.

While his letter was being delivered at the Residency, Général Béthouart proceeded to Moroccan Army Headquarters. Général Georges Lascroux, the commander of the military forces in Morocco whose post Général Béth-

ouart was actually assuming, was sent to Meknès under nominal guard. Général Auguste Lahoulle, commanding the air forces in Morocco, was also soon placed under arrest.

In the meantime, in Casablanca, a similar letter was handed to Amiral François Michelier, the commander of all French naval units in Morocco and Commander-in-Chief of the Casablanca defence sector. He was urged to join with Général Giraud in receiving the Americans without resistance as a preliminary to joint action against the Axis. Michelier wanted to confirm the veracity of the message but when he could not find any corroborating report of an imminent landing he assumed that Béthouart was the victim of a hoax, possibly a German plan to invade Morocco. He still double-checked at intervals during the night but each time the Amiral assured Général Noguès and others by telephone that no large armada had been seen approaching the shore.

With no landings being reported as taking place at the time given by Général Béthouart, it all seemed to be a false alarm. While President Roo-

sevelt's radio broadcast and his letter to Général Noguès would have dispelled doubts, the former was not heard at the Residency and the later was delivered far too late.

As a result, Noguès had Béthouart's orders cancelled and instead he put into effect the standing defence directives. All army units were ordered to move to prescribed locations, and naval forces were alerted for action, as were air force units. Général Noguès communicated by telephone with the commanders of the Meknès and Marrakech military sectors to stress that they remained subordinate to his authority rather than accepting the leadership of Général Béthouart as the latter had claimed.

At Rabat, the Residency was divested of the cordon that had surrounded it. Général Lascroux was reinstated in his post of commander of the military forces, Général Lahoulle as commander of the air forces, and Général Raymond Desré took over command of the Division de Casablanca. Général Béthouart and his leading associates were held in custody in the Residency until evening and then sent to Meknès to stand trial.

In the early morning of November 8, Général Béthouart, the commander of the Division de Casablanca and the leader of the pro-Allied organisation in Morocco, took over and had Général Lascroux, the commander of the military forces in Morocco, and Général Lahoulle, commanding the air forces in Morocco, placed under house arrest. However, he failed to convince Amiral Michelier that the Americans were about to land and the orders he had issued were soon cancelled and instead the standing defence directives were put into effect. Générals Lascroux and Lahoulle were reinstated in their commands and Béthouart and his leading associates arrested. Unfortunately, no photographs exist to illustrate those hectic hours, this picture of the officers who failed to join with the Allies on D-Day being taken on November 11 when discussions for an armistice were underway in Fédala. Colonel Hobart R. Gay, Patton's Chief-of-Staff, is talking to Général Noguès. Général Lahoulle is on the right and Général Lascroux, carrying a briefcase, is behind Gay. Général Béthouart is notably absent as he was still in custody awaiting trial.

Capturing Safi

Under Rear Admiral Lyal Davidson, the Southern Naval Task Group comprised six troop transports and two destroyer-transports, screened by a squadron of three destroyers, and six minesweepers and other auxiliaries. The fire-support group comprised the battleship *New York*, the cruiser *Philadelphia* and the destroyers *Mervine, Knight* and *Beatty*. Air support was furnished from the carrier *Santee*, which was in turn protected by two destroyers. Naval air support from the *Santee* was to be supplemented soon after D-Day from Port-Lyautey airfield by aircraft of the XII Air Support Command flown in from Gibraltar.

By November 7 the Southern Naval Task Group was zig-zagging on station far off shore after its two-week voyage across the Atlantic. That afternoon the transport *Lyon* dropped astern of the destroyer-transports *Bernadou* and *Cole* (destroyers converted for high-speed transport operations classified as APD — AP for transport and D for destroyer) and within two hours had transferred to them by means of landing craft the bulk of Companies K and L of the 47th Infantry who were to be the first to land.

That night all the transports and warships reached their assigned areas about eight miles offshore with Safi's lights visible on the horizon. Debarkation nets

Flying from the USS *Santee*, US Navy photographer, Lieutenant Bristol, pictured the landing operations on Yellow Beach at Jorf el Houdi, eight miles south of Safi.

were dropped over the sides, the landing craft lowered, and men started boarding.

Designated Sub-Task Force Blackstone, the Safi landing force numbered nearly 6,500 men. It was commanded by

Major General Ernest N. Harmon, the commander of the 2nd Armored Division. The force was organised into two Battalion Landing Teams (BLTs) for amphibious assault; one Armored Landing Team (ALT) for early commitment;

Another of Bristol's shots taken on November 10 shows the main landing beaches at Safi. Red Beach is on the left with Blue Beach left of centre, and Green Beach centre right at the bottom of the harbour. The town of Safi is on the extreme right. The ships present are (L-R): the Fleet Auxiliary USS *Dorothea L. Dix*; the Attack Transports USS *Calvert* (AP-65) and USS *Harris* (AP-8): the Troop Transport USS *Lyon* (AP-71), and the tanker, USS *Housatonic* (AO-35).

This photograph, also from November 10, was taken from the top of the cliff just north of Safi. It shows Blue Beach — the large expanse on the left — and Green Beach which lay within the harbour at the base of the long jetty.

one infantry battalion and one tank battalion in reserve; and miscellaneous other detachments. The two battalion landing teams consisted of the 1st and 2nd Battalion, 47th Infantry, while the 3rd Battalion was in reserve. The Armored Landing Team consisted of elements of the 2nd and 3rd Battalions, 67th Armored Regiment (36 M-3 Stuart light and 54 M-4 Sherman medium tanks), supported by two batteries of self-propelled 105mm howitzers, a bridge company, and signal and supply detachments. In addition, light tanks from Company B, 70th Tank Battalion, were attached to the two BLTs.

The few beaches available at Safi lay for the most part at the base of high rocky bluffs that provided no exit for vehicles. Within the harbour, however, was a short stretch of soft sand designated as Green Beach, and just outside the harbour, extending northward from the mole for almost 500 yards, was a longer strip of sand labelled Blue Beach. A third patch of sand, Red Beach, ran for a shorter distance along the base of the cliffs to the north-west of Blue Beach. Passage inland from this beach was possible for vehicles only from the southernmost portion.

Eight miles south of Safi, at Jorf el Houdi, a fourth beach was earmarked and labelled Yellow Beach. Below rugged but not insurmountable bluffs and near a road, it was considered during the planning as giving a possible

landfall for a march on Safi from the south. Its approaches were to be reconnoitred by submarine in time to be reported to the task force commander during the first hours after arriving off Safi. Should the report be favourable, the 2nd Battalion, 47th Infantry, would be sent to land there.

After reconnaissance, the assault was scheduled to open with surprise landings in the harbour itself from the *Bernadou* and the *Cole*. Following on from the line of departure 3,500 yards offshore, at intervals of not more than 50 feet so as to keep each other in sight, were a wave of landing ships carrying

A wonderful vantage point to overlook the Safi landing beaches can be obtained from the Café Corniche on the Avenue Mohammed Belkhadir. Red Beach is hidden below the cliff in the foreground.

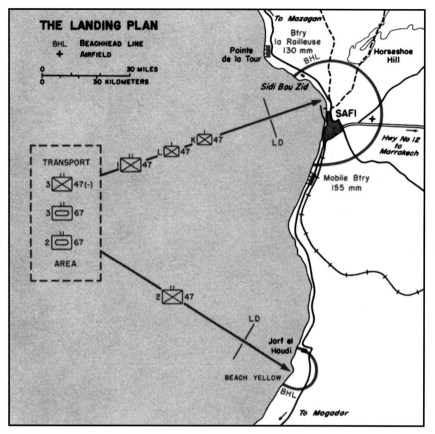

THE LANDING PLAN

BHL BEACHHEAD LINE
+ AIRFIELD

The assault by Sub-Task Force Blackstone at Safi. The operation was scheduled to begin before 5 a.m.

five light tanks for Green Beach and three successive waves of infantry of the 1st BLT intended for Blue, Red, and Green Beaches. The assault phase was to take from 13 to 16 minutes. Three more assault waves were to wait at the line of departure. The first two to be released at proper intervals while the last was to remain in floating reserve until summoned from shore. As first light was expected at 5.36 a.m. and sunrise at 7 a.m., the time for starting the run to the shore was set for 3.30 a.m.

The French garrison at Safi consisted of one battalion of infantry, one armoured battalion with 15 obsolete Renault FT17 tanks and five equally obsolete armoured cars, and two batteries of artillery, one with four 75mm howitzers and the other of four 155mm guns. Total manpower was some 500 officers and men. On the Pointe de la Tour, a headland less than a mile above Red Beach, a coastal battery known as La Railleuse comprised two operable and two inoperable 130mm guns in concrete circular emplacements. Air support could be summoned from inland aerodromes but ground reinforcements would have to come from Marrakech nearly 100 miles away.

Warnings of the approach of shipping reached Safi shortly after 3.20 a.m. The alert was sounded and the commanding officer, Capitaine de Vaisseau François Deuve, rushed to his command post located just above the port.

Surprise landings were to be carried out in the harbour itself by two companies which were being carried aboard the USS *Bernadou* and USS *Cole*. This shot of the *Bernadou*, with the signalman sending a message with semaphore flags, shows how the ship's mast was removed to facilitate her role in the operation.

D-DAY LANDINGS

The submarine USS *Barb* took station a little over two miles from Pointe de la Tour and during the night the scout detachment aboard set out in a rubber dinghy to land on the end of the long jetty, ready to mark the harbour entrance by infrared signals to assist the *Bernadou* and the *Cole*. In complete darkness, the party lost its way and entered the harbour itself by mistake. They quickly came under fire from sentries and had to take cover.

It was some time before 1 a.m. that the 1st Battalion of the 47th Infantry started to board but navigating the landing craft alongside and lowering vehicles, ammunition, and equipment in the dark and heavy swell proved unexpectedly difficult. Also, weighed down by cumbersome 60lb packs and weapons, the men were slow to clamber down the nets and board the bobbing craft. Consequently, operations fell behind schedule necessitating H-Hour being put back by 30 minutes. Even then, only four of the five tank lighters planned for the first wave, and only the first three personnel waves, had been loaded and despatched to the rendezvous area. Finally, they left the line of departure at 4 a.m.

Meanwhile Ensign John J. Bell in a scout boat from the transport *Harris* set out for the tip of the jetty to assist the approach. He closed the harbour at minimum speed, cutting his engine now and again to listen. Reaching the correct spot about 4.10 a.m. he turned his infrared light on to face seaward.

As the *Bernadou* neared the harbour mouth, the French flashed the signal 'VH' and she responded at once with the same signal. However, faced with ships of unknown nature threatening the harbour, at 5.15 a.m. Capitaine de Vaisseau Deuve ordered his defences to open fire. As the *Bernadou* passed the northern end of the jetty, and was about to enter the harbour, the 75mm battery at the Front de Mer opened up, as well

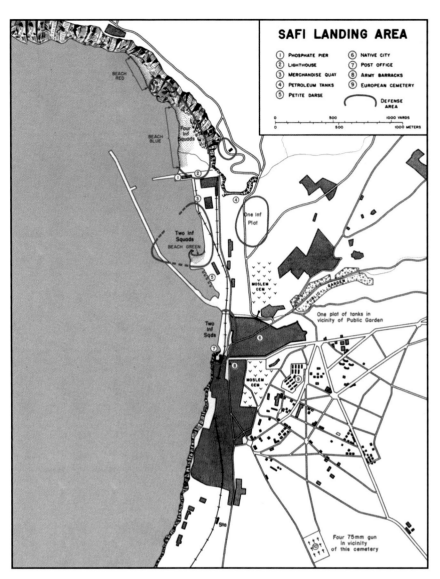

SAFI LANDING AREA

① PHOSPHATE PIER   ⑥ NATIVE CITY
② LIGHTHOUSE   ⑦ POST OFFICE
③ MERCHANDISE QUAY   ⑧ ARMY BARRACKS
④ PETROLEUM TANKS   ⑨ EUROPEAN CEMETERY
⑤ PETITE DARSE

DEFENSE AREA

After the assault had taken place in the harbour, four waves of landing craft were to follow at intervals of not more than 50 feet to keep each other in sight. One wave was to carry five light tanks for Green Beach, with three waves of infantry for Blue, Red and Green Beaches.

Although the wartime caption for this shot taken on November 8 in vague, only describing the soldiers as 'patrolling the coast', the high cliff backing the beach is a feature not found elsewhere, so one can be pretty sure that it was taken overlooking the Safi beaches.

as machine guns emplaced along the bluffs and the high ground east of the port. Riflemen on the wharves and jetty also joined in. From its hidden position south of Safi, the 155mm battery opened up as well as the 130mm battery on Pointe de la Tour. The *Bernadou*'s gunners replied while the ship continued on her way as a flare with an American flag attached was released above the harbour in the hope of moderating the hostile reception, but this had no effect.

The two destroyers escorting the assault force, the *Mervine* and the *Beatty*, quickly opened up to counter the French artillery. Meanwhile the *Philadelphia* shelled the supposed site of the 155mm battery to the south and the *New York* engaged the battery on top of Pointe de la Tour with her 14-inch guns. A lucky shot soon knocked out the fire control tower.

Meanwhile, as the *Bernadou* was entering the harbour under intense fire, she found access to the quays obstructed by ships already tied up alongside the wharves. She therefore

111

The coastal battery on the Pointe de la Tour, a headland less than a mile north of Red Beach, was known as La Railleuse, taken from the name of the destroyer that accidently blew up in Casablanca harbour in March 1940. The main armament of the ship was then removed to be installed in the battery that was built to cover the harbour. It comprised four 130mm guns in concrete circular emplacements but in November 1942 there was a shortage of personnel so only two guns were manned. The battery opened up at the American fleet at first light on November 8. The *New York* soon answered back and at 8 a.m. a 14-inch shell smashed through the fire control post. Although it failed to explode, it still killed the battery commander, Lieutenant de Vaisseau Jean Laporte, and one of his men. American tankers moving from Safi arrived at 11.30 a.m. and spiked the guns.

Looking northwards from the second gun emplacement past the ammunition storage shelter wrecked by a shell. The first gun emplacement is in the middle distance.

Hastily built in the summer of 1940, the battery command post was situated on the highest point at the northern end.

When a university was built just a few hundred yards away, the old battery fortunately escaped demolition .

Having suffered her first casualties on November 8 when two TBF Avengers crashed while taking off, the *Santee* suffered appalling losses on November 9 and 10 when some of its pilots were unable to locate the carrier's position. With fuel running low, the aircraft had to make emergency landings on the airfield at Safi but its muddy surface caused many of the planes to nose over. By the end of the day on the 10th, the Santee was down to three SBDs, four F4Fs, and one TBF. *Above:* This shot of the airfield taken on the 12th shows the deep ruts and three stranded machines, two SBD-3 Dauntless and one TBF-1 Avenger.

made for a small mole between Green Beach and the Petite Darse. She released a landing net and at approximately 4.45 a.m. Company K scrambled ashore. One section immediately rushed to the central post office to take over the telephone and telegraph system and cut communications with the rest of Morocco. On the way, they captured some French troops moving toward the port and also seized an anti-tank gun and disarmed civil police.

Unable to see clearly in the dark, the *Cole* mistook the *Beatty* for the *Bernadou* and turned on the wrong course before being signalled to stop. Ensign Bell then guided her into the harbour by radio.

By this time, the tank lighters had moved ahead of the *Cole* and although one temporarily fell behind with engine trouble, the other three continued into the harbour. They reached Green Beach some 20 minutes after the *Bernadou*.

Running the gauntlet through a renewed outburst of French machine gun and small-arms fire, the *Cole* swung alongside the merchandise quay to put Company L ashore. They quickly spread out through the dock area, scattering the defenders. By daylight, the harbour, railway station, post office, and roads leading into the town from the south were in American hands.

A wonderful comparison taken by François Denis from an ultralight during a sortie along the Moroccan coast in 2007. At this time, Safi aerodrome was still open though already in poor shape. It later closed, the whole area being designated for redevelopment.

This Avenger was the mount of Lieutenant Commander Joseph A. Ruddy, the commander of VGS-29. His crew comprised Radioman Harold K. Curtis and George S. Hinckley, the Ordnance officer. Ruddy had landed at Safi on the 10th as Hinkley was in need of urgent medical aid but then got bogged in. Here GIs struggle to extricate the machine with the help of steel matting. Note the Dauntless in the background that has ground-looped trying to land on the soft surface.

In the meantime, the first three waves of the 1st BLT under Major Frederick C. Feil, each with more than 200 men in a group of six LCPRs (Landing Craft Personnel Ramp), had landed on Red, Blue, and Green Beaches, more or less at the designated spots by 5.30 a.m. Reaching land, they advanced up the beaches against minor resistance from higher ground.

With daylight, the large fleet of ships offshore were now revealed to the gunners of the battery on Pointe de la Tour and the two 130mm guns quickly resumed firing. They first concentrated

Three Wildcats from VGF-29 also came a cropper at Safi on November 10. Two of the pilots, Ensign Alfred Fecke and Ensign Joe M. Galanno, had been ordered not to return to the *Santee* as the ship had suspended flight operations to refuel the cruiser USS *Philadelphia*, and both were damaged during their landing. Also the third man, Ensign John Thompson, had to make an emergency landing at Safi after taking hits in his oil cooler.

on the *Mervine* but without the help of the fire control station destroyed during the night the shelling was inaccurate. Nevertheless, the *Mervine* was straddled several times and her steering gear damaged from a near miss astern. After returning the fire she then moved out of range as did the transports.

The fourth and fifth waves, held up by various difficulties, did not reach Red, Blue, and Green Beaches before daybreak, the first at 7.45 a.m. and the second at 9.05 a.m. At Green Beach, the tank lighters were several hours late, only three having reached the beach on time, a fourth arriving much later after repairing an engine problem. Once ashore, many of the tanks were found to be suffering from waterlogged engines and/or faulty batteries. Also the steep, soft sand did not help and it was after 8 a.m. before they were finally ready for action.

On the right wing, lowering and loading of landing craft in the heavy swell for Yellow Beach fell considerably behind the schedule. The assault wave of Major Louis Gershenow's 2nd BLT did not set out for the beach until 8 a.m. and it was noon before the 2nd Battalion of the 47th Infantry was finally ashore and ready to move to Safi along the coastal road.

Disembarkation of the 3rd BLT under Major John B. Evans from the *Lyon* began just before 8 a.m. and the first wave started in for Green Beach an hour later but the unit was still not all ashore and reorganised until noon.

About 9 a.m. the second wave of the Armored Landing Team was ordered to start sending the lighters carrying tanks to the beach. Within an hour, one platoon had cleared Green Beach and was en route for Pointe de la Tour to investigate the situation there.

By mid-morning one more platoon of five tanks had landed on Blue Beach but thereafter no more were brought ashore. The rest of the armour remained on board until the ships could enter the harbour and be unloaded direct from ship to quay.

Some time after 10.30 a.m., the 155mm battery two miles south of Safi renewed its

GIs pictured at the entrance to the Safi aeroclub which lay at the north-western corner of the airfield. There is even an old civilian biplane, seen here on the extreme right, which gives a link between this shot and the photo on the top of page 113.

When Jean Paul visited Safi he found that only the streets had been completed for the new redevelopment project at the old airfield. The old wall has disappeared alongside Avenue Chahid Abdel Ali Ben Chekroune but this corner still shows signs of where it once ran.

Jerrycans of aviation spirit were offloaded from the *Titania* and transported to the airfield to fuel up the five planes that were still operational. This is Lieutenant Donald A. Pattie's Dauntless.

Another nice comparison by François Denis when he dropped in to the aerodrome during his Fly Aventure exploit in 2007. His could well have been one of the last aircraft to land and take off at Safi.

shelling of the harbour in one final bombardment. The *Philadelphia* answered back while an observation plane helped to pinpoint the camouflaged target. To complete the destruction of the battery, bombers from the *Santee* worked it over and one direct hit was reported. Later investigation indicated that the French gunners had spiked their own guns.

After the shelling ceased, unloading was resumed, and once the channel had been swept early in the afternoon, both the seatrain *Lakehurst* and the *Titania* moved to dockside moorings.

In the town, the army barracks area just south of the harbour appeared to be the main centre of resistance and Company K and Company I were ordered to attack only to be quickly pinned down by machine gun and rifle fire. The French defenders counter-attacked with three light tanks but two were quickly knocked out with rifle grenades while the stunned driver of the third collided with a wall. The tanks were seized by the Americans and the guns then turned onto the barracks. Early in the afternoon, a section of 81mm mortars began lobbing bombs on the barracks and the garrison finally surrendered at 3.30 p.m.

When night fell on Safi, the beach-head extended about 5,000 yards from the port. Unloading of cargo was completed as rapidly as possible but provision for setting up inland dumps was slow and the docks and beaches became congested.

With the planes unable to take off from the muddy airfield, a makeshift airstrip was created along a portion of the main road inland from Safi, a bulldozer levelling some trees on either side. Warming up the engine of his Dauntless Lieutenant George L. Schein prepared to take off with his radio/gunner Joseph P. Haggerty.

American engineers later laid down a 5,600 feet hard runway at Safi. The remains of it could still be seen in 2004 . . .

. . . but today the new developement has spread right across the flying field.

With a man sitting on the wing to guide him, Lieutenant Pattie taxies his Dauntless onto the narrow road. Out of five attempts to take off, three ended in failure, Pattie being one of the two successful pilots.

When Ensign DeClinton C. Nichols attempted it, the wind caught him and he ended up in the field beside the road with a bent prop and the landing gear badly damaged.

Lieutenant George L. Schein Jr. then had a go but he also came off the road into the field. Only Pattie and Lieutenant William R. Staggs returned safely to the *Santee*.

Under full power with restricted forward vision, pilots must have struggled to keep the aircraft straight on the narrow road

and the right-hand wheel of this machine caught the soft shoulder, dragging it off the road.

Experience had shown that trying to fly off aircraft under their own power was no longer an option, so the few machines still worth saving were transported to the harbour. *Left:* Although purposely designed to save space on aircraft carriers

(it actually increased carrying capacity by 50 per cent), the ability to fold the wings was an unsuspected advantage when trying to negotiate the narrow streets of Safi. *Right:* Avenue Moulay Youssef with the old native town on the left.

NOVEMBER 9

At dawn on November 9, as the coast was shrouded in thick fog, a French Douglas DB-7 bomber of GB II/32 from Agadir made a determined low-level attack on the *Lakehurst* moored in Safi harbour. A small warehouse used to store ammunition was hit and was soon ablaze with ammunition exploding. Anti-aircraft fire quickly brought down the bomber and it crashed on Red Beach.

In the afternoon, Wildcats and Dauntlesses from the *Santee* were sent to attack the airfield at Marrakech. Hangars were set on fire and the pilots claimed to have destroyed ten aircraft on the ground but in reality only one DB-7 had been hit.

While approaching the Marrakech targets, and again on their return, the aircraft also attacked convoys carrying reinforcements toward Safi, dispersing them though inflicting no losses. With fuel running too low for the return to the *Santee*, six planes had to land on the small airfield at Safi but many nosed over having struck soft ground. (The machines that were still flyable — most of them Dauntless bombers — were taxied to the main road some two miles to the north-east where a bulldozer had levelled the trees on either side.

The convoy has reached the T-junction in front of the Ksar el Bahr in the heart of Safi. The old fort, built by the Portuguese in the 16th century, was restored in 1963 and gives spectacular views from the top of the ramparts.

Left: Horse-drawn transport was cleared to enable the Jeep towing the plane to reach the quayside. *Right:* The monument in the

middle of this roundabout recalled that the 'Ra' papyrus boat built by Thor Heyerdahl started from Safi to cross the Atlantic in 1970.

After having lost 21 aircraft in three days — ten Wildcats, four Dauntlesses and seven Avengers — out of the 31 that she started out with, the *Santee* was hard hit. Lieutenant Commander John T. Blackburn was the commander of VGF-29, and on November 8 he was leading a flight of six Wildcats on patrol over Safi. They encountered no hostile aircraft and did not engage any ground targets but two hours into the mission Lieutenant George Trumpeter lost oil pressure. Failing to find the carrier, he had to crash-land on the beach. Blackburn also had to ditch in the sea having run out of fuel. Due to their limited navigational skills, the remaining four pilots got lost and had to make emergency landings near Mazagan. All the aircraft were damaged and the pilots taken prisoner by the French. Blackburn spent 60 hours in his life raft before being rescued by the destroyer USS *Rodman*. He was then transferred to the minelayer *Monadnock*. *Right:* Here he is being swung from the minelayer to USS *Santee* using a breeches-buoy. Blackburn was hospitalised for severe cold-water immersion as his feet were close to becoming gangrenous. (He later became an ace in the Pacific with 13 Japanese planes to his credit and was later to command the aircraft carrier USS *Midway* in the late 1950s.)

French troops counter-attacked in the afternoon using three Renault FT light tanks. Two were knocked out with rifle grenades while the third one became a casualty when trying to argue with a wall! *Right:* Though mature trees now make the place very difficult to recognise, Jean Paul traced the spot at the junction of Avenue Mohamed V with Rue Allal al Ilan.

However, of the five attempts at take-off on the morning of the 11th, only two were successful. One Avenger torpedo-bomber was towed down to the harbour with its wings folded to be loaded onto a transport but the fate of the remaining aircraft remains unclear.)

Armoured elements were then sent eastward from the bridgehead to intercept the French column coming from Marrakech and the first contact was reported at 5 p.m. over one mile east of Bou Guedra where a machine gun outpost was eliminated and a bridge was secured. General Harmon then came in to survey the situation at Bou Guedra first hand and he decided that one light tank company — Company B, 70th Tank Battalion — could alone contain the French and protect the unloading operations at Safi. Late in the afternoon he directed that the main force disengage after dark and start out northwards next morning for Casablanca via Mazagan.

When the Americans began firing mortars at the barracks, the garrison finally surrendered during the afternoon. The GIs then had an opportunity to inspect the disabled tanks like *Le Champagne* (No. 73160) pictured here.

Left: **While searching the interior of *Le Lorraine* (No. 74553), this soldier shows one of the shells to a local. The 37mm gun in the tank was devised specifically to engage infantry and machine** gun nests and it did not have the penetrating power to pierce armour. *Right:* **The spot on Rue Allal al Ilan where *Le Lorraine* was disabled, lay just across the street from *Le Champagne*.**

Above: **This GIs stands in front of the shops that once fronted the Ksar el Bahr in what was then the commercial centre of Safi. He is still wearing one of the American flag brassards on his sleeve which were issued to the troops in the initial phase although they appear to have been soon discarded. It is interesting to see that this soldier is wearing the early-pattern herringbone twill (HBT) uniform issued in 1941. This was initially intended only for wearing during fatigue duties but which soon proved to be much better material than the normal uniform for hot weather and tropical climates. So it became very commonly used as combat clothing.** *Right:* **To enlarge the square and bring the old fortress to prominence, the shopping parade was demolished sometime in the 1970s.**

Late on the afternoon of the 9th, Major General Ernest N. Harmon *(right)*, the commander of Sub-Task Force Blackstone, directed Combat Command B to start out from the Safi bridgehead next morning, moving north towards Casablanca via Mazagan. The force began its march at 9 a.m. on November 10 and made uneventful progress during the day. At 7.30 a.m. the following morning, the armoured column reached Mazagan where the garrison surrendered without a fight.

NOVEMBER 10

At 9 a.m. on November 10, Combat Command B of the 2nd Armored Division began its march from Bou Guedra to the north over the road leading to Mazagan. The force made steady, uneventful progress during the day. In the evening, a naval force comprising the cruiser *Philadelphia* and the destroyers *Cowie* and *Knight* started northward

Earlier in the morning, an offer from the French to terminate hostilities was received at American headquarters at Fédala at which point orders were sent out for an immediate cease-fire.

along the coast to give fire support to the armoured column. The *Bernadou* and *Cole*, laden with men, ammunition, and supplies, each escorting six landing craft carrying fuel in cans, departed that same evening to bring supplementary fuel and ammunition for the armoured vehicles.

At 4.30 a.m. on November 11, under a starlit sky, the armoured column halted close to Mazagan. Fortunately, the bridge across the steep-sided Oum er Rbia river valley was intact and apparently undefended and by 7.30 a.m. tanks had reached the town. Quickly and without a fight the garrison surrendered.

At the same time, a French delegation was being received at the Western Task Force command post in Fédala, signifying the readiness of Général Noguès to cease resistance. With this the need for Task Force Blackstone to hurry northward to assault Casablanca came to an end.

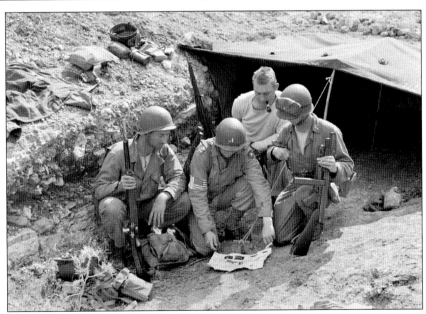

The cease-fire agreement was signed that afternoon at Fédala so halting Task Force Blackstone's drive to Casablanca.

The Capture of Port-Lyautey

The primary mission of Sub-Task Force Goalpost landing at Port-Lyautey was to gain possession of the aerodrome which lay in a loop of the Sebou river.

The Northern Naval Task Group under Rear Admiral Monroe Kelly comprised eight troop and cargo transports, one destroyer-transport, and five minesweepers and other auxiliaries. The fire-support group was led by the battleship *Texas*, the cruiser *Savannah*, and six destroyers. Air support was furnished from the carrier *Sangamon,* which was protected by two destroyers, and sailing in company was the carrier *Chenango* with 76 P-40s on board.

The primary mission of Sub-Task Force Goalpost was to gain possession of the aerodrome at Port-Lyautey for use as a base for the P-40s ferried aboard the *Chenango*, and for the aircraft of the XII Air Support Command that were waiting at Gibraltar. The plan was that the airfield was to be available by nightfall on D-Day to be ready to support the main attack on Casablanca.

The plan of attack provided for five simultaneous landings in the Port-Lyautey sector, two at beaches north of the mouth of the Sebou river and three to the south at Mehdia. The force comprised three Battalion Landing Teams of the 60th Regimental Combat Team for the actual amphibious assault; one Armored Landing Team of the 66th Armored Regiment for early commitment; and one battalion of engineers, in all some 9,000 men.

The most northerly landing was to be made by a third of the 3rd BLT on Red Beach located over four miles north of the Sebou river. This detachment was to gain the bluffs north of the airfield before daylight. From that point, it was to neutralise any defences on the airfield, reconnoitre to the north and east, and send a detail to block or gain possession of the bridge over the Sebou just north of Port-Lyautey. Eventually the detachment would cross the river in rubber boats and participate in a co-ordinated attack on the airfield itself, planned for 11 a.m.

The main force of the 3rd BLT under Lieutenant Colonel John J. Toffey would land on Red 2 Beach, less than 1,000 yards north of the river's mouth. This force was to occupy positions on the northern bank of the river opposite Mehdia from where it could provide supporting artillery and mortar fire for the attack on the Kasba, the old walled fortress that dominated the entrance to the river on its south bank. Then, continuing along the northern bank of the river, it was to join the other part of the 3rd BLT in the attack on the airfield.

Major John H. Dilley's 2nd BLT was to land just south of the river on Green Beach and capture the coastal defences at Mehdia before daylight, i.e. before 6 a.m. If the initial attempt failed, naval and air bombardment would be called down by General Truscott at 6.15 a.m. followed by a second ground assault. Meanwhile, the main body of the 2nd BLT was to push on north-eastwards to reach the hill south-west of the airfield and participate in the co-ordinated attack to be launched at 11 a.m. If all went well, the airfield would be in American hands, either by French consent or by capture, before nightfall.

The mouth of the River Sebou as seen from the Kasbah today, this comparison taken for us by El Maroqui. The fish cannery on the bank of the river was used for few days as a camp for French prisoners. In 1942, a boom then barred access to the river.

On the right wing, four to five miles south of the Sebou, the 1st BLT of Major Percy DeW. McCarley was to land simultaneously on two beaches, Blue and Yellow. It was to rapidly push overland to block the western exits to Port-Lyautey and also participate in the attack on the airfield. At the same time, detachments were to reconnoitre five miles to the south and south-east and to protect the south-western flank.

The Armored Landing Team — 65 M-3 Stuart light tanks of the 66th Armored Regiment — would also land on the Mehdia beaches during the day to support the operations, particularly in the area south-west and south of Port-Lyautey.

Naval aircraft from the carrier *Sangamon* would assist the advance and the attack on the airfield. If urgent air support was required, the *Chenango* was prepared to launch some of the P-40s it carried for emergency strikes followed by landings in the open countryside.

Surprise was out of question for by now the messages from President Roosevelt and General Eisenhower had been broadcast from London, and the landings in the Mediterranean were well advanced before those at Mehdia had even begun. It was planned to land two emissaries with the first wave, Major Pierpont M. Hamilton and Colonel Demas T. Craw, who were to drive by Jeep to Port-Lyautey and hand Colonel Jean Petit, the French commander, a letter similar to the President's broadcast. If the response was negative, the airfield was to be taken right away by a co-ordinated attack from three or four sides, from the air, and with the aid of naval gun-fire.

The French defence of the Port-Lyautey sector was estimated to comprise one infantry regiment of around 3,000 men with supporting artillery. These troops could be reinforced within a day by 1,200 mechanised cavalry and elements of a tank battalion from Rabat, additional reinforcement being able to march from Rabat and Meknès within a few days.

No photographer appears to have landed with Sub-Task Force Goalpost, not even with the follow up waves on D+1 or D+2. This general view of Blue Beach showing wreckage of landing craft was taken in May 1943 when Signal Corps photographer Carpenter was directed to report on the landing at Port-Lyautey.

THE LANDINGS BEGIN

The Northern Naval Task Group arrived off Mehdia just before midnight. The lights ashore were shining brightly and the shore was clearly visible from the transport area 15,000 to 16,000 yards out. While the *Texas* and *Savannah* took up positions to the north and south, the transports sought their designated stations in which to begin disembarkation of the assault troops. However, the transports had lost formation during the last stage of the approach and delays ensued in forming up the waves for the actual landings. As a result, General Truscott had no option but to agree to postpone H-Hour for 30 minutes to 4.30 a.m. The craft that were ready were then sent in while the others being formed up in improvised waves for the follow-up.

Colonel Craw and Major Hamilton came ashore at first light as planned and started out for Port-Lyautey under a flag of truce. French troops near the Kasba directed them toward the town but as the reached an outpost at a fork in the road, the surprised guards opened up, killing Colonel Craw. Major Hamilton was then conducted to the headquarters of Colonel Petit where his reception, though amicable, led to an inconclusive reply. Hamilton was initially detained but was eventually permitted to speak by telephone to Petit's superior, Général Maurice Mathenet at Meknès. The atmosphere at the French headquarters was one of sympathy toward the Allied cause and distaste for the current fighting but Colonel Petit said he could do nothing to stop it, pending orders to do so.

Instead of coming ashore on Blue and Yellow Beaches, a navigational error led to the major part of the 1st Battalion Landing Team of Major Percy DeW. McCarley landing at this spot, some two kilometres south of the mouth of the Sebou. A nice comparison of this deserted Atlantic coast beach was taken by Hanane.

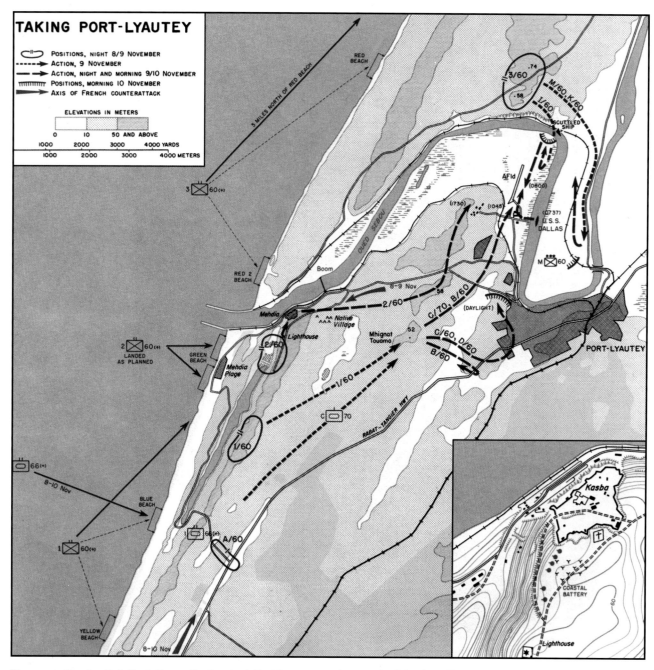

TAKING PORT-LYAUTEY

- ⌒ Positions, night 8/9 November
- ---▶ Action, 9 November
- —▶ Action, night and morning 9/10 November
- ⊓⊓⊓⊓ Positions, morning 10 November
- ➤ Axis of French counterattack

ELEVATIONS IN METERS

| 0 | 10 | 50 AND ABOVE |

1000   2000   3000   4000 YARDS

1000   2000   3000   4000 METERS

The operation by Sub-Task Force Goalpost at Port-Lyautey involved five simultaneous landings at two at beaches north of the mouth of the river (Red 1 and Red 2), and three to the south at Mehdia (Green, Blue and Yellow).

THE 2nd BLT ATTACKS IN THE CENTRE

In spite of delays and confusion in debarkation, the 2nd BLT's first three waves started toward Green Beach in time to land before 6 a.m. Almost simultaneously with the touch-down of the first wave, a French searchlight came on; a red signal rocket was fired from the jetty, and the coastal guns near the Kasba (Batterie Ponsot with two 138mm guns) opened up. The naval commander, Rear Admiral Monroe Kelly, signalled 'Batter Up' at 6.15 a.m. and ordered the destroyer *Eberle* to return fire. A few salvos from the destroyer knocked out the searchlight and temporarily silenced the coastal guns. Orders to 'Play Ball' — the signal for general naval attack by the whole task force — were then received from Admiral Hewitt at 7.10 a.m.

After reorganising, the 2nd BLT pushed on inland but naval shells soon started to scream overhead as the warships returned fire against the guns near the Kasba. (The ships had orders to reply at once to coastal guns firing to seaward without giving advance warning to troops ashore who might be in the target area.) The leaders of the 2nd BLT, inexperienced in the effects of such fire, and apparently uncertain of its control, melted back into cover in considerable disorder and waited for the shelling to stop. Once the naval bombardment ceased the 2nd BLT resumed its advance toward the high ridge and the area near the lighthouse was secured after a brief firefight. They were just about to attack the French position near the Kasba when the naval gun-fire began again. When a green flare — the signal to cease fire — failed to have any effect, the Americans beat a hasty retreat. Although the fire-power of the US ships was much greater than that of the French coastal guns — some 15 American shells being fired for each French one — the naval gun-fire still did not effect complete neutralisation of the battery.

The 2nd BLT finally resumed its drive eastward at midday, reaching the native settlement just east of the Kasba. They then came under counter-attack from a small force of French infantry. Naval shelling and bombardment from the air was brought down on the French artillery supporting the attack, but the French pressed on, committing three old tanks during the afternoon. Two of the tanks were knocked out by grenades and the third withdrew, but the 2nd BLT troops kept on pulling back piecemeal and the French took a substantial number of prisoners from a detachment covering the withdrawal.

In his May 1943 tour of the historic spots of the operations of November 8-11, Carpenter pictured this nondescript building on the Mehdia beach, explaining that it was used as the first American headquarters, set up on the beach on November 8.

Since the war, the area above Mehdia Beach has been extensively built up and building work was still taking place when Jean Paul visited Mehdia in 2019. The high fence, enclosing the excavation for a new residence, made this comparison difficult to take.

THE 1st BLT ATTACK ON THE SOUTH WING

Navigational errors brought most of the 1st BLT ashore about 2,800 yards north of Blue Beach instead of on Blue and Yellow Beaches; then, as a result of the mistake, its second wave landed ahead of the first. Fortunately, the 1st BLT was able to reorganise without French interference.

It then started a three-mile detour around the southern end of the lagoon, and five hours after the landings began it was able to start advancing north-east along the high ground on the far side of the lagoon. Machine guns pinned down the column on a ridge until late in the afternoon but artillery shelling finally broke up the French resistance just before nightfall. During the evening, the French tested the American outposts on the southern flank and soon drove them back.

General Truscott then paid a visit to Major McCarley, the 1st BLT commander, and directed him to establish contact at once with the 2nd BLT to the north and, at first light, to resume the attack toward the airfield.

THE 3rd BLT ATTACK ON THE NORTH WING

North of the Sebou river estuary, the 3rd BLT experienced similar difficulties in getting ashore. In the dark the organisation of the landing craft into waves became confused; loading the men was slow and the whole process fell so far behind schedule that it was not until 6 a.m. that the first wave headed towards the mist-covered shore. During the run in, two French fighters swept low over the formation, strafing two of the landing craft but without causing any casualties.

In the confused embarkation, the boats had ended up too far north so that the actual landings took place five miles to the north-east of Red Beach. As the men hurried up the sandy slopes to the high ground, Dewoitine 520 fighters resumed strafing attacks, two French aircraft being shot down into the sea.

Checking their maps, Lieutenant Colonel Toffey and his staff then realised that their troops had not been

Another shot by Carpenter captioned as 'the area of tank battle'. At first light on November 9, seven Stuarts stopped a counter-attacking French force comprising infantry and 15 Renault R-35 tanks. It was an uneven fight as the frontal armour of the Stuarts proved too thick for the French shells, the Americans knocking out the four leading tanks and inflicting severe losses among the infantry.

The U-Bend in the road turning around the lagoon provides a perfect link with the past. The beach is only a few hundred metres off to the left.

In the grey light of dawn on the 10th, with a raider detachment of 75 men, and a French pilot (René Malevergne) on board, the destroyer *Dallas* made her way slowly up the Sebou, coming under cannon and small-arms fire throughout. She reached the bend of the river sometime after 7.30 a.m. and put her troops ashore on the eastern perimeter of the airfield. This picture of the *Dallas* was taken the day after she had made her way up the river. Note the landing craft beached at the seaplane facility in the foreground with French aircraft lying between the hangars in background.

landed on Red Beach but miles farther north. The men had to undertake an arduous cross-country march, hand-carrying everything over ridges and through scrub, so that it was not until noon that the 3rd BLT was finally in position on Hills 74 and 58 overlooking the northern bend of the Sebou river.

A naval control party then set up radios and adjusted fire from the *Savannah* onto a 155mm gun battery observed to be in action south-west of the airfield while the *Texas* targeted an ammunition dump.

OPERATIONS ON THE SECOND DAY

At sunset the wind increased, and the swell and surf were soon running too high to unload further tanks and heavy weapons onto the beach. Boats had much difficulty in landing and leaving the beaches and misplaced troops contributed to the general confusion.

At Green Beach, all available men were taken from the shore party during the night of November 8/9 and organised into provisional units to defend the ridge-line east of the beach. The seven Stuart tanks of the 66th Armored Regiment that were already landed, under Lieutenant Colonel Harry H. Semmes, were directed to the southern wing of the beach-head to take up positions blocking the Rabat—Port-Lyautey highway. In the first grey light of a cold

dawn, Semmes's tanks were taking positions astride the highway south-east of the lagoon.

About 6.30 a.m. on November 9, the leaders of a French force comprising 15 Renault R-35 tanks and two battalions of infantry, approaching along the road from Rabat, came into view of Semmes's tanks. The Americans pulled back behind a slight rise and opened fire, destroying the four leading tanks and inflicting severe losses among the infantry. Frontal armour on the Stuart tanks was too heavy for the French shells to pierce.

Meanwhile, gun-fire from the *Savannah* was directed by her spotter plane to target the French assembly area in a little wood near the highway. This accurate fire forced the French to break off the attack and to temporarily withdraw. General Truscott then attached ten or more light tanks from Company C, 70th Tank Battalion, and one section of anti-tank guns to Colonel Semmes's force in time to help repulse a second French attack at about 9 a.m.

Throughout the day, the battle on the southern flank of the bridgehead continued on a diminishing scale, and during the afternoon the threat in this sector had so moderated that Company C, 70th Tank Battalion, was released to the 3rd BLT in the hope that the force could thereby push through to the airfield before nightfall.

In the centre, the French advanced along the southern bank of the Sebou river as far as Mehdia at the northern end of the beach, overwhelming the 2nd BLT outposts on the ridge. Fire from American positions near the lighthouse halted the French temporarily but they then brought up some 75mm guns and mortars, forcing the Americans to abandon the lighthouse area. The rest of the day passed in a sort of stalemate with the 2nd BLT unable to mount a co-ordinated attack despite the availability of artillery, naval gun-fire, and air support.

In the meantime, moving from the south, the 1st BLT resumed its advance toward the airfield and by 3 p.m. its leaders reached the crest of Mhignat Touama, a 100ft-high hill midway between the beaches and Port-Lyautey. They were pinned down there by mortar and machine gun-fire but American artillery and the timely arrival of the ten light tanks of Company C forestalled the threatened counter-attack. As the 1st BLT organised to resume its advance, a Navy plane — possibly one of the Wildcats from VF-9 that reported having bombed and strafed French convoy near Port-Lyautey — dropped two bombs among the troops. Artillery fire from an unidentified source then started to fall in the area and the disruption that ensued delayed preparations until it was too late to start the tank-infantry attack.

When news of the landing arrived, the French commander at Port-Lyautey, Colonel Jean Petit, sent his 1er Bataillon to take positions on the height above Mehdia beach. He then set out to assess the situation for himself. Meanwhile, having landed with the first wave, Major Pierpont M. Hamilton and Colonel Demas T. Craw, started out by Jeep to Port-Lyautey. Petit's car was approaching the Kasba when his intelligence officer in the leading vehicle suddenly made a U-turn and came back waving a warning. Petit spotted a greenish-grey vehicle approaching so his driver also turned around. When the two vehicles reached the leaders of the 1er Bataillon now advancing up the road, they immediately opened fire at it as it appeared that at first sight to be chasing the two French cars. The Jeep pulled over to the side of the road whereupon Colonel Petit walked back to meet the officer who stepped down. Major Hamilton explained in fluent French that they were emissaries coming on behalf of the commander of American forces then landing to discuss a cessation of the fighting. Mortally wounded, Colonel Craw lay sprawled in his seat. When Hamilton pointed out the three flags on the front of the Jeep — one white, the other in the colours of France and the United States — Petit apologized for the unfortunate clash but insisted that, coming at such a speed, the flags could not be seen so the vehicle was inevitably identified as a threat. In January 1943, during his stay at Casablanca, President Roosevelt came to lay a wreath at the foot of the cemetery flagpole that we discern in the background. Both Hamilton and Craw were soon awarded the Medal of Honor.

Having suffered from decades of neglect, the Kasba was nicely restored between 2010 and 2012 thanks to a grant of $100,000 from the American Ambassador's fund for 'Cultural Preservation'.

NIGHT OPERATIONS

On the left wing, the 3rd BLT sent Companies K and M in the afternoon to march down the spit of flatlands in the bend of the river just east of the airfield toward the western end of the bridge at Port-Lyautey. After dark, they drove the French defenders from the western end of the bridge but were in turn repulsed by artillery fire. A machine gun platoon was left in position to control the bridge while the rest of the detachment returned to Hill 58. Meanwhile, Company I crossed the river from the northern bank in rubber boats but lost its bearings and eventually dug in on the river bank near the point of the crossing to await daylight.

About 9.30 p.m. a boat carrying a demolition party was sent from the *George Clymer* to cut the boom that was still barring access to the Sebou river. The party proceeded as planned and the main cable was cut. The smaller signal wire then broke and the boom parted. As guards ashore opened heavy fire, the boat returned to the *George Clymer* by 4.30 a.m.

At 5.30 a.m. the destroyer-transport *Dallas* carrying a raider detachment began working her way into the mouth of the Sebou guided by René Malevergne, a local river pilot whom the Office of Strategic Services had spirited out of Morocco with just such a mission in mind. In the grey light of dawn, the ship steamed up to the boom, knifed through it, and continued up the river, the muddy bottom of the river sucking at her hull and shells from the Kasba smacking into the water near her. The *Dallas* then turned round the bend of the river, passing a scuttled ship. Some time after 7.30 a.m. she hove to in shallow water near the seaplane base on the eastern perimeter of the airfield and the raider detachment quickly went ashore in rubber

In May, Carpenter pictured Colonel Craw's grave in the field cemetery that had been established near the Kasba. Today Craw has an 'In Memory' stone in Oakwood Catholic Cemetery in Traverse City, Michigan, although it is not clear whether his remains were cremated or buried at sea.

The US Army headquarters in Port-Lyautey pictured by Carpenter in May 1943.

boats. With Company I moving in from the north, they quickly took control and by 8 a.m. the Americans had finally taken possession of the airfield.

The French then blew out three spans of the bridge to Port-Lyautey.

Without waiting for word back on conditions on the ground, the P-40s were then launched from the *Chenango* and the first began arriving at 10.30 a.m. The conditions on the airfield were bad, however, with many bomb craters on the concrete runway and pools of water on the grass, and all the aircraft launched in this first wave suffered varying mishaps on landing. The *Dallas* finally managed to radio through to the *Chenango* not to send any more aircraft.

TAKING THE KASBA

On November 10, shortly before the attack on the aerodrome, the 2nd BLT, reinforced by two self-propelled 105mm guns, moved out at first light to clear the entrenchments and machine gun nests outside the walls of the Kasba. The two guns fired at point-blank range at the gates of the fort but it still failed to stop intense machine gun and rifle fire coming from within. With the attack still thwarted, Lieutenant D. C. Dressendorfer, the naval air liaison officer, then radioed the *Sangamon* for air support and a flight of eight Dauntless bombers from VGS-26 on its way to Meknès was instead diverted to Port-Lyautey. Dressendorfer guided the flight by radio and the bombers dropped their loads where smoke-shells had marked the target. Before the French could recover from the shock, the Americans rushed the gates while the smoke and dust were still thick and the surrender of the 250 defenders followed quickly.

By noon patrols with tanks had brought Port-Lyautey and the high ground south-west of the airfield under American control. Colonel Petit was captured and he immediately ordered the force under his command to cease-fire.

As he had now received instructions from Algiers to end the fighting, at 10.30 p.m. Général Mathenet telephoned Colonel Petit's headquarters to speak with Major Hamilton. He expressed his wish to meet General Truscott to discuss the cessation of hostilities in the whole sector. Together with Colonel Léon Lebeau, Colonel Petit's deputy commander, Major Hamilton drove to a point on the airfield where troops and tanks of Company C of the 70th Tank Battalion were assembled. Using the radio in one of the tanks he was able to make contact with Colonel Semmes on the southern edge of the beach-head. The latter went along the beach to General Truscott's command post and a meeting with the French was then arranged for 8 a.m. the following morning near the gates of the Kasba.

In the meantime, the same message saying that Général Mathenet requested an interview as soon as possible was relayed by Aldis lamp from the airfield to the *Dallas* anchored close by in the Sebou river.

The battle at Port-Lyautey came to an end at 4 a.m. on November 11 and the formal meeting at the Kasba later that morning was a brightly coloured pageant of French colonial uniforms and Arab costumes. Général Mathenet accepted that French troops would remain in their barracks, with the Americans holding on to what they had won until ultimate peace terms were agreed at higher levels. He also agreed to hand over Rabat-Salé airfield without further delay.

On November 12, the 33rd Fighter Group moved to the airfield at Casablanca-Cazes and those P-40s still on the *Chenango* were launched and landed at Cazes. (No more P-40s had been dispatched from the carrier after the abortive start on November 10, the surviving planes at Port-Lyautey progressively reaching Cazes after damage suffered in landing had been repaired.)

Meanwhile, HMS *Archer* arrived off Casablanca with 35 more P-40s, the 'advance attrition' of the 33rd Fighter Group. On November 14, the *Archer* successfully catapulted off the first 15 aircraft but the next 15 struggled to get airborne. When it came to launching number 31, the catapult failed to propel the aircraft with full force and the plane landed in the sea, the pilot being rescued by a destroyer. The 30 aircraft landed at Cazes airfield without further incident. Two days later an attempt was made to launch the remaining four aircraft. The first two made it off the deck but the third failed to gain airspeed and ditched. The last aircraft was launched on November 18 as *Archer* was about to reach Casablanca to unload her passengers and cargo.

The building where the US headquarters once stood has now gone so it was a real challenge to trace the location. However, the church tower in the background was a valuable clue and checking old post cards finally brought the author to the Avenue Georges Clémenceau, now renamed Avenue Mohammed V. Closed in 2000 due to diminishing attendance the church was demolished and replaced by a bank.

During the morning of November 8 there was some discussion on board *Chenango* about delaying any action due to the complete lack of intelligence concerning conditions ashore but Lieutenant Colonel William W. Momyer, the 33rd Fighter Group commander, would have none of it. Shortly after 10 a.m. he ordered the launch of two P-40s — those of Captain Daniel B. Rathbun and his wingman — to check on the condition of the airfield at Port-Lyautey. Rathbun: 'The sight that interested me the most involved several bomb craters on the concrete runway, all made by our Navy planes in an effort to immobilize French aircraft. There were grass fields on both sides of the north-south runway but they had been flooded and pools of water remained on the grass. While the craters were big and the debris field on the north end of the runway covered the entire width of the runway, I decided to try to land just beyond the first crater and then slip past the crater farther down the runway. Alas, the plane stalled just as I reached the first crater, dropping the wheels into the crater and wiping off the landing gear. I came to rest out on the grass on the west side of the runway, shaken but not injured. My wingman, Harry E. Dowd, saw what happened so he decided to try the grass on the west side of the runway. He made a good landing, but the wheels sank into the muddy ground and he nosed up, damaging the

propeller and knocking the engine out of line. I knew that I had to stop the other planes. I ran to the *Dallas* tied up to a pier in the river that formed the northern and eastern edges of the airfield and asked that the ship send a message to the *Chenango* that further launches should be cancelled.' Rathbun then went up to a tank that reached the airfield and asked if they could attempt to fill in the craters by locking one track and then sweeping sideways but the repair effort had very limited success. In the meantime, without waiting for a report back on conditions ashore, Lieutenant Colonel Momyer had 15 more aircraft launched from the carrier and they soon arrived over the airfield. Seeing the two wrecked aircraft, Momyer decided to attempt a landing on the extreme northern end of the runway but he came in too low and his wheels caught the end of the concrete strip, wiping off his landing gear. The rest of the pilots then tried their luck on the muddy grass east of the runway with no better success and all suffered varying degrees of damage and injury. By this time the *Dallas* had managed to get a warning through to the *Chenango* so no further aircraft were launched. Rathbun later testified that Momyer 'oblivious to the chaos he had helped create by his foolhardy, too early, departure from the carrier', strode up to him and declared: 'Rathbun, if you had used your head, you could have prevented all of this!'

The operation having ended in complete failure, the launch of further aircraft from the *Chenango* was immediately discontinued. Seventeen P-40s lay wrecked on the ground at Port-Lyautey, one had ended up ditching in the Atlantic after taking off, and another just vanished into the fog. No P-40s had gone into action on D-Day as planned and the remaining aircraft still on the *Chenango* were not launched until November 12 when Cazes airfield was available near Casablanca. After the damage

suffered in landing had been repaired, the surviving machines at Port-Lyautey progressively reached Cazes. British carrier *Archer* then arrived off Casablanca with 35 more P-40s for the 33rd Fighter Group. The first aircraft were launched on November 14 and 30 landed at Cazes, one plane having ditched. Two days later two more planes were launched, one of which ditching after take-off. The last P-40 was successfully launched on November 18.

Landings at Fédala

Sub-Task Force Brushwood launched the main amphibious assault at Fédala, 15 miles north-east of Casablanca, with plan to swing south-west to capture the town. Meanwhile the cruiser USS *Tuscaloosa* supported the landing by shelling French forces.

The main amphibious assault for the capture of Casablanca was to be launched at Fédala, 15 miles to the north-east. Sub-Task Force Brushwood — the 3rd Infantry Division, reinforced by an armoured landing team from the 67th Armored Regiment of the 2nd Armored Division, some 18,800 men, and 79 M-3 Stuart light tanks — was to establish itself on shore, seize the small port, and then swing south-westward to capture Casablanca. At the same time, from its landings at Safi, Combat Command B of the 2nd Armored Division would advance to the southern side of Casablanca.

Sub-Task Force Brushwood was under the command of Major General Jonathan W. Anderson who was the Commanding General of the Atlantic Fleet's Amphibious Corps and had been long identified with Army troop training for amphibious operations. The Centre Naval Task Group comprised 15 troop and cargo transports, screened by a squadron of six destroyers, and seven minesweepers and other auxiliaries. The fire-support group comprised the cruisers *Augusta* and *Brooklyn* and the destroyers *Wilkes*, *Swanson*, *Ludlow* and *Murphy*. Air support was furnished from the carriers *Ranger* and *Suwannee* which were in turn protected by the cruiser *Cleveland* and five destroyers. Naval air support from the two carriers was to be supplemented soon after D-Day by aircraft operating from Port-Lyautey airfield.

The four main landing beaches — identified from west to east as Red 2, Red 3, Blue, and Blue 2 – lay on the long crescent sandy beach that extends from the breakwater of Fédala harbour to the Cherqui headland three miles to the north-east. Except for Blue 2 which was on the shore of a cove at the mouth of the Nefifikh river, all four beaches had an easy gradient through sand dunes to flat land above.

Three other beaches were considered for later or optional landings. Closer of Fédala harbour, Red Beach

On the *Augusta*, Major General Geoffrey Keyes, Patton's deputy commander, was pictured addressing Brigadier General John K. Cannon, commanding general of the XII Air Support Command, who was about to fly a reconnaissance mission on board a SOC Seagull floatplane.

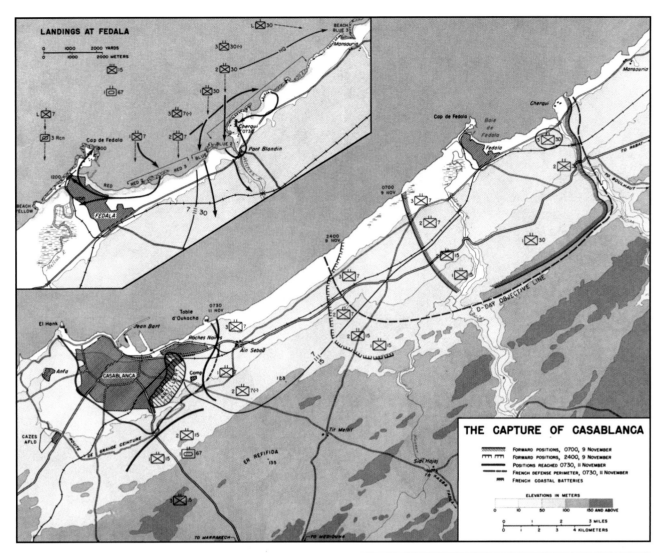

LANDINGS AT FEDALA

THE CAPTURE OF CASABLANCA

FORWARD POSITIONS, 0700, 9 NOVEMBER
FORWARD POSITIONS, 2400, 9 NOVEMBER
POSITIONS REACHED 0730, 11 NOVEMBER
FRENCH DEFENSE PERIMETER, 0730, 11 NOVEMBER
FRENCH COASTAL BATTERIES

ELEVATIONS IN METERS

was bordered by a ten-foot seawall so was reserved for follow-up landings once the whole sector was under American control. Smaller units could land at Yellow Beach, near the mouth of the Mellah river just west of Fédala, and on Blue 3 Beach, in the Mansouria inlet about three miles north-east of the Cherqui headland.

The Fédala sector was believed to be manned by 2,500 French troops. The nearest reinforcements were at Rabat, 43 miles to the north-east, and there was the 4,500-strong garrison to consider at Casablanca. Also, the advance along the coast might have to face upwards of another 6,500 troops.

The greatest hazards facing the landing force were the coastal batteries that could enfilade all the four main landing beaches. Known as the Batterie du Pont Blondin, the most powerful battery on the Cherqui headland comprised three 138mm guns. On Cap de Fédala, across the bay where the major landings were planned, two 75mm guns could shell all the beaches as could the battery with three 100mm guns emplaced near the base of the cape. Silencing the coastal batteries was therefore to be the first priority.

Another possible threat was from French naval units, especially submarines, based at Casablanca. Though the partly completed battleship *Jean*

Sub-Task Force Brushwood comprised the 3rd Infantry Division reinforced by an armoured landing team from the 67th Armored Regiment — a complement of some 18,800 men with 79 M-3 Stuart light tanks. On the eve of the landing, troops of the division were pictured drawing their ammunition on board USS *Joseph T. Dickman* (AP-26), the first transport on the left wing of the assault fleet.

Off Fédala, the fire-support group comprised the cruisers *Augusta* and *Brooklyn* and four destroyers. At 7.10 a.m., the *Augusta* opened up with her 8-inch guns, firing 72 rounds in a dozen minutes from a range of 12,000 yards in an attempt to silence the Batterie du Port. *Right:* A salvo from the French battery lands near the *Augusta*. The launch hanging from the crane is probably the one being prepared to take Patton and his staff ashore. This photograph was taken some time before the cruiser opened fire because the blast from its guns simply blew the boat to pieces!

Bart could not move, the 380mm guns in her single turret could easily reach the Fédala area. However, the battleship had no fire control system and no range finder so the shots could only be adjusted via radio and telephone lines with two coastal observation posts.

Task Force Brushwood was organised into three regimental landing groups (RLGs). These were based on the 7th (Colonel Robert C. Macon), the

Off Casablanca, the Covering Group comprised the cruisers *Tuscaloosa* and *Wichita* and the battleship *Massachusetts*. This is a view from her after-deck taken during a lull in the artillery battle on the morning of November 8. The single turret remaining operative on the *Jean Bart* began firing from about 7 a.m., as did the El Hank battery, and at 7.04 a.m. the *Massachusetts* let go her first 16-inch salvo in reply at the *Jean Bart*. The battleship and the *Tuscaloosa* concentrated on trying to silence the French battleship from a range of 24,000 yards, increasing to 29,000 yards, while the *Wichita* shelled the El Hank battery from 21,800 yards.

west of the town and hold the bridges over the Mellah river. BLT 1-30 was to come ashore on Blue Beach and push four miles to the south to occupy a long ridge beyond the main Casablanca—Rabat highway. BLT 2-30 was to land on Blue 2 Beach and move to occupy the Cherqui headland and capture the Batterie du Pont Blondin. It was then to secure the bridges over the Nefifikh river and form a defence line on the eastern bank.

The third battalion of each of these two regiments would form a floating reserve. The entire 15th RLG would be in Task Force reserve prepared to land two hours after the assault battalions and assemble ashore in the 7th RLG's zone to advance south-westward. Once the port at Fédala was captured, it was to be used first for unloading armoured vehicles and heavy equipment and then for other stores.

THE LANDINGS BEGIN

The assembly area was six to eight miles offshore but an unexpected current carried the fleet a few miles from the desired location with the result that the transport formation became badly deranged. A series of emergency manoeuvres then took place to try to re-establish the planned formation.

15th (Colonel Thomas H. Monroe), and the 30th (Colonel Arthur H. Rogers) Infantry Regiments.

The landing plan as laid down was as follows. BLT 1-7 — the 1st Battalion Landing Team of the 7th Regimental Landing Group — was to land on Red 2 Beach and take the town of Fédala, then continuing on to the cape to seize the two batteries there. BLT 2-7 was to land on Red 3 Beach, clear the sector south and

A near miss from a salvo fired by the El Hank battery at the USS *Mayrant*, one of the four destroyers assigned as the screen for the Covering Group. (The gunnery officer of *Mayrant* was Lieutenant Franklin D. Roosevelt Jr., the son of the President.)

Just before dawn on D-Day, the *Ranger* and the *Suwannee* began to launch their aircraft, this shot showing the activity on the flight deck of the *Ranger*. A Wildcat to be used as a spotter plane is being prepared for launch.

Reports of the slow pace at which landing craft were being loaded as the men clambered down the sides of the ships, weighed down by all their equipment, and the consequent delay in the landing craft assembling at the rendezvous points, made it necessary to impose a half hour's delay. Orders were then issued to the transports to use their own landing craft to disembark as large a proportion of the assault BLTs as possible and not to wait for the arrival of further landing craft from other transports. (None of the transports carried enough landing craft to land the troops on board which necessitated the temporary use of boats and crews from other vessels.) In spite of this, another postponement of 15 minutes had to be ordered so it was nearer 4.45 a.m. when the assault started out towards the shore.

The four control destroyers, the *Wilkes*, *Swanson*, *Ludlow*, and *Murphy*, shepherding the landing craft for which each was responsible, moved to a line of departure 4,000 yards offshore. At the sound of engines approaching, searchlights on Cap de Fédala and Cherqui lit up the sky in quest of aircraft, but as vertical beams had been specified in General Eisenhower's broadcast to be shown as a sign of non-resistance, the sight brought a brief moment of hope. However, having

The radio/gunner of this Dauntless of VS-41, Photographer's Mate 2nd Class M. D. Mokos, gives a thumbs-up as Lieutenant Cecil V. Johnson prepares to embark on a reconnaissance mission from the *Ranger*.

133

Left: **Ensign C. C. Bevis Jr. pilot of of a Dauntless of VS-41, and his radio-gunner, Aviation Radioman 3rd Class W. J. Sackelford. On November 8, 15 Dauntless SBDs of VS-41 attacked a French naval force comprising the light cruiser *Primauguet* and** three destroyers. The caption to this photograph claimed that Ensign Bevis scored a near miss on the cruiser. *Right:* **Lieutenant Edward Micka pictured aboard his Wildcat of VF-9 on the flight deck of the *Ranger*.**

found nothing in the sky, the searchlights then turned instead to sweep the sea. The vessels escorting the landing craft opened up on them and the lights were soon doused. The faulty navigation caused many LCAs to come ashore miles from their designated touch-down locations, some encountering rocky obstructions or reefs rather than sandy beaches. The surf swept boats against the rocks with such destructive force that many either capsized or were smashed.

The first men to land at around 5 a.m. were elements of BLT 1-7. Due to land on Red 2, they ended up partly on that beach, partly on Red 3, and partly on the rocky shore that lay between them. The loss in landing craft was heavy but, despite these losses, all three rifle companies were ashore by 6 a.m. In particular, the boat crews of

French reports indicate that five Curtiss H-75s, six Dewoitine 520s and three DB-7s were lost on the Médiouna airfield to strafing attack by US Navy planes. This is one of the H-75s from GC II/5. On November 9 Lieutenant Micka participated in an attack on the airfield, south of Casablanca, together with a dozen Wildcats. The American aircraft conducted strafing runs at low altitude in sections of two as the French bombers and fighters were well dispersed. However, Micka's Wildcat was caught in the explosion of a French Douglas DB-7 that he was attacking and his aircraft was blown out of the sky. The French recovered his body and buried him on the spot with full military honours, Lieutenant Micka, from Great Neck, New York, now lies buried in the cemetery at Médiouna, Casablanca. He was posthumously awarded the Navy Cross.

The first men to get ashore were elements of BLT 1-7, part of which landed on Red 3 Beach.

Joseph T. Dickman had the best record, losing only two out of 27 craft on Blue 2 Beach in the initial landing of BLT 2-30, and retrieving the others promptly for a second trip.

The *Massachusetts*, the *Wichita*, and the *Tuscaloosa* catapulted spotter seaplanes and steamed along the coast at a range of some 20,000 yards from Casablanca harbour. The *Ranger* and the *Suwannee*, ten miles further out, began to launch their aircraft just before dawn and a squadron of Daunt-less dive-bombers from the *Ranger* was soon circling 10,000 feet above Casablanca, prepared to attack any French destroyers or submarines which tried to leave the harbour, or to blast any anti-aircraft batteries which opened fire. One squadron of Wildcats from the *Ranger* was also in position to attack the airfield at Rabat and another to strike Cazes aerodrome at Casablanca. The *Suwannee*'s aircraft were aloft to protect the vessels off Fédala from air or submarine attack.

Just after 6.30 a.m. leaflets containing General Eisenhower's proclamation fluttered down over Casablanca. An hour later a cordon of French guards had been placed around the US Consulate.

A few minutes before 7 a.m. anti-aircraft guns in Casablanca harbour opened up against one of the observation planes and French fighters started driving others out to sea. One Curtiss H-75 from GC II/5 attacked a Vought Kingfisher floatplane from the *Massachusetts*, forcing it to ditch off Ain

Then Red Beach 3 . . . now Plage Monica, a photo by El Akramine.

On D+1, a Signal Corps photographer pictured the first 'American flag planted on the beach-head at Fédala'.

Sebaa. The pilot succeeded in taxi-ing the plane to the beach where he was taken prisoner while the observer, wounded during the fight, was taken to hospital.

At 8 a.m. Colonel William H. Wilbur, a member of Patton's staff, arrived at the French Admiralty building after a trip from Fédala in a vehicle bearing a huge flag of truce, his mission being to persuade Amiral Michelier to co-operate. Colonel Wilbur found out that Général Béthouart, with whom he hoped to make contact, was under close arrest and that the Navy was in charge. An officer offered to take him to see Amiral Michelier but when the admiral refused to meet him, Wilbur headed back to the American lines in Fédala.

Just then, the battery on the El Hank headland west of the city (comprising four 194mm and four 138mm guns) opened up against the assault armada, as did the turret on the Jean Bart and various guns on other ships in the harbour. In reply shells from the Massachusetts and the Tuscaloosa began to target the Jean Bart while the Wichita opened fire on El Hank, using her spotting plane.

During the morning, the German armistice commission in Casablanca under Generalleutnant Heinz-Hellmuth von Wühlisch left the city in haste, taking off from Cazes airfield in three Heinkel He 111s and a Junkers Ju-52.

NAVAL ACTIONS ON D-DAY

The Massachusetts fired nine 16-inch salvos, some 120 shots, at the Jean Bart and made five hits. One exploded below the after control station, completely wrecking it and making a large hole below the waterline. Another hit the 380mm turret before ricocheting into the city, the impact jamming the turret and silencing it for 48 hours. Meanwhile, the Tuscaloosa turned on the submarine berthing area in the harbour, soon joined by the Wichita which had by then silenced, temporarily as it was soon to appear, the El Hank battery.

Amiral Michelier ordered the submarines and destroyers to sortie from Casablanca and attack the armada off

The toll of landing craft was heavy at Fédala as can be seen in this picture taken 'on the first day of landings'. Many of the landing craft and much other equipment lies scattered all along the beach.

With Battalion Landing Team 1-7 having secured Fédala by 6 a.m., the 3rd Platoon of Company C under Lieutenant Floyd L. Hardy halted a car and a truck carrying nine German officers and men, all members of the German Armistice Commission. They had fled from the Hôtel Miramar and, according to one account, had been captured while running across the golf course in order to hop a plane.

Fédala, and break up the landing operations there.

Eight submarines quickly dropped moorings and sailed to action. At 8.15 a.m., the commander of the 2ème Escadre Légère, Amiral Raymond Gervais de Lafond, aboard the destroyer *Milan* led seven destroyers out of the harbour. (He later told Admiral Hewitt that when this first sortie commenced he was still ignorant of the nationality of the ships he had been ordered to fight.)

Undeterred by repeated attacks by Wildcats from the *Ranger*, the destroyers approached the American ships off Fédala and opened fire, hitting the destroyer *Ludlow* and forced her and the *Wilkes* to fall back on the cruisers. At 8.30 a.m., when the French destroyers were some four miles from the transports off Fédala, Admiral Hewitt ordered *Augusta* and *Brooklyn* and the destroyers *Wilkes* and *Swanson* to intercept them. Action opened at 18,500 yards at 8.48 a.m., rapidly closing to 17,600. At about 9 a.m. the French destroyers retired towards Casablanca.

Augusta and *Brooklyn* broke off and returned to guard the transports, while the destroyers engaged the guns on Cap de Fédala, which had reopened fire. In the meantime, the French destroyers managed to lay up a heavy smoke screen and followed the excellent tactics of charging out of it to fire at their formidable opponents, then in again to throw off the spot planes and range finders.

The minutes from 10 a.m. were the hottest part of this action, with so many things happening almost simultaneously. The light cruiser *Primauguet* sortied to assist the destroyers, two of which then peeled off from the smoke screen group and headed north to deliver a torpedo attack on the Cover-

ing Group. *Massachusetts*, at a range of about 11 miles, and *Tuscaloosa*, at a little less, landed a couple of salvos on the van destroyer *Fougueux* that blew up and sank.

About the same moment a shell from the El Hank battery hit the *Massachusetts* on the main deck forward and exploded below, injuring nobody.

Aircraft from the *Ranger* intervened, bombing and strafing the French ships while salvos from El Hank guns and torpedoes from French submarines added

to the complexity of the naval battle. At 11.07 a.m. the submarine *Méduse* fired a spread of four torpedoes at the *Massachusetts*, and then another salvo at the *Tuscaloosa*, narrowly missing both, while at 11.10 a.m. the submarine *Amazone* fired five torpedoes at the *Brooklyn* at a range of not over a thousand yards but the submarine's firing impulse bubbles were seen from the cruiser that dodged the torpedoes wake by a timely 90-degree turn.

Massachusetts soon returned to battle and at 10.35 a.m. she landed a salvo on the *Boulonnais*, who promptly rolled over and soon sank.

At about 11 a.m., the *Primauguet* took a bad beating from *Augusta* and *Brooklyn*. Holed five times below the waterline, and with her No. 3 turret disabled by a 8-inch shell, she retired toward the harbour and anchored off the Roches Noires. *Milan*, with five hits, at least three of them 8-inch, was burning and had to beach too off Roches Noires in the afternoon; Amiral Gervais de Lafond then transfered onboard the *Primauguet*. The *Brestois* was hit by fire from the *Augusta*, she managed to make the harbour jetty in the afternoon where planes from the *Ranger* strafed her and that night she rolled over and sank.

The three destroyers still in action outside the harbour, the *Frondeur*, *Alcyon*, and *Albatros*, formed up about 11.15 a.m. apparently with the intention of delivering a torpedo attack on the cruisers, but they were soon reduced to ineffectual zigzagging behind a smoke screen by the fire of the *Tuscaloosa* and *Wichita*. The El Hank battery took part and after a number of straddles and near misses, it scored one hit on the *Wichita* at 11.28 a.m. Ten minutes later the cruiser dodged a spread of three torpedoes from a submarine.

US Signal Corps photographer, Lieutenant Robert J. Longini, was on hand to photograph the bemused German prisoners still stunned by the sudden change in their fortunes. They were soon taken aboard the transport USS *Ancon* lying off shore and then shipped to the United States, the first German prisoners to be taken by US forces on land in World War II.

137

In mid-afternoon on November 8, after Cap de Fédala had been occupied, the harbour was inspected and four of the docks and two paved slipways were found to be usable. *Left:* **A Jeep** drives ashore under its own power. *Right:* **This is the same view today, looking north-west, with the base of Cap de Fédala in background.**

The *Frondeur* then took a hit aft and limped into port down at the stern and she was soon finished off by aircraft strafing. The *Albatros* was hit twice at 11.30 a.m., but with only three of her guns functioning she still zigzagged behind a smoke screen, she shot at the *Augusta*. At that moment some Dauntless bombers from the *Ranger* succeeded to plant two bombs amidships and one engine room was quickly flooded; a hit from the *Augusta* then flooded the second engine room and the *Albatros* went dead in the water.

Out of the eight ships which took part in this morning engagement, only the *Alcyon* returned to her berth undamaged.

In the afternoon, the French sent three avisos (large patrol boats) — *La Grandière, La Gracieuse*, and *Commandant Delage* — to pick up survivors from the sunken destroyers. Their course however worried the Americans and the *Brooklyn* and *Augusta*, and destroyers, engaged them at 1.12 p.m., range 17,200 yards, rapidly closing to 14,300. The American ships proved unable to trace their target in the protective smoke screen however, though a plane damaged *La Grandière* with a bomb, and all three ships returned to harbour safely.

During this action a brave little tug attempted towing in the *Albatros*, who was bombed and strafed on the way, and finally beached at the Roches Noires near the *Primauguet* and *Milan. Primauguet* suffered several bombings and strafings from *Ranger*'s planes that afternoon, and her whole forward half was completely wrecked. A direct hit on her bridge killed her captain, Capitaine de Vaisseau Léon Mercier, and eight officers; Amiral Gervais de Lafond was seriously wounded.

Of the submarines, three were sunk by plane bombing or naval gun-fire at their berths in the harbour. Of the eight that succeeded to sail out in the morning to turn to action, the *Sidi-Ferruch, Conquérant*, and *Sybille* were sunk, two of them as a result of depth-charging by American planes and destroyers. The *Amazone* and the *Antiope* made Dakar safely but the *Méduse* was damaged by ships and planes from the *Santee* and she had to beach near Mazagan. *Le Tonnant* made for Cadiz in Spain where her captain scuttled her on the 15th. Only the *Orphée* was able to return to her berth unscathed.

The slipways were fine for disembarking vehicles from ramped lighters and, with a railway running along the full length of the dock which was normally used by trawlers, supplies could be loaded directly into rolling stock. At 11 a.m. on the 9th the transport *Arcturus* arrived and tied up at the tankers' dock, and by 2.30 p.m. vehicles of the 1st Battalion, 67th Armored Regiment, were being swung ashore.

CLEARING FÉDALA CAPE

Having assembled at the inland edge of Red 2 Beach, before daylight elements of the 1st Battalion, 7th Infantry, set off towards Fédala. One company of the 6ème Régiment de Tirailleurs Sénégalais was surprised and quickly captured and by 6 a.m. Fédala was under American control. The German Armistice Commissioners in Fédala were surprised in their headquarters at the Miramar Hôtel and they fled just before an American platoon entered the building. They were soon captured as they tried to leave the town.

A few minutes after 6 a.m., with many naval targets becoming visible in the dim first light of day, the guns on Cap de Fédala and the Cherqui headland opened fire. As a result, the transports had to suspend debarkation and unloading to move further out to sea. The *Wilkes*, *Swanson* and *Ludlow* remained to give fire support but the *Murphy*, still only about 5,000 yards from the headland, drew heavy fire which first straddled and then struck her, forcing her to withdraw. The cruiser *Brooklyn* sent up a spotter plane and at 6.22 a.m. opened up with a salvo from her 6-inch guns. Her shells soon struck the fire control position on the Cherqui headland, rendering it useless, and another shell hit one of the emplacements, putting that gun out of action. In the meantime ground troops had surrounded the battery. As soon as the naval bombardment lifted, they attacked the position from several sides and at 7.30 a.m. Captain Mackenzie E. Porter, commander of Company H, 30th Infantry, received its surrender.

At the Fédala cape, naval counter-battery fire against the French guns was hampered by the proximity of petroleum tanks that the Americans wanted to leave undamaged but a stray shell from one of the destroyers struck one tank setting it on fire. Naval shelling silenced the cape battery for a while but the guns came to life at irregular intervals during the morning. The 100mm guns of the Batterie du Port also resumed fire, especially against the beaches across the bay where the 30th RLG was landing.

Lieutenant Colonel Roy E. Moore, commanding BLT 1/7, repeatedly requested that naval gun-fire on the cape be suspended to permit him at mount an attack but Colonel Rogers, commanding the 30th RLG which was under intermittent fire from the French, wanted the bombardment to continue until the guns were neutralised. When the naval shelling failed to silence the guns, Moore's recommendations were finally approved and an infantry attack, supported by four light tanks of the 756th Tank Battalion, went in at 11.40 a.m. At noon the fire control station and the 100mm battery surrendered to Company A of the 7th Infantry, but the 75mm guns and machine guns in concrete emplacements on the tip of the cape held out until 3 p.m.

General Patton first prepared to leave the *Augusta* for the Fédala beachhead with some of his staff at 8 a.m. Their personal baggage had already

Patton wanted to go ashore early on the morning of November 8 but as we have seen the muzzle blast from the *Augusta*'s guns destroyed the boat he was going to use, so it was early afternoon before he and Rear Admiral Hall (seen behind Patton) and some of his staff finally stepped onto dry land.

Spending the night at the Hôtel Miramar, Patton was up before daylight on November 9 to check the situation on the beach for himself.

About 2 p.m. on D+1, the *Ranger* launched three US Army L-4A Cubs to carry out reconnaissance for the 3rd Infantry Division. The leader of the flight was Captain Ford E. Allcorn (pictured with *Elizabeth,* serial 236389), the two other Cubs being flown by Lieutenant John R. Shell and Lieutenant William A. Butler.

En route for the Fédala racetrack from which they were due to operate, they flew over the cruiser *Brooklyn.* The crew were unaware of the identity of the three aircraft, and failing to find anything like them in his book of aircraft silhouettes, the gunnery officer ordered his men to open fire. Every other ship followed and the Cubs received more friendly fire from the ground troops as they crossed the coast. As Allcorn headed inland his plane was riddled by machine gun-fire from every American unit he overflew. His windscreen disintegrated and the engine burst into flames. Although wounded in his right leg, he managed to sideslip the Cub and get down before the aircraft exploded. He was picked up shortly afterwards by friendly civilians and taken to an American first-aid post. Facing the same friendly fire, Butler had to crash land his plane near a fort within French lines only to be captured and held prisoner with his passenger, Captain Breton A. Devol Jr. Meanwhile, Shell managed to reach the racetrack that was their objective, but when he attempted to take off again to begin spotting for the artillery, he encountered such concentrated small-arms fire that he had to land back immediately.

Although all three Cubs carried the official markings for identification during Operation 'Torch' — a yellow surround to fuselage star and yellow-painted engine cowlings — these efforts were completely in vain — a lesson which led to the adoption of wide black and white stripes for the Normandy landings in 1944. Here the machine lifts off easily in a 35-knot headwind.

The aftermath of the naval battle on the first morning in Casablanca harbour. Seven French destroyers left at around 8.15 a.m. to attack the American transports off Fédala, 12 miles to the east, and coming in range, began shelling landing craft off Yellow Beach. About 10 a.m. two destroyers headed north to deliver a torpedo attack on the Covering Group but the *Massachusetts* and the *Tuscaloosa* soon scored a couple of hits on the *Fougueux* which blew up and sank. The *Massachusetts* then landed another salvo on the *Boulonnais* causing her to promptly roll over and sink. About 11.00 a.m., the badly hit *Milan* had to return to the harbour, soon followed by the equally-damaged *Brestois*. She reached the jetty but then aircraft from the *Ranger* strafed her and she floundered during the night. *Right:* This photograph was taken on November 11 by one of the *Ranger*'s planes: the *Milan* is in the right foreground, the *Albatros*, centre, with the *Primauguet* beyond.

been loaded on a landing craft but before it could be lowered the cruiser was called on to open fire. The first muzzle blast of the *Augusta*'s rear turret blew the waiting landing craft to pieces but fortunately the general's two ivory-handled pistols had just been retrieved for him to wear. Patton finally reached Fédala at 1.20 p.m.

Colonel Hobart R. Gay, Patton's Chief-of-Staff, travelled from Fédala under a flag of truce to Casablanca to try again to persuade the French to cease hostilities. The French Army leaders were eager to have the fighting stopped, and some of them even suggested a course of action for the Americans to adopt if a surrender of the city had to be gained by force, but Amiral Michelier still refused to talk to the Americans.

NOVEMBER 9

Spending the night at the Miramar Hôtel, from where the German control commissioners had fled early that morning, General Patton was up before daylight on November 9. He first went with his aide, Lieutenant Al Stiller, to check the situation at the beach and, in his own words, 'the situation we found was very bad. Boats were coming in and not being pushed off after unloading. There was shell-fire and French aviators

The forward superstructure of the beached *Milan* was largely burned out.

Early on the 8th, the *Jean Bart* opened fire on warships covering the landings with the four 380mm guns of her only operational turret. US Navy aircraft arrived to attack her sometime after 7.15 a.m., one bomb hitting a catapult and another the nearby quay. The *Massachusetts* then took over and just after 8 a.m. one of its 16-inch shells hit the working turret, jamming it (it was repaired after several hours of strenuous effort). Ten minutes later another shell exploded below the after control station, blasting a large hole below the water-line. The *Jean Bart* still fired back and she was only silenced when nine Dauntless bombers achieved two direct hits with 1,000-pound bombs on the afternoon of the 10th. This photo was taken on November 16.

141

were strafing the beach. Although they missed it by a considerable distance, our men would take cover and delay unloading operations, particularly the ammunition which was vitally necessary as we were fighting a major engagement not more than fifteen hundred yards to the south.'

He remained on the beach until after noon and then returned to the *Augusta* to see Admiral Hewitt while sending his deputy commander, Major General Geoffrey Keyes, and most of the staff ashore. By mutual understanding with the Admiral, command responsibility in Morocco now passed to General Patton, and when he returned to shore later that afternoon, Advanced Headquarters for the Western Task Force had been set up in the Hôtel Miramar in Fédala.

During the morning, 15 French bombers (mostly Lioré et Olivier 451s from GB II/23 flying from Meknès) attacked the assault fleet off Fédala but, dropping their bombs from high altitude, they achieved no hits. Wildcats from VF-9, USS *Ranger*, then attacked their escort and, in the ensuing dogfight, four Curtiss H-75s from GC I/5 were shot down for the loss of one Wildcat.

On D+1 the force moved into positions in preparation for a co-ordinated attack on Casablanca the next morning. The advance was only lightly resisted, with only occasional strafing by low-flying aircraft, and one French reconnaissance patrol advancing along the Rabat—Casablanca highway was driven off during the morning. By midnight the troops were in position for the action scheduled to start at 7 a.m. on November 10.

The assault was to be made on a four-battalion front with the 7th Infantry on the right (north) and the 15th Infantry on the left. From north to south the four BLTs in the front were BLTs 3-7, 2-7, 2-15 and 1-15. BLT 1-7 was positioned behind BLT 2-7 as regimental reserve and BLT 3-15 was in a similar role behind BLT 2-15. To aid the main attack in the 7th Infantry's zone, Companies A and C of the 756th Tank Battalion were also attached. The eastern side of the bridgehead was held by BLTs 2-30 and 1-30, the former on the left (north-east), the latter on the right (south-east).

Unloading had much improved on November 9 with the use of the docks and two inclined slipways in Fédala port, and a captured French trawler also began taking men ashore, about 200 at a time, supplementing the few remaining landing craft and their exhausted crews.

NOVEMBER 10

The American artillery in the bridgehead opened fire at 7 a.m. to support the attack on Casablanca but the guns immediately came under French counter-battery fire. Soon French infantry launched an attack on the American artillery positions with machine guns and hand-grenades, one of the casualties being Lieutenant Colonel Kermit Davis, the commanding officer of the 10th Field Artillery Battalion. Lacking infantry protection, the

The liner *Porthos*, 12,633 GRT, carrying refugees from Dakar had just arrived at Casablanca when the shelling started. She managed to reach the tip of the Môle du Commerce and the refugees disembarked as best they could before a huge shell from the *Massachusetts*, intended for the *Jean Bart*, struck the ship. The *Porthos* sank while jammed against the quayside with 26 victims on board.

artillery battalion dropped back to new positions more than 1,000 yards to the east.

Shortly before 11 a.m. the avisos *Commandant Delage* and *La Gracieuse*, each armed with a single 100mm gun, sailed out of Casablanca harbour. Moving east, only a short distance offshore, they kept bringing down enfilade fire on BLT 2-7 until the *Augusta* and four destroyers drove them back into the harbour. However, the *Augusta* was

Out of the 11 French submarines based at Casablanca, seven were sunk during the battle, two succeeded in reaching Dakar, and *Le Tonnant* made for Cadiz in Spain where her captain scuttled her. The *Orphée* cast off immediately the alarm was raised on November 8 but, failing to find a target, she returned to port on the night of the 10th. Hastily resupplied, she was then ordered to make for Dakar. It was still dark when she set off early on November 11 but she was recalled when hostilities ended in Morocco. Here she enters the Bassin Delande with the grain silo in left background. The other ships are the cargo vessel *Fauzon* that was damaged and the oilers, *Le Lot* and *Elorn*, which both came through unscathed. Further along the quay on the left is the cargo ship *Île de Noirmoutier*.

Another shot taken from one of the *Ranger*'s aircraft shows the harbour cluttered with hulks. On the left are two destroyers, the *Simoun* and *Frondeur* (capsized), while in the background is the light cruiser *Primauguet* (left centre), and the destroyers *Albatros* and *Milan* (closest to the beach). Among the merchant ships visible are *Vendome* (left), *De la Salle* (centre, inboard) and *Wyoming* (centre, outboard), all portraying neutrality markings. So many French and neutral merchant ships had been hit or sunk that Admiral Hall commented that he 'earnestly wished the *Massachusetts* had stayed home'.

now within range of the *Jean Bart* whose determined crew had managed to get the 380mm turret operational again and subjected the *Augusta* to a series of very near misses.

In the afternoon, Wildcats from the VF-9 strafed the harbour, aiming at the *Jean Bart* and the nearby anti-aircraft guns, followed by nine Dauntless bombers from VS-41. The bombers achieved two direct hits with 1,000-pound bombs on the French warship and several near misses finally silencing her.

In spite of these difficulties and persistent French artillery fire, the attack made good progress during the day, and late on November 10 both the 7th RLG on the right and the 15th RLG over on the left had reached the eastern and southern outskirts of Casablanca.

The attack next morning would be opened at 7 a.m. with bombardment followed with the ground assault being launched 30 minutes later.

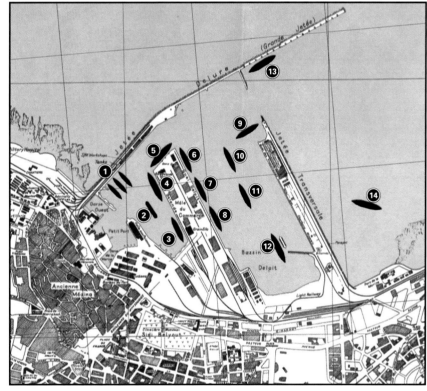

Damaged and sunken ships in Casablanca harbour. (1) Submarines *L'Amphitrite*, *La Psyché*, and *L'Oréade*, sunk. (2) Large floating dry dock, scuttled. (3) Cargo ship *Fauzon* sunk by two 16-inch hits. (4) *Jean Bart* with her stern resting on the bottom. (5) *Porthos*, rolled over against the dock. (6) The liner *La Savoie*, sunk by two 16-inch hits and one bomb. (7) Cargo ship *Lipari*, sunk. (8) Tanker *Île d'Ouessant* sunk by two 16-inch hits. (9) Prison ship *Saint Blaise*, sunk. (10) Cargo ship *Schiaffino* suffered bomb damage. (11) Italian cargo ship *San Pietro*, sunk. (12) Destroyer *Frondeur*, capsized. (13) Destroyer *Brestois*, sunk. (14) Light cruiser *Primauguet*, beached.

Hostilities End in Morocco

An M3 is photographed patrolling Casablanca shortly after the surrender on November 11. This photo was taken on the Place des Nations Unies.

At Gibraltar, the fragmentary reports from the Western Task Force which filtered through the overburdened communications system to General Eisenhower had become increasingly disturbing. On November 10, in a personal communication, he informed Patton that Algiers had been won in two days; Oran's defences were rapidly crumbling, and the only 'tough nut' was in Patton's hands. 'Crack it open quickly and ask for what you want', the message said.

In the afternoon, Général Noguès was informed that Amiral Darlan had issued orders in the name of Maréchal Pétain to stop the useless fighting in

American and French commanders met at the Hôtel Miramar in Fédala, now taken over as the HQ for the Western Task Force, and an informal understanding for an end to hostilities was quickly agreed. French officers leaving the hotel after the negotiations. In dark uniforms were Vice Amiral Michelier and Général Auguste Lahoulle, Air Force Commander in Morocco.

The Western Task Force flag which flew in front of the hotel is now on display at the General Patton Museum in Fort Knox, Kentucky, autographed by the General and his men. The Hôtel Miramar closed in 1995. *Right:* Jean Paul ventured into the garden to take this comparison but he was quickly apprehended and told that the place was a Royal Residence and all photography was strictly forbidden. Sometime later, while the two guards were elsewhere, he surreptitiously took this shot of the entrance.

Sometime later Patton went to meet General Clark at his headquarters which had been established in the art déco Shell building in Casablanca.

Constructed in 1934, the building at the junction of Boulevard Mohammed V and Rue Rue Azilal has now been converted into the luxurious Hotel Imperial.

North Africa. While awaiting confirmation, Noguès telephoned Général Lascroux and advised him of this turn of events. Accordingly, Lascroux radioed orders to Marrakech and Casablanca to refrain from further hostilities against the Americans pending the negotiation of an armistice. The exact text of Darlan's orders was telephoned to Noguès at 7.15 p.m. and transmitted by him to Généraux Lascroux and Lahoulle and to Amiral Michelier. They were instructed to arrange for a meeting with the American commander.

At about 2 a.m. on November 11, a French vehicle coming from the direction of Rabat approached an outpost of Company G, 30th Infantry, north-east of Fédala. It had its lights blazing and was flying white flags while one of the occupants was blowing a bugle. The group, made up of two officers and two enlisted men, was conducted to the regimental command post and thence to task force headquarters at the Hôtel Miramar. The four Frenchmen were allowed to continue to Casablanca but they were warned that they must return quickly with an agreement to negotiate an armistice if the city were to be spared the consequences of the attack scheduled to begin at daybreak.

The French agreement to terminate hostilities, and a request to arrange terms at an afternoon conference in Fédala, was received at Headquarters, Western Task Force, just before the attack was scheduled to begin. Orders to cease-fire were immediately sent out although they did not reach every American unit in time.

The French forces in Casablanca, represented by Amiral Pierre Ronarc'h and Général Raymond Desré, surrendered to General Anderson shortly before noon. At General Patton's request, Amiral Michelier was escorted by Brigadier General William W. Eagles, General Anderson's assistant, to Fédala to participate in the negotiations. The presence of Michelier, the naval Commander-in-Chief, led Admiral Hewitt to come ashore to join the discussion. With the arrival of Général Noguès from Rabat formal negotiations began just after 2 p.m.

These photos were taken in January 1943 just after Clark took command of the newly created US Fifth Army. Patton and Clark were friendly in public although Patton believed Clark was 'too damned slick' and 'much too concerned with himself'.

In spite of the name changes that have taken place in North Africa, this roundabout is still known as the Rond-Point du Général Patton.

Left: **On December 19, Général Noguès and General Patton reviewed French and American troops on parade in Rabat.**

The occasion was a local native festival. *Right:* **The ceremony was held Place Lyautey in front of the railway station.**

Hotchkiss H-39 and Renault R-35 tanks of the 1er Régiment de Chasseurs d'Afrique rumble past the viewing stand.

An American Howitzer Motor Carriage — a 105mm howitzer mounted on a M3 half-track chassis — followed along Avenue Dar el Makhzen.

The buildings on the corner remain unchanged although Avenue Dar el Makhzen has been renamed Boulevard Mohammed V, and Rue Delpit is now Avenue Abou Inane.

The generals were welcomed by the Sultan of Morocco to his palace. In 1957 he became King Mohammed V and his son (centre) was crowned King Hassan II after his father's death in 1961.

Today, the Royal palace cannot be visited and, although Jean Paul could see the building that would make the link with the past, he had to be content with this shot from just outside.

The Allied Combined Chiefs-of-Staff had already prepared two sets of armistice terms, one presupposing only token French resistance, the other envisaging prolonged fighting resulting in the destruction of French military power but, in the circumstances, both were considered inappropriate. Instead an informal understanding was adopted — a gentleman's agreement as it were. This stated that the Americans would occupy those areas required for security and for future operations; that prisoners should be exchanged; that French troops should not be disarmed but be confined to barracks, and that without General Eisenhower's approval, no punishment should be inflicted on anyone for having assisted the Americans. Lasting terms were to be determined in negotiations which were already in progress in Algiers.

U-Boats were now closing in on the concentration of shipping off the coast of Morocco and on November 11, *U-173* torpedoed the *Joseph Hewes* (*AP-50*), off Casablanca. (The *U-173* was sunk in turn five days later by American destroyers.) On November 12, Korvettenkapitän Ernst Kals, the captain of *U-130*, managed to evade powerful escort and sunk three combat loaders off Casablanca, *Edward Rutledge* (*AP-57*), *Hugh L. Scott* (*AP-4*), and *Tasker H. Bliss* (*AP-42*).

A Guard of Honour was provided by a company of the 82nd Reconnaissance Battalion with the band from the 3rd Infantry Division. Lined up at the entrance to the palace was a company of tanks, a battery of 105mm self-propelled and 75mm assault guns. Patton wrote that 'Général Noguès and I rode in a reconnaissance car with top down, and we stood up. The escort of honour had a profound effect on the populace, it being the first time I ever heard the Arabs cheer.'

Left: Two months later, Brigadier General Arthur Wilson, Chief of the Service of Supply in the Western Task Force, and Général Georges Lascroux saluted the American colours in Casablanca during the parade to celebrate George Washington's birthday.

At the same time, guns and vehicles were ceremoniously handed over to the French army. *Right:* The author established that this parade had been held in Avenue du Général d'Amade, now Avenue Hassan II.

Taking Bougie and Bône

Operations began at Bougie early on the morning of November 11, a Royal Navy photographer, Lieutenant John Hampton, being present to picture troops landing in the harbour.

Assuming maximum French co-operation, Allied strategists had initially made plans to employ parachute troops and commandos for the seizure of the airfields at Bône in eastern Algeria, and at Bizerte and Tunis in Tunisia on November 11, 12, and 13. Those reserves that had not been committed at Algiers would be sent by sea to the Golfe de Bougie for the capture of the port of Bougie and the neighbouring aerodrome at Djidjelli on November 12. This would then obtain a forward base to provide fighter protection against Axis bombers capable of striking from Sicily.

On November 9, however, with French co-operation still uncertain, it appeared unwise to send commandos and paratroops so far ahead of Allied ground forces. Instead, the British 78th Division, under the command of Major-General Vyvyan Evelegh, undertook to first occupy Bougie and Djidjelli, and then to rush as many troops as possible overland via Sétif and Constantine to a railhead at Souk Ahras in Tunisia. Meanwhile an air and seaborne operation would take Bône. The aircraft carrier *Argus* was to provide initial air cover but once the Djidjelli airstrip had been taken, fighters from Maison Blanche would take over.

The distance involved was huge — about 100 miles from Algiers to Bougie and 160 miles more to Bône — and the country in between very rugged.

In the evening of November 10, a fast convoy of four infantry landing ships (*Karanja, Marnix van Sint Aldegonde, Awatea* and *Cathay*) carrying the 36th Infantry Brigade Group (which had been the floating reserve) with escorting warships (the cruiser *Sheffield*, four destroyers, two frigates and two minesweepers) left Algiers for Bougie. They soon overtook a slower

When friendly signals were received from the coastguard station at Bougie inviting the British ships to enter, the destroyers *Bramham* and *Wilton* entered the harbour soon after 7 a.m. to check on French intentions. As a result of the ensuing conversations with the French commander, the four troopships — *Karanja, Marnix van Sint Aldegonde, Awatea* and *Cathay* — were directed to anchor in Bougie Bay. Three transports — *Urlana, Glenfinlas* and *Stanhill* — soon followed. Samir took this nice comparison along the sea front.

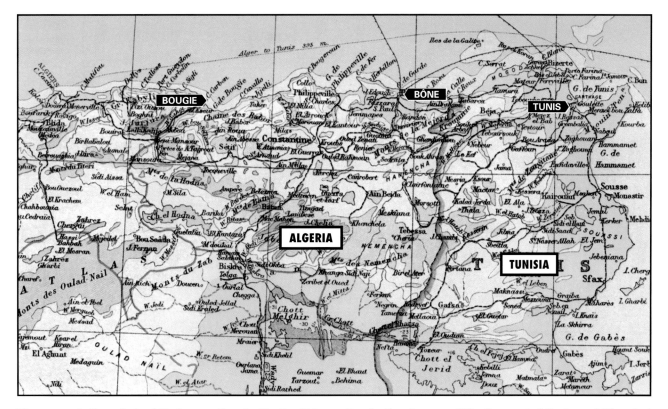

The crux of the whole Allied operation in North Africa depended on the swift capture of major ports in eastern Algeria: Bougie, some 460 miles west of Tunis, and Bône, just 300 miles away.

group of five cargo vessels and warships (the monitor *Roberts*, two destroyers, a corvette and three trawlers) which had set out at 5 p.m. A covering force to the north (Force O with aircraft carrier *Argus*, cruisers *Scylla* and *Charybdis* and two destroyers) added more support.

The convoy arrived off Cap Carbon at 4.30 a.m. on November 11 to begin landing operations on D White Beach which was outside the range of any coastal gun. Troops of the 6th Battalion, Royal West Kent Regiment, struggled through heavy surf to the shore and first troops landed at about 6.15 a.m. How-

ever the second part of the operation, in which the *Awatea* was to set down troops near Djidjelli for them to speed ahead to take control of the airfield from friendly French forces, soon went awry as the surf was too heavy and it proved impossible to make landfall. The troops had to be taken back to the west

During the afternoon of November 11, Italian SM 79 and German Heinkel He 111 torpedo bombers and Junkers Ju 88 bombers, came in to attack the Allied shipping anchored in the bay. The *Awatea* and the *Cathay* were both hit and caught fire, the former sinking that evening and the latter burning all night. More Ju 88s returned next morning when the *Karanja* (above) was hit. An oil fire broke out on board and by 8.30 a.m. the ship had to be abandoned.

149

Left: **At dawn on November 12, the destroyers *Lamberton* and *Wheatland*, with the guidance of a friendly local pilot, slipped into the port at Bône and put ashore No. 6 Commando.**

The landing was unopposed and the port was swiftly secured, this photograph being taken early in December. *Right:* **Nice comparison by Jalel, looking north.**

to go ashore at Bougie but as they would then be over 40 miles from the airstrip, they were too far away to capture it that day. So the RAF had to be held back till the following day.

The *Argus* was hit by a bomb in the afternoon of the 10th which left her with only seven serviceable Seafires so at dawn on the 11th Admiral Burrough ordered that the *Avenger*, then in Algiers with engine trouble, put to sea and fly off two flights of four Sea Hurricanes to reinforce the *Argus*. One of the two flights was unable to locate *Argus* and returned to the *Avenger*.

Next day the Spitfires of No. 154 Squadron were able to fly to the Djidjelli airstrip from the Maison Blanche (where they had flown from Gibraltar on November 8) although they remained grounded for lack of fuel. Although no fuel was available, the squadron was able to mount one sortie in defence of Bougie with what was left in their tanks. (Fuel finally arrived the following night.)

As it was too risky to leave the *Argus* so far east, Force O had to be withdrawn which left the shipping at Bougie without air cover.

A German air attack that afternoon did no harm but a heavier raid by 30 Ju 88s and He 111s followed at dusk. The transports *Cathay* and *Awatea* were hit and sunk and the monitor *Roberts* damaged. Shortly before dawn, the anti-aircraft ship *Tynwald* was sunk by a mine, and soon afterwards the transport *Karanja* was set on fire during another raid. She soon sank.

At dawn on November 12, the destroyers HMS *Lamberton* and HMS *Wheatland*, with the guidance of a friendly local pilot, slipped into the port of Bône, 125 miles east of Bougie, and put ashore No. 6 Commando. Later that day, two companies of the British 3rd Battalion, 1st Parachute Regiment, were dropped from American aircraft on the small airfield near Bône. Both arrivals were unopposed and the port and airfield were swiftly secured.

Providing accommodation for at least 22 ships, and having a connection with

Another shot by Lieutenant Parnall of the destroyer HMS *Bicester* alongside a jetty in the dockyard.

Bône harbour today, a comparison by Matthew, looking south.

The Eastern Air Command was quickly built up in eastern Algeria. By November 14, the Spitfires of Nos. 81 and 111 Squadrons were based at Bône airfield and those of Nos. 154 and 242 Squadrons at Djidjelli. Meanwhile, bomber wings were moved from England to the Mediterranean. On November 15, Flying Officer Kenneth Waud of No. 81 Squadron, standing on the wing, checks the damage of the Heinkel that he had just shot down near Bône.

the main Algiers—Tunis railway line, the port of Bône was highly valued by the Allies as a major point of tranship-ment for the supplies and reinforce-ments needed for Tunisia. However, the downside was that Bône was within easy range of enemy aircraft from Sar-dinia and Sicily.

Axis aircraft inflicted additional losses to shipping off Bougie, the freighter *Glenfinlas* was bombed and sunk in the harbour on the 13rd and the transport *Narkunda* on the 14th. On the 15th, the minesweeper HMS *Algerine* was torpedoed by the Italian submarine *Ascianghi* as she was clearing mines off Bougie and she went down with heavy loss of life.

Empty transports returning from Operation 'Torch' were sunk by U-Boats including the troop transport *Nieuw Zeeland* torpedoed by *U-380* some 80 miles east of Gibraltar on November 11. U-Boats also closed in from the west, in the Atlantic, and on November 12 *U-515* torpedoed and sunk the depot ship HMS *Hecla* and damaged the destroyer HMS *Marne*, blowing off her stern. On the 14th, *U-413* sunk the troopship *Warwick Castle*. On November 15, some 120 miles north-west of Gibraltar, Kapitänleut-nant Adolf Piening led his *U-155* close to the north bound convoy MKF-1Y and fired a spread of four torpedoes. He was not able to make visual observa-tions but heard three detonations. The torpedoes actually hit and sunk the troop transport *Ettrick* and the carrier HMS *Avenger*. The impact on her started a fire and an immediate explo-sion in the bomb-store. The *Avenger* sank quickly with a heavy loss of life, 516 men perishing with only 12 sur-vivors. The third ship hit was the trans-port *Almaack (AK-27)*; she was badly damaged and was towed back to Gibral-tar on the 17th.

Casualties

Allied casualties during the first six days of Operation 'Torch' — November 8 to 13 — amounted to 2,300 for army, navy and air forces: 1,181 killed, 74 missing, and 1,087 wounded. Of those who lost their lives, 540 were British, 543 American, and 98 Dutch; the wounded being 178 British, 890 Ameri-can and 19 Dutch. (The Dutch losses were all at sea when destroyer *Isaac Sweers* was torpedoed and sunk on November 13.) French losses for the same period amounted to approxi-mately 3,300, 1,350 killed and 1,950 wounded.

Meanwhile the squadrons of the 33rd Fighter Group which had landed in Morocco in November, progressively moved east to airfields in Algeria in December. This P-40F, 'one of the latest American fighter planes' claimed the official caption, was pictured at La Sénia on December 14 while en route to Telergma. Piloted by Lieutenant Bill Day, *Dammit* was one of the P-40s which had been launched from the *Chenango* on November 10.

THE RACE FOR TUNISIA

Axis Reaction

The Axis reaction to the 'Torch' landings was to organise a massive build-up by air and sea to move troops and supplies to Tunisia. Here a formation of Junkers Ju 52 start their return journey to Italy and Sicily.

The Allied landings in North Africa had taken the Axis command by surprise. No guiding principles had been laid down to face such an event, and there had been no planning for any operation in French North Africa. However, the Germans lost no time in reacting, and right from the evening of November 8 preparations were in full swing to ship troops to Tunisia. On the 10th, Hitler directed the policy to be undertaken to counter the new situation. A bridgehead was to be quickly established in Tunisia in a race to beat the advancing Allied forces. This front was to be short, based on defensible terrain, and a convenient distance from the harbours.

With France's Mediterranean coast now vulnerable to Allied attack, a take-over of the unoccupied southern part of France was the logical German military response to Operation 'Torch' and at midnight on November 10-11, Axis forces began to cross the demarcation line and enter the southern part of the country.

Above: **Skimming low over the coastline, this flight was photographed overflying one of the most remarkable relics remaining in North Africa from the Roman era. The circular port at Carthage comprised two parts: an outer rectangular harbour for merchant shipping leading to an inner circular harbour, some 325 metres in diameter, designed for the Carthaginian naval fleet. Comprising docking bays and warehouses, altogether the complex could house up to 220 ships. During the Third Punic War (149-146 BC), a naval battle fought outside the port in the summer of 147 BC ended in victory for the Carthaginians but the Romans then laid siege to Carthage. In the spring of 146 BC, the Romans broke through the city wall but the Carthaginians resisted with courage born of despair and the battle was fought street by street, house by house. The Romans finally captured the city, killing hundreds of thousands of inhabitants (sources put the figure at 350,000) and selling into slavery an estimated 50,000 survivors. They then completely laid waste to the town.** *Right:* **Remarkably, 2,000 years later, the two harbours stand as historic landmarks of a bygone era.**

One round trip from Naples and two from Sicily were made each day, the first Sicilian flight arriving before 7 a.m. and the second late in the afternoon. When the formations arrived off the Golfe de Tunis, they separated into sections destined either for Bizerte or Tunis *(above)*. At the peak of the air transport operation to Tunisia, the daily flights consisted of an average of 200 Ju 52s and 15 of the six-engine Messerschmitt Me 323s. The tonnage transported daily amounted to over 500 tonnes.

While the Ju 52 could carry 1.8 metric tons, the gigantic Me 323s could carry 10 tons. It would appear that these two Daimler-Benz aircraft engines were to be transported back to Italy for major overhaul. This shot shows how the huge aircraft rested on its rear wheels when empty, the weight of the cargo progressively loading the front wheels.

By the end of November, the Luftwaffe units based in Tunisia comprised nine squadrons of Bf 109G fighters (six belonging to Jagdgeschwader 53 and three to II./Jagdgeschwader 51), three squadrons of Ju 87 dive-bombers of the II./Sturzkampfgeschwader 3 and a reconnaissance squadron, the 2./Aufklärungsgruppe 14 flying Bf 109F. There were also seven squadrons of Focke-Wulf FW 190s, three of the II./Jagdgeschwader 2, a fighter unit, and four of the III./Zerstörergeschwader 2. The first Focke-Wulf FW 190s sent over were those of the II./Jagdgeschwader 2, a fighter unit, and the III./Zerstörergeschwader 2, a ground attack unit. This one in a shelter inherited from the French might be from the latter unit, based at Sidi Ahmed near Bizerte. The tail of a second FW 190 also parked in this same shelter can just be seen on the extreme right.

Meanwhile, the OKW (Armed Forces High Command) had directed the transfer of three divisions to Tunisia: the 10. Panzer-Division and Division General Göring from France, and the 334. Infanterie-Division then being readied for duty at Grafenwöhr, Germany. Units that were immediately available in Italy — most coming from the pool of reinforcements held there for Rommel's forces fighting in Libya — were also prepared for immediate departure.

As to the French authorities and armed forces in Tunisia, the German

Left: **General der Panzertruppen Walther Nehring, who had been receiving treatment in Germany for wounds received in Egypt in August 1942, was in Rome on November 17 when his orders to return to Rommel's Panzerarmee Afrika in Libya were cancelled and he was diverted instead to Tunisia to take command of the LXXXX. Armeekorps. Though on November 9 the German representatives at the Armistice Commission sitting in Wiesbaden assured the** French delegates that the Italians would not be permitted to establish military forces in Tunisia, the very next day the Italians sent a first batch of fighters to Tunisia. The first two transport ships docked in Bizerte on the 12th and Axis ground troops progressively landed. *Right:* **Italian troops soon occupied the coastal defences like this one which had been built by the French in order to oppose the Italian claim to take over Tunisia.**

By November 25 the German forces under LXXXX. Armeekorps totalled nearly 16,000, of which around 9,000 were Italian troops. They were dispersed in two bridgeheads around Bizerte and Tunis, with a small reserve held in the Tunis area. By then the German ground elements consisted of two parachute infantry regiments; a battalion of parachute engineers; one Luftwaffe guard battalion and three Army field battalions; one tank battalion and part of another; two reconnaissance companies, one with armoured cars; a motor-cycle company; one motorised antitank company; one field artillery battalion; and about two and a half anti-aircraft artillery battalions.

policy formulated by November 11 was to gain their co-operation. The claim was that the forces sent to Tunisia were there to protect the French interests against the depredations of the Allies. As the French were keen to oppose the long-standing Italian plans to annex Tunisia, at first the operation was to be seen as solely German.

The German and Italian armistice commissions having imposed the strict application of the conditions of the armistice on the French forces in Tunisia, they now comprised only 13,000 men (of whom 6,600 were natives). This was a tenth the size of the force in Tunisia in June 1940 when France was ready to counter an Italian attack on the country. By November 1942, the weak units of the Division de Tunis under Général Georges Barré were all badly lacking in modern weapons and equipment. They had neither heavy artillery nor anti-aircraft and anti-tank guns and only a single company of 15 obsolete Renault D1 tanks.

Amiral Jean-Pierre Estéva, the Resident General in Tunisia, had made clear to the American consul upon receiving the letter from President Roosevelt when the landings began in Algeria and Morocco on November 8 that he was going to strictly comply with his orders from Vichy. The first directives he had received that day from the Army command in Algiers reminded him of the

The author established that this photo of a German infantry platoon was taken here at the western entrance to Tunis, at the Bardo Square, near the Tunisian Parliament and the Bardo museum.

standing instructions to defend Tunisia from all sides, but orders from Vichy on the 9th told him to open the airfields in Tunisia and eastern Algeria to Axis aircraft.

Half an hour after midday the first German aircraft began landing at El Aouina near Tunis. Colonel Paul Bergeron, commanding the Tunis sector, immediately directed units, including two platoons of Renault D1 tanks, to surround the airfield to hold the Germans there. By evening 90 aircraft had landed.

Most sea traffic was unloaded at Tunis (seen *left*) and at Bizerte. Cranes were generally lacking and the transport vessels had to use their own on-board lifting gear and improvise as best they could. As a result, the process was slow and the unloading rate for one day was 1,500 metric tons. This meant that the larger vessels remained at quay long enough to face the risk of one or more raids. Also, the labour in the ports was generally unreliable, abandoning their posts rather than risk being caught in air raids, and few of the Tunisian Italians promised to Nehring for stevedore service ever appeared. In the end German labour troops and Hamburg dockers had to be imported. *Right:* By November 25 Italian ground elements in Tunisia included three regiments of infantry (the first elements of Divisione Superga,

Generale Dante Lorenzelli); two assault gun and two anti-tank gun battalions; and staff and service units from the XXX Corpo d'Armata, Generale Vittorio Sogno. Following orders from Général Juin in Algiers, Général Barré ordered his Division de Tunis to pull back westwards on the night of November 13-14 to occupy defensive positions in the hills west of Bizerte and Tunis and the Medjerda river valley. Oberst Martin Harlinghausen, the commander of the Tunis bridgehead, could then seize key positions in the city. At Bizerte, Amiral Derrien failed to comply with orders from Algiers and his naval forces hold out for nearly a month, forcing the Germans to retain some forces away from the front in the west, but he was finally forced to surrender his command on December 8.

The German airlift continued throughout November 10 and 11, and on the 11th aircraft started to land at Sidi Ahmed near Bizerte. That day, motor launches entered harbours at Bizerte and Tunis bringing Italian port engineers ready to clear the blockships sunk by the French in the approaches of the ports.

In the meantime, the French authorities in Tunisia were subject to a series of changing and confusing instructions. On November 10, after Amiral Darlan's first armistice agreement, new directives from Algiers stated that the Anglo-American forces were not to be resisted. On November 11, from Algiers, Général Juin ordered Général Barré to pull back all his forces to form a covering line in western Tunisia and forbid Axis access to Algeria.

Among the forces rushed to Tunisia was the schwere Panzer-Abteilung 501 equipped with the new Tiger tanks. The battalion had then 20 Tigers and 16 PzKpfw IIIs and was organised in two companies. It entrained in Germany on November 10 for transport to Italy and the first trains reached Reggio on the 18th. While the tanks were being loaded onto ships, the crews were being flown to Tunisia from the 20th. Major Hans Georg Lueder, the battalion commander, arrived in North Africa on the 22nd and the first three Tigers landed in Bizerte on board the *Aspromonte*, an Italian train ferry, on the following day. A fourth tank was delivered to Tunis by Marinefährprahm 477 on

November 27 with the remainder arriving piecemeal at Bizerte over the next six weeks: two on December 1, one on the 6th, another on the 13th and four on the 25th. Five followed on January 8, one on the 16th and the last two on the 24th. *Left:* Tiger '142', commanded by Hauptmann Eberhard Deichmann (seen sitting on the turret), being paraded through the city after having been delivered to Tunis harbour on November 27. It was still in transport condition with narrow tracks and no side skirts. The serial number, 250015, has been stencilled by the factory on the muzzle cover. *Right:* Avenue Habib Bourguiba with Tunis Theatre on the left.

Left: **In spite of all difficulties, heavy equipment was progressively arriving in Tunisia like this eight-wheel SdKfz 233 armoured car armed with a short barrelled 75mm gun. It was part of those first elements of the 10. Panzer-Division to have landed.**

Right: **This 21cm Mörser 18 was so large that it had to be transported in two sections. This is the barrel section on its separate travelling trailer being towed by a SdKfz 8 heavy prime mover.**

Later that evening Général Barré evacuated Tunis with his staff and moved during the night to establish his command post at Souk el Arba, some 130 kilometres to the west.

While the movements of French forces towards the west accelerated in the night, on November 12 Amiral Louis Derrien commanding the Bizerte naval station decided to retain forces to defend the harbour and operate the coastal batteries. To this end he retained one section of the Division de Tunis as well as the naval troops under his command, some 3,000 all told.

On the 12th, as the troops withdrawing took positions along the prescribed lines west of Tunis and Bizerte, at Béja, Medjez el Bab, Teboursouk and Sidi Nsir, Général Juin gave orders to open fire on any Axis force attempting to push westwards.

November 12 was also the day when the first two Axis transports, *Catarina Costa* and *Città di Napoli*, docked in Bizerte. Tunis harbour was cleared by November 15 and from then on Axis vessels arrived daily.

Meanwhile, a strong force of transport aircraft continued to ferry troops to Tunisia at a rate of 750 men per day. Two companies of Fallschirmjäger-Regiment 5 were flown in on the 12th, the majority of the regiment's two battalions following over the next three days. The Italians began to send over a new division, Divisione Superga, on the 12th and Fallschirmjäger-Pionier-Bataillon 1 arrived on the 14th.

By the end of November, Nehring had to accept that with the small forces available, the Axis had enlarged the bridgehead as far as they were able, so he decided to wait for more reinforcements before launching a new counter-thrust against the Allied forces moving west from Algeria. This picture shows German paratroopers at the very tip of the German advance in western Tunisia but, as the photographer's captions have not survived, it is impossible to know precisely when and where it was taken. However, it is quite possible that it shows the leaders of the force comprising some 300 paratroopers from the third battalion of Fallschirmjäger-Regiment 5 under the command of Hauptmann Wilhelm Knoche which was awaiting orders to attack the French positions at Medjez el Bab on the morning of November 19.

Right: General Nehring quickly issued a proclamation in French and Italian addressed to the 'Tunisians, Algerians, Moroccans, soldiers of France'. Calling the population to remain calm and disciplined, he urged the French soldiers to fight side by side with the Germans to repel the invaders. *Below:* In their strategy for the Middle East, the Germans played upon the anger of the Arab population against France and Britain, the old colonial overlords. In their hasty and unprepared engagement in Tunisia, the Germans hoped to quickly win over the Neo-Destour Party, a nationalist movement. Most of its leaders had been imprisoned by the French, and after the Germans entered the former 'Zone Libre' in southern France, they swiftly had them liberated. In December, OKH considered transferring a battalion of the Arab Legion (a unit created in 1941 by recruiting Arab volunteers from the Middle East to assist the pro-Nazi revolt in Iraq) from the Eastern Front to Tunisia, with plan to use it as the core of a new unit of North African Muslim volunteers. However, the Italians complained when they heard of the plan as they wanted the French ousted from Tunisia so that they could take their place rather than see Tunisian nationalists gain independence. The Germans reassured the Italians that they recognised their primacy in North Africa but moved ahead regardless with their preparations for deploying units of Arab volunteers in Tunisia. Time was short and supplies lacking but by February 1943, some 2,000 Arabs had volunteered for service and three battalions were formed. Nevertheless, the front-line deployment of these hastily assembled units in April proved to be far below German expectations, with the general fighting ability poor and a sizable number of the volunteers quickly defecting.

To recruit volunteers in Tunisia, the German propaganda machine capitalised on the anger of the indigenous population against France and they lost no time in issuing details of the release of the Destourian nationalists from French captivity. The news was received with great enthusiasm among the population and joyful demonstrations took place on the streets. However, while the Germans harped on that they supported the Arab stand against the colonial powers, they were posing a major problem to the Axis partnership for in neighbouring Libya the colonial power was Italy, Germany's ally! *Right:* It is unclear when this parade of a party of Fallschirmjägers took place but it was clearly staged to impress both the French authorities and the Arab population and may have been part of the effort to recruit Arab volunteers. *Centre:* The parade started from the Kasbah square, just west of the Medina, the old indigenous town, and moved southwards to circle it on Avenue Bab Jedid.

By the 15th Oberst Martin Harlinghausen, the newly-appointed Fliegerführer Tunisien (Luftwaffe Officer in Command in Tunisia) had a total of 81 fighters and 28 Stukas at his disposal. These were quickly employed in protecting the air and naval forces and in attempts to slow the Allied advance from Algeria.

After a succession of temporary commanders, Oberst Friedrich von Broich took over on the 18th as German Army's commander of the bridgehead, the patchwork command in Tunisia being then designated Division von Broich. Meanwhile a new German headquarters, which was to be called LXXXX. Armeekorps, was being set up under General der Panzertruppen Walther Nehring. He had been wounded on August 31 during an air raid near Alam el Halfa in Egypt but now, after convalescing in Germany, he was en route to Libya. Generalfeldmarschall Albert Kesselring, the Oberbefehlshaber Süd

Left: Getting into their stride, the paratroopers march to the square at the end of the avenue. The officer leading the parade is unidentified. *Right:* The building nearest the camera has since been completely rebuilt, and the trees which lined the street have all been cut down, so it was the balconies in middle distance that were the clue to pinpoint the location.

161

A crowd of Arabs now accompanied the paratroopers, many of them giving the Nazi salute. These photos underline a remarkable clash of history: while the indigenous population enthusiastically welcomed the Germans, apparently there were no Europeans to be seen on the streets. No one had any idea that in a little over a decade this colonial world was to suddenly end. In 1956, Tunisia obtained from France the signature putting an end to the Protectorate, thus obtaining independence.

(Commander-in-Chief South), caught up with him in Rome. Though Nehring had not yet fully recovered, the urgency of the Tunisian situation was such that Kesselring cancelled Nehring's orders and diverted him instead to Tunisia to take command of the new corps. His remit was the establishment of a bridgehead, if possible, as far west as the Algerian-Tunisian border.

With just a single staff officer, at first Nehring established his headquarters in the former US Consulate in Tunis. No signal communications had been set up so the French telephone system had to be used despite the risk of hostile surveillance. There was no one to tell him which units had arrived, where they were, or who commanded them. With the limited forces available, Nehring planned to establish two bridgeheads around Tunis and Bizerte as far inland as his forces could maintain.

Meanwhile, mobile detachments advanced westwards, some moving on Béja from Sidi Nsir, while others were approaching Medjez el Bab, Goubellat, Bou Arada and Pont du Fahs. A first clash with French forces occurred late on November 14 when a German scout car followed by a truck with some 20 men coming from Mateur in the direction of Béja broke through several road-blocks and shots were exchanged.

By previous arrangement, Général Barré came to Medjez el Bab from Souk el Arba in the early hours of November 19 to meet an emissary from

Dr Rudolf Rahn, the German diplomatic agent in Tunis. The diplomat, Eitel Friedrich Moellhausen, gave him an ultimatum from General Nehring: French troops must withdraw westwards to the meridian of Tabarka or hostilities against them would begin at 7 a.m. Général Barré's response — which was that he would give his decision at 7 a.m. — was interpreted at Nehring's headquarters as an effort to gain more time before openly joining the Allies. The time for the showdown

arrived on the 19th when a German column, some 300 men strong, moved on to capture the bridge over the Medjerda river at Medjez el Bab. The bridge and this sector of the river were held by a French-American force: a company of the 4ème Régiment de Chasseurs d'Afrique and a battery of American artillery and two platoons of US anti-aircraft artillery. The Germans attacked during the morning after a Stuka attack and established positions across the river.

A timeless comparison in Tunis by Amine Bouattour. Then the street was called Place de la Gare but it has now been renamed Place Mongi Bali.

162

Right: Reaching the western end of Avenue Jules Ferry, the parade proceeded straight ahead along Avenue de France. Among those nationalists liberated from French prisons due to German intervention was the Neo-Destour party leader, Habib Bourguiba. He finally reached Tunisia at the beginning of April 1943, travelling via Italy, and he immediately went into hiding. He was one of the very few Arab leaders who did not join in any common action with the Axis. In 1955 Bourguiba began negotiations for independence from France which was finally achieved on March 20, 1956, so ending the 75-year-old French protectorate. He then served as the Prime Minister of the Kingdom of Tunisia before proclaiming the Tunisian Republic in 1957. He became the first President, remaining in power for the following 30 years before being deposed by his prime minister, Zine El Abidine Ben Ali, in November 1987. He was later kept under house arrest in Monastir, where he remained until his death on April 6, 2000.

However, as it proved difficult to supply them, the British and American elements were pulled back during the night leading the French commander, Colonel Guy le Couteulx de Caumont, to do the same. The Germans occupied Medjez el Bab on the 20th although the French blocked their armoured cars when they tried to push further west to Oued Zarga.

In the meantime, General Nehring used the small forces available to him to organise protection for the long line of communication with Rommel's forces in Libya. On November 17 and 18, small German garrisons were sent to occupy Sousse, Sfax and Gabès, the major towns along the coast south of Tunis. Those in Gabès were joined on November 20 by Italian troops retiring from Libya after an exhausting overland march. To impede any Allied thrust toward Gabès or Sfax, German demolition teams parachuted in during the night near Gafsa and along the roads between Gafsa and Tébessa.

After independence the Tunisians renamed the main streets after heroes of the struggle for liberation, Avenue Jules Ferry being renamed Avenue Habib Bourguiba. However the names of many of the streets in the capital were left unchanged and this one is still called Avenue de France.

Left: The parade finally reached the Bab el Bahr (the Gate to the Sea) which marks the dividing line between the Medina and the European city just to the east of it. *Above:* The French pulled down most of the walls that once surrounded the old city and the gate now stands isolated in the middle of a large pedestrian area. Nicely renovated, it is one of the most popular tourist landmarks in Tunis.

Advance into Tunisia

On December 6, V Corps took over command of the Allied forces pushing into Tunisia. This shot of a Crusader of the 6th Armoured Division was taken later that month.

General Anderson's orders for Operation 'Torch' were for the Eastern Task Force to first occupy the port of Algiers and the adjacent airfields and then 'to build up rapidly a striking force through Algiers and adjacent ports' and 'occupy Tunisia at the earliest possible date'.

The first follow-up convoys arrived at Algiers from November 12 with men and equipment in order to bring the two infantry brigades initially landed up to strength. First ashore was a regimental group of the 6th Armoured Division, a parachute brigade, some anti-aircraft units, and two RAF wings.

The steady build-up continued so that by December 6, Anderson had the 78th Infantry Division with three brigades (the 11th, the 36th, and the 1st Guards); the 6th Armoured Division now nearly up to strength; the complete army headquarters (not yet officially named First Army) and the nearly-complete staff of the V Corps, together with ten thousand vehicles, impressive supplies of ammunition, fuel and bombs.

Meanwhile, American units were sent forward from Algiers and Oran to join with the Eastern Task Force, while fighter and bomber squadrons were progressively shifted eastward from November 12 to operate from airfields at Souk el Arba (RAF fighters), Bône (RAF and USAAF fighters), Youks les Bains (USAAF fighters and bombers), and Canrobert (RAF bombers). The distance of these airfields from the front was a serious disadvantage for the Allies, as it was 60 miles from Souk el Arba airfield to Tebourba, 120 miles from Bône and 140 miles from Youks les Bains, when it was only 20 miles from the Axis airfields near Tunis and Bizerte.

On November 16, B-17s of the 97th Bombardment Group based at Maison Blanche began a series of airfield raids — on Sidi Ahmed at Bizerte, El Aouina near Tunis, and airfields near Cagliari in Sardinia. Axis night attacks on Algiers continued without interception until November 27 when a flight of Beau-

fighters equipped with radar went into action for the first time, shooting down three German bombers.

Heavy rain on November 24 and 25 gave a foretaste of what would happen to the airfields in the forward area as only Bône had a concrete runway and the rainy season just beginning.

In Algiers, following the agreement of November 13, Général Giraud was now the Commander-in-Chief of all the French forces in North Africa and he lost no time in ordering full mobilisation. His first directive on November 15 was that all available forces must now take on a covering role along a general line leading from Tabarka on the coast to Tébessa, behind which the Allied force moving from the west could concentrate for an attack against Bizerte and Tunis. Key points along this line were Tabarka, Souk el Arba, Le Kef, Tajerouine, Djebel Dyr, and passes east and south of Tébessa. The forces then available were Général Barré's troops in Tunisia and the Division de Constantine under Général Joseph Welvert in eastern Algeria. Before long, the Division d'Alger and the 1ère Brigade Légère Mécanique (BLM) were also to come forward and assume sectors along this front.

On November 14, General Anderson pushed on eastward with the forces he then had available. On the 15th, 'Hart Force' comprising units of all arms from the 11th Infantry Brigade, made mobile by pooling available brigade transport, was directed to advance along the coastal highway from Bône to Tabarka and then on to Djebel Abiod. It would be followed by the 36th Infantry Brigade. Inland, advanced parties of the 11th Infantry Brigade and 'Blade Force' — an armoured regimental group from the 6th Armoured Division including the tanks of the 17th/21st Lancers, B Squadron of the 1st Derbyshire Yeomanry, artillery, anti-tank and anti-aircraft guns and engineers, under the command of Lieutenant-Colonel Richard Hull — were directed on Souk el

Arba through Souk Ahras. Plans called for reconnaissance and delaying action against Axis attempts from Tunisia to penetrate farther west, and to establish contact with the French forces in the sector.

To support the overland march, the British 1st Parachute Battalion was to be flown from Algiers on the 15th to seize the railway centre of Souk el Arba but bad weather delayed the drop. Another airborne operation took place on November 15 when C-47s of the 60th Troop Carrier Group dropped the 2nd Battalion of the US 509th Parachute Infantry Regiment at Youks les Bains, near Tébessa, right down on the southern flank. Under Colonel Edson D. Raff, the battalion had assembled at Maison Blanche after its unfortunate experience at Oran. The improvised operation was a swift success thanks to a friendly French reception. Part of the American force then continued to Tébessa and farther east into Tunisia.

Dropping from 32 C-47s of the 64th Troop Carrier Group, the 1st Parachute Battalion finally came down near Souk el Arba on November 16 and the French local command provided them with lorries to move eastwards. By nightfall, Allied forces had crossed into Tunisia in three areas: along the coast where the 36th Infantry Brigade was at Tabarka and the leading 'Hart Force' at Djebel Abiod; inland with the 1st Parachute Battalion at Souk el Arba and approaching Souk el Khemis with 'Blade Force' following; and further south where the paratroop force under Colonel Raff was closing on Bou Chebka. At each point the French troops encountered were all helpful and well disposed, proof that Général Barré's forces were willingly complying with Général Giraud's order to fight alongside the Allies.

The first ground engagement against Axis forces took place on November 17 near Djebel Abiod when a leading patrol from 'Hart Force' was attacked

Left: **This crew of a Valentine of the 6th Armoured Division are reading their mail which has recently arrived in Tunisia.** *Right:* **An M3 Lee medium tank in a bivouac area of the US 1st Armored Division near Souk El Arba on November 21. The 2nd**

Battalion, 13th Armored Regiment, was the first American unit to reach the Tunisian border having travelled by road from Oran to Algiers, then shipped by sea to Bône, from where they travelled by road to the front.

at a bridge and road intersection by a small German-Italian battle group. The next day, the leaders of the 1st Parachute Battalion ambushed a German reconnaissance party of six armoured cars near Sidi Nsir.

In the south, a German airborne demolition team landed near Gafsa on the evening of November 20 while an Italian motorised force headed towards the town over the main road from Gabès. The garrison in Gafsa, which was made up of a French command and a small detachment of Colonel Raff's paratroops, retired to Fériana after being alerted by telephone. On Novem-

ber 22, now reinforced, the unit returned to Gafsa, drove out the few Germans there, and continued toward Gabès. It encountered the Italian motorised column near El Guettar forcing it to turn back.

On November 21, a German armoured column cleared the way for an Italian security detachment to occupy Kairouan, advancing south-westwards the following day to drive a weak French garrison out of Sbeïtla. The German column then pulled back to the north leaving a small Italian force in possession of the town. A detachment of Colonel Raff's command then

attacked at midday and expelled the Italians before withdrawing to Kasserine and Fériana, leaving a French force to take up the defence of Sbeïtla.

After an unsuccessful attempt on November 24 to regain Sbeïtla, Nehring accepted that the motley forces at his command had enlarged the bridgehead as much as they were able. He then had no option but to wait for reinforcements before resuming counter-thrusts toward western Tunisia. By the end of November, his strength had built up to more than 15,000 German and 9,000 Italian troops deployed in the Bizerte and Tunis areas.

Left: **On December 25, men of the 2nd Battalion, Coldstream Guards, returned to Medjez el Bab after taking part in a night**

attack on Longstop Hill. *Right:* **Here they are questioning an Arab who had just emerged from the German lines.**

The understanding achieved in Algiers with Darlan on November 13 received the approval of the President, Prime Minister, and Combined Chiefs-of-Staff, but when revealed to the public it immediately raised a storm of protest in the United States as well as in the United Kingdom. The thrust of the argument was because the Allies had dealt with a senior man from Vichy, a man who had been the chief of a government that collaborated with Germany.

Back at Gibraltar after his visit in Algiers, General Eisenhower was confronted with the first wave of official doubt and public indignation from Washington and London. He promptly sent a message to General Marshall, Chief-of-Staff of the US Army, to justify his decision on military grounds. He pointed out that French sentiment in North Africa had been largely misjudged. Giraud was impotent and acknowledged it while Darlan was the only representative who was generally acceptable. Without him the Allies' hopes for a quick conquest of Tunisia could not be realised.

The Clark-Darlan Agreement

On November 22, an agreement was signed between the Allies and the French command in North Africa, sealed with a handshake by Clark and Darlan. In the background a portrait of Marshal Pétain.

Marshall stood firmly behind Eisenhower and hurriedly summoned a conference of press and radio commentators on the morning of November 15 to quell the critics. Churchill and Roosevelt also joined in to placate the situation on a political level, the line being that the understanding with Darlan could 'only be a temporary expedient, justifiable solely by the stress of battle'.

Darlan realised how the Allies intended to use and then discard him and he complained to Eisenhower that they were decreasing his usefulness by weakening his influence. Yet he continued to negotiate detailed agreements governing future relations between the French colonies and the Allies, arrangements pertaining to civil administration, French shipping, and economic activity, and to enlist the support of French West Africa for his programme of active warfare against the Axis powers.

The negotiations with Darlan resulted in the signature on November 22 of the first of the detailed arrangements between the Allies and the French. Known from its signatories as the 'Clark-Darlan Agreement', its 21 articles set forth the basis of co-operative action in the months ahead. Most of it was phrased in language taken from letters written before the landings by Murphy (as the President's personal representative) to Giraud and other friendly French officers, while the text for other articles came from the draft armistice terms approved in advance by the Combined Chiefs-of-Staff.

The terms provided for the closest possible co-operation in the effort to expel the Axis forces from North Africa, to liberate metropolitan France, and 'restore integrally the French Empire'. The fiction of a paramount American position in the campaign led

to frequent reference to Eisenhower as the Commanding General, US Army, 'with supporting forces'.

The agreement generally left any civil officials in Algeria and Morocco — all of them named by Vichy — to retain their positions undisturbed. This choice was justified on military grounds, the Americans considering that the anti-Darlan groups were not in a position to control North Africa if given that choice.

Consequently, nothing was done to identify and restrain Axis sympathisers and the members of fascist societies like the Service d'Ordre Légionnaire and the Parti Populaire Français. With others in less formal associations, they were left to spread propaganda against the Allies and their supporters, whether Giraudist or Gaullist. Some even seemed prepared to assist an Axis counter-invasion. Denunciation of these

Sealing the agreement, a Franco-British-American ceremony was held in Algiers at the First World War memorial.

Following Algerian independence in 1962, Boulevard Laferrière had its name changed to Mohamed Khemisti.

Left: **Amiral Darlan, General Eisenhower and Admiral Cunningham.**
Right: **The First World War memorial was designed by sculptor Paul Landowski, who is better known for the huge statue of Christ the Redeemer in Rio de Janeiro. Inaugurated in 1928, the Algiers memorial jointly commemorated both the Arab and European soldiers killed during that war. However, after the country gained its independence, the memorial was not deemed acceptable and in** **1978, to clear the place before the African Games due to be held in Algeria, the authorities ordered it to be removed. Algerian sculptor Mohamed Issiakhem was given the job but he could not bring himself to destroy it, so he carefully wrapped it and had it buried inside the concrete of the new statue. This featured two hands breaking the chains of colonialism, the new memorial deemed more in keeping with the current climate.**

anti-Allied individuals to American civilian officials was of little or no avail for their hands were tied by military control.

In Morocco, Amiral Michelier and Général Noguès remained in their positions in spite of the fact that they had followed Vichy's orders and actively opposed the Allies for four days. General Patton strongly supported them as being indispensable.

On the other hand, Général Béthouart and his associates, who from the beginning had given their support to the Allies, were now left to face French military discipline. Général Noguès initiated measures to bring them to trial and Patton did nothing more than insist that no action whatsoever must be taken against Béthouart without the approval of Eisenhower. When Béthouart's plight was made known through American channels to Général Giraud — and thence to General Eisenhower on November 15 — he interceded to request his immediate release and that of 'any others now in prison for the same kind of reason'. On November 17, Béthouart and Colonel Pierre Magnan, the commander of the troops that had taken over at Rabat on the night of the unsuccessful coup, were finally released and flown to Algiers by the Americans.

However, in general, the American military leadership showed little concern as to the fate of their pre-invasion friends, and less prominent officers and men remained in custody for an undue length of time. Early in December, when Général Giraud visited French Morocco, he ensured that French enlisted men who had deserted to the Americans during the November fighting in Morocco were returned to their units without punishment.

One of the official photos of Darlan and Eisenhower taken during the ceremony that day also includes Colonel Julius C. Holmes, the head of Civil Affairs Branch for Operation 'Torch'. He had actually been one of the participants at the secret meeting at Messelmoun earlier in October (see pages 46-54).

On December 18, French photographer Marcel Viard took this shot of the two key men in the new French administration now fully aligned with the Allies: Amiral Darlan, the High Commissioner and Commander-in-Chief of Naval Forces, and Général Giraud, Commander-in-Chief of Ground and Air Forces.

167

On November 24, as two brigades of the 78th Infantry Division were reaching the Tunisian front, Anderson directed Major-General Evelegh to first occupy the line Tebourba—Mateur before advancing on Tunis and Bizerte.

Evelegh directed the 36th Brigade (Brigadier Arthur L. Kent-Lemon) to move towards Mateur while the 11th Brigade (Brigadier Edward E. Cass) was to take Medjez el Bab and then to advance on Tebourba and Djedeïda. 'Blade Force' was to operate in between to reach Sidi Nsir and make flanking attacks on Tebourba. The attack was due to start on the night of November 24-25.

'Blade Force' met little opposition and successfully passed Sidi Nsir and soon reached the Chouïgui Pass, north of Tebourba. In the afternoon, Stuart tanks from the US 1st Armored Regiment (attached to 'Blade Force' from

The Allies engage the Axis

The first clash between German and Allied forces in Tunisia took place in the afternoon of the 17th when paratroopers probing west clashed with the leaders of 'Hart Force' at Djebel Abiod.

Top: **When Kriegsberichter Arppe pictured this motorcycle approaching Djedeïda, the leading Allied forces were then only a few kilometres away.** *Left:* **Mines were quickly prepared to** bar the crossing of the bridge over the Medjerda river. *Right:* **A new bridge now bypasses the old one which was saved from destruction (off to the right in this shot).**

November 21) raided the Axis airfield at Djedeïda, destroying 17 Stukas before withdrawing to Chouïgui.

On the left wing, torrential rain forced the 36th Brigade to delay their attack while in the south the 11th Brigade met stiff resistance and failed to reach Tebourba.

The raid at Djedeïda airfield, carried out only 30 kilometres from Tunis, alarmed Nehring who decided to pull back his forces at Medjez el Bab to strengthen the sector at Tebourba. Consequently, when the 11th Brigade pushed to Medjez el Bab on November 26, they found that the town had been evacuated by the Germans. The 1st Battalion, East Surrey Regiment then advanced on to Tebourba but were counter-attacked early on the 27th. Being widely extended, the Surreys suffered heavy losses. In the north, the 36th Brigade advanced slowly, reaching Sedjenane on the 27th.

Major-General Evelegh then devised a new plan. The 11th Brigade was directed to take Djedeïda on the 28th while the 2nd Parachute Battalion (Lieutenant-Colonel John D. Frost) was to drop at Depienne, 26 miles

In the south, Gafsa changed hands twice between November 20 and 22, alternating between a small German airborne unit and a French command backed by a detachment of Colonel Raff's paratroopers. The town was finally taken by an Italian motorised force moving from Gabès. This heavily censored photo was probably taken at that time.

The drop by the 2nd Parachute Battalion at Depienne, some 45 kilometres south of Tunis, on November 29 turned out to be a complete failure and the force finally withdrew during the night of November 31/December 1. It reached friendly lines near Medjez el Bab on December 3. *Left:* The frustration can be seen on the faces of Captain Stark, Lieutenant Braylet and Major Ashford pictured near Béja after returning from the operation. *Right:* The wounded had to be left behind, with a small detachment to guard them. This captured paratrooper pictured by German PK Biedermann might well be one from that rear guard.

The paratroopers rested for a time near Béja. *Left:* Sergeant Frank Tucker of Maidstone, Kent, was pictured washing mud off his boots at the local drinking trough. *Right:* The huge railway viaduct still stands with the line in regular use.

south of Tunis, on the following day to take the landing ground at Oudna and later link up with 'Blade Force'. Meanwhile, on the other flank, the 1st Commando was to land from the sea near Sidi Moudjad, 14 miles west of Bizerte, on the 30th and harass the German forces opposing the advance of the 36th Brigade.

The results, however, were disappointing. Over 500 men of the 2nd Parachute Battalion were dropped near Depienne by C-47s of the 62nd and 64th Troop Carrier Groups on the afternoon of the 29th. That night they proceeded to the landing ground at Oudna only to discover that it was not even in use. Meanwhile, the 11th Brigade failed to take Djedeïda and 'Blade Force', to which the paratroopers were to join, failed to advance at all. The paratroopers made their way back to Medjez el Bab as best they could, suffering nearly 300 casualties. (Many of the 266 missing returned later.)

Put ashore without opposition in the early hours of December 1 near Sidi Moudjad, the British and Americans of the 1st Commando advanced to their designated objectives on the Bizerte—Mateur road. The object was to deny its use to the Axis for at least three days but, running low on

More successful, if less spectacular, was the engagement of the 2nd Battalion of the US 509th Parachute Infantry Regiment. After their first drop at Oran on November 8, the battalion jumped on the 15th to secure the airfield at Youks les Bains. The force then successfully operated with French forces in southern Tunisia and for a time contributed to preventing German and Italian detachments from taking Gafsa and Sbeïtla. In January 1943, the battalion commander, Colonel Edson D. Raff, was awarded the Légion d'Honneur by Général Joseph Welvert.

On November 28, the 5th Northamptons prepared to attack Djedeïda, with the 2nd Battalion of the 13th Armored Regiment in support, but they came up against resolute defence and soon had to pull back, having lost five tanks. Pictured by PK Friedrich of the Propaganda Zug 'Tunis', the M3 medium tank was of the original American design with the turret mounting a small cupola on top with a machine gun. The tank was named General Lee by the British.

supplies and harassed by the Germans, they were finally forced to withdraw to Sedjenane where the last elements arrived on December 5. On November 30 Evelegh decided to pause for two or three days to wait for more air support.

BUILDING THE BRIDGEHEAD

On November 27, the Germans tried to take over the French Fleet in Toulon harbour on the other side of the Mediterranean. In the early hours, armoured battle groups approached the naval base but the French sailors were ready and they scuttled or destroyed their ships before the Germans could seize them (see *After the Battle* No. 76). One battleship, two battle-cruisers, four heavy and three light cruisers, 24 destroyers, 16 submarines and a number of smaller craft were sunk or seriously damaged by their own crews. Five submarines succeeded in escaping, though the *Venus* could only reach deep water off Toulon and scuttled herself there, while the *Iris* reached Barcelona where the Spanish interned her. The *Casabianca* and the *Marsouin* reached Algiers, and *Glorieux* made for Oran, and all three immediately joined in on the side of the Allies.

In Tunisia, the Germans now abandoned the fiction that they were supporting French interests against the excesses of the Allies and on November 30 Nehring was ordered to disarm the French. Général Barré's forces were beyond reach but Admiral Derrien's command, trapped in Bizerte, was a threat in the rear that must be cleared. It took some time to assemble the necessary task force as units had to be sent back from the front in the west, but on December 8 Amiral Derrien was forced to surrender the 3,000 men under his command. This included coastal batteries, an arsenal, three torpedo boats, nine submarines, two dispatch boats and some artillery. The Axis command

Five Crusader IIIs were lost on December 1 when the 17th/21st Lancers were sent to assist 'Blade Force' which was being overrun in the Chouïgui sector.

then began preparations to recruit an Arab legion in Tunisia and to cultivate leaders of the Destourian movement for Arab independence to organise sabotage by pro-Axis Arabs.

General Evelegh's decision taken to wait came almost simultaneously with a decision by the Axis command to strike back at Tebourba. Disapproving Nehring's withdrawal from the Medjez el Bab sector, on the 28th Kesselring ordered him to push the British back. Nehring entrusted Generalleutnant Wolfgang Fischer, part of whose 10. Panzer-Division was just arriving, with an enveloping attack of the Tebourba sector. In fact, Fischer only had a small part of his division available as his two panzergrenadier regiments and other units were yet to arrive, but he devised a plan to launch an ambitious enveloping attack on the morning of December 1 with what forces he had available.

He organised his force into four battle groups called Hudel, Lueder, Koch and Djedeïda, the last initially in reserve. Group Hudel, (possessing two companies of tanks, two companies of anti-tank guns, and a company of dismounted motorcycle troops) was to destroy the Allied armoured force at Chouïgui, and then, in conjunction with Group Lueder (comprising one company of tanks, one field artillery battery of three guns, one company of dismounted motorcycle troops), attack Tebourba from the west. In the south, Group Koch (made up of

This M5 was probably one of the six claimed destroyed on December 2 by Kampfgruppe Lueder in the Chouïgui sector. Markings identify it as belonging to Company C of the 1st Armored Regiment.

seven companies of parachute infantry, three companies of infantry, one German and one Italian anti-tank company, two field artillery pieces, engineers and bicycle troops) was to attack El Bathan and then push to the west. At Djedeïda, a fourth group (Group Djedeïda) would

pursue the Allies if they pulled back during the tank operations north of Tebourba but otherwise would await General Fischer's order to move. Group Djedeïda included one company of parachute infantry, two companies of infantry, two anti-aircraft companies,

On the afternoon of December 28, flying their last mission of the day, P-38s of the 14th Fighter Group clashed with Messerschmitt Bf 109s from Jagdgeschwader 1 over Pont du Fahs. 2nd Lieutenant Livie F. Mullinax claimed one Bf 109 shot down but in turn he was shot down, probably by Oberfeldwebel Otto Schultz. The German pilots claimed four P-38s shot down but said that they suffered no loss. Mullinax was taken prisoner and was in a POW camp in Italy when the Italians surrendered in September 1943. *Above:* The wreck of Mullinax's P-38 — *Tangerine*, 41-7654 of the 48th Fighter Squadron — was featured by one of the German photographers who took a series of photos of this wreck.

From November 24, while his Tigers were progressively moving to the sector of Djedeïda, Major Lueder, the commander of schwere Panzer-Abteilung 501, was temporarily given command of a battle group comprising two companies from Panzer-Abteilung 190 and one motorcycle company from the 10. Panzer-Division to support the paratroopers of Kampfgruppe Koch in the Medjez el Bab sector. Kampfgruppe Lueder finally started operations at Djedeïda just before midday on December 25.

a motorcycle engineer platoon, two PzKpfw III tanks and the two Tiger tanks which had successfully made the overland trip from the port to the battle-front.

About 8 a.m., led by Fischer personally, the Hudel and Lueder groups advanced on Chouïgui from two directions causing 'Blade Force' to disperse. To the south, the 1st Surreys beat off the infantry of Group Koch trying to take the bridge near El Bathan. The day ended with the 11th Infantry Brigade holding its position, though its northern flank was exposed.

On December 2, Groups Hudel and Lueder assaulted Tebourba but then they were attacked on their right flank by elements of the US 13rd Armored Regiment. The Americans lost heavily but their action, and intense artillery shelling, halted any more progress by the German battle groups. Meanwhile, Group Djedeïda had launched an attack on the 2nd Hampshires east of Tebourba but the Hampshires held their ground throughout the day.

Fischer continued with his assault on December 3. The 1st Surreys and 2nd Hampshires fought back, Major Wallace Le Patourel, the commander of the latter unit being awarded the Victoria Cross for his conduct, but both formations were finally forced to fall back. Meanwhile Evelegh had ordered the 11th Infantry Brigade to withdraw to the high ground on each side of the Medjerda river west of Tebourba.

Major Lueder then had three of his Tigers and four of his PzKpfw III assembled just east of Djedeïda. Top: PK Dullin of the Propaganda Kompanie 'Afrika' pictured Tiger '142' commanded by Hauptmann Deichmann — we saw it photographed in Tunis on page 158. Above: It is not clear whether it was Dullin or another photographer that took this series of photos of Tiger '141' immobilised in a remote Tunisian field while the maintenance team were changing the engine. Here the crew take a break while they wait for the breakdown unit. The Tigers of schwere Panzer-Abteilung 501 were painted in sand-olive and were marked with large three-figure numerals on the sides of the turret.

The 12-cylinder Maybach HL 210 P45 engine used to power the Tiger was rushed into production before all the bugs had been ironed out with the result that it could not be reliably operated at its maximum power output of 3,000rpm. Though the engine developed 650hp, the heavy Tigers were still underpowered and from the 251st onwards, the HL 210 engine was replaced by the upgraded HL 230 P45 that gave an additional 50 horsepower.

By midday on December 4 the German attacks from both east and west broke into Tebourba and contact was soon established with Group Koch pushing northward from El Bathan.

The aggressive Axis defence ended in a real success, the Allies having been halted in their tracks and turned back. Allied losses over the four days were heavy, and according to an estimate by General Fischer, these amounted to 55 tanks, four armoured cars, four anti-tank guns, six 100mm guns and six 120mm guns, 38 machine guns, 40 mortars, 300 motor vehicles and quantities of ammunition of many kinds. Over a thousand men had been taken prisoner.

On December 2, General Anderson reported that his forces were stretched to the limit. Next day Eisenhower advised the Combined Chiefs-of-Staff that a breathing space was essential and that he hoped to resume the advance about December 9. He pointed out that the ground units pushing eastwards 'in a pell-mell race for Tunisia' had gone 'beyond the sustainable limit of air capabilities' to support them. He said that although the 'air forces have been working at maximum pace' they could not 'keep down the hostile strafing and dive-bombing which is so largely responsible for breaking up all attempted advances by ground forces'.

General Nehring now found the means to launch another assault beyond Tebourba, attacking up the Medjerda river valley, and on December 6 elements of Fischer's command attacked to clear the Allies from Djebel el Guessa, forcing Evelegh into another withdrawal along the river. Now the 11th Brigade was to occupy the high ground of Djebel el Ahmera while Combat Command B from the US 1st Armored Division took up positions at Djebel Bou Aoukaz on the far side of the river.

After a new German probe on December 10, Combat Command B was ordered to pull back north of the river and a light engagement with a small German force then ensued near the bridge at Bordj Toum. False reports from the head of the CCB column led the force to take instead a narrow dirt track along the eastern bank of the river. This decision ended in a major disaster as many vehicles soon bogged down, the crews finally abandoned 18 tanks, 41 guns and 150 vehicles, having to continue to Medjez el Bab on foot.

The replacement engine was brought up by a SdKfz 9 heavy half-track with a Büssing-NAG type 4500 lorry to provide the heavy lift. The largest of the German half-tracks to enter service — it weighed 18 tons when laden — the SdKfz 9 was designed both as a tank-recovery vehicle and also as a prime mover for heavy artillery. The Büssing-NAG lorry mounted a Bilstein swing crane that had a maximum lifting capability of three tons.

Kriegsberichter Fenske pictured the Tigers of schwere Panzer-Abteilung 501 as they drove into action west of Djedeïda in the afternoon of December 1. *Left:* Tiger '111', the mount of Hauptmann von Nolde, the commander of the 1. Kompanie, has pulled up just before crossing this bridge, perhaps to check if it had been mined. *Right:* The author was delighted, not only to track down the location, but to find the bridge ramp still exactly the same as it was in 1943.

On December 6, V Corps under Lieutenant-General Charles Allfrey took over command of the Allied forces in Tunisia. They then comprised the 6th Armoured Division (one armoured brigade and one infantry brigade); the 78th Division (three infantry brigades); Combat Command B from the US 1st Armored Division; the 1st Parachute Brigade, and the 1st and 6th Commandos.

On the opposing side, the LXXXX. Armeekorps headquarters was elevated to that of 5. Panzerarmee on December 8 and a new commander, Generaloberst Hans-Jürgen von Arnim, arrived to take over. Nehring was repatriated to Germany as Kesselring found his attitude too cautious when he directed him to enlarge the fragile Tunisian bridgehead. In particular, Kesselring said that Medjez el Bab should have been defended on November 26 rather than being abandoned.

On December 13, considering that the Allied threat in the Tebourba—Mateur area had been destroyed, von Arnim decided to go on the defensive in this sector. The 5. Panzerarmee front was then organised into three parts, held in turn by Division von Broich from the coast to the area of the Tine river valley; by the 10. Panzer-Division

The attack of Kampfgruppe Djedeïda west of Djedeïda was carried out with four PzKpfw IIIs *(photo left)* and three Tigers *(above)*.

That afternoon, the panzers claimed nine Allied tanks destroyed. Von Nolde was killed by a shell burst while running to reach another Tiger, and Hauptmann Deichmann, the commander of Tiger '142', was shot by a sniper as he left his tank to obtain a clearer view. Nikolai von Nolde and Eberhard Deichmann are now buried in the German War Cemetery at Bordj-Cedria, 25 kilometres east of Tunis. *Right:* Looking eastwards along the same old bridge crossing the Medjerda river.

The German attack captured Hill 186, a commanding hill just east of Tebourba, during the morning of December 3. A counter-attack in the afternoon by the 2nd Hampshires to restore the line was only partly successful and, after a last attempt by the 1st Surreys, the British force evacuated the town that evening. *Left:* German war photographer Wörner pictured German troops entering Tebourba on the morning of December 4 and reaching the church in the centre of the town. *Right:* No longer a place of worship, the building today houses a public library.

to a point ten miles west of Zaghouan, and by the Divisione Superga in the south and east. The southern flank, beginning at a point south-west of Enfidaville, was under command of the 50a Brigata Speciale.

THE RACE IS LOST

On December 15, AFHQ estimated the effective strength of combat troops in North Africa at 20,000 British, 11,800 American and 7,000 French, facing Axis forces of around 25,000 combat and 10,000 service troops, most of them in the Tunis bridgehead. The report noted that the Allies had more tanks than the Axis (crediting the Germans with 80) while recognising that the strength of the Axis aviation was superior to that of the Allies.

After postponements in the rate of build-up caused by adverse weather, General Anderson, under Eisenhower's prodding, concluded that the offensive should be launched on December 22-24 in order to take advantage of a full moon for mounting a night infantry attack.

The plan was prepared by V Corps. The 6th Armoured Division under

These British POWs are being marched along the main street in Tebourba towards the railway station. Among those captured was Major Wallace Le Patourel, commanding the 2nd Hampshires. Initial reports suggested that he had been killed so he was awarded the Victoria Cross posthumously but in fact he had been wounded and taken prisoner. He received his VC after he was repatriated in 1943.

Left: German infantry moving on through Tebourba on December 4. *Right:* The main street is now named Farhat Hached after a leader of the Tunisian liberation movement who lost his life in 1952. A plaque on the right-hand side of the street now explains that in June 1954 two Tunisian independence fighters machine-gunned a café which was then a popular venue for French settlers. Bullet holes are still visible on the walls of the café.

175

FIRST ALLIED ATTEMPT
TO REACH TUNIS

1st phase 15th-21st November .... — — →
2nd phase 22nd-30th .... ———→
5 Corps' front on 1st January 1943 ...... ━ ▪ ━
Clash with enemy troops .... ➡

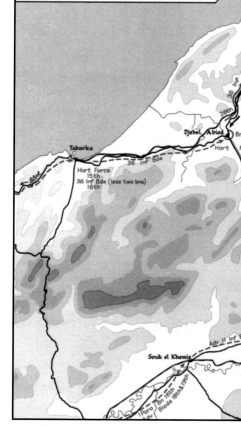

After postponements caused by adverse weather slowing the build-up, General Anderson now decided to launch the offensive. The plan for the operation was designed to take a number of tactical points in succession, starting with Djebel el Ahmera. The 2nd Coldstream Guards captured the hill on the 22nd but the Germans retook it on the 23rd. The Guards then retook the top of the hill on the 24th but the Germans regained it on Christmas Day. That afternoon V Corps finally ordered the operation to be broken off, pulling back Allied forces to the start line from where they had set out two weeks earlier. Djebel el Ahmera had been dubbed 'Longstop Hill', Sergeant Stubbs picturing men of the 2nd Battalion, Coldstream Guards, attacking it on December 25.

Major-General Charles F. Keightley was to make the main thrust to Tunis via Massicault, while the 78th Infantry Division was to protect the left flank by securing a number of tactical points in succession, starting with Djebel el Ahmera (soon to be known as Longstop Hill), and El Aroussa height above the

Left: Lieutenant-General Charles Allfrey, the commander of V Corps, took command of the Allied forces in Tunisia on December 6. This photo shows him in conversation with Brigadier Raleigh Chichester-Constable, then commanding the 139th Infantry Brigade, 46th Division. Right: A memorial by the side of the C50 road commemorates the units that fought for the hotly-contested hill ('Longstop' being translated in French as 'Colline du Long Arrêt'). During the French tenure of Tunisia, many monuments and memorials were erected commemorating battles fought in the country and fortunately most have survived following independence. Sadly, this is not the case in Libya and Algeria.

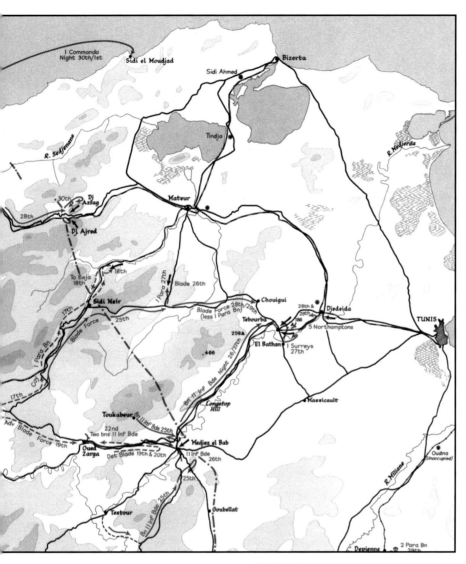

after three days of indecisive fighting, Allied forces withdrew to Medjez el Bab, right back to the line they had set out from two weeks earlier.

The Axis command had shown a remarkably prompt and effective reaction to the slow advance of the Eastern Task Force and they had certainly won the race in Tunisia. On the 26th, General Eisenhower signalled to the Combined Chiefs-of-Staff that there was no chance of an immediate attack on Tunis as adequate supplies and reinforcements had first to be built up.

On January 1, 1943, the Eastern Task Force was officially renamed British First Army. Eisenhower as the Commander-in-Chief, Allied Force, assumed direct command of military operations on the entire front and an advanced command post was established at Constantine.

The First Army was located on the left wing in the coastal sector while the US II Corps was positioned on the right wing in central Tunisia. In between, the detachment of French forces was commanded by Général Juin, who controlled two zones: that of Général Barré's Tunisian Troop Command in the north and the XIXème Corps d'Armée under Général Koeltz in the south. Units of the three nationalities that were in areas assigned to another nation were to be adjusted and concentrated with forces of their own nationality, but during the intervening period some units would have to accept being attached to the command of whatever zone they happened to be in. The XIXème Corps d'Armée was thus to hand over to II Corps the Division de Constantine while the Tunisian Troop Command was to make five battalions of infantry available to the First Army.

The advance of Allied forces in their attempt to reach Tunis in November and December 1942. The red dashed arrows show the first phase of the advance (November 15/21); the red arrows the second phase (November 22/30) while the black arrows illustrate the clashes with Axis forces. The front line is shown as dotted dashed red line as it was on January 1, 1943.

Tebourba Gap. The 1st Guards Brigade, (Brigadier Felix A. V. Copland-Griffiths) of the 78th Division was given the first of these tasks to be launched on December 22, with the 5th Northamptons following on one day later. The 6th Armoured Division was to attack on the 24th.

The 2nd Coldstream Guards took Longstop Hill on the 22nd, but the Germans retook it on the 23rd. While V Corps postponed the second phase of the attack for 48 hours, it confirmed that the operation to secure Longstop Hill was to continue. The Guards recaptured the top of the hill during the afternoon of the 24th but failed to take Djebel el Rhaa just to the east where the main German positions were sited. After the Germans regained the upper part of Longstop Hill on Christmas Day, that afternoon V Corps ordered the operation to be broken off. Thus,

On December 26, Eisenhower had to advise the Combined Chiefs-of-Staff in Washington that there was no chance of an immediate attack on Tunis. This picture of him enjoying C Rations during an inspection tour of the Tunisian front was taken later in 1943.

The Axis evacuates Libya

One thousand miles to the east, Rommel evacuated Tobruk on November 12, the leaders of the 4th Light Armoured Division entering the town the following day.

In Egypt, the battle of El Alamein ended on November 11 with a decisive victory for the Eighth Army. It marked the watershed of the campaign in the Western Desert and resulted in General-feldmarschall Erwin Rommel, the commander of the Deutsch-Italienische Panzerarmee, withdrawing his German and Italian armies as fast as the dire supply situation permitted. Axis forces soon abandoned Tobruk and the leaders of the Eighth Army entered the town on November 13. The same story applied at Benghazi on the 20th.

In three weeks, Rommel had successfully pulled back his forces over 1200 kilometres in the face of a vastly superior enemy. 'Evacuation of Cyrenaica was complete' he proudly noted.

Realising that he was far too weak to hold his present position near Mersa Brega, 160 miles along the coast behind Benghazi, on November 17 Rommel sent a report about the state of his force. He stressed that Buerat, and Homs and Tarhuna, were the best places to make a stand, the latter location was only some 50 miles in front of Tripoli.

As far as the Italians were concerned, abandoning Libya — their colony —

Top left: **British troops found Tobruk almost totally destroyed but the Officers' Club, masquerading as the 'Tobruk Tavern' provided a welcome watering hole amid the devastation.** *Top right:* **The tell-tale iron support for the sign was still there to identify the nondescript building.** *Above:* **The Pioneer Corps worked hard to clear the streets of rubble.**

Left: **Despite months of shelling and bombing, the church was still standing although in poor shape with the tower condemned as unsafe. When this photo was taken some weeks after the recapture of the town, the square in front of the** church had been cleared up and unknown hands had even found time to touch up with humour the paintwork on the oil drum. *Right:* **Seventy years later the church is still there although no longer a place of worship.**

British forces entered Benghazi, 220 miles further to the west, on November 20. *Left:* A Bren Carrier roared down Via Roma. *Above:* This street is now Sharia Omar al Muhktar, the main figure of the struggle against the Italian colonisation in the 1920s.

was too much to bear and at first they refused to follow Rommel's advice. When Hitler confirmed on November 22 that the Mersa Brega position was to be held at all costs, Rommel decided to fly to Germany to explain his views to the Führer face to face. The conference was frustrating for Rommel as Hitler refused to listen to his reasoning, insisting that it was a political necessity to hold a major bridgehead in North Africa. Rommel then went to Rome to confer with Mussolini and his staff and he found the Italians 'far more reasonable than our own higher command'. The Italians accepted that initial preparations for a possible retreat to Buerat should be made and steps must be taken to move the non-motorised Italian infantry back to this position.

Rommel returned to Africa and directed the first steps of the withdrawal, beginning on December 5. He recorded that 'the move swallowed up practically all the meagre amount of petrol we did receive, and transport of ammunition to the front virtually ceased'. To his relief, he was granted more time than he expected as Lieutenant-General Bernard

On November 26, Sergeant Flack pictured these Stuart tanks — most probably from the Royal Scots Greys — on the waterfront in Benghazi. The Italians had named the esplanade Viale della Vittoria: Victory Avenue.

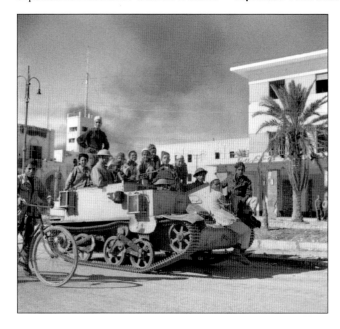

Left: Arab children were given rides along the promenade. *Above:* The road is now Sharia 23 July, commemorating the anniversary of the Egyptian Revolution of 1952. The signal office and the building nearby have both been replaced, but the third building remains as a link with the past.

After the epic 1,450-mile march from Egypt, the leaders of the Eighth Army entered Tripoli on January 23. Pushing along the inland road, the 11th Hussars were the first to enter the city. Their War Diary explains that 'we arrived in Tripoli about 0500 hours and it appeared a dead city, all the windows were shuttered and there was no living thing about, not even a stray dog.' *Above:* Close second, arriving along the coastal road, was C Squadron, 50th Royal Tank Regiment, carrying two companies of the Gordon Highlanders, with Piper George Ramsey standing on the leading to pipe them through the town.

Montgomery took three weeks to concentrating his forces after the 800-mile advance of the Eighth Army from El Alamein.

On December 13 Montgomery launched a wide outflanking manoeuvre across the desert with the aim of cutting the coastal road well west of El Agheila. Rommel urged the last covering forces to pull back and by dawn on the 16th, when the leaders of the New Zealand Division reached the coastal road, the last of the Axis forces had just escaped. The operation was a disappointing failure, the total bag between December 13 and 17 being only of 450 prisoners, and 18 tanks.

The Axis High Command decreed, once again, that the present defence along the Buerat line was to be held 'to the last' but again Rommel insisted that this would not be possible. On December 17, he reported to OKW and Comando Supremo that to avoid the destruction of his army, and open the road to Tunisia for the British, the Deutsch-Italienische Panzerarmee must pull back to positions near Gabès, far to the west in Tunisia. As a stop-gap measure, withdrawal to the hilly country between Homs and Tarhuna should be considered.

Generale Ettore Bastico, the Italian Commander-in-Chief for North Africa, supported Rommel's thinking in most

In background, the Red Castle Museum which hosts Libya's Antiquities Department and the National Museum with a collection of Phoenician, Greek and Roman artefacts.

Above: **Montgomery arranged a victorious parade in Tripoli on January 26, seen here returning the salute as his car drives through the then Piazza Italia.** *Above right:* **A nice comparison in 2010 with the marquee then used by the late Muammar Gaddafi to review his parades. Known as Piazza Italia during the colonial rule, Independence Square during the monarchy, then Green Square during the Gaddafi era this major landmark of Tripoli was renamed the Martyrs' Square at the end of Gaddafi's rule in 2011.**

of its essentials, and Bastico's efforts to gain some understanding of the danger of the situation finally got through to Berlin and Rome. On December 31 an order from Comando Supremo gave Bastico a free hand stating that if the Panzerarmee was faced by a powerful offensive, it could retreat as he thought fit. Bastico met Rommel at midday to convey him the news.

On January 6 Maresciallo Ugo Cavallero, Chief-of-Staff of the Italian Armed Forces, came personally to Africa to outline Mussolini's latest strategic vision. Accepting that it was impossible to supply both the Libyan and Tunisian theatres, the Duce had decided that Tunisia was the more important to the Axis war effort and therefore Tripolitania was to be evacuated.

By the evening of January 18, worried about the threat of encirclement, Rommel decided it was time to abandon the Homs—Tarhuna line and pull back to southern Tunisia. Another stormy meeting with Kesselring and Cavallero ensued as Rommel ordered Tripoli to be abandoned on the night of January 22/23. British troops entered the town unopposed early on the 23rd.

The last sizeable action of the war in Libya was fought near Zuara, some 30 miles east of the border with Tunisia, where the leaders of the 7th Armoured Division were held up for four days by rearguards of the 90. leichte Afrika-Division. By early February, Rommel had managed to extricate most of his much-depleted Deutsch-Italienische Panzerarmee — then numbering about 30,000 German and 48,000 Italian troops — into Tunisia where they began to establish at the Mareth Line south of Gabès.

Pressing westwards along the Via Balbia, Eighth Army transport passes through Buerat, halfway to the Tunisian border.

With photography in Libya a risky business, and as the radio aerials in the background indicated that this was a military site, the author swiftly snapped this comparison before speeding on his way.

Unrest over the Allied affiliation with Darlan had not abated and, as Christmas approached, Churchill reminded Roosevelt of the admiral's 'odious record' and added that 'we must not overlook the serious political injury which may be done to our cause, not only in France, by the feeling that we are ready to make terms with local Quislings'.

The problem of what to do about Darlan was solved unexpectedly by a young Frenchman, Fernand Bonnier de la Chapelle. On December 24 he managed to reach the admiral's office in his headquarters in the Palais d'Été in Algiers and promptly shot him to death. The perpetrator was arrested and quickly tried and convicted by a French court, being executed by firing-squad two days later.

Officially, Bonnier de la Chapelle acted alone but unofficially there has been no end to the speculation as to the secret intrigues at work and who might have manipulated the young idealist. Sir Stewart Menzies, the wartime head of MI6 who hardly ever left London, just happened to be in Algiers at the time but no solid evidence has ever surfaced to prove any British involvement, nor that de Gaulle ordered the assassination.

Admiral Darlan Assassinated

Amiral Darlan, the key man in the agreement reached with the French in North Africa, made his last public appearance on December 22, two days before he was killed.

For the Allies, Darlan's death was a blessing and Clark later wrote: 'It is too bad that he went that way but, strategically speaking, his removal from the scene was like the lancing of a troublesome boil. He had served his purpose, and his death solved what could have been the very difficult problem of what to do with him in the future. Darlan was a political investment forced upon us by the circumstances, but we made a sensational profit in lives and time through using him.'

In his history of the Second World War, Churchill was even more to the point: 'Darlan's murder relieved the Allies of their embarrassment for working with him and left them with all the advantages he had been able to bestow.'

Général Giraud then took over as High Commissioner.

Above: **The parade was held in front of the Hôtel Aletti (now Hotel Safir), at the junction of Rue Alfred Lelluch (now Rue Asselah Hocine) and the parallel Boulevard Bugeaud (now Boulevard Mustapha Ben Boulaid). Darlan was on his way to greet Muslim elders that he had invited for the Muslim feast of Aid el Kebir held at the Colysée cinema just across the street.** *Left:* **On December 16, a French reporter pictured the admiral in headquarters in the Palais d'Été, and this office is most probably where he was shot on December 24 by a young idealist Fernand Bonnier de la Chapelle. He was waiting in the corridor when Darlan and his Chief-of-Staff, Capitaine de Frégate Jean Hourcade, arrived and entered their offices without paying attention to the young man. He then burst into Darlan's office and shot him dead. The palace was the former summer residence of the Dey of Algiers, but was taken over by the French in 1830 for the Governor General's residence. Renamed the Palais du Peuple after the independence of Algeria, it is now owned by the State and is out of bounds, all requests to picture the office where Darlan was assassinated being refused.**

The funeral service was held the following day. High officials of the Allied forces surrounded the coffin that was exposed before service at the Cathedral in Algiers.

Darlan had kept his promises to the Allies most effectively and in General Eisenhower's own words, he has been 'the source of all our practical help'. *Above:* On December 25, the day after the murder, a Signal Corps photographer took this picture of 'the entrance to the office of the late Admiral Darlan'. He added in his caption that 'entering this doorway, the assassin fired shots that resulted in death'. *Right:* The same day people were pictured paying homage to the late Admiral as his coffin lay in state, topped by his naval head-dress in the Gouvernement Général building.

Left: The majority of the Allied leaders attended the funeral. L-R: General Eisenhower, Admiral Cunningham, General Clark and General Walter Bedell Smith, Chief-of-Staff of AFHQ. *Right:* Darlan was first laid to rest in a casemate within the Admiralty in Algiers but in 1964, just before Algerian independence it was decided to move the body to the French Military Cemetery at Mers el Kebir where the 1,300 sailors killed during the Royal Navy bombardment in July 1940 were buried (see page 12). However, it appears that when the coffin was being removed from the Admiralty, it was discovered that the casemate door had been forced and the coffin was empty. One unofficial account indicates that when it was decided that Darlan was to be moved, naval personnel had secretly buried him at sea, and that when the reburial took place at Mers el Kebir, the coffin was weighted with sand. Only his son was party to the secret. Sadly, the Algerian authorities failed to maintain the French war cemetery and since the 1990s it has been regularly desecrated. The worst incident took place in 2005 when nearly all of the 1,300 graves were destroyed, crosses smashed, and the remains disinterred and strewn across the landscape.

At Casablanca, the French having very efficiently moved every ship that was seaworthy to moorings outside the harbour and cleared up the dock area, on November 13 the five transports of the Centre Group, which by then were more or less empty, were ordered into the harbour to complete unloading. On November 15 the five transports sailed back to the USA while the rest of the Centre Group seven transports and cargo vessels entered the harbour together with five transports of the Northern Group. However, for several days, order was totally lacking and the unloading conditions at Casablanca were shockingly bad. On November 15, Admiral Hewitt sent a staff officer to warn Patton that conditions in the docks were scandalous whereupon the general assigned two battalions of infantry and one of engineers to help with the unloading. On the morning of November 18, the first follow-up convoy UGF-2 with 20 cargo vessels and four transports — arrived at the harbour. On November 23 a US Navy salvage expert, Captain William A. Sullivan, was flown in from the States only to discover that all but one of the berths were still unusable. The largest job proved to be the clearing of two wrecks that were blocking the whole length of the eastern side of the Môle du Commerce: the cargo ship *Lipari* and the liner *La Savoie*.

The *Lipari* had practically broken in two so raising her in one piece required an innovative approach. To reduce the total weight, the superstructure was cut down and removed piecemeal. Then an anchor chain was run along both sides of the ship and secured wherever evidence of strength remained and she was successfully re-floated with the ends hanging together. In the end, the clearance teams removed or salvaged 13 wrecked ships from the harbour: five large cargo or passenger vessels; the battleship *Jean Bart*, the destroyer *Tempête* and two floating dry docks. *Left:* Taken from the Quai des Phosphates, this shot shows the wrecks blocking Bassin Delpit. In the mid-distance were (L-R) the destroyer *Tempête* and the cargo ships *San Pietro* and *Schiaffino*. *Right:* In the background, the grain silo still stands to provide continuity with the past.

For weeks, an acute shortage of motor transport prevented the forward movement of supplies from the port causing a huge backlog in the docks. However, the Atlantic Base Section progressively surmounted all difficulties and established a smooth supply operation. *Left:* The *George Clymer (AP-51)* unloading stores and ammunition at the Quai des Phosphates. *Right:* Modern handling machinery now lines this quayside; this is the *Ultra Agility*, a modern bulk carrier of 34,830 GRT.

German and Italian prisoners, most of them airmen, were marched down to the harbour at Algiers for embarkation.

Comparison by Omar Mecheri. In the background is the tower of the lift which links the town with the harbour down below.

In Algeria, the main port was Algiers where a steady sequence of convoys brought in men and matériel to build up the Eastern Task Force. Occasionally ships went straight through to Bône but usually cargoes were trans-shipped at Algiers into smaller vessels to be carried forward the 230 miles to Bône. There was a similar arrangement between Oran and Philippeville. From Bône and Philippeville, transport to the front was by road and rail, while some was taken the 30 miles from Bône eastwards to Tabarka using LCMs and LCTs. The Italian Navy devised an ambitious operation to attack shipping in the Algiers harbour. On the evening of December 10, the submarine *Ambra* brought to Algiers three manned torpedoes and ten commando frogmen armed with limpet mines. The submarine approached the entrance at a depth of 18 metres with two frogmen swimming to scout on the surface. Guiding the submarine by phone, they led her toward a position 2,000 metres from the southern entrance to the harbour. At 9.45 p.m. they reported spotting six steamers so the frogmen and the three manned torpedoes were ordered into action. Mines were placed on several ships before the alarm was sounded. In spite of the intense reaction from the harbour defences, the submarine waited till 3 a.m. — one hour after the original time set — in the hope of recovering the operatives but none returned. The scout swimmers were then recalled and the submarine departed for La Spezia. At 5 a.m. the time-fused mines began to explode. The *Berta*, 1,493 GRT, sank within five minutes, and three other ships, the *Empire Centaur*, 7,041 GRT, *Harmattan*, 4,587 GRT, and *Ocean Vanquisher*, 7,174 GRT, were damaged, the latter very badly. The six crewmen on the manned torpedoes (Giovanni Badessi, Guido Arena, Giorgio Reggioli, Carlo Pesel, Ferdinando Cocchi and Colombo Pamolli) and the ten divers (Agostino Morello, Botti, Rolfini, Ghiglione, Evangelisti, Feroldi, Boscolo, Lugano, Lucchetti and Luciani) were all captured.

Axis bombers regularly attacked Algiers harbour. *Left:* The original caption of this impressive shot of an anti-aircraft barrage indicates that two German bombers were shot down on this night. *Right:* One of the craters left in the street near the harbour.

185

During November, Allied fighter and bomber squadrons were progressively built up in eastern Algeria. The fighters comprised two squadrons of Hurricanes, No. 225 at Bône and No. 253 at Philippeville, while two squadrons of Spitifires, Nos. 72 and 93, were based at Souk el Arba. P-38s of the 14th Fighter Group took over at Youks les Bains. Between November 12 and 17, three squadrons of Blenheim V medium bombers from No. 326 Wing were based at Blida while the B-17 heavies of the US 97th Bombardment Group were at Maison Blanche from the 13th and those of the US 301st Bombardment Group at Tafaraoui, near Oran, from the 26th. By the beginning of December all suitable airfields in eastern Algeria were being used to capacity: Bône held 76 fighters; Youks les Bains 37; and Souk el Arba 45. Some distance to the rear, Canrobert and Djidjelli together had a total of 19 fighters and light bombers. In the Algiers area, Maison Blanche and Blida together hosted 150 aircraft, and four fields around Oran had 180, mostly at Tafaraoui and La Sénia. However, operations on many of these airfields were incapacitated by soft ground in the winter rainy season.

To provide an all-weather airfield for the heavies, US engineers were flown to Biskra, an oasis on the edge of the desert 200 kilometres inland from Bougie. It was ready for operations to begin on December 13, and on January 7 *Life* photographer, Margaret Bourke-White, took this picture of the damage done by a German bomb to a B-26 bomber from the 17th Bombardment Group.

On December 11, the headquarters of XII Bomber Command was established at Constantine in the city's art museum, pictured here by Signal Corps photographer, Tech/3 Charles Q. Coffman.

Built in the 1920s, the Cirta Museum displays artefacts discovered in and around the city, its name coming from the time when Constantine was part of the Kingdom of Numidia before Roman rule.

Left: American airmen in front of the famous Légion Étrangère barracks at Sidi Bel Abbès, 60 kilometres inland from Oran. *Right:* It is now occupied by unit of the Algerian Gendarmerie and all of our requests to take a photograph were refused. However, this old postcard from the Foreign Legion days provides a good stand-in comparison.

The rate of replacement at the front line airfields in eastern Algeria was very unsatisfactory, and the current shortage of pilots and crews caused a serious lowering of morale. Following an urgent request from Eisenhower to the War Department in December, Admiral King agreed to use the *Ranger* to ferry P-40s to Morocco. The 325th Fighter Group was given 72 new P-40Fs and the pilots were given three days training in their new aircraft on a runway in the States, marked off to simulate the take-off from a flight deck. On January 7, the P-40s were hoisted aboard the *Ranger* for the voyage to North Africa. *Left:* Support personel loading the wing machine guns of a P-40 while en route. Note that the canopies were painted with a dark protective coating. *Right:* Major C. T. Tinker, Captain Calvin T. Durgin, the captain of the *Ranger*, and Lieutenant Colonel Gordon H. Austin, the 325th Fighter Group commander, have a final review of the launch plan prior to the take off on January 19.

Launched in six successive flights, the 72 aircraft landed at Cazes, near Casablanca, where they stayed until the 23rd before being sent on to Médiouna. The next day they flew protective cover for President Roosevelt's party at Casablanca.

The 'Symbol' Conference

Stalin having made known that he could not leave Russia for the time being so Roosevelt and Churchill agreed to meet without him at Anfa, a western suburb of Casablanca.

In December, with expectations of an early end to the whole campaign in North Africa, Roosevelt and Churchill agreed to meet to plan Allied strategy for the next phase of the war in Europe. Stalin was invited but he declined to attend, explaining that the ongoing conflict in Stalingrad required his presence in the Soviet Union. From January 14 to 24, 1943, President Roosevelt and Prime Minister Churchill met in French Morocco for the 'Symbol' Conference in Casablanca.

At first, de Gaulle was not present at Casablanca. While he was personally facing American hostility, and also the fact that they were giving full support to Général Giraud, he also found himself as a pawn in the game played by Churchill to oppose Roosevelt's great post-war design to put an end to colonial empires. Roosevelt saw through this and was convinced that the French general had not come because Churchill

The conference was held in the Anfa Hôtel, an idyllic location far from the sounds of battle. Nevertheless, soldiers patrolled the hotel and the perimeter was protected by barbed wire entanglements with the two entrances guarded by sentries.

In spite of its historic importance, the hotel was unceremoniously demolished in 1972 for the construction of a complex of five buildings inside the large roundabout. This is a view from the north-western corner.

A number of properties close to the hotel were requisitioned to house the President and Prime Minister and the high-ranking participants. On the south-east corner of the roundabout, which circled the hotel, the Dar es Saada villa was secured for the President's residence. Flying in a Pan American Boeing 314 flying boat, Roosevelt left Florida on January 11, becoming the first President to travel on official business by air. The aircraft touched down in the Caribbean before continuing down the southern coast of South America to Brazil. From there, it crossed the Atlantic to Gambia. On the morning of the 14th, the President took off from Yundum Field in a C-54 transport that flew along the coastline in order to afford him a view of Dakar. The plane landed at Médiouna airfield, near Casablanca, at 6.20 p.m. and by seven o'clock the President was installed in the Dar es Saada villa. *Above:* Air Chief Marshal Sir Charles Portal, Lord Louis Mountbatten, Admiral Sir Dudley Pound and Admiral Ernest J. King, the Commander-in-Chief, US Navy, are on their way to see the President at the villa. This photo was taken on the evening of January 14 when Roosevelt had dinner with the Prime Minister and some of the high ranking staff.

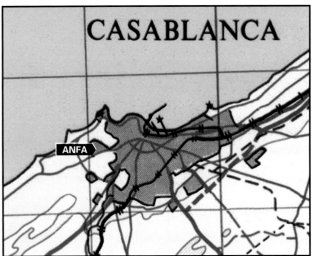

Left: During a break in discussions on January 17, General Patton, Field-Marshal Sir John Dill, General George C. Marshall and Lieutenant General Henry H. Arnold were pictured in a jovial mood outside in the street, just in front of Roosevelt's villa. *Right:* Although the hotel has disappeared, the road layout with the roundabout remains unchanged.

Security was very tight around the President and Michael F. Reilly, chief of the White House Secret Service detail, personally came to Casablanca to deal with security arrangements. On January 21 Roosevelt was driven the 85 miles to Rabat to inspect US troops. He set off at 9.20 a.m. in an olive drab Daimler limousine escorted by motorcycles, reconnaissance cars, and a pair of Jeeps bristling with Secret Service agents. Just outside Rabat, agents erected a privacy screen and lifted Roosevelt from the car into the front seat of a Jeep. (Roosevelt had been struck down in 1921 with a paralytic illness that left him partially paralysed from the waist down. He was careful that his disability was not overtly publicised, especially when aids had to lift him from vehicles. Even though he had difficulty in standing, nevertheless, he entered the race for the presidency and was elected in 1937.) *Right:* The inspection of the 2nd Armored Division lasted for over half an hour, the President being driven past the troops, followed by Secret Service agents, including some in the following Jeep with their submachine guns at the ready.

Left: This shot of Roosevelt in a Jeep in front of his villa was taken on January 18 when he left with Patton to inspect the troops detailed to guard the Anfa camp. *Right:* Villa Dar es Saada . . . then and now.

had not asked him to attend. Finally, called in by Churchill, de Gaulle arrived from London on January 22 and two days later, on the last day of the conference, he and Giraud were persuaded by Roosevelt to shake hands for the benefit of the Press.

As to future strategy, Roosevelt lobbied for a cross-Channel invasion of Europe in 1943 but Churchill felt the time was not opportune, and favoured instead an Allied assault on Sicily followed by an invasion of mainland Italy. As a compromise, Roosevelt acceded to Churchill's proposal for Europe and the Prime Minister's Italian strategy was agreed while the Prime Minister pledged more troops and resources to the Pacific and Burma.

After co-ordinating preparations for one of the large meetings, Field-Marshal Sir John Dill was pictured by Signal Corps photographer, Sergeant Robert A. Edwards as he left Villa Dar es Saada.

The target date for Operation 'Husky' — the invasion of Sicily — was fixed for July with General Eisenhower as Supreme Commander.

A few hours before the final meeting, news arrived that the Eighth Army had entered Tripoli, a happy contrast to the previous meeting between the President and the Prime Minister seven months earlier when the report of the loss of Tobruk had come through at the worst possible moment.

The conference produced a unified statement of purpose: the Casablanca Declaration. The most far-reaching announcements were that the Allies would accept nothing less than the 'unconditional surrender' of the Axis powers. Responsibility for this doctrine rests exclusively with Roosevelt and behind the scenes Churchill did not fully subscribe to it. Roosevelt had borrowed the term 'unconditional surrender' from General Ulysses S. Grant who had communicated this stance to the Confederate commander at Forts Henry and Donelson during the

The Prime Minister's residence was the Villa Mirador situated on the north-east corner of the roundabout. This is a view of it from the hotel.

The Prime Minister, accompanied by his son Randolph, leaves for a meeting with President Roosevelt.

The Villa Mirador is now the private residence of the US Consul General in Morocco.

Left: **A short walk took him to Roosevelt's Dar es Saada villa.** *Right:* **In Villa Mirador, Churchill's map room has been** preserved as a museum documenting his presence here in 1943, complete with his original desk.

The President, together with General Clark and Robert Murphy, first conferred with Général Giraud in the afternoon of the 17th. They held a second conference on the morning of January 19, after which the President and the Général appeared on the terrace for a photo call. *Above left:* **This picture taken by Signal Corps photographer, Sergeant Victor W. Groshon, shows that Roosevelt was still wearing the black armband of mourning for his mother who had died in December 1941. Giraud had another audience with Roosevelt on January 24 when he was given a signed 'Agreement in Principle' by the President, to deliver the matériel required for three armoured and eight infantry divisions, as well as 1,000 first-line airplanes.** *Above right:* **This corner of the garden of the Dar es Saada villa is still exactly the same.**

American Civil War. The President explained what the term meant in a radio address on February 12: 'We mean no harm to the common people of the Axis nations. But we do mean to impose punishment and retribution upon their guilty, barbaric leaders'.

The conference also formulated a revised structure for the Mediterranean theatre. Currently, the frontier between Libya and Tunisia separated the military area under the Commander-in-Chief, Allied Expeditionary Force (General Eisenhower), from that of the British Commander-in-Chief, Middle East (General Sir Harold Alexander). Now it was decided that when the Eighth Army crossed this boundary it would pass into

Centre right: **Just after midday on January 22, President Roosevelt conferred the Medal of Honor on Colonel William H. Wilbur. After the failure to approach the French command on November 8 (see page 136), Wilbur headed back to the Fédala beach-head where he personally led an attack to capture an artillery battery still firing at Allied shipping. While General Marshall looks on, General Patton helps to fasten the award. That evening, the President invited the Sultan Mohammed V to join him for dinner along with Churchill and Général Noguès, giving credibility to Moroccan aspirations for independence and an intimation that the end of the colonial empires was not far away.**

The present-day owner of villa Dar es Saada, Aziz Lazrak, kindly gave us permission for Jean Paul to enter the garden of his house to take these historical comparisons.

On January 22, the Press were called in to take the official photographs of the President and Prime Minister and the Combined Chiefs-of-Staff. This was probably the only occasion during the entire war when so many of the top brass were assembled together in one place. Prominent in this shot taken by Signal Corps photographer Robert A. Edwards are Field-Marshal Sir John Dill, General Sir Alan Brooke, Admiral Sir Dudley Pound, Air Chief Marshal Sir Charles Portal, Lieutenant-General Sir Hastings L. Ismay, Commodore Lord Louis Mountbatten, Brigadier Edward Jacob, General George C. Marshall, Admiral Ernest J. King, General Henry H. Arnold, and Brigadier General John R. Deane.

General Eisenhower's control. At the same time, a newly-formed 18th Army Group under General Alexander would be created to command both the First and Eighth Armies. Then, General Mait- land Wilson would succeed Alexander as Commander-in-Chief, Middle East.

After the conference was over, Churchill flew on to Turkey, via Cairo, for meeting with Ismet Inönü, the Turkish President, on January 30. The Prime Minister returned to Cairo on January 31 and then stopped off at Tripoli where he reviewed units of the Eighth Army.

The art deco villa Dar Es-Saada was built about 1935 by architect Erwin Hinnen for Mrs Besson-Maufrangeas who was still the owner in 1943 when Eisenhower requisitioned it to house the President. Roosevelt found the house 'comfortable in every way' and he wrote a warm letter to his host at the close of the conference: 'I want you to know that I am very grateful to have had the use of your charming house as my headquarters. I thank you again for your hospitality.' Having discovered a French-language edition of Emil Ludwig's popular biography of him, the President autographed it, adding the inscription: 'For Mme R. Maufrangeas-Besson, from the subject of the book'.

The conference lasted from January 14 to January 24 when the President and the Prime Minister took a photo-call for the war correspondents covering the conference. During those ten days, the leaders and advisers held 15 formal sessions. Some of the deliberations were concerned with current operations in Tunisia but the major purpose of the conference was to determine the Allied objectives for 1943 and to establish priorities between the various theatres. Behind the scenes, however, the conflict between Churchill and Roosevelt over their opposing views of the post-war world reached another climax. In his book *As He Saw It*, Elliott Roosevelt, the son of the President, tells how his father confided to him that he was going to press the issue during the conference. 'Churchill may have thought I wasn't serious, last time. He'll find out, this time.' Also, though it was officially reported as an accord between the Prime Minister and the President to demand the 'unconditional surrender' of the Axis powers, the responsibility for the doctrine rested with Roosevelt while Churchill did not fully subscribe to the inflexibility of it. The last meeting was held during the evening of January 23 when the President, the Prime Minister, and the American and British military, naval, and air chiefs conferred in the dining room of Roosevelt's villa. The conference ended just before 8 p.m. Later in the evening, Roosevelt dictated some background material to the Chief Clerk Frank Terry that he planned to give to the correspondents who were to attend the press conference scheduled for 11 a.m. the following day.

Much like it does today, the Anfa neighbourhood in 1943 comprised a cosmopolitan patchwork of wealthy Moroccans and expatriates from around the world. The historic hotel that stood inside the roundabout in 1943 has now disappeared but the road layout remains the same with five new buildings within the loop. (1) Site of the Anfa Hôtel. (2) Villa Dar es Saada. (3) Villa Mirador.

In the early hours of the 24th, Terry met Churchill with Roosevelt's dictation and over the next two hours the final draft of a cable to Stalin reporting on the highlights of the meeting was agreed, as was the text of a joint communique to be issued to the Press. Just after midday, the President and the Prime Minister gave their concluding statements as they sat on the lawn behind the villa. The most significant point was that unlike the armistice that had ended the First World War, this time the Allies would accept nothing less than the unconditional surrender of the Axis powers.

At the end of December, after the death of Darlan, de Gaulle made overtures to Giraud for a merger into a single organisation for the achievement of victory, and he proposed that they meet on French soil to discuss the problem. Giraud was well disposed towards the idea but he asked de Gaulle to wait until the military situation in French North Africa had become less demanding and political conditions less disturbed. When Churchill explained on the very first day of the conference that de Gaulle had refused to come, Roosevelt smiled and later told his son Elliott he knew the real reason: it was because 'our friend Winston has not thought hitherto to ask him to do so'. He explained that in order to counter his post-war ambition to put an end to colonial empires, Churchill was using the coincidence of English and French interests in keeping the status quo. The President insisted that de Gaulle attend. Elliott said that on January 21 Churchill 'bounced' in Roosevelt villa and announced that de Gaulle agreed 'to come down and join our talks'. De Gaulle arrived the following day and had a first meeting with Roosevelt late in the evening, 'father being charming'

noted Elliott, and 'de Gaulle non-committal'. Two days later the President first received Giraud at his villa and it took half an hour of pressing diplomacy to urge him to agree to work with de Gaulle. Giraud then left whereupon de Gaulle was introduced. Roosevelt once again did his best to convince him to work with Giraud before calling the latter back. Finally, the two French generals agreed to shake hands. Churchill then arrived and Roosevelt urged all four to go outside and sit together for an official handshake photograph for the benefit of the Press. As the two French leaders discussed a basis of unification at Casablanca, the basic contrast in their positions was evident. Giraud believed in rallying every kind of Frenchmen who could contribute to liberation, postponing accountability for earlier actions until France had been freed. In contrast with such views, de Gaulle and the Free French wished to immediately sweep from office high officials who had accepted Marshal Pétain's authority. As a result, the two French leaders decided to continue on their separate ways, maintaining liaison through representatives in Algiers and London, but hoping one day to achieve unity.

The conference ended on a sad note, as on January 25, an aircraft carrying 14 Allied war correspondents to Casablanca mistakenly flew over Larache in Spanish Morocco and was fired upon by a Spanish anti-aircraft battery. Hits were registered on the plane and one bullet struck Edouard Beaudry of the Canadian Broadcasting Corporation in the forehead. A military funeral was held the next day in the American war cemetery near Port Lyautey. Today his grave lies in Ben M'Sick European Cemetery where Field-Marshal Sir Claude Auchinleck is also buried.

Left: **A parade of US troops in Algiers late in December 1942.** *Right:* **The Hôtel Albert 1er remains in business at the corner of Avenue Pasteur and Boulevard Mohamed Khemisti.**

Vichy without Pétain

It was soon apparent that Giraud was not the best man to handle the complex situation. Though his position required him to get involved in politics, he made clear that he refused to take political responsibility, his only priority being the reconstruction of the French Army to resume the fight against the Axis. To get rid of the Vichy regime was not a priority for him and the American willingness to make a deal with Darlan, leaving the Vichy men and administration in power, did nothing to encourage him to act otherwise. He even failed to remove the Vichy racist laws or to liberate the regime's political prisoners in the south Algerian camps. When in January 1943 he decided to replace Yves Châtel, the Governor General of Algeria and one of the most compromised men of the Vichy administration, he chose Marcel Peyrouton who had been Minister of Interior in the Vichy government. As far as North Africa was concerned, it was 'Vichy without Pétain'.

On the other hand, to the Gaullists, any Frenchman who had accepted the authority of the Vichy regime should now be proscribed and those responsible put to trial. To them, any such connection with Vichy was a certain disqualification for responsible service against the Axis. De Gaulle's entourage made no mystery of their feelings towards Giraud during the Casablanca Conference. Also Général Leclerc (Philippe de Hauteclocque, Leclerc being his nom de guerre), the distinguished Gaullist officer who had fought with the Eighth Army, was equally frank when he met Giraud later at Montgomery's command post.

From February, however, under Allied guidance, particularly through Jean Monnet, Giraud progressively separated himself from the Vichy regime.

Jean Monnet was a French economist who had been sent to the USA in August 1940 by the British Government as a member of the British Supply Council sent to negotiate the purchase of war supplies. He was soon close to President Roosevelt and was officially sent from the United States to assist in the French re-armament plan.

The death of Darlan brought an end to the arrangement which had freed Général Giraud from political matters that he considered a nuisance. He was at a military command post in Le Kef, about to supervise the forthcoming French attack, when he heard about the assassination whereupon he immediately started back to Algiers that night, arriving on the afternoon of Christmas Day. He then succeeded Darlan as a leader of the French who accepted a voluntary association with the Anglo-Americans in north-west Africa. However, he was soon to prove less competent than his predecessor in the bewilderingly complex role of administering territories populated by such discordant elements, both native and European.

Colonel Harold B. Willis, chief of the French Liaison Section of the Allied Air Forces in North Africa, had been a member of the Lafayette Escadrille during the First World War. Visiting the air base near Casablanca shortly after the end of the fighting in November 1942 he was astonished to see his old 'Indian Head' insignia painted on the Curtiss H-75s of the Groupe de Chasse II/5. Willis then conceived the idea of re-equipping the French group with modern American aircraft and having the unit quickly join the fight against the Axis. The first 12 P-40 fighters were officially delivered to the Groupe de Chasse II/5 at Algiers Maison Blanche airfield on January 9, 1943.

In March Giraud announced the termination of the Imperial Council of Provincial Governors, and that Vichy organisations like the Service d'Ordre Légionnaire be suppressed. He also directed that political prisoners were to be released from detention.

As far as reconciliation with de Gaulle and the Free French in Britain was concerned, Giraud arranged for one of de Gaulle's leading adherents in Algiers, René Capitant, to go to London on his behalf. He had the task of furnishing de Gaulle with a trustworthy, first-hand report of conditions in French North Africa, and to open negotiations for a merger with the Fighting French in London. Pressure on both factions by the Allies contributed to progressive compromises although major points of contention remained like the overall control of the French armed forces.

Left: **The French are presented with the American colours.** *Right:* **The swift creation of the new Escadrille Lafayette delighted Général** **Giraud whose paramount concern remained with the rebuilding of the French Army, and the military operations in Tunisia.**

THE FIGHT IN TUNISIA

Aggressive Defence by the Axis

Faced with the failure to speedily seize Tunisia, the Allied leaders meeting at the Anfa conference in January pushed for an early resolution of this final phase of Operation 'Torch'.

In late January Hitler expanded the functions of Generalfeldmarshall Kesselring, the Ob. Süd (Commander-in-Chief South), as he was now to represent the views of the Führer and of the OKW (Armed Forces High Command) on the conduct of operations in the central Mediterranean in negotiations with Mussolini and Comando Supremo. He was to report back to OKW and OKH (Army High Command) with any requests and/or recommendations from Rommel and von Arnim, or by Comando Supremo, as he was also responsible for the provision of all the supplies for German troops in the theatre. Having installed his operations staff with Comando Supremo in Rome, Kesselring now began to function as the C in C of the armies in Tunisia.

In the meantime, the defeatist elements in the Italian hierarchy finally succeeded in getting rid of Maresciallo Cavallero, the Chief-of-Staff of the Italian Armed Forces, who they considered too pro-German, and on February 4 Generale Vittorio Ambrosio replaced him. One of Ambrosio's first steps was to protest to Kesselring about the size of the German staff contingent at Comando Supremo.

In spite staggering losses to shipping, the Axis still managed to send a remarkable number of troops and tonnage of equipment to Tunisia.

The bulk of cargo was transported from Naples to Tunis and Bizerte in ships ranging from 1,500 to 8,000 tons, the voyage taking about 36 hours, while ferries and landing-craft took the shorter 14-hour route from Trapani and Marsala in Sicily. The convoys kept well to the west while crossing the Tyrrhenian Sea, trying to keep out of range of torpedo-bomber planes from Malta.

In January 41,115 men (29,203 Germans and 11,912 Italians) were shipped to Tunisia as well as 35,505 tonnes of supplies, 50 tanks, 2,017 vehicles and 249 guns. German troops were sent by sea and air but the Italians were mostly transported by sea.

By the end of January the strength of the 5. Panzerarmee had reached a total of more than 100,000 men, of whom 74,000 were Germans and 26,000 Italians. Also supplies brought in by air and sea between November and January amounted to 100,000 tonnes.

Early in February the boundary between Rommel's army and the Axis forces in Tunisia was shifted northwards to run from a point on the coast, ten miles north-east of Sfax, through Mezzouna and Sened to the Kebir river north-west of Gafsa.

Top left: **On January 2, 1943, Sergeant Price and Fusilier J. Crowther of the 2nd Battalion, Lancashire Fusiliers, 11th Brigade, were pictured keeping the Axis lines under observation in the sector of Medjez el Bab.** *Top right:* **Later in the month, in the area of Rebaa, a mortar crew from the 6th Battalion, Royal West Kent Regiment of the 36th Brigade, was in action, firing from the bed of a dried-up wadi.** *Above:* **While the Allies planned to resume their offensive, so also did the Axis command and on January 18, Generaloberst von Arnim launched Operation 'Eilbote' in the Kebir river valley. On the right wing, in the sector of Bou Arada, a diversionary attack by Kampfgruppe Burk was caught in the middle of the plain by elements of the 6th Armoured Division and suffered painful losses. Sergeant Frederick Wackett pictured this disabled PzKpfw IV from Panzer-Regiment 7 with the turret blown away exposing the decapitated body of a crew member.**

The topography of Tunisia is dominated by three connected mountain chains that form a vast inverted 'Y'. The fork lies south of Pont du Fahs and the stem extends northward to Cap Bon. One arm, the Eastern Dorsale, projects southwards for over 200 kilometres to Maknassy; the other, the Western Dorsale, extends still further to the south-west to reach Fériana. Across the wide southern opening of the Y is the east-west chain lying on either side of the oasis at Gafsa.

The stalemate of the Allies main effort in the direction of Tunis now encouraged both sides to extend southward, each attempting to balance the other's build-up along the Eastern Dorsale.

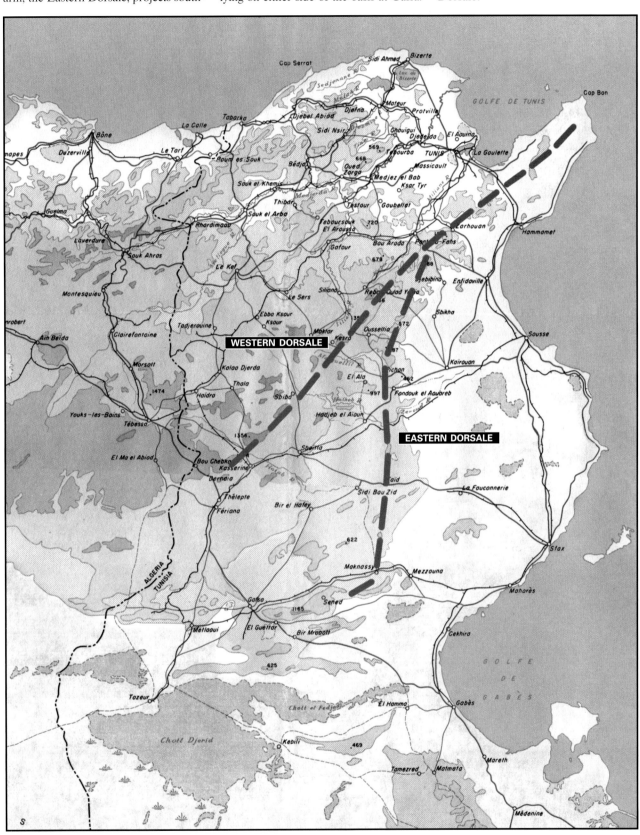

Topography of Tunisia is dominated by three connected mountain chains forming a vast inverted 'Y' structure with a great triangular region within the outspread arms of the Western and Eastern Dorsales. Between the Eastern Dorsale and the sea, the coastal plain spreads to a width of about 70 miles south of Enfidaville but narrows north of Gabès to a bottleneck. This narrow gap, and the neck between Enfidaville and Hammamet further north, are vital points of control.

Having been moved from France to Italy, and then to Tunisia as quickly as transport was available, the 10. Panzer-Division was the most potent of the German forces to arrive in response to the Allied landings. This division had been rehabilitating in France when the Allies landed in North Africa and, after initially being involved in the occupation of southern France, it was rushed to Tunisia. The bulk of its Panzer-Regiment 7 landed at the beginning of December 1942 although the vessels carrying most of the 5. Kompanie and 8. Kompanie were sunk on December 3. Out of its original regimental strength of 21 PzKpfw IIs, 105 PzKpfw IIIs and 20 PzKpfw IVs, losses in transit were two PzKpfw IIs, 16 PzKpfw IIIs, and 12 PzKpfw IVs. This photograph shows one of the PzKpfw IIIs that successfully made it all the way through to Tunisia in January 1943.

The Axis had seized the tactical initiative in December and, still thinking in terms of aggressive defence, von Arnim planned Operation 'Olivernernte' to be mounted early in January to capture Medjez el Bab. However bad weather and chronic shortage of transport and artillery caused the operation to be postponed for two weeks.

In the south, after a preparatory air strike in two waves and a powerful artillery bombardment, a German battle group with tanks of Panzer-Abteilung 190 in support launched a determined assault on January 3 to capture the Fondouk el Aouareb, a gap in the Eastern Dorsale due west of Kairouan. The well-co-ordinated attack soon overwhelmed the French defenders with the loss of more than 300 men and several guns.

Some 20 miles to the north two successive French offensives on December 27-30 and January 12-15 had already gained important positions in this same sector on either side of Karachoum gap and Kairouan pass, defiles across the Eastern Dorsale which led to the coastal plain and south-eastward to Kairouan. German reinforcements were sent to bolster the lines of Divisione Superga and were able to check any tendency of the French to carry the attack beyond the mountains. By January 13 von Arnim was concerned about losing more ground in this sector so decided to launch a limited attack to regain control of this part of the Eastern Dorsale. It was due to begin on the 18th but as the troops for this new operation had to be drawn mostly from those assembled for Operation 'Olivernernte', that plan to capture Medjez el Bab had to be abandoned.

Generalmajor Friedrich Weber, the commander of the 334. Infanterie-Division, was put in command of this operation (code-named 'Eilbote I') and he planned to employ three battle groups. On the right wing, the first, under Weber himself, was to push south-westwards from Pont du Fahs and take Djebel Mansour. This group consisted of his own Gebirgsjäger-Regiment 756, reinforced by a detachment of schwere Panzer-Abteilung 501 with four PzKpfw IIIs and four Tigers, with artillery, engineers and anti-aircraft units.

This series of photographs features new arrivals smiling at their first encounter with camels, so perhaps we can surmise that this is the first time in North Africa for these paratroops (note the shooting star emblem on the car).

The 10. Panzer-Division was commanded by Generalleutnant Wolfgang Fischer, pictured here conferring with Generaloberst von Arnim during the Tebourba battles in December. Fischer was to be killed on February 2 when his car drove into a badly-marked Italian minefield.

Another potent unit rushed to Tunisia was schwere Panzer-Abteilung 501 which was equipped with the new Tiger tanks. After their first engagement in the Tebourba sector in December, the Tigers were assembled near Manouba where the first eight tanks of the 2. Kompanie finally joined the battalion. From mid-January, the 1. Kompanie was directed to the Pont du Fahs area in preparation for Operation 'Eilbote'. *Above:* Tiger '122' was one of the early December arrivals to Tunisia.

The second battle group under Major Hans-Georg Lueder was to move up the Kebir valley and then swing south to the El Glib crossroads. It would then turn east toward the Karachoum gap. It consisted of a company from schwere Panzer-Abteilung 501 with ten PzKpfw IIIs and five Tigers, a battalion of armoured infantry (II. Abteilung of Panzergrenadier-Regiment 69) with a platoon of engineers, and some anti-aircraft units.

On the left wing, the third group was to advance westwards on an axis perpendicular to the main effort with the intention of completing the destruction of the French units trapped on the heights. Commanded by Oberstleutnant Harald Stolz, it was a combined Italian-German force with a regiment from Divisione Superga and a company from Panzer-Abteilung 190.

To support this effort, and protect the exposed northern flank, a holding attack was to be launched in the sector of Bou Arada by elements of the 10. Panzer-Division (Kampfgruppe Burk with three companies of Panzer-Regiment 7 and some engineers and anti-aircraft units) and elements of Fallschirmjäger-Regiment 5.

All preparatory movements were carried out at night in order to conceal the build-up, the attacks going in early on the morning of January 18. The main assault headed down the Kebir valley

For the operation, the Tigers were attached to Kampfgruppe Weber and it certainly raised the spirits of the infantry to find that they had the protection of such powerful machines. *Left:* This view of Tiger '132' shows how the number of each was displayed for easy identification using large three digit numbers, painted in red with white borders, on each side of the turret. *Right:* Servicing the huge 88mm gun of Tiger '122', the barrel measuring almost five metres in length.

An unknown PK photographer took these two photos of a disabled convoy. *Above left:* A Morris C8/MG, officially described as Truck 4×4 AT Portee, meaning that a QF 2-pounder anti-tank gun was carried on the vehicle and taken off when needed. *Above right:* The addition of a pipe from the radiator cap to what looks like a two-gallon can was to capture and condense steam being vented, the same arrangement seen on many desert vehicles with the Eighth Army. This view also shows the battleaxe symbol of 78th Infantry Division painted on the right mudguard. The marking '62' in green identified the vehicle as belonging to the 3rd Battalion of the division's second infantry brigade. The presence of the 2-pounder gun might be explained by the fact that the anti-tank section of the battalion had been given the 2-pounders when the Anti-Tank Regiment received 6-pounder and 17-pounder guns. *Right:* Another German photographer saw this burning Carrier as good opportunity to take some propaganda shots.

and, although the poorly-equipped French units facing them held their ground, by the evening of the 19th the leaders of Kampfgruppe Weber were near Sidi Saïd. Kampfgruppe Lueder had reached the El Glib crossroads and Kampfgruppe Stolz was controlling Djebel Chirich. The French units regrouped on Djebel Mansour and Djebel Bargou but some troops were isolated in the hills near the Karachoum Gap.

By evening, Général Juin reported the seriousness of the situation and asked for reinforcements whereupon Combat Command B of the US 1st Armored Division was moved northwards to Maktar and some elements of the V Corps began to move south.

In the meantime, hampered by lack of transport, the German attack lost momentum although Kampfgruppe Lueder advanced as far as the Ousseltia—Kairouan road just west of the Kairouan Pass. At this point the 5. Panzerarmee decided that the operation had achieved its main aim that was the control of the passes west of Kairouan, so during the night of January 23/24 forces withdrew to a much-improved sector running along Djebel Mansour, Djebel Bou Kril and Djebel er Rihana.

As the photographer's captions to these prints did not survive the war, it is difficult to say if they were taken in December 1942 or January 1943. This particular roll of 35mm negatives ends with some frames showing British prisoners being assembled and picked up by trucks, the battleaxe insignia being seen on the shoulder of one of the men.

Although Eisenhower's directive of January 20 limited operations on the southern flank for the time to defence, nevertheless General Fredendall *(left)*, the commander of II Corps, still devised an attack to take Maknassy, 80 kilometres east of Gafsa. *Right:* Sergeant Charles Bowman, who took this shot of a Sherman of the US 1st Armored Division moving through Gafsa, used a little poetic licence in his caption as he stated that it was 'on the way to the front' but it turns out to have been taken some time later! *Below:* Another shot by Sergeant Bowman of an Italian captain being taken to US headquarters in Gafsa for questioning.

THE US II CORPS RAID AT SENED

On December 27, General Alexander in Cairo reported to Eisenhower that by late January the Eighth Army pursuing Rommel's forces were expected to reach southern Tunisia. Operations to weaken or destroy the German-Italian force there should then be launched.

To this end, the Americans favoured the idea of sending an armoured force to disrupt the Axis line of supply in southern Tunisia. An outline plan for Operation 'Satin' — an attack toward Sfax — was therefore approved at AFHQ on December 28.

Under General Fredendall, the headquarters of II Corps began moving from Oran to Constantine on January 4. One week later its main section was up and running there near the headquarters of First Army, while an advance command post was located some 120 miles to the south-east in Tébessa. While plans for Operation 'Satin' were being prepared, the troops who were to come under

Left: Some distance west of Gafsa, the destruction of this line was the work of one of the German demolition teams that parachuted into this sector back in November 1942 with the purpose of impeding any Allied thrust from Gafsa toward Gabès or Sfax.

Right: Kilometre markers along railways in present-day Tunisia are still the same as they were during the French administration, so that the '161' sign enabled the author to take this remarkable comparison about four kilometres west of Sened. We are looking east.

Before launching his attack, Fredendall decided to first undertake a hit-and-run raid on Sened, a small railway halt about halfway along the road to Maknassy. The raiding force started out early on January 24. The small station and the settlement of a few houses were swiftly taken and by evening the battle group was back in a bivouac area near Gafsa. Several Signal Corps photographers were active in this sector but unfortunately their captions are generally very vague, without a date or location, making it difficult to determine the exact circumstances or when this photo of a disabled Semovente M41 75/18 self-propelled gun was taken.

Fredendall's command were relocated from northern Tunisia or brought forward from Morocco and Algeria.

On January 11, Generals Anderson, Juin and Fredendall met with Eisenhower at Constantine to finalise the coming operation, the basic plan being for II Corps to act aggressively against the enemy line of communication in the direction of Sfax, interrupting its use as much as possible. D-Day was tentatively set for January 22. At Malta, ships were loaded ready to be sent into Sfax harbour when II Corps specified, thus supplementing the overloaded line of supply through Tébessa from Algiers.

General Fredendall planned to attack with the bulk of his command from Gafsa to Gabès and thence push north along the coast to Sfax. He also planned to station a mobile force in the area between Hadjeb el Aïoun and Sbeïtla to forestall any Axis counter-attack that may come from the Kairouan sector.

Although the plan received Eisenhower's tentative approval, when he met Alexander at the 'Symbol' conference, he learned that the Eighth Army would not enter southern Tunisia by the end of January as previously anticipated. By then, it would only have reached Tripoli, over 150 miles to the east; consequently, Eisenhower decided that the II Corps attack on Sfax would have to be cancelled for the time being.

Eisenhower returned to Algiers on January 16 and two days later, at a commanders' conference in Constantine, he reiterated that operations on the southern flank must be defensive for the time being and that as much as possible of II Corps — particularly the 1st Armored Division of Major General Orlando Ward — was to be held as a mobile reserve ready to fend off any hostile counter-measures.

He issued a directive to this effect on January 20 but Fredendall decided to postpone the assembly of the 1st Armored Division until all elements of the division had had a taste of combat. To this end he devised an operation from Gafsa to take Maknassy, 50 miles to the east on the road to Sfax, and the pass through the Eastern Dorsale just to the east of it. However, the division was already largely committed to other operations. Combat Command A (Brigadier General Raymond E. McQuillin) was assembling near Sbeïtla to join the French in an operation planned for the 23rd to regain the Fondouk gap, and Combat Command B (Brigadier General Paul Robinett) had orders to move to the Ousseltia valley in support of another operation by the XIXème Corps d'Armée.

To carry out the Maknassy attack, General Ward had to assemble a Combat Command C under Colonel Robert I. Stack, commander of the 6th Armored Infantry Regiment, made up of a battalion from the 6th Armored Infantry, a company of the 81st Reconnaissance Battalion and one from the 13th Armored Regiment, plus contingents of engineers, artillery and signals.

Before launching the attack, Fredendall decided to first undertake a hit-and-run raid on Sened, a railway station midway to Maknassy along the same road. In spite of the fact that both General Ward and Général Joseph Welvert, the commander of the Division de Constantine (which held the II Corps line south of the 1st Armored Division), pointed out that such an operation would warn the enemy of the planned Maknassy attack, nevertheless Fredendall ordered it to go ahead.

The raiding force started out from Gafsa at 4 a.m. on January 24. The small settlement of a few houses and olive trees was soon taken and by 6 p.m. Combat Command C was back in bivouac area near Gafsa. Losses were quite small with the capture of 96 prisoners.

II Corps then finalised its plans for the main attack on Maknassy, scheduled for February 1. Combat Command C was to advance north-eastwards to approach Maknassy from the north via the Maïzila Pass while a temporary Combat Command D under Colonel Robert V. Maraist would simultaneously strike eastwards from Gafsa by way of the Sened station. (CCD was to be made up of the 3rd Battalion of the 13th Armored Regiment less Company G; the 1st Battalion, 168th Infantry Regiment (detached from the 34th Infantry Division); the 701st Tank Destroyer Battalion less Companies A and B, plus engineers and artillery units.)

However, the mountain range in the background (Djebel Meloussi) provides a nice reference point for this comparison taken just outside the hamlet around Sened station, looking north-eastwards.

This M3 medium tank from the 13th Armored Regiment was disabled by mines in Sened during the January 24 raid.

Although the round shed disappeared years ago, this is the wartime scene as it appears today.

Another interesting photo, taken this time by Signal Corps photographer Corsner, although in his captioning he gives no explanation as to what happened to cause this half-track to get knocked out.

THE LOSS OF THE FAÏD PASS

Meanwhile the Germans were finalising plans to take the Faïd Pass, a broad opening in the Eastern Dorsale through which ran the road from Sbeïtla to Sfax. The objective was to seize the pass, set up holding positions at key points north and south of there, and then reconnoitre westwards halfway to Sbeïtla. The attack was to be launched by the 21. Panzer-Division assisted by elements of the Italian 50a Brigata Speciale. Defending the pass, as well as one north at Sidi Khalif and another to the south at Aïn Rebaou, was a detachment of about 1,000 men of the Division de Constantine.

Oberst Hans von Hildebrandt, the commander of the 21. Panzer-Division, organised two battle groups for the operation. Commanded by Major Hans Pfeiffer, Kampfgruppe Pfeiffer was subdivided into northern, centre and southern task forces. The small northern force was to take the Sidi Khalif Pass and secure the northern flank; the main central force was to attack the Faïd Pass

There is nothing in the foreground that could help locate the spot but the mountain range in far distance gives a good clue for this comparison, looking towards the north-east, some ten kilometres west of Sened.

On February 13, Generals Eisenhower and Anderson came to confer with Fredendall at his headquarters near Tébessa. During the night, Eisenhower travelled by road as far as Sbeïtla and Sidi Bouzid, returning to Tébessa just before daylight. Light aircraft were a more convenient mode of travel, although not without risks. *Left:* Here Eisenhower is pictured stepping out of his plane just after landing while General Anderson, commander of the First Army, came in his Auster *(right)* for the meeting.

from the east, while the southern task force was to seize the Aïn Rebaou Pass and protect the southern flank from the French forces on Djebel Ksaïra. (Djebel is the customary term in North Africa for high hill or mountain.)

Further south, Kampfgruppe Grün, commanded by Hauptmann Werner Grün, was to make a long encircling march through the Maïzila Pass to hit the French garrison at the Faïd Pass from the rear. In addition, Aufklärungs-Abteilung 580 was to precede the Kampfgruppe and then, having reached the supporting position at Djebel Boudinar, turn due west and reconnoitre as far as Bir el Hafey.

The attack began early on January 30. The northern and southern task forces of Kampfgruppe Pfeiffer attained their objectives quickly but the central force and Kampfgruppe Grün were held up for five hours by stubborn French resistance. The French defenders were finally pushed back after which the Germans took the village of Faïd and sealed off the pass although the French still held the pass itself.

In mid-February, Anderson withdrew the 6th Armoured Division for his Army Reserve, with plans for it to exchange its Valentines for new Shermans. The crew of this Valentine are relaxing near Bou Arada. The circle marking on the turret indicates that this tank belonged to a C Squadron.

Left: Sergeant Bowman pictured another Valentine tank reaching Bou Arada. *Right:* This is Bou Arada today, looking northwards along the road to Medjez el Bab. Remarkably, some of the houses in the right background are still standing.

Following a request from Anderson to discuss the situation with him, Eisenhower came to Telergma airfield on the morning of February 1. Anderson explained that the failed attacks at Faïd and Maknassy were an indication that the Allies were spreading their forces too thinly. He proposed that the Allies shorten their lines by withdrawing from 'exposed places like Gafsa, Maknassy, and Faïd' to permit the desired concentration of force on the southern flank. However, Eisenhower insisted that 'if Maknassy is not taken by tonight', the whole 1st Armored Division should be withdrawn 'into a central position and kept concentrated'. This M3 half-track from the division's 1st Armored Regiment mired in sand near Sidi Bouzid was one that had to be recovered by a Sherman.

In spite of early and repeated demands from the French for reinforcements, General McQuillin was slow to react, only despatching cautious reconnaissance patrols in the morning. At 2.30 p.m. he decided to postpone a counter-attack until the following morning.

Combat Command A's counter-attack finally began at 7 a.m. on the 31st. On the left, one force under Colonel Alexander N. Stark consisting of the 1st Battalion of the 26th Infantry Regiment; the 3rd Battalion of the 1st Armored Regiment (less Company G); a platoon from the 701st Tank Destroyer Battalion and one of anti-aircraft artillery. Stark's force advanced from Djebel Lessouda against Faïd. On the right, another force under Lieutenant Colonel William B. Kern made up of the 1st Battalion of the 6th Armored Infantry (less Company B); Company G of the 1st Armored Regiment; Company A of the 701st Tank Destroyers, plus a platoon of engineers, moved out from Sidi Bouzid to strike at the Aïn Rebaou Pass.

During the night, the Germans had positioned their tanks in defile positions and dug in guns, mortars and machine guns with the result that both attacking forces were quickly brought to a halt and repulsed. Tanks of Company H were lured within range of anti-tank guns, at least eight being lost. With the American counter-attack halted, the Germans were finally able to overwhelm the French defenders and capture Faïd Pass.

In the early afternoon of January 30, Combat Command C was ordered to intervene in the Faïd battle by advancing north-eastward from Gafsa toward Sidi Bouzid and to attack 'in [the] flank the force of enemy tanks and infantry thrusting at Sidi Bouzid from the east'. Combat Command C bivouacked for the night 30 miles to the south-west of Sidi Bouzid, ready to resume its advance the following morning but still out of communication with McQuillin.

However, during the day, II Corps misinterpreted what was happening at Aïn Rebaou, assuming that friendly troops were advancing northwards when in actual fact they had been repulsed. Failing to understand that the Faïd battle was being lost, II Corps then returned to its plan for the Maknassy attack. At 4 p.m., Combat Command C, which was then nearing the Faïd battle area, was radioed a change of orders. Now they were to turn south and proceed with the Maknassy attack in co-ordination with Combat Command D. This meant that Combat Command A alone resumed the attack against Faïd at noon on February 1.

General McQuillin ordered Colonel Stark to bring his 26th Infantry south toward Sidi Bouzid and then to attack eastwards on an axis converging with Lieutenant Colonel Kern's advance toward the Aïn Rebaou Pass. Rather than risk his tanks against the German anti-tank guns, he planned to open with a very strong artillery barrage, followed by an infantry assault. McQuillin had set the time of attack late so as not to have the sun low in the eyes of his advancing force. The tanks were to be held in reserve for a later sweep against Faïd.

The infantry of both forces was methodically advancing behind the artillery barrage when suddenly a group of 15 German tanks emerged from Faïd village and hit the American northern flank, throwing the infantry back into confusion. The 3rd Battalion, 1st Armored Regiment, was directed to get the attack going again but the tanks soon came up against fire from well-concealed guns. Colonel Stark's force pulled back some distance east of Sidi Bouzid while Kern's southern group turned south-west and occupied Djebel Ksaïra. The following day, February 2, having received instructions to now go on the defensive, McQuillin organised positions on Djebel Ksaïra and set up a line east of Sidi Bouzid.

Meanwhile, as ordered, Combat Command C had opened its attack on the Maïzila Pass on the morning of February 1 but no sooner had it done so than another change of orders arrived from II Corps, postponing full commitment. Fredendall's indecision continued until 2 p.m. when he finally confirmed the instructions to secure the Maïzila Pass. Preparations were being made to mount the attack the following morning when the orders from II Corps were abruptly revised yet again, Combat Command C now being ordered north to Hajeb el Aïoun.

Judging that the American endeavours at the Maïzila Pass and Sened might interfere with the operations of his 21. Panzer-Division in the Faïd Pass, Oberst Hildebrandt despatched a provisional battle group under his Chief-of-Staff, Oberstleutnant Helmuth Strempel, to set up aggressive defensive actions from Djebel Matleg, north of Maknassy, to Djebel Bou Hedma to the south.

Strempel's counter-stroke against Combat Command D began at about 4 p.m. on February 2, heralded by a dive-bombing raid by Stukas that stunned the American infantry. At the same time 15 German tanks advanced on the left flank. Some of Maraist's troops panicked and started fleeing, jamming the road with vehicles heading west, but they were quickly checked and turned around. Five panzers managed to get through to the main American position but were driven back by tanks and tank destroyers and by 7 p.m. the situation had been restored.

Despite the German intervention, the American attack toward Maknassy was resumed at daylight on February 3 and by noon the forward elements — reconnaissance patrols of the 701st Tank Destroyer Battalion — were six miles from the town. During the afternoon, a flight of 15 B-25s first attacked Axis tanks near Maknassy but then turned to bomb Sened station which was in American hands.

During a conference with Anderson on the morning of February 1, Eisenhower directed that the central front must be securely held by employing the 1st Armored Division as a concentrated force, even if that involved pulling back from the Eastern Dorsale and evacuating Gafsa. And so, on the afternoon of the 3rd, II Corps ordered Colonel Maraist to break off the attack and return Combat Command D to Gafsa. The withdrawal was completed before daylight on February 4. This marked the end of the Maknassy undertaking.

The commander of this M3 light tank of the 13th Armored Regiment surveys the route ahead as the tank moves into position near El Guettar. This shot was possibly taken on January 24 when a raiding force started out from Gafsa to strike at the station at Sened before returning in the evening.

Meanwhile, the corps continued its attack on Maknassy using Combat Command D alone and Colonel Maraist's force assaulted Sened station on January 31. However, Axis aircraft repeatedly harassed the preparatory moves and a dive-bombing attack by eight Stukas at 1.30 p.m., and another later in the afternoon, shook the infantry and caused many casualties. By now it was too late to form up for an assault so it was decided to reorganise during the night for another attack at dawn.

The renewed attack proceeded slowly and it was 5 p.m. on February 1 before Combat Command D finally entered Sened station, the Axis defenders pulling back toward Maknassy. The Americans renewed their advance next morning and proceeded rapidly until 9.30 a.m. when their tanks were stopped by another dive-bombing attack. The force then deployed along a ridge, prepared to meet a counter-attack. At this point, Fredendall urged Colonel Maraist to put his infantry on the heights some six miles east of Sened by 10 a.m. next morning, reproaching him that 'too much time has been wasted already'.

Sbeïtla — the ancient Roman Sufetela — was a key crossroads across the southern opening of the Y-shaped mountain chains that marked the topography of Tunisia. A German photographer pictured the exotic names shown on this road sign just east of Sbeïtla, as it showed the 10. Panzer-Division insignia (a 'Y' with three tick marks) fixed to it.

ALLIED DISPOSITIONS

On the Allied left wing, in the north the First Army undertook to reorganize its V Corps. This was to restore the many small units that had become separated from their parent organisations, and also to create the long-deferred establishment of an army reserve. It was the arrival of the British 46th Infantry Division in the forward area, coupled with the introduction of elements of the US 34th Infantry Division into the French sector, that made it possible to consider withdrawing the British 6th Armoured Division from the Bou Arada valley into army reserve. Orders on February 12 specified that the division was to move to Rhardimaou to be refitted with new Sherman tanks that were being brought in via Bône. This day, the 16th/5th The Queen's Royal Lancers began to leave its old tanks at a depot at Ebba Ksour, south of El Kef, preparatory to receiving the Shermans.

Its own lighter tanks were to be handed over to the French.

The 18th Infantry Regiment was withdrawn from the V Corps on February 13-14 to prepare for transfer to the French XIXème Corps d'Armée, and the 26th Infantry Regiment was to be withdrawn from II Corps at the beginning of March and join with it. Once these moves had taken place, the 1st Infantry Division would be reunited after three months of being fragmented.

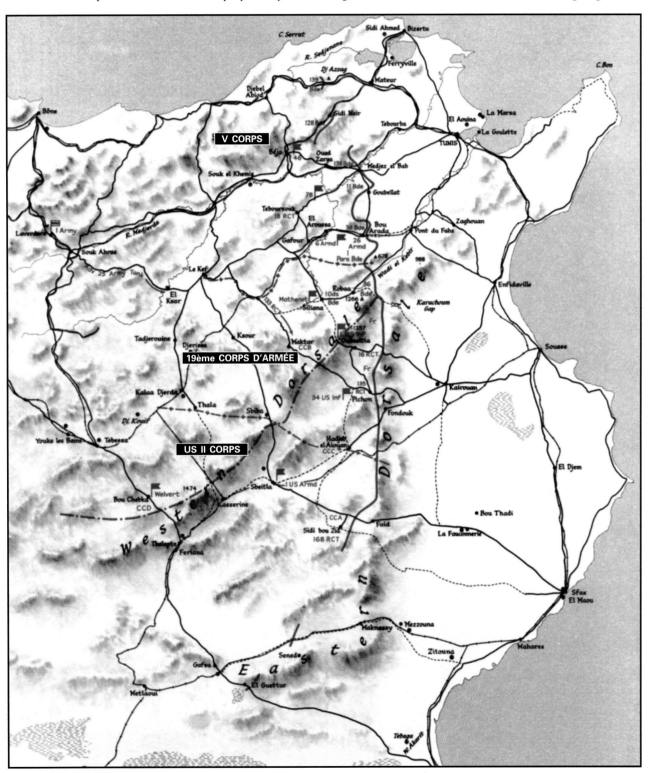

The dispositions of the First Army as they were on February 14 are indicated by a solid red line. From north to south they are the V Corps, the XIXème Corps d'Armée and the US II Corps.

The front line four days later, after the withdrawal of the right flank from the Eastern Dorsale to the Western Dorsale, is shown with dashes.

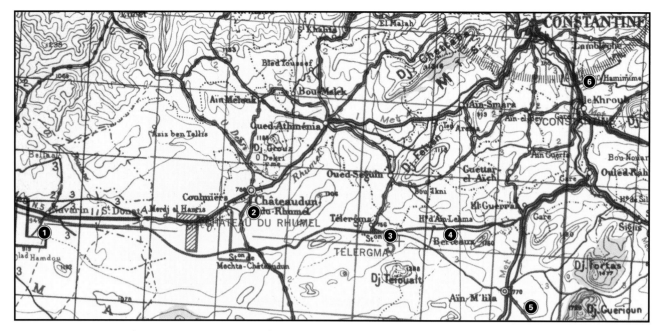

The interlude before attempting a second drive toward Tunis was due to the lack of Allied air support, but this had much improved by February. Steel matting for runways had been brought up, as well as fuel and other supplies, and new forward airfields began operations south-west (the sector on this map) and south-east of Constantine.

Meanwhile, the US 34th Infantry Division was moving up from the Oran area, its 133rd and 135th Infantry Regiments making the long journey to Tunisia during the second week of February. They were then to relieve the 1st Infantry Division to permit the division's consolidation into First Army reserve.

The southern flank of the French Corps was covered by Combat Command B of the 1st Armored Division. This force, which included 110

In addition to the B-25s of the 310th Bombardment Group established at Telergma [3] and the Spitfires of No. 152 Squadron established at Constantine [6] in December, B-17 squadrons from the 97th, 99th and 301st Bombardment Groups moved in during January and February to be based at Navarin [1], Châteaudun du Rhumel [2] and Aïn M'lila [5]. *Above:* Having moved in January to Berteaux [4], the 310th Bombardment Group was soon the main attacking force in the Allied offensive against Axis shipping supplying Tunisia launched from the 11th. On February 12, these B-25s were pictured taking off from Berteaux. *Right:* On January 9, B-25s from the US 12th Bombardment Group took part in a mission — together with Baltimore IIIs from the RAF's No. 232 Wing — to bomb the Mareth Line. In the foreground, 41-12863 was the aircraft of Captain Douglas W. Spawn, serving with the 82nd Bombardment Squadron.

Left: **At Youks les Bains, engineers are working with a bulldozer to fill in a bomb crater. By mid-February, units assigned to Youks les Bains comprised the 47th Bombardment Group manning A-20 bombers, the 33rd Fighter Group with P-40 fighters, and the 54th Observation Squadron flying P-38s. The Beaufighter** **seen here probably belonged to one of the two RAF night fighter squadrons (Nos. 153 and 600) based at Sétif, some 100 kilometres to the west.** *Right:* **The airfield was located about 150 kilometres south-east of Constantine but today has merged into the obscurity of a patchwork of agricultural fields.**

medium tanks, and was directly under First Army control, was positioned east of Maktar. Next to it on the southern side lay Combat Command C, a somewhat weaker group, and even further south was Combat Command A, reinforced by the 168th Infantry Regiment, both combat commands controlled by II Corps. At the same time, a small force was assembling at Fériana under command of Colonel Stark. At Gafsa, and southeast of it at the village of El Guettar, lay the extreme southern wing of the active Allied front.

The arc running from Sbeïtla through Kasserine and Fériana to Gafsa and El Guettar was screened by security detachments, and beyond them by roving patrols. The latter were conducted for II Corps by Squadrons B and D of the 1st Derbyshire Yeomanry.

After some argument, the Allied high command determined that Gafsa could not be strengthened enough to hold it against an Axis attack. If it came to it, the Gafsa force would have to be pulled back toward Fériana from where a counter-attack in sufficient strength could be mounted.

On February 13, Generals Eisenhower and Anderson met at General Fredendall's headquarters located near Tébessa to review the complete disposition of American, British and French forces. Eisenhower concluded that they were 'as good as could be made pending the development of an actual attack and in view of the great value of holding the forward regions, if it could possibly be done'. During the night, Eisenhower then travelled forward as far as Sbeïtla and Sidi Bouzid, returning to Tébessa a little before daylight.

First Lieutenant Ronald G. Macdonald of the 346th Fighter Squadron was shot down on February 17 while he was strafing a German convoy. Fortunately, Major Chuck Miller, a military **policeman with the 1st Armored Division, reached him before the Germans, helping him destroy the P-39. A German photographer was soon on the scene to picture the smoking wreck.**

The Germans launched their Operation 'Frühlingswind' on February 14, attacking westwards from the Faïd Pass. The US Combat Command A counter-attacked on the first morning but the attempt ended in utter disaster, the 3rd Battalion of the 1st Armored Regiment losing 44 of its 55 tanks. Combat Command C's attack the following day was also catastrophic, the 2nd Battalion of the 1st Armored Regiment suffering the loss of 46 Shermans.

Left: German army cameramen were soon on the spot to picture the wrecks of the two shattered American tank battalions. While the pictures they took are devoid of any caption material, fortunately this frame in the sequence showed a mountainous skyline in the background which helped pinpoint the location. *Right:* The photographer must have stood here, just south of the village of Faïd, looking eastwards towards Djebel Bou Dzer.

THE BATTLE OF SIDI BOUZID

At the beginning of February, Rommel reasoned that he could expect a fortnight's lull at Mareth, thanks to Montgomery's practice of methodically stockpiling supplies before an attack. So he intended to make full use of this and on February 3 he proposed that a spoiling attack should be launched to prevent Allied forces from striking from Gafsa towards the coast. Kesselring came to Tunisia on February 9 to confer with Rommel and von Arnim near Gabès and the two army commanders then adjusted their plans. The 5. Panzerarmee, using the 10. Panzer-Division and the 21. Panzer-Division, was first to break through the Faïd Pass, taking Sidi Bouzid and starting a drive for Sbeïtla (Operation 'Frühlingswind'). In the south, Kampfgruppe DAK,

Instrumental in breaking the 1st Armored Division counter-attack on February 14 was the 1. Kompanie of schwere Panzer-Abteilung 501, a force of six Tigers and nine PzKpfw IIIs. Attached to the 10. Panzer-Division on the 8th, the company started southwards from the sector north of Kairouan, where it had assembled after its involvement in Operation 'Eilbote'. After several night marches, the force joined up with Kampfgruppe Reimann on the 13th.

The Tigers took a sizeable share in the destruction of the 1st Armored's 3rd Battalion on February 14, the crews claiming to have knocked out 20 of the Shermans. The other losses presumably fell to the guns of the other components of Kampfgruppe Reimann: one platoon of Panzerjäger-Abteilung 90, the Sturmgeschütz-Batterie, and one platoon of Flak guns from Panzer-Artillerie-Regiment 90. The Tigers did not take part in any of the fighting on the 15th but on the next day, February 16, they moved in to scatter odd American elements near Sidi Bouzid where the company's commander, Oberleutnant Schmidt-Bornagius, was killed.

a composite German and Italian force of division strength created on February 10, was to follow this up by taking Gafsa in Operation 'Morgenluft'. Comando Supremo revised its directive on the 11th and Kesselring approved the plans to execute it.

Operation 'Frühlingswind' was launched on the morning of February 14 when two battle groups from the 10. Panzer-Division — Kampfgruppe Gerhardt and Kampfgruppe Reimann — debouched from the Faïd Pass to the west. Combat Command A counterattacked near Sidi Bouzid but the operation ended in utter disaster, the 3rd Battalion of the 1st Armored Regiment losing 44 of its 51 tanks. Combat Command C went in the following day but the 2nd Battalion was destroyed in turn, only four of its Shermans managing to escape. In the first two days of the German offensive, two tank battalions of the 1st Armored Division and a considerable portion of its artillery had been lost, and over 2,600 men were trapped on the hills near Sidi Bouzid.

On the evening of the 14th, the First Army decided to give up Gafsa. That night in a rainstorm, the American and French troops pulled back north-westwards as far as Fériana in the company of hordes of locals herding sheep, mules, and camels.

This blown-up M3A1 Stuart light tank lying by the side of the road between Faïd and Sbeïtla most likely belonged to the 1st Battalion of the 1st Armored Regiment. There was another tank battalion in the 1st Armored Division equipped with light tanks, the 1st Battalion, 13th Armored Regiment, but that unit was not deployed beyond Sbeïtla.

The failure of the American counter-attacks left two task forces — Lessouda Force on Djebel Lessouda and the 168th Regimental Combat Team on Djebel Ksaïra and Djebel Garet Hadid — isolated. Though his subordinate commanders pressed him to allow both forces to be withdrawn immediately, General Fredendall held off giving permission for two days. It was not until the afternoon of February 15, through messages dropped by air on Djebel Lessouda, that Lieutenant Colonel John K. Waters was finally told to get his force back during the night. A substantial group managed to infiltrate the enemy's outposts, and by dawn, 231 men had succeeded in reaching Djebel

Hamra, bringing with them some prisoners. Others got through to the north or south. However, in the end only around 250 of its 1,000-strong force managed to make their way back to friendly lines. The force commander, Lieutenant Colonel Waters was General Patton's son-in-law, and he was among the prisoners;. Meanwhile, some distance to the south, the 168th Combat Team remained stranded in two groups on Djebel Ksaïra and Djebel Garet Hadid for another day. Being kept under pressure, and crowded into smaller and smaller areas on each hill, by the evening of the 16th they were thirsty and hungry, finally being ordered to withdraw during the following night.

The Germans captured over 2,400 men on February 16 and 17 and the milestone provided the clue as to the location.

This is now highway P13, just west of the village of Faïd, looking westwards.

By mid-morning, Drake reported that men were abandoning their artillery positions and deserting the battlefield in panic. 'They're only shifting positions,' General McQuillin told him curtly. 'Shifting positions, Hell,' Drake radioed. I know panic when I see it.' Having destroyed all the weapons and equipment that could not be carried, the two groups of the 168th Combat Team worked their way down the slopes of Djebel Ksaïra and Djebel Garet Hadid. In complete darkness, they then started out across the plain, marching westwards toward Djebel Hamra about 15 miles away. However, when dawn broke they were still on the plain when German motorised troops opened up with heavy machine guns. In the official account of the events of February 17, Colonel Thomas D. Drake reported that his mixed command of some 400 men returned fire 'with the weapons that they had', confessing that only half of them were still armed. They began surrendering in small groups as the Germans closed in.

Around 800 prisoners were taken in the first group and 600, including Colonel Drake, in the second. All but a few of the 1,650 men of 168th Combat Team were captured. None of the photos in the film taken by the Germans confirm Drake's post-war claim that many of his men were barefooted because the Arabs had taken their footwear! They do confirm however, not surprisingly, that the men were terribly thirsty as the Germans did not have much water to spare. *Above:* The rest-stop over, the group starts out eastwards again. After spending a night in the desert where the temperature can drop to almost freezing, they were picked up by trucks early on the 18th and taken to Tunis. *Right:* The same view 70 years later. Djebel Bou Dzer stretches south from the Faïd Pass which lies off the picture to the left.

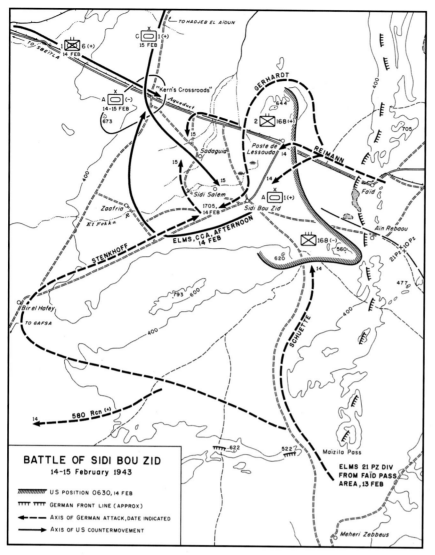

BATTLE OF SIDI BOU ZID
14-15 February 1943

///////// US POSITION 0630, 14 FEB

ㅜㅜㅜ ㅜㅜㅜ GERMAN FRONT LINE (APPROX)

◀ --- ◀ AXIS OF GERMAN ATTACK, DATE INDICATED

▶ AXIS OF US COUNTERMOVEMENT

Today Sidi Bouzid is best known as the birthplace of the Arab Spring uprising for it was there that Mohamed Bouazizi set himself on fire in December 2010 to protest against unfair treatment suffered at the hands of Tunisia's corrupt government. The repercussions of that tragic act were to resonate throughout the Arab world.

ment, but in the early hours of the 17th, the situation was such that Anderson permitted Fredendall to abandon Sbeïtla and Fériana.

Having re-organised their battle groups during the morning, the Germans resumed their advance shortly after noon and the leaders entered Sbeïtla at 5 p.m. on the 17th.

Meanwhile, in the south, Operation 'Morgenluft' was launched with Kampfgruppe DAK striking for Gafsa on the 15th. Commanded by Oberst Kurt von Liebenstein, the battle group then comprised Panzergrenadier-Regiment Afrika, the I. Abteilung of Panzer-Regiment 8, Aufklärungs-Abteilung 33, plus the usual artillery, engineers, and Flak detachments. (Although it was called the Afrikakorps Battle Group, it should not be confused with the main Afrikakorps.) This force was joined by mobile Italian elements stationed near Él Guettar.

The Allies having evacuated Gafsa, the town was swiftly entered on the evening of the 15th. Pressing on, after a short skirmish Kampfgruppe DAK captured Fériana around noon on February 17. Continuing the pursuit northwards, the German leaders pushed on to Thélepte where the Americans had some 120 aircraft based on two airfields: two A-20 squadrons of the 47th Bombardment Group, three Spitfire squadrons of the 31st Fighter Group, and two P-39 squadrons of the 81st Fighter Group. Those operational aircraft were hastily flown out but many were left behind — 34 according to the US Army official history — and they were destroyed after 60,000 gallons of aviation fuel was poured on them from storage tanks. Nevertheless, the Germans reported to have seized 20 tonnes of aviation fuel and 30 tonnes of lubricants.

In their first battle against the Wehrmacht, the US Army had suffered a painful defeat having lost 2,546 men killed or captured and 103 tanks, 18 field guns, and 280 vehicles captured or destroyed.

Despite urgent pleas from his subordinate commanders that the forces trapped on the hills near Sidi Bouzid be withdrawn immediately, General Fredendall withheld permission for two days. By the time he agreed, only around 250 out of the 1,000 men of Lessouda Force — a force of infantry, tanks, artillery, and tank destroyers, commanded by Lieutenant Colonel John K. Waters, executive officer of the 1st Armored Regiment — were able to make it back to friendly lines, and virtually the whole of the 168th Combat Team — some 1,650 strong — was captured. Some 2,400 American soldiers became POWs in this sector on February 16 and 17.

In the afternoon of the 16th, two battle groups of the 21. Panzer-Division began advancing toward Sbeïtla in conjunction with Kampfgruppe Gerhardt, soon hitting screening forces of Combat Command A. The situation quickly got out of hand and before long the Sbeïtla road was a mass of vehicles of Combat Command A streaming back through the town. Some elements stood fast, including tanks of the 3rd Battalion of the 13th Armored Regi-

Survivors of the Sidi Bouzid disaster, these three battered GIs were pictured on their return to American lines after travelling for three days across no-man's-land. The background suggests that the photo was taken in Kasserine.

Hitler's order in late January expanded the remit of General-feldmarshall Kesselring, and from then on he behaved as the C-in-C of the Axis armies in North Africa. On the evening of February 18, supporting Rommel's proposal earlier in the afternoon, he radioed to von Armin and Rommel, the two army commanders in Tunisia: 'I consider it essential to continue the attack toward Tébessa and northward by concentrating all available forces on the left wing and exploiting our recent successes with a blow that can still have vast consequences for the enemy'. Early in the morning of the 19th Kesselring flew to Tunisia to confer with von Arnim and Rommel.

The plan was for Kampfgruppe DAK to strike into the Kasserine Pass in a surprise attack at daybreak on February 19, while 30 kilometres to the east, a battle group of the 21. Panzer-Division would set out towards Sbiba. Oberst Bayerlein, Rommel's Chief-of-Staff at the Deutsch-Italienische Panzerarmee since December 1942, stands on the left next to Rommel's former Chief-of-Staff, Generalleutnant Alfred Gause. He was soon to become Chief-of-Staff of Heeresgruppe Afrika. The other officer standing is Generale Giuseppe Mancinelli, the liaison officer with the Italian command. Kesselring is hidden behind Rommel.

BATTLE OF THE KASSERINE PASS

The Allies completed their withdrawal to the Western Dorsale during the night of February 17/18 and American, British and French forces were then deployed to each of the areas of possible Axis penetration: Sbiba, Kasserine, and Tébessa.

Encouraged by air reconnaissance that revealed that the Allies were withdrawing westwards, on February 17 Rommel proposed a wide sweep around the north-west through Tébessa with the ultimate objective of Bône, outflanking the reserves that the Allies were feeding into their lengthening southern front and disrupting their lines of communication. Rommel's proposal met with full approval from Kesselring who had just returned to Italy from a visit to Hitler at his headquarters in East Prussia. Kesselring radioed to the two army commanders in Tunisia: 'I consider it essential to continue the attack toward Tébessa and northward by concentrating all available forces on the left wing and exploiting our recent successes with a blow that can still have vast consequences for the enemy. This is for your preliminary information. I shall speak in this sense to the Duce and Ambrosio today.'

The directive from Comando Supremo reached Rommel and von Arnim in the early hours of the 19th. Stating that 'a unique opportunity is

Thrown together ten days previously from various units, the makeshift Kampfgruppe DAK comprised Panzergrenadier-Regiment Afrika (formed from Sonderverband 288, initially a special unit formed for service in Iraq); the I. Abteilung of Panzer-Regiment 8, and Aufklärungs-Abteilung 33 (from the 15. Panzer-Division); the Luftwaffen-Jäger-Brigade 1 (the remnants of the famed Fallschirmjäger-Brigade Ramcke, another unit withdrawn from El Alamein); one group from Artillerie-Regiment 190; three batteries from Werfer-Regiment 71, plus engineers, Flak detachments, and elements of Italian infantry, armour and artillery. However, the surprise attack planned at daybreak fell behind schedule and it was not until the morning of the 19th that the leading elements of Panzergrenadier-Regiment Afrika finally moved up. This PzKpfw III belonged to the I. Abteilung of Panzer-Regiment 8 commanded by Hauptmann Hans-Günther Stotten.

Kampfgruppe DAK resumed the attack on the morning of February 20. While the attackers prepared to jump off *(left)*, six-barrelled Nebelwerfer 41 rocket launchers from Werfer-Regiment 71 opened up *(right)*. These particular photos precisely match the description

that Rommel gives in his diary. For example, on February 20 he wrote: 'From midday onwards the attack was resumed in fierce hand-to-hand fighting. Nebelwerfer were brought into action for the first time in Africa and proved very effective.'

now offered to force a decisive success in Tunisia', the order directed a deep thrust northward to threaten the rear of the British V Corps and force its withdrawal to the Algerian frontier. Using all the available mobile troops from his own Deutsch-Italienische Panzerarmee, and the 10. and 21. Panzer-Divisions from the 5. Panzerarmee now assigned to him, Rommel was directed to attack northwards with El Kef as his initial objective. Von Arnim was ordered to immediately recall those elements of the 10. Panzer-Division from the Fondouk—Kairouan area where he had just sent it. Also, he was told to harass and pin down the enemy with local attacks on his front.

The directive disappointed Rommel as he believed that to strike at El Kef, instead of making the wide circling movement through Tébessa toward Bône that he advocated, was 'an appalling and unbelievable piece of short-sightedness'. Knowing however that time was more valuable than objections, he ordered the attack to begin at first light on the 19th.

The plan was for the Kampfgruppe DAK, now commanded by General-major Karl Bülowius, formerly the Afrikakorps artillery commander, after

Rommel recorded that 20 tanks and 30 half-tracks had been captured on February 20. These M3 half-tracks were most probably those of the 3rd Battalion of the 6th Armored Infantry that were hastily abandoned by their drivers at the southern entrance to the pass, leaving the scattered infantrymen to try to pull back on foot through the German positions.

In the logistic situation that the Axis forces were facing in North Africa, the Germans were quick to put any captured vehicles back into use. When time permitted, German crosses were added.

This photograph was taken some distance before reaching the bridge over the Wadi Hatab, looking south. Djebel Chambi lies in the background.

This SdKfz 10 half-track is seen towing a captured British 25-pounder and ammunition trailer, moving in the direction of the Kasserine Pass.

This is the plain at the bottom of the pass, not far from the junction of the Tébessa and Thala roads. The view is looking north with Djebel Semmama in the distance.

Oberst Liebenstein was wounded by a mine explosion on February 16, to strike into the Kasserine Pass in a surprise attack at daybreak while the 21. Panzer-Division advanced from Sbeïtla through Sbiba to El Ksour, 80 kilometres north on the road to El Kef. The 10. Panzer-Division was to concentrate at Sbeïtla, ready to exploit the success of either the 21. Panzer-Division at Sbiba or Kampfgruppe DAK at Kasserine. (Following the death of Generalleutnant Fischer, who had been killed when his car drove into a minefield on February 1, Oberst von Broich was now in command of the 10. Panzer-Division.)

Early in the morning, February 19, Kesselring flew to Tunisia to ensure prompt execution of Comando Supremo's directive. He found that von Arnim had prepared a counter-proposal with a concentric attack toward El Kef, and thence down the Medjerda river, with Béja as the objective. Such an attack, von Arnim argued, would engage all the Allied forces instead of, as Rommel's plan would do, merely force them to fall back toward their centres of supply. Kesselring unequivocally rejected von Arnim's concept.

On the morning of February 21, while on the road to Thala, a force from the 10. Panzer-Division encountered a patrol from the 17th/21st Lancers and quickly knocked out six of their Crusaders. Together with Bayerlein, Rommel was soon on the spot to inspect them, this Crusader III with a triangle insignia denoting that it belonged to the A Squadron.

These photos were taken on February 21 when Rommel wrote that he went 'forward to the 10. Panzer-Division with Bayerlein and Horsters'. (Professor Hans Horsters was a doctor sent out to Africa in the summer of 1942 specifically to stay with Rommel and treat his debilitating health problems.) *Left:* When they came across these disabled M3 self-propelled 75mm anti-tank guns by the side of the road to Thala, Rommel explained in his diary that they 'had driven onto their own mines'. *Right:* Looking south by the side the P17 road, the Kasserine Pass is about one kilometre away from this bridge over the Wadi Hatab.

Left: **Oberst Otto Menton, the commander of Panzergrenadier-Regiment Afrika, checks his position with one of his subalterns.** *Right:* **The mountainous skyline of Djebel Semmama** helped establish the spot for this comparison taken near the P13 road to Tébessa some distance north of the junction with the road from Thala.

Back to the road to Thala, some distance away from the bridge over the wadi, the photographer pictured a platoon of PzKpfw IVs of Panzer-Regiment 7 pushing north into the pass. Firing the Panzergranate 40 armour-piercing shell which had a muzzle velocity of over 990 metres per second, the long-barrelled 75mm gun could penetrate five inches of armour at a range of 1,000 metres, easily knocking out the American Sherman and British Crusader and Valentine tanks that opposed them in Tunisia. *Right:* The pictures were taken about a kilometre from the bridge over the Wadi Hatab, looking south. A quarry has now chewed up the mountainside, completely changing the foreground, but the knolls of Djebel Semmama on the horizon still provide a perfect match.

The PK photographer then climbed the rocks by the side of the road for a grandstand view. This seemingly endless column of armour is the battle group of the 10. Panzer-Division is driving northwards into the pass.

At Rommel's urgent request, during the night of February 19-20 Comando Supremo followed up its directive with an order for reorganisation of command. Under the designation Gruppe Rommel, he was now to command the combined forces of the 1a Armata, charged with the defence of the Mareth position, and a force comprising the 10. Panzer-Division, the 21. Panzer-Division, and the Kampfgruppe DAK. The change went into effect at 6 a.m. on February 20.

At 9 a.m. on February 19, a battle group of the 21. Panzer-Division started north from Sbeïtla down the Sbiba road. The advance was uneventful until the leaders reached a belt of mines across the road. A passage was cleared through the mines and the advance resumed until it came upon another minefield, this one covered by strong British artillery. His main column stopped, Oberst Hildebrandt sent a

Amazingly, Rommel was then pictured driving past a captured M3 half-track in his Kfz 21 Kommandeurs-Cabriolet. Of his visit to the 10. Panzer-Division that day, Rommel wrote that 'the division was not getting forward fast enough and I had to be continually at them to keep the speed up; they did not seem to realise that they were in a race with the Allies reserves.

To form my own judgement of the situation I drove forward to the leading scouts to see what was happening.' *Right:* The author discovered that the photograph had been taken from the top of the escarpment lining the road with the Wadi Hatab in middle distance. A new bridge has since been built over the capricious wadi.

Generalmajor Karl Bülowius, the commander of Kampfgruppe DAK, established his command post at the southern entrance to the Kasserine Pass. At noon on the 22nd, Kesselring came to confer with Rommel at Kasserine. 'We agreed that a continuation of the attack towards El Kef held no prospect of success and decided to break off the offensive by stages.' Shortly before midnight that day, the appropriate orders were issued.

Having identified the mountain in background as Djebel Chambi, the author was able to track down exactly where the command post for Kampfgruppe DAK had been located. A convenient underpass below the railway line that ran down the pass off to the west of the road provided fitting shelter from artillery shelling and also from the winter rain.

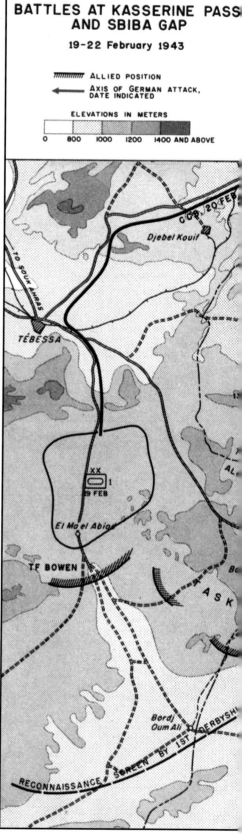

BATTLES AT KASSERINE PASS AND SBIBA GAP

19-22 February 1943

////// ALLIED POSITION

⟵ AXIS OF GERMAN ATTACK, DATE INDICATED

ELEVATIONS IN METERS

0   800   1000   1200   1400 AND ABOVE

battalion of Panzer-Regiment 5 — about 25 tanks and some lorry-borne infantry — in an attempt to sweep to the east, out of range of the British artillery, and then north.

At the Kasserine Pass, the surprise attack planned at daybreak was behind schedule and it was later in the morning when the two battalions of Panzer-grenadier-Regiment Afrika finally moved up. One climbed the eastern flanking hill of the pass, Djebel Semmama, while the other moved along the floor of the pass. The attackers took Point 974 — a prominent knoll up the shoulder of Djebel Semmama — but heavy fire from the American artillery prevented them from continuing down the mountain's western face. On the valley floor, the attackers pushed as far as Wadi Zebbeus, a tributary of the main Wadi Hatab, but were then stopped by artillery fire. The attack continued during the afternoon of the 19th as the grenadiers pushed slowly and persistently higher up the shoulder of Djebel Semmama.

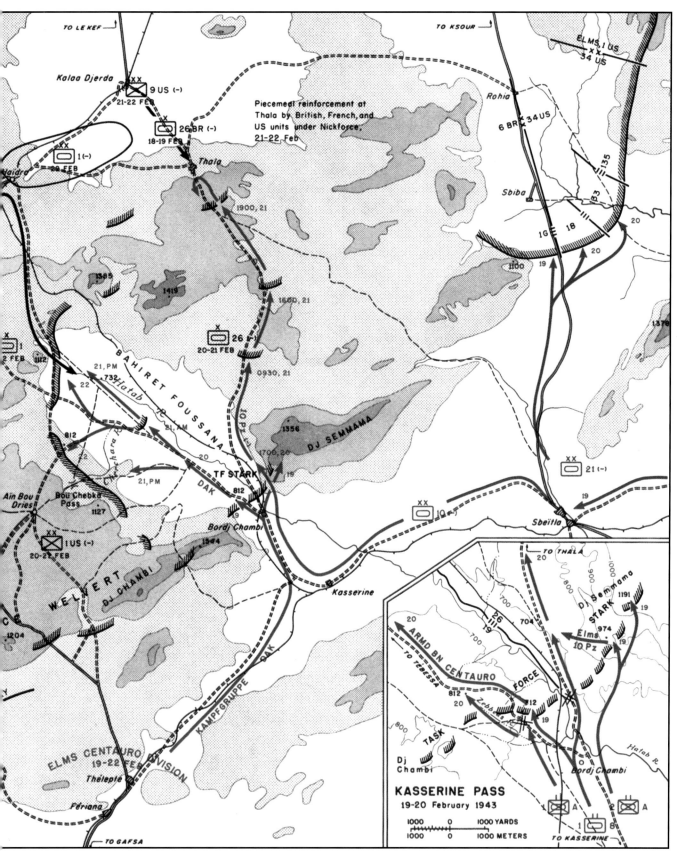

KASSERINE PASS

19-20 February 1943

| 1000 | 0 | 1000 YARDS |
| 1000 | 0 | 1000 METERS |

Faced with strong opposition at Sbiba where the leaders of the 21. Panzer-Division were still blocked, on the evening of the 19th Rommel ordered the 10. Panzer-Division to move to the Kasserine Pass and then head north along the Thala road. However, delayed by poor roads and bad weather, the 10. Panzer was slow

and by nightfall on February 19 its advance elements had not even reached Kasserine.

At 8.30 a.m. on the 20th, General-major Bülowius resumed the offensive at Kasserine, sending a force of tanks and infantry through the minefield on the Tébessa road. By noon, the American troops in this sector

were falling back, followed by their tanks and tank-destroyers. From Thala where it had just arrived, the 26th Armoured Brigade sent a detachment south to Kasserine. Comprising a squadron of the 2nd Lothians and Border Horse with 11 Valentine and Crusader tanks, the force was dubbed 'Gore Force'.

February 23 passed without pressure being applied on the withdrawing Axis forces. *Left:* A British photographer, Sergeant Bourne, pictured Allied shells exploding on a German-held position at the Kasserine Pass. *Right:* The same view today from beside the P17, a few kilometres from the entrance to the pass, with Djebel Semmama in the background.

Rommel now drove to Bülowius's headquarters to confer with him and Oberst von Broich. Rommel made clear that he was 'extremely angry' about the slow advance of von Broich's leading troops and complained that 'valuable time was being squandered'. He instructed that an all-out attack was to be launched at Kasserine that afternoon with Kampfgruppe DAK on the left and the available elements of the 10. Panzer-Division on the right.

The American defence soon disintegrated under this assault. The attackers first opened the road to Tébessa, along which armoured elements of Divisione Centauro pushed some eight kilometres without finding any Allied troops. At the same time on the right side of the pass, von Broich's troops forced back Gore Force towards Thala, destroying all 11 tanks.

Sizeable American forces were now cut off on Djebel Semmama, including the 3rd Battalion of 6th Armored Infantry whose armoured personnel carriers stood parked near the base of the mountain. The drivers had taken

The time finally set for the Allied counter-attack was 6.30 a.m. on February 25. The day before, in preparation for the attack, this squadron of Shermans from the 16th/5th Lancers moved forward down the Thala road.

With American forces on the right wing and British on the left, the Allied attack moved into the pass during the morning only to find it free of any Axis forces. *Left:* While a sapper of Royal Engineers' 8th Field Squadron removes mines from the road, infantry and carriers of the 3rd Battalion of the Grenadier Guards pass by over difficult terrain *(right).*

On the right wing, the advance was made by CCB, 1st Armored Division, with the 16th Infantry Regiment from the 1st Infantry Division attached. The Axis rearguards, which had barred occupation of Djebel Zebbeus until late on the previous evening, had all pulled out during the night, and the artillery preparation drew no response. However, progress was slow because of road demolitions, mines, and booby traps.

Left: **On February 26, Signal Corps photographer George McGray pictured elements of the 2nd Battalion, 16th Infantry, moving down the Kasserine Pass along the road from Tébessa after they had 'cleared the roads and fields of mines'.** *Above:* **This winding stretch of the P13 road near Boulaaba, the village at the junction of the road from Tébessa with that from Thala, makes for a perfect comparison.**

off, leaving the scattered riflemen to infiltrate back on foot. By nightfall the Germans were in firm possession of the Kasserine Pass and about 20 tanks and 30 troop carriers had fallen into their hands.

Further north, the Kampfgruppe of the 21. Panzer-Division had also resumed its attack at Sbiba on February 20 but extremely difficult terrain, with deep wadis and extensive soft areas, and powerful Allied artillery fire, brought this advance to a standstill.

At noon on the 20th, Kesselring came to confer with Rommel at his advanced

command post located at the entrance to the Pass. The two field marshals agreed that the Axis forces must break out of the pass during the day if the operation was to succeed.

The Allies finally took significant measures to man and organise their defences in the rear of the Kasserine Pass during the night of February 20/21. Fredendall ordered Combat Command B to move over to the right wing where its commander, Brigadier General Paul Robinett, was to take charge of all the troops in an area south of Wadi Hatab to defend the secondary passes at

Djebel el Hamra and stop the German advance toward Tébessa. On the left wing, Brigadier Charles Dunphie, the commander of the 26th Armoured Brigade, was to lead all the forces remaining on the north side of the wadi to protect the way to Thala.

On February 21, the leaders of the Kampfgruppe DAK surprised elements of Combat Command B near the Bou Chebka Pass and forced them to pull back, leaving five 105mm howitzers and 30 vehicles in German hands. US artillery soon pinned down the attackers on Point 812, the Americans

Left: **Signal Corps photographer Lorenzo Alcock pictured Private Vincent Biondi, Private Andy Parillo and Corporal Robert Posner, from Company D, 16th Armored Engineers, checking Kasserine** railway station for mines. *Right:* **Most of the railway lines built in Tunisia during the period of French colonisation are still running and the station at Kasserine has survived unscathed.**

227

Left: Touring the battlefield on February 26, Sergeant McGray pictured a GIs inspecting this disabled PzKpfw IV. The clues to which unit it belonged are the 'Wolfsangel' emblem, denoting Panzer-Regiment 8, and the triangle divided by a vertical bar on the turret, the sign of the 15. Panzer-Division. This panzer was one of the seven reported lost by the regiment on February 20. *Right:* The mountain face of Djebel Semmama across the valley gave a perfect reference point to trace where the tank had been knocked out: beside the Tébessa road near the village of Boulaaba.

counter-attacked and the German leaders fell back toward the Kasserine Pass, abandoning the guns and vehicles captured earlier.

By daylight on the 22nd, the leaders of Panzer-Regiment 7 on the northern wing were just south of Thala when heavy shelling hit them. Expecting a counter-attack, von Broich decided to postpone any offensive drive on the town, a decision soon approved by Rommel after he had personally reconnoitred the position. Kesselring then visited Rommel at his command post and both agreed that the time had come to break the operation off and withdraw their forces. Comando Supremo was so advised and, shortly before midnight on the 22nd, the appropriate orders were issued.

The II Corps took no action on February 23 and 24 to try to kill or capture the vulnerable retreating forces and the withdrawal of the Axis force that was north-west of the Kasserine Pass was soon successfully completed. A timid pursuit finally started on the morning of the 25th, halting at the line Hajeb el Aïoun—Sidi Bouzid—Gafsa which the Axis forces were to hold for the next fortnight.

On his way back to Rome Kesselring stopped at the Tunis airfield where he summoned von Arnim to meet him. He later recollected that he censured him for withholding sizeable elements of the 10. Panzer-Division from Rommel, thus weakening the attack. There here is no contemporary record to confirm this

German materiel losses in south-western Tunisia for February 16-24 were comparatively light: just 20 tanks and 61 motor vehicles. AFPU photographer Sergeant Wackett photographed this PzKpfw III of the 10. Panzer-Division at the side of the Thala road which, by the size of the explosion, appears to have been subjected to a demolition charge. Another shot of the same tank shows its turret bearing the bison insignia indicating that it belonged to Panzer-Regiment 7.

On February 24, on the road to Tébessa, Staff Sergeant Alcock pictured American and French soldiers inspecting this disabled M14/41 Italian tank. Armed with a 47mm gun, the tank proved unreliable in the difficult African terrain and it caught fire easily when hit.

Alcock then photographed these GIs trying hard to start the engine of a Horch 901. The vehicle had belonged to an army signal unit and the telescopic antenna aroused some curiosity. When fully extended, the Kurbelmast (KM8) could be raised to eight metres.

however and in post-war interview, von Arnim insisted that the elements he was accused of withholding were already in contact with Allied forces in the Med-jerda valley, not in reserve, and that the 10. Panzer-Division was sent as it stood at the time orders were received. In later years Kesselring was to attribute the Axis failure in part to von Arnim's departure from orders, although holding Rommel responsible for not having insisted on full compliance.

German personnel losses in the sector were comparatively light with 201 men killed, 536 wounded and 252 missing. Twenty tanks were lost, as well as 61 vehicles and six armoured vehicles. (Italian losses are not known.) *Left:* The price of defeat on the road to Thala. Sergeant McGray of the Signal Corps came across the body of a dead crewman lying beside a PzKpfw III, and British photographer Sergeant Bowman just happened to picture the same body *(below).*

Although the Axis objective to bring about a westward withdrawal of the First Army by penetrating its southern flank had been frustrated, nevertheless the attack inflicted substantial losses in men and matériel on the Allies. Most heavily hit was the 1st Armored Division. Its 1st Armored Regiment had suffered such losses to its 2nd and 3rd Battalions that they temporarily had to be combined in a provisional 23rd Battalion. At the same time, one company each from the 81st Reconnaissance Battalion, 16th Armored Engineer Battalion, and 91st Armored Field Artillery Battalion, had to be completely re-equipped. Losses by the 168th Combat Team of the 34th Infantry Division also ran high. Incomplete German reports give an idea of the number of prisoners taken and the matériel destroyed or captured for the period February 14-22 as 4,000 prisoners, 235 tanks, 110 self-propelled guns and reconnaissance vehicles, 95 personnel carriers, 67 anti-tank guns, and large numbers of anti-aircraft guns, heavy mortars and machine guns. Around 45 tons of ammunition were captured, with 25,000 gallons of fuel and a large amount of engineer equipment.

The 18th Army Group was created on February 20 with General Alexander in command. By the beginning of March, he had three headquarters subordinated to him: the Eighth Army which was approaching the Axis Mareth Line in southern Tunisia; the First Army which was in northern Tunisia making slow progress eastwards towards Tunis, and the US II Corps deployed in southern Tunisia, licking its wounds after the setbacks at Sidi Bouzid and Kasserine.

On February 21, Alexander announced that the tasks of his army groups would now have two phases. The first was for the Eighth Army to break through the Mareth Line, while the First Army would help by mounting timed attacks to draw off Axis reserves which could otherwise be used against the Eighth Army. In the second phase, both armies would direct their efforts to wipe out the Axis forces in their last bridgehead. Also, as decided at Casablanca, the campaign in Tunisia had to end by April 30 latest so that Operation 'Husky', the invasion of Sicily, could be launched before August.

The Axis command was now facing a dramatic supply situation. During January and February 1943, the Allies had progressively gained control over the vital triangle of the Mediterranean bordered by Sardinia, Sicily and Tunisia and waters and ports of the Tyrrhenian

Oberst Rudolf Lang (centre), the commander of Kampfgruppe Lang, with Oberst Walther Barenthin, commanding Fallschirm-Regiment Barenthin, at a staff meeting.

Fighting for the Initiative

Sea as well. Axis shipping suffered increasing risks of air, submarine and surface attack, added to the increasingly difficult task of vessels navigating through their own and British mine-fields. Though not many ships struck mines, the narrow swept channels left little room for manoeuvre when convoys were subjected to bombing. Against mounting Allied opposition, less than 30,000 men were transported to Tunisia in February, and deliveries were only 33,000 tonnes of supplies, not including the 52 tanks, 1,483 vehicles and 157 guns delivered.

Operation 'Ochsenkopf' was designed to take the initiative in the north. Kampfgruppe Lang comprised 14 Tigers, 20 PzKpfw IVs and 40 PzKpfw IIIs. The latter tanks came from the II.

Abteilung of Panzer-Regiment 7, and the schwere Panzer-Abteilung 501, which had just consolidated with it, being redesignated as the regiment's third battalion.

The long-prepared reorganisation for an Axis united command in Tunisia was put into effect during the night of February 19/20. The Deutsch-Italienische Panzerarmee was inactivated and replaced by the 1a Armata which took over the defence of the Mareth Line under Generale Giovanni Messe, Oberst Fritz Bayerlein being appointed as his Chief-of-Staff. On February 23, Heeresgruppe Afrika was created, commanded by Rommel, and its headquarters created from that of the former Deutsch-Italienische Panzerarmee. The new army group commanded the 1a Armata and the 5. Panzerarmee. Knowing that his days in Africa were numbered, Rommel only agreed to take on the position after he had been assured that he could set his own date for relinquishing command to von Arnim.

On February 26 von Arnim warned Rommel that in the dire logistical situation, the 1a Armata and 5. Panzerarmee should be concentrated to have a chance to successfully defend a smaller area. Messe was on the same wavelength when he wrote on the 27th that the 1a Armata was too weak to hold the Mareth Line and suggested a retreat to Wadi Akarit, just north of Gabès, while there was still time.

On March 1 Rommel forwarded these observations to Comando Supremo, OKW, and Kesselring, together with his own views. Heeresgruppe Afrika was far too weak for its long front and the supply situation was desperate. While he would do what he could with spoiling attacks, the Allies would probably move at the next full moon when they would easily drive a wedge between his two armies. The only remedy was to withdraw the armies into a smaller bridgehead in northern Tunisia that could then be held for some time. Any other policy would lead to the destruction of the 1a Armata and 5. Panzerarmee and the loss of the Axis presence in Africa.

Kesselring disagreed with these views, stressing that widely-ranging mobile formations would check the Allies and gain time for reinforcements and equipment to arrive to strengthen the front. On March 6 he informed Rommel that Hitler and Comando

In heavy rain, a column of German troops escorting British prisoners leaves Sidi Nsir heading north along the railway tracks.

This railway line is now disused yet the author found the crossing and the station (in the background) still looking much as it did during the war.

Left: **This battle group has halted near the station but it is difficult to determine when the photos were taken as it could be either on February 27 or 28 when Lang waited in vain for the Grenadier-Regiment 47 to achieve an enveloping movement in** the Djebel Zebla to dislodge the British at Hunt's Gap just to the west. A captured American half-track, now in German service, has joined other lorries and motorcycles parked near the station. *Right:* Time has stood still in this corner of North Africa.

231

Left: **The station building was taken over for a field hospital, wounded German and British soldiers being brought in using this Kübelwagen, prominently marked with red crosses** although it was hardly an ideal vehicle for carrying stretcher cases. *Right:* **Closer inspection of the building revealed it to be quite derelict.**

Supremo rejected his advice to pull back and concentrate the two armies into a smaller bridgehead.

Unwilling to give up the 10. and 21. Panzer-Divisions to the 1a Armata, as the directive from Comando Supremo on February 23 had ordered, von Arnim flew to Rome on the 24th (without informing Rommel) to gain Kesselring's backing for a major offensive in the north. The underlying assumption of his plan was that the Allies had greatly weakened their front in this sector by moving troops to oppose Rommel's drive on Thala. Kesselring supported the plan and on the 25th von Arnim issued orders for Operation 'Ochsenkopf'.

Korpsgruppe Weber was to launch the main blow toward Béja, Teboursouk and El Aroussa (from north to south).

Left: **Co-incidently, this direction sign nearby pointed towards the objective of the operation — Béja — and to Ksar Mezouar where the German advance was soon to be halted in its tracks.** **The emblem of the schwere Panzer-Abteilung 501, a stalking Tiger, can be seen on the left support.** *Right:* **Lightly wounded men were laid on the platform.**

On the right wing in the northern coastal sector, Division von Manteuffel was to launch a thrust aimed at Sedjenane and Djebel Abiod. (Following the death of Generalleutnant Fischer, and the taking over of the 10. Panzer-Division by Oberst von Broich, from the 7th Generalmajor Hasso von Manteuffel assumed command of the Division von Broich which then changed its title to Division von Manteuffel.)

Operation 'Ochsenkopf' began on February 26. On the left wing, in the Teboursouk—El Aroussa sector, Korpsgruppe Weber made some progress on the first day but Allied counter-attacks soon restored the line. On the corps right wing, Kampfgruppe Lang, trying to capture Béja, came up against a detachment of the 5th Hampshires and the 155th Battery Royal Artillery at Sidi Nsir. The British force was overrun during the afternoon and all the field guns were lost.

Oberst Rudolf Lang resumed his advance the following day along the road to Béja with his tanks inter-

In front of the station, infantry appears to be packing up, possibly part of this force of Grenadier-Regiment sent to the enveloping movement in the Djebel Zebla.

Left: Lang later recalled how Allied aircraft were very active — hence the 20mm anti-aircraft gun set up at the intersection. *Right:* The main road runs south to Béja which was once the objective of Kampfgruppe Lang.

spersed with lorry-borne infantry and armoured cars. As they drove into a défilé at Ksar Mezouar they ran straight into an ambush as the 128th Infantry Brigade had emplaced five batteries of field artillery and one battery of anti-tank guns along a line of commanding ground. Overnight rain had turned the fields into mud so the Germans were unable to leave the road to outflank the British gunners. Tank after tank was knocked out and any that tried to risk the soft ground on either side were soon bogged down. After the Germans withdrew, leaving behind many disabled tanks including several Tigers, British engineers went in to disable as many as possible to prevent their recovery.

By March 1, Kampfgruppe Lang was down to just seven tanks fit to fight. Although many of the losses were later recovered and repaired, leaving the net loss 22 including seven Tigers, the setback caused turmoil in Heeresgruppe Afrika headquarters. Rommel later noted that 'It made me particularly angry to see how the few Tigers we had in Africa were thrown into attack through a marshy valley where their principle advantage, the long range of their heavy guns, was completely ineffective'.

Oberst Lang resumed the advance along the road on the 27th but the leaders came up against six batteries of the 128th Infantry Brigade at Ksar Mezouar. These comprised five batteries of field artillery and one of anti-tank guns, emplaced along a line of commanding ground. Also as rain had turned the fields into mud, any tank that tried to leave the road to outflank the British gunners soon became bogged down.

The Germans persevered with their attack throughout the night but to no avail. Major Lueder, the battalion commander, was wounded, as were several of his officers. Many panzers were left immobilised including seven Tigers, and by the 28th the Tiger battalion was down to two Tigers, three PzKpfw IIIs and two PzKpfw IVs. Some of the stranded tanks were later recovered, as was Tiger '813' seen here, but the net loss of this operation amounted to 22 tanks, including seven Tigers.

Nevertheless, the battle continued for the next four days in the vicinity of Ksar Mezouar, the Germans pushing on further up the defile, but the men were exhausted and soon had to dig in defensive positions in the hills.

On the right wing, Division von Manteuffel made a slow, yet sizeable advance over the next three weeks, pushing the 139th Infantry Brigade back and taking El Aouna on March 1, Sedjenane on the 4th and Tamera on the 17th.

On March 1 the Germans finally gave up in this sector giving the Royal Engineers the opportunity to finish off the panzers left behind with demolition charges. GIs were later photographed inspected the damage to '823' and '833'. When the schwere Panzer-Abteilung 501 was consolidated with Panzer-Regiment 7 before Operation 'Ochsenkopf', and was redesignated as the regiment's third battalion, the former 1. Kompanie of Tigers then became the 7. Kompanie and the 2. Kompanie became the 8. Kompanie. American engineers came in to finish the job, the destruction wrought at Ksar Mezouar being very impressive.

Left: **The original captions to this series of photos taken in March 1943 by Signal Corps photographer Sergeant Victor W. Groshon give no clues as to where he took the photos. Some authors have previously described them as being taken in** Casablanca and it was a real challenge to track down the correct location. *Right:* **The author finally worked out that they were actually taken in Rabat, in front of Chamber of Commerce building at No. 2 Rue Ghandi.**

PATTON ENTERS THE FIGHT

General Alexander's judgement of the performance of General Fredendall, the US II Corps commander, during the recent battle was unfavorable, and he made his opinion known to Eisenhower. At Eisenhower's request, Major General Bradley carried out an inspection of II Corps, and in early March Eisenhower had further confirmation about Fredendall at a command conference at Tébessa. Eisenhower asked Bradley: 'What do you think of the command here?' Bradley replied, 'It's pretty bad. I've talked to all the division commanders. To a man they've lost confidence in Fredendall as the corps commander.'

When his Chief-of-Staff, General Walter B. Smith, and his G-3, Brigadier General Lowell W. Rooks, all confirmed the poor performance by Fredendall.

The photographs were taken just prior to Patton's departure for the Tunisian battlefront when he said goodbye to his staff officers in the building that housed the headquarters of the I Armored Corps. *Above:* **From L-R: Colonel Irving C. Avery, Captain John M. Thistle of the MP Company, and 2nd Lieutenant M. A. Graupner from the Provost Marshal's section.** **Also present at the ceremony, but not seen in this shot, were Brigadier General William H. Wilbur, I Armored Corps commander; his Chief-of-Staff, Colonel Hobart R. Gay; Major General Ernest Harmon, commanding officer 2nd Armored Division, and Brigadier General William W. Eagles, deputy commander, 3rd Infantry Division.**

Meeting Patton at Algiers on March 5, Eisenhower told him to go to Constantine to confer with his new superior, General Alexander, commander of 18th Army Group. He acquainted Patton with the plans for the Eighth Army to attack the Axis holding the Mareth Line in southern Tunisia. Patton was to launch a supporting effort from the west to attract Axis forces from the Eighth Army front. Patton spent the night in Constantine and then made for II Corps headquarters where he arrived about 10 a.m. *Right:* Witnesses later describe him arriving at Djebel Kouif, a small mining town 25 kilometres north of Tébessa where the II Corps HQ was located, standing 'erect like a charioteer' in the leading vehicle of a siren-blaring caval-cade of armoured vehicles. Eisenhower came to see Patton on March 16 to confirm his promotion to Lieutenant General and award him the extra star, although the caption did not state where the meeting had taken place. To make it even more diffi-cult, it was exactly when Patton left Djebel Kouif to establish his new HQ at Fériana.

When the author was researching this for *The Desert War Then and Now*, he ordered an overexposed print of this photo *(left)* so that the view outside the window became visible *(centre)*.

From this it was possible to ascertain that the photo had been taken at Djebel Kouif as it showed the power station *(right)* for the phosphate mine, which had closed down decades ago.

Eisenhower was now determined to bring in a new corps commander. The choice fell on General Patton who was then commanding US I Armored Corps in Morocco, and was busy detailing plans for Operation 'Husky', the invasion of Sicily scheduled for later in the year. Warned on March 4 that he was to immediately depart for Tunisia where he would be the new, temporary, comman-der of the II Corps, Patton noted in his diary: 'Well, it is taking over rather a mess but I will make a go of it'.

Patton took command of II Corps on March 6, bringing with him a new Chief-of-Staff, Brigadier General Hugh J. Gaffey, and other staff officers. General Bradley then became the deputy corps commander, being designated to succeed Patton as soon as operations in southern Tunisia were completed.

Summoned to Algiers, Patton met Eisenhower on the airfield on March 5. Patton was told to take command of II Corps and get it back on its feet with all possible speed. He was to restore American prestige, give the soldiers back their self-respect, and prove their ability to defeat the Germans. He was to institute intensive training, re-equip-ping and re-organisation, applying all

In an informal ceremony, Eisenhower awards the extra star to a delighted Patton.

On February 20, the 18th Army Group was created with General Alexander in command, having three headquarters subordinated to him: the First Army, the II Corps, and the Eighth Army. This shot of him with General Patton was taken later in 1943, during Operation 'Husky', in company with Rear Admiral Alan C. Kirk on board USS *Ancon*.

the 34th and 9th Divisions, with the 1st Infantry and 1st Armored Divisions training and recuperating to the rear. With the 13th Field Artillery Brigade and the 1st Tank Destroyer Group that had been parcelled out to the four divisions and to corps reserves, in all the force comprised about 88,000 men.

With the prescribed push eastwards due for mid-March, Patton had a little more than a week to knock II Corps into shape. He immediately travelled throughout the corps sector in a motorcade of armoured cars and motorcycle escorts, visiting every battalion in his four divisions, inciting commanders and giving pep-talks to the troops. He issued strict orders that all men must wear helmets, ties and leggings at all times, personally carrying out inspections and fining officers and men for infractions. At the same time he saw to it that new equipment, uniforms and mail arrived speedily and improved the men's living conditions by insisting on better rations and well-prepared meals.

On March 12, Patton was promoted to lieutenant general. He lost no time in unpacking a three-star flag and adding a third star to his helmet, collar insignia and to the red flag on his vehicles.

the lessons learnt thus far. He was to have no qualms about removing inefficient commanders. Also, as his corps would be fighting under British command, he should instil in his men a spirit of genuine partnership with the British.

Following the Sidi Bouzid and Kasserine setbacks, Alexander lacked confidence in the capacity of II Corps to execute the operation under its own responsibility and he made sure to carefully instruct Patton as to the limitations of his task. He was to seize Gafsa and take the key passes leading through the Eastern Dorsale at El Guettar and Maknassy but he was not to proceed into the coastal plain. Also, at all times, all II Corps movements were to be subject to 18th Army Group's approval. Patton later complained in a letter to General Marshall: 'All I have is the actual conduct of the operations prescribed.'

On the morning of March 6, Patton arrived at the II Corps command post at Djebel Kouif near Tébessa and formally relieved Fredendall, handing him a hand-written letter from Eisenhower. Fredendall left immediately afterwards. (He would return to the States, be promoted to lieutenant general and take command of an army in training.)

Present at the corps headquarters was Major General Omar N. Bradley, who had been sent there by Eisenhower as his 'eyes and ears' beside Fredendall during the height of the Kasserine crisis. Patton was uncomfortable with Bradley's status and, with Eisenhower's approval, he made him his Deputy Corps Commander. Later on, at an appropriate time, Bradley was to take over the corps to allow Patton to return to planning the invasion of Sicily.

The II Corps then comprised four divisions holding a 60-mile line which ran from Hajeb el Aïoun in the north via Sidi Bouzid to Gafsa in the south. They were

On March 17, Eisenhower and Alexander arrived at Fériana to confer with Patton. The author traced the correct building, which had originally built by the French as a tax office, but it now lay within the perimeter of a Tunisian army barracks. Unfortunately, a polite request to the commanding officer to take a comparison photograph was met by an equally polite refusal.

237

Flak guns were set up to protect the Luftwaffe airfield near El Djem, between Sfax and Sousse.

This was a difficult comparison to take as the old Roman amphitheatre is now hemmed in by the modern city.

THE BATTLE OF MEDENINE

We must now leave the First Army and II Corps sectors for a moment to catch up with what had been happening in southern Tunisia where the 1a Armata was up against the Eighth Army.

While Montgomery was building up his reserves, the Axis had made the most of the hiatus to build defences with such scanty materials as could be procured. Following his agreement to Kesselring on March 1 that he would do what he could with spoiling operations, Rommel then turned to attack Medenine, an important road junction in the centre of the Eighth Army front. Generale Messe and the staff of the Afrikakorps were to devise the final plan of the operation which envisaged cutting through the British deployed in front of the Mareth Line, and to divide and destroy them. Code-named Operation 'Capri', it provided for the commitment of two main groups in co-ordinated blows from the north-west, west and south-west, using 140 tanks and 10,000 infantry.

Allied air superiority in Tunisia had one remarkable moment on April 7 when British fighter-bombers unbeknowingly strafed a vehicle in which the new Chief-of-Staff of the 10. Panzer-Division was riding. Oberstleutnant Claus Schenk Graf von Stauffenberg had only taken over a few weeks previously after the division commander, Generalleutnant Fischer, had been killed and his Chief-of-Staff, Oberstleutnant Ulrich Bürker, seriously wounded when their car triggered a mine. Severely wounded in the air attack, von Stauffenberg was evacuated to Germany, finally losing his left eye, his right hand, and two fingers of his left hand. As time would show, these injuries keeping him away from the front were to allow him to play a leading role in the July 1944 plot to kill Hitler. Here he is seen (right) in North Africa with Oberst von Broich, the 10. Panzer-Division commander.

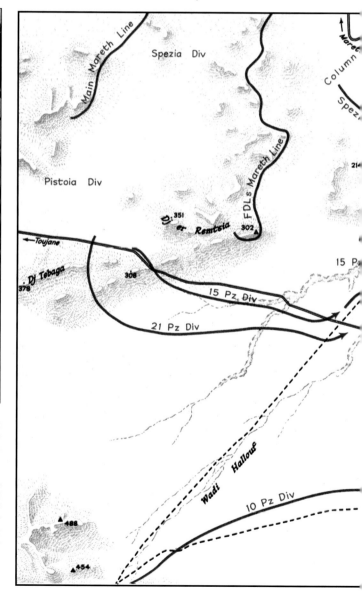

The Afrikakorps (taken over from March 5 by Generalleutnant Hans Cramer) was to launch the main attack. In the centre, moving from the Toujane area, the 15. Panzer-Division had the objective of Zemlet el Lebene and Hir Ksar Kourine, while on its right the 21. Panzer-Division was to aim at two ridges that were believed to be occupied by British artillery. On the right wing, debouching from the Hallouf Pass, the 10. Panzer-Division was to take Metameur. On the left (northern) wing, between the Mareth—Medenine coastal road and the sea, a battle group under the command of Generalmajor Theodor von Sponeck, the commander of the 90. leichte Afrika-Division, was to push southwards in the direction of Zemlet el Lebene and Hir Ksar Kourine with four German battalions in the centre, the Trieste Battle Group on the left and La Spezia Battle Group on the right. On the far right (south), reconnaissance elements were to block the road from Foum Tatahouine to prevent the arrival of reinforcements.

Supplies of ammunition and fuel were very short, and any hope for making a surprise attack was lost through Ultra decrypts and air reconnaissance

Operation 'Capri', the Axis offensive launched in the Medenine sector, ended as a complete failure, losing 40 tanks on March 6 and 7 for no gain whatsoever. The overwhelming superiority of the British gunners had secured the victory as illustrated by these three burning PzKpfw IIIs.

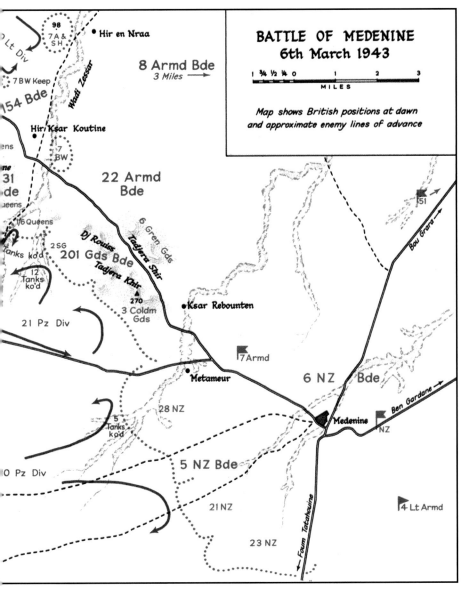

BATTLE OF MEDENINE
6th March 1943

MILES

Map shows British positions at dawn
and approximate enemy lines of advance

spotting the approach of the panzer divisions, particularly the 10. Panzer-Division moving from Gabès through Matmata towards the Hallouf Pass.

The attack was aimed at the front occupied by the XXX Corps. On the right, the 51st (Highland) Division held a sector about 15 miles wide from the Mareth—Medenine road to the coast with the 8th Armoured Brigade three miles behind. In the centre — the Axis main objective — lay the 7th Armoured Division, with the 131st Infantry Brigade occupying the Zemlet et Lebene ridge, the 201st Guards Brigade the Tadjera Khir heights, and the 22nd Armoured Brigade behind them. On the left (south-western) wing, the New Zealand Division and the 4th Armoured Brigade guarded the approaches to Metameur and Medenine, with the 5th New Zealand Brigade up front.

The corps had, in round numbers, 460 anti-tank guns, 350 25-pdr and medium guns, 300 tanks, all with plenty of ammunition. Men and guns were well dug in and were under centralised control for shelling pre-arranged areas in response to calls from observers.

The Axis attack opened at 6 a.m. on March 6 in a heavy mist that at first masked the attacking columns. On the right wing, the 10. Panzer-Division quickly came in contact with New Zealand out-posts south-west of Metameur, losing five tanks. In the centre, the 15. Panzer-Division, advancing along the Hallouf River, came under a heavy artillery bombardment and had to halt to wait until its own artillery could come forward in support. The leading tanks of the 21. Panzer-Division also came under a very strong artillery fire and were brought to a halt while still three kilometres from their objective, the Tadjera Khir heights.

On the left (northern) wing, the attack by the 90. leichte Afrika-Division and the Italian battle groups met some initial successes but were soon driven back by counter-attacks from the 154th Brigade.

The attack was renewed in the afternoon with the 15. and 21. Panzer-Divisions trying to push along both sides of the Hallouf river but the British artillery fire was devastating, halting the advance after a few hundred metres.

Faced with lack of progress against the much stronger defences, Messe proposed in the evening calling off the battle. Rommel agreed and at 8.30 p.m. he gave the order to stop but the disengagement was difficult and more tanks were lost in the process.

Altogether, Heeresgruppe Afrika had suffered 650 casualties on March 6 and 7 and lost 40 tanks, compared to just 50 prisoners taken and six tanks and 32 guns destroyed. The overwhelming superiority of the British gunners had secured the victory.

This costly reverse was Rommel's last battle in Africa. On March 10 he was succeeded by von Arnim who, in turn, yielded command of the 5. Panzerarmee to General der Panzertruppen Gustav von Vaerst.

Rommel had departed from Sfax airfield the previous day, flying via Rome to Hitler's Wolfsschanze HQ in East Prussia. There he met the Führer on the evening of the 10th. Hitler confirmed that the Tunisian bridgehead must be held but he refused Rommel's request to return to Africa. Instead he ordered him to go on sick leave. Rommel then flew back to Germany to begin his long-overdue medical treatment at the hospital at Semmering.

His departure was kept a secret and for weeks, Allied press reports continued to present the Axis forces in Tunisia as Rommel's famous Afrikakorps. It was only after the final defeat in May 1943 that the public, German included, was to discover that the well-publicised Generalfeldmarschall Rommel had not been leading operations in North Africa for the past two months.

Barring the gap south of Mareth, the French defensive line was about 30 kilometres long and comprised 28 strong-points numbered from 'P1' near the sea to 'P28' on the lower slope of the hills. Each strong point comprised gun and machine gun casemates, and concrete command posts and shelters protected by mines and barbed wire.

THE BATTLE AT MARETH

On the basis of the reconnaissance made in January and February to investigate the routes west of the Matmata mountains, which revealed that a large force could reach the El Hamma gap along this flanking approach, General Montgomery finalised his plan to breach the Mareth Line. It was code-named Operation 'Pugilist Gallop'.

The provisional New Zealand Corps under Lieutenant-General Sir Bernard Freyberg was to outflank the Mareth Line well inland via Ksar Rhilane to reach the El Hamma gap. After breaking through there, they were then to turn east and disrupt the enemy's rear. In the meantime, the main attack by the XXX Corps (Lieutenant-General Sir Oliver Leese) would be launched near the coast. Once the infantry was through the Axis defence line, two

armoured divisions would cross to exploit northwards, Sfax being given as the objective. The operation would begin on the night of March 20/21 when moonlight would facilitate a night assault.

The Eighth Army had over 600 tanks to the 150 available to the Axis, 1,480 guns to 680, with air superiority of at least two to one.

From March 18, air reconnaissance reported massive movement by Allied forces and the Axis command concluded — correctly — that an attack at the El Hamma gap could be expected in three or four days, coinciding with a main assault against the Mareth Line. To counter it, the 164. leichte Afrika-Division was moved westwards to the Tebaga—Djebel Malab position and the 10. Panzer-Division was moved south to Maharès.

By mid-March, General Montgomery had finalised his plans to outflank the Mareth Line by attacking well inland via Ksar Rhilane to reach the El Hamma gap. This photo of him was taken in Benghazi in front of the Cathedral.

While the New Zealand Corps launched its 'left hook' over the edge of the desert, the XXX Corps attack opened with a heavy artillery bombardment from over 300 guns on the evening of March 20. After this the 151st Brigade advanced. It was expected to establish three crossing points of the Wadi Zigzaou, one for each of two infantry battalions and another for the 50th Royal Tank Regiment that was following.

At first the leading tanks bogged down attempting to cross the wadi but a further attempt later in the day was successful and 42 Valentines finally made across. A battle group of the 15. Panzer-Division counter-attacked in the afternoon although the waterlogged ground slowed its progress. The British held on until nightfall but then began to pull back across the wadi leaving behind 30 disabled tanks and 200 prisoners in Axis hands. In the meantime, the New Zealand Corps had carried out the left hook and by the afternoon of March 22 the force was ten miles south-west of El Hamma.

Montgomery realised that the attack by the XXX Corps had not been successful so he altered his plan during the night of March 22/23 to turn the flanking manoeuvre by the New Zealand Corps into the main effort, and he directed the 1st Armoured Division to use the route used by the New Zealanders. The new operation, code-named 'Supercharge', was set for March 26.

From Allied movements observed late on the 23rd, and again on the 24th, the Axis command correctly interpreted Montgomery's intention to switch the focus of the attack to the El Hamma gap. Therefore, towards evening on March 23, the 15. Panzer-Division and other elements started to pull back from the Mareth Line for new positions about 15 miles south-west of Gabès. From there they would be able to intervene either on the Mareth Line or into the El Hamma gap.

The commander of the 164. leichte Afrika-Division, Generalmajor von Liebenstein (who had returned on March 13, promoted to Generalmajor,

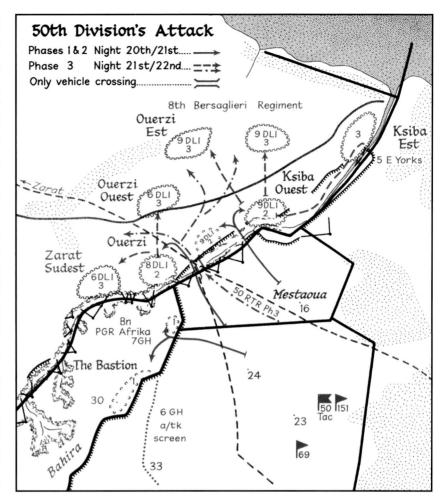

The 50th Division's attack on the Mareth Line entrusted the capture of Ksiba Ouest to 9th Durham Light Infantry and Ouerzi to the 8th Durhams. At the same time the 50th Royal Tank Regiment was to cross Wadi Zigzaou (a dry river bed) and then fan out with the 6th Durham Light Infantry following them.

after being wounded), was put in command of the whole sector, his division being ordered into a defensive position astride the track from Kebili to El Hamma with the 21. Panzer-Division on its left.

However, the Axis command finally realised that it was time to retreat to Wadi Akarit and on the morning of the 24th Heeresgruppe Afrika directed Messe to pull the 1a Armata back to

this new line of defence. The move was to begin the next day, and was to be completed in 72 hours. Messe protested that lack of transport would not allow him to move that quickly but von Arnim insisted on the timetable.

Operation 'Supercharge' opened at 4 p.m. on the 26th by a strong artillery barrage and the tanks of the 8th Armoured Brigade then pushed along the track from Kebili. With the sun in

Left: The leading Valentine bogged down while attempting to negotiate Wadi Zigzaou, so blocking the way until the sappers could create a bypass around it. This allowed four tanks to finally get across. Captain Keating later came to picture the bogged down Valentine. *Right:* A road now crosses the wadi at the point where the 50th Royal Tank Regiment made their crossing.

Left: **Some time after the attack on the night of March 20/21, Captain Keating staged this re-enactment with men from the 5th East Yorkshires, 69th Brigade, assaulting one of the** bunkers of the Mareth Line. *Right:* **This shot of the machine gun casemate of strong-point 'P3' just west of the 50th Royal Tank Regiment crossing-point was taken by Alan Waters.**

their eyes, and a strong wind blowing dust kicked up by shelling and bombing in their faces, at first the Axis defenders could not see what was coming. 'Supercharge' quickly reached its first objectives and the two centre battalions of the 164. leichte Afrika-Division were soon overrun. The gap was open and with the 2nd Armoured Brigade in the lead, the 1st Armoured Division passed through late in the afternoon. The tanks had penetrated over two miles before nightfall so they waited for the moon to rise to resume the advance about midnight.

Von Liebenstein managed to scrape together an anti-tank screen (three 88mm and four 50mm anti-tank guns and four 100mm field guns) south of El Hamma. With this, together with elements from the 21. Panzer-Division, he was able to check the British advance.

The Eighth Army then lost a day while the next move was being planned which gave the Axis a welcome breathing space. Their forces successfully

Another re-enactment by the Army Film and Photographic Unit was this one by infantry of the 151st Brigade, following the attack on the night of March 20/21. Following the heavy bombardment carried out by more than 300 guns, they demonstrate how they used ladders to scale the sides of Wadi Zigzaou.

abandoned the Mareth position on the 27th, but as the Eighth Army did not follow up, there was little fighting on the 28th. The Axis rearguards pulled back north of El Hamma and Gabès during the night of March 28/29, and on the following night moved even further back into the Akarit positions.

That position was a narrow opening in the coastal plain north of Gabès. The passage was blocked partly by hills and also by the steep-sided stream bed of the Wadi Akarit, while the great salt marsh (Chott El Fejal) lay on the western flank and the sea on the other side. Time was short however and little had been done to build and organise the 18-mile-wide position. An anti-tank ditch had been dug across the plain to extend the wadi to the nearest hill (Djebel Roumana) and other shorter trenches were dug zig-zagging across the openings between the various hills. About 4,000 mines had been laid, most of them between the coastal road and Roumana, and in small patches between Roumana and Fatnassa.

There was little fighting on the 28th as Generals Horrocks and Freyberg were still debating the best plan of action when the Axis forces pulled back. These two Italians who failed to withdraw in time were captured by the 5th Queen's Own Cameron Highlanders.

Above left: **The same day, March 29, Crusader tanks of the 9th Lancers, 2nd Armoured Brigade, were photographed advancing through El Hamma.** *Above right:* **The photo was taken at the western entrance of the village where the P16 road starts westwards to Djebel Tebaga and Kebili, but unfortunately new buildings now hide most of the features. Nevertheless, the Y-shaped junction still makes for a good reference point.** *Right:* **Time for a welcome cuppa in Gabès on March 29. This Valentine was one of the few tanks remaining in operation with the 50th Royal Tank Regiment after the painful losses suffered on the 22nd (see page 241). The shadows appearing in the foreground of the photo betray that this nice 'housekeeping' scenery was somewhat staged by Captain Geoffrey Keating. Before the war, he was on the staff of the** *Daily Sketch* **and was the prominent figure with the AFPU in North Africa. He was on the stage right from September 1939 when he was the first cameraman to accompany the British Expeditionary Force to France. He took part in the campaigns in Norway, France and Crete and was then posted to North Africa. His photos and those of his fellow cameramen of No. 1 Section, Army Film and Photographic Unit did much to raise the profile of the yet unknown Montgomery, finally making him a national hero.**

Gafsa, Maknassy and El Guettar

While these events were taking place in the south on the Eighth Army's front, the US II Corps was readying operations for the drive eastwards. The plan of attack, drawn up by the corps and code-named Operation 'WOP' was as follows.

The attack was to start on March 15. On that day, the 1st Infantry Division was to advance to Gafsa and seize the town. Meanwhile the 1st Armored Division was to clear the Thélepte sector which had been lost in the Kasserine battle, and then — if the 1st Division was successful at Gafsa — launch a drive from north of Gafsa north-eastward to Maknassy and the pass that lay behind it. In the northern half of the corps sector, the 34th Infantry Division was to advance towards the Fondouk Pass.

In this sector of the Axis front, there were only the few elements of Divisione Centauro that had been left to hold Gafsa when the Axis broke off their February offensive, with small forward units at Faïd and Maknassy.

On March 8, II Corps passed from First Army's control to 18th Army Group's direct control. Tentative plans for Operation 'WOP' were then approved by the 18th Army Group and General Alexander and his Chief-of-Staff, Major-General Richard McCreery, spent the next two days at Patton's headquarters while inspecting units of the corps. On March 13, to bring it closer to the Eighth Army's attack scheduled for March 20, Alexander shifted the operation's start date from March 15 to the 17th.

During the night of March 16/17, the 1st Infantry Division was transported in trucks from its concentration area at Bou Chebka over 40 miles southwards via Fériana to assembly points outside Gafsa. The divisional plan of attack called for the 18th Infantry to climb over the eastern mountain and approach the town from the east, while two battalions

of the 16th Infantry were to climb the opposite hill and moved in from the west. At the same time a motorised task force from the 26th Infantry was to skirt the eastern mountain and advance upon the town from the south-west.

Although the Axis garrison was seen to be already pulling back from Gafsa and the surrounding area, the launch was held back until 10 a.m. to await a scheduled air bombardment. At 9.45 a.m., a formation of B-25s appeared to bomb the target and at H-Hour the troops moved off. Shortly after noon the leaders entered Gafsa from the north-west. While mines and booby traps were plentiful, the town itself was found to be free of defenders.

The Italian garrison of 1,200 had abandoned the town early that morning and, screened by German troops of Aufklärungs-Abteilung 580, established new defensive positions 12 miles to the east on the heights east of El Guettar.

The Axis garrison having pulled out, the US 1st Infantry Division swiftly captured Gafsa on the morning of March 17 and Patton soon moved his II Corps headquarters to the town. *Above left:* **On April 3, he was pictured chatting with Major General Dawson Olmstead, the US War Department's Chief Signals Officer, on the veranda outside the HQ.** *Above right:* **Lieutenant-General Sir John Gort, then Governor of Malta, also visited Patton at Gafsa. The General's immaculate dress exemplified the strict regime that he had enforced since he had taken over II Corps. Quite by chance the author recognised the balcony with its columns on the first floor of a building now the barracks of the National Guard. Based on past experience, Jean Paul anticipated a negative response to any request to take photographs so he snapped a quick comparison *(below)* while the sentry was taking shelter from the hot sun. He then knocked to ask if he could access the balcony and stand for a few minutes in Patton's footsteps, but when he asked if he could take pictures, the tone turned icy and he was quickly ejected from the building!**

The same street, Rue Amor Ben Slimen, in Gafsa today.

East of El Guettar, the 18th Infantry Regiment, 1st Infantry Division, dug-in in the hills south of the Gabès road.

II Corps. In addition to taking Sened and Maknassy, Patton was now to seize the high ground east of Maknassy and send a light armoured raiding party to Mezzouna, another 12 miles further east. However, as before, no large forces were to pass beyond the safety of the Eastern Dorsale mountains.

Following these new instructions, the 1st Armored Division launched an attack on Maknassy on the 21st. As Combat Command C advanced on the village along the road from Sened, over on the left wing Combat Command B moved eastwards along a camel trail to reach an area from which it could flank the attack and assist in preparatory artillery fire on the village. The lead elements of Combat Command C approached Maknassy before midnight and started to shell the town but it was not until the following morning, March 22, that reconnaissance units finally discovered that the village was completely empty.

General Ward decided to wait to reinforce and reorganise before pushing on to the El Guettar Pass to the east. Though Patton later regretted not having gone forward himself that day to urge Ward on, there is some inconclusive evidence that he had approved Ward's

Patton had plans to resume the advance on Maknassy on the 19th but torrential rain turned the ground into thick mud which made cross-country travel impossible for wheeled vehicles. Reluctantly he was forced to accept a postponement by one day. On the 19th, with most of the 1st Armored Division still bogged down in mud, Patton drove through the downpour to review the situation with the division commander, Major General Ward. He then ordered the attack to go ahead next morning.

The offensive got off to a good start early on March 20. The 60th Regimental Combat Team climbed the western slopes of Djebel Goussa, the mountain that dominated the valley through which ran the railway from Gafsa via Sened to Maknassy. This forced the Italians to abandon their entrenched positions near Sened station and Sened village. Meanwhile, Combat Command C moved round the north of Djebel Goussa to reach the exit from the valley some eight miles north of Sened. On the right, Combat Command A, starting out from Zannouch Station north-east of Gafsa, advanced along the dirt road that ran parallel to the railway until it got to a minefield west of Sened station. By evening the small Axis force had been driven out of the station area by artillery fire, some troops escaping north-eastwards only to run headlong into Combat Command C. They took 70 prisoners after a brief engagement at dawn on March 21. Another part of the garrison took refuge in the village of Sened, located some five miles to the south of the station, where it finally surrendered on March 23, the final bag consisting of 542 Italian prisoners.

When Patton returned to his headquarters in Fériana after his rain-sodden visit to Ward on the 19th, he found General McCreery waiting with Alexander's new plans and orders for

Another shot from the series of photos taken on March 21: men of Company D of the 18th Infantry digging slit trenches.

The mountain range in the far distance to the south, Djebel El Asker, enabled the author to locate the hillocks on the south side of the road to Gabès.

245

The artillery of the 1st Infantry Division played a major role in halting the 10. Panzer-Division attack on March 23, the score of nearly 30 panzers destroyed being shared with the 601st and 899th Tank Destroyer Battalions. This shot of a crew loading a 155mm howitzer was taken 'east of El Guettar' on March 23.

proved to be strongly defended, with a minefield barring the approach to the crest, and covered by machine guns both on the hill and on adjacent slopes to the left and right. After one company commander was killed, the attack was halted and the men ordered to dig in and wait for daylight.

The 3rd Battalion renewed the assault next morning, March 23, but, just as the German defenders, by then reduced to only 80 infantrymen, were beginning to fall back, Oberst Lang arrived. He was able to make the small force hold on until elements of his Kampfgruppe joined them. That evening the Americans launched a succession of attacks but all to no avail.

A stronger force was concentrated in the night for a renewed assault and three battalions of infantry, supported by two companies of tanks and four battalions of artillery, attacked Djebel Naemia from the north, west and south on the morning of March 24. Yet, in spite of hard fighting, the Americans were still unable to dislodge the German defenders.

That evening, Patton telephoned General Ward to order him to personally lead an attack next morning, telling him in no uncertain terms that it had to succeed. Obeying this unorthodox order, early on the 25th Ward led an assault on Hill 322 by three battalions of the 6th Armored Infantry. They won some ground but could not seize the hill and by noon Ward (who had been wounded in the eye) decided to call off the attack.

cautious decision during a roadside conference with him just west of Maknassy after the capture of the village.

At this point, the role envisioned for II Corps was modified for on the previous day, March 21, when the Eighth Army was about to assault the Mareth position, Montgomery had suggested to Alexander that the Americans could be of assistance by sending an armoured thrust eastward across the Gabès plain to cut the coastal road. Though he considered such an idea to be too ambitious, Alexander nevertheless issued instructions to II Corps on the morning of March 22. Thus in the afternoon Patton verbally relayed instructions to General Ward to seize and hold the Maknassy Pass while a small armoured column was to be sent to raid Mezzouna. In addition, a second armoured force was to be kept in readiness to push to Maharès on the coast, more than 50 miles east of Maknassy. He ordered that the attack on the pass be made that night.

Ward relayed the orders for the assault to begin at 11.30 p.m. Combat Command C with the 3rd Battalion, 60th Infantry, attached was to seize Djebel Dribica (Hill 209) and Djebel Naemia (Hill 322) north of the pass, while the 60th Regimental Combat Team was simultaneously to gain control of Djebel Bou Douaou (Hill 753) beyond and south-east of it.

The night attack started as planned. No opposition was met in securing Djebel Bou Douaou, and Djebel Dribica was taken against only light opposition. However, Djebel Naemia

General Patton was at El Guettar on the afternoon of March 23 when the 10. Panzer-Division renewed its assault. Seeing the attackers advancing under a hail of mortar, machine gun and artillery fire, he is reputed to have remarked: 'My God, it seems a crime to murder good infantry like that'.

Well aware of the risk of an attack by the II Corps in the flank of the forces facing the Eighth Army, Kesselring had meanwhile employed two measures to counter the danger. First, part of the 5. Panzerarmee reserves near Mareth and others at the El Hamma gap were to be deployed in holding the heights east of Maknassy, and then the 10. Panzer-Division was to be released from Heeresgruppe Afrika reserve to join with the Afrikakorps which was to mount a counter-attack toward Gafsa.

The 10. Panzer-Division first assembled during the night south of Djebel Ben Kheïr, east of El Hafay, and in the early hours of March 23 moved westwards along the axis of the Gabès—Gafsa road. The force comprised the I. Abteilung of Panzer-Regiment 7 with 50 tanks, two battalions of infantry (one each from Panzergrenadier-Regiment 69 and Panzergrenadier-Regiment 86), and one battalion of Panzer-Artillerie-Regiment 90. The plan was that having broken through the American positions, the attack was to push north-westward against the southern flank of the 1st Infantry Division.

Contact with the Americans was made about 5 a.m. while it was still dark, the Germans sweeping the foothills and the lower ground north of the road before launching the main attack. Daylight revealed German tanks and self-propelled guns, interspersed with infantry in carriers, rolling westward in a hollow square formation at a slow but steady pace. Behind them, a column of trucks drove to a predetermined point at the western end of Djebel el Mcheltat to unload more infantry which closely followed the armoured rectangle ahead of them. The 3rd Battalions of both the 18th and 16th Infantry were under direct attack.

Then the German force separated into three. One group turned northwest among the foothills east of Hill 336 overrunning the 32nd and part of the 5th Field Artillery Battalions; another continued along the road, while the third and largest force tried to sweep the hills and northward along the edge of the Chott el Guettar salt lake.

The engagements east of Hill 336 brought some fierce hand-to-hand encounters, and heavy American losses, the artillerymen defending their guns with rifles and grenades. The German group advancing along the highway reached a new minefield just laid from the base of Hill 336 along the Wadi Keddab and across the highway to the Chott el Guettar salt lake. There, the tide of battle changed. Rushed in from reserve at El Guettar, the 2nd Battalion of the 16th Infantry de-trucked at the fork of the roads just east of the village and moved into position on either side of the 3rd Battalion line. Reserves from II Corps began arriving too, including the 899th Tank Destroyer Battalion of full-tracked 3-inch M10 guns and the 17th Field Artillery Battalion.

American artillery and the tank destroyers then knocked out nearly 30 panzers and the minefield stopped eight more. By mid-morning the German attack had stalled and began pulling

Captain Michael Paulick, commander of the Reconnaissance Company of the 601st Tank Destroyer Battalion. On March 23, the 601st played a critical role in the effort that day to halt the 10. Panzer-Division counter-attack, even though it cost the loss of 21 out of its 31 tank destroyers. The M3 tank destroyer was a hasty creation of marrying the already proven M3 half-track with the 75mm gun. This TD was pictured in one of the defile positions from where the battalion struck at the the panzers.

back a few kilometres, towing some of their disabled tanks. In the early afternoon, Company E of the 16th Infantry made a limited counter-attack that retook the former positions of the 32nd Field Artillery and contact with the 3rd Battalion, 18th Infantry, south of the Gabès highway was re-established.

'Infantrymen preparing to go on patrol.' Signal Corps photographer Park added in his caption that he had taken the photo in Maknassy although unfortunately he failed to record the date. We think it was most probably taken on March 22, the day the Americans entered the village and found it devoid of any defenders.

'A Yank looks off into the distance from his position on top of a light tank.' Equally vague, is the caption to this photo by Park, but at least we know that the M3 light tank belonged to the 13th Armored Regiment.

Preceded by an air strike, the 10. Panzer-Division renewed its attack in the late afternoon. The Germans got to within 300 yards of the American positions but the now well-prepared force within the pass crucified them with mortar, machine-gun and artillery fire, compelling the panzers and panzergrenadiers to retreat in disarray.

American losses amounted to six 155mm and six 105mm guns, 24 half-tracked tank destroyers, and seven M10 tank destroyers. From their original 50, the Germans had had 32 tanks put out of action, half of which they managed to recover, the others being later blown up by the Americans.

In spite of this reverse, the Germans pursued their aggressive defence and on the 24th they made some progress in the high ground on the southern side of the Gabès highway, where the 1st and 2nd Battalions of the 18th Infantry were holding Djebel Berda. On the 25th the Germans regained Hill 772, one of

Berda's north-eastern buttresses. Even with the 1st Ranger Battalion in support, the two battalions of the 16th Infantry, tired and badly cut up by two days of fighting, were unable to hold their positions and during the night of March 25/26 Corps ordered them to withdraw through the Rangers.

The Eighth Army's attack on the Mareth Line was scheduled to enter a crucial phase on the night of March 26/27 and at noon on the 25th the 18th Army Group issued a new directive to II Corps to assist in tying down Axis forces. Patton was ordered to abandon his attempts to break through east of Maknassy, where the corps was making disappointing progress, and instead concentrate three divisions — the 1st and 9th Infantry and the 1st Armored — at El Guettar for an attack south-east towards Gabès. The two infantry divisions were to attack and open the El Guettar Pass, thus allowing the 1st Armored Division to roll through the

gap and thrust toward the coastal plain. Meanwhile, the 34th Infantry Division was to attack the Axis-held pass at Fondouk el Aouareb, some 85 miles further to the north. This was in order to secure a starting point, beyond the mountains, from which a force could later be launched to cut off an Axis northward retreat, if and when that occurred.

The road to Gabès branches off to the south-east at a fork just east of El Guettar then passes between jumbled hills at the northern end which rise to the horseshoe-shaped complex of Djebel el Mcheltat and the Djebel Berda. The Gumtree road continues at the fork along the southern base of Djebel Orbata to reach the coastal plain and Maharès on the coast.

The II Corps offensive started on March 28. The 1st Infantry Division, on the left of the road, launched the 16th and 26th Infantry in an attack on Djebel Mcheltat but they were quickly hurled back from the wired-in, well-defended

Men of the 1st Armored Division take a breather at Maknassy's railway station soon after the occupation of the town.

The station has changed little, many trains now using this line to carry phosphate from mines from Gafsa to the port at Sfax.

positions. Resuming the attack the following day, the 26th Infantry advanced to within assaulting distance of Hill 482, finally taking this key position on March 30 but with heavy losses. The 16th Infantry, operating south of the horseshoe rim, made equally slow progress. Meanwhile, to the north, the 18th Infantry was advancing along the Gumtree road. After taking Djebel Hamadi (Hill 567), they moved south to cover the flank of the 26th Infantry by attacking the position of Hill 574.

On the right of the Gabès road, the 9th Infantry Division moved to attack Djebel el Kheroua and its northernmost peak, Hill 369, which dominated the pass from the south. The 47th Infantry assembled as planned at the western base of Djebel Berda in a series of night moves. Attacking at H-Hour, the 1st and 3rd Battalions mistook a nearby ridge (Djebel el Hamra) for Hill 369 and captured the wrong feature. (They used maps that were re-photographed French sheets surveyed in 1903, and at a scale of 1:100,000. The blurred copies showed mountains, ravines and wadis all looking alike which made orientation a very difficult task.)

The operation miscarried even further when the regiment's 2nd Battalion, which was to come in from the south,

A 1st Infantry Division situation report dated March 23 records that about 700 prisoners were taken that day, mostly Italians.

Left: This column of Italian prisoners are being marched through El Guettar by men from Company B of the 18th Infantry Regiment. Right: El Guettar has seen a lot of changes since the war, many new buildings having sprung up hiding many of the distinguishing features in the wartime photographs. This view is looking north-west with Djebel Orbata in the background.

The wartime caption to this photo in particular praised 'the deadly marksmanship of the US Army Air Force bombers', pointing out that direct hits had been scored on warehouses, terminals and the pier head at Sousse. Although a date and unit for the raid are not given, we believe it shows the operation mounted on January 2 when A-20 medium bombers hit Sousse in two waves during the morning, returning for a further attack in the afternoon.

became lost for about 36 hours among the rough hills between Djebel el Kheroua and Djebel Lettouchi. Caught in machine-gun cross-fire, the battalion lost its commander, its intelligence officer and communication officer, its entire Company E, and the commanders of two other companies. In all, 232 enlisted men and ten officers were taken prisoner.

The division hastily committed the 1st Battalion, 39th Infantry, from reserve and sent it out to seize Hill 772. The feature had been held by the Americans until two days earlier but it was now in German hands, and the battalion became lost in the maze of djebels for more than a day.

The 9th Infantry Division then committed the 2nd Battalion of the 39th Infantry to try to take Hill 369 from the north. However, the lorry column bringing the battalion forward down the Gabès highway drove much too close to Hill 290, which was Italian-held and it received heavy fire. Badly demoralised, most of the column pulled out and scurried back all the way to the starting point. The remainder was pinned down and unable to move in daylight, and only managed to struggle back 36 hours later. Hill 369 remained in Axis hands, preventing any passage for the armour down the road to Gabès.

No longer at war — this is the port of Sousse today, courtesy of Google Earth.

250

The Axis in Trouble

By the end of March the position of the Axis in Tunisia was desperate. On the morning of March 29 von Arnim signalled to OKW, sending a copy to Kesselring and Comando Supremo: 'Supplies shattering. Ammunition only available for 1-2 days, no more stocks for some weapons such as medium field howitzers. Fuel situation similar, large-scale movements no longer possible.'

Meanwhile in Rome, arguments over strategy continued. On the 29th, Generale Ambrosio believed that preparations should begin for a retreat to a line on the hills between Djebel Mansour and Enfidaville, well north of the Akarit Line, but Kesselring disagreed stating that this would be contrary to Hitler's order that the Akarit position was the final defence line. Oberst Siegfried Westphal, Kesselring's Chief of Operations, flew to Tunisia the next day to talk to von Arnim but the meeting just resulted in a heated exchange of views, Westphal saying that the Heeresgruppe Afrika seemed always to be 'squinting over its shoulder' to which von Arnim angrily replied that he was squinting for ships.

The preparations being made for retreat did not escape the notice of the troops and by April 5 Comando Supremo expressed concerns that there were signs of 'retreat mindedness' in Tunisia. Consequently, 1a Armata was warned that any idea that the Akarit Line was only a delaying position must be dismissed at once.

Units were disposed in the Akarit position more or less as they had been at Mareth. On the left wing, the XX Corpo d'Armata, Generale Taddeo Orlando, held the sector from the coast road to Fatnassa with (from east to west) Divisione Giovani Fascisti, two battalions of the 90. leichte Afrika-Division astride the coast road, and Divisione Trieste and Divisione La Spezia. West of Fatnassa, the XXI Corpo d'Armata, Generale Navarini, had Divisione Pistoia covering the Haidoudi Pass through which the road to El Guettar and Gafsa passed. A detachment of the 15. Panzer-Division was deployed in the mouth of the pass, and next to it were positioned the remnants of the 164. leichte Afrika-Division. On the extreme western flank lay the Raggruppamento Sahariano. The few reserves were Panzergrenadier-Regiment 361 and Panzerjäger-Abteilung 190 of the 90. leichte Afrika-Division in the Fatnassa area, and the 15. Panzer-Division (less a detachment) and Panzergrenadier-Regiment 200 (90. leichte Afrika-Division) north of Roumana, but they had only 22 German and four Italian tanks between them.

Over on the Allied side, the 18th Army Group revised on March 29 — for the fourth time — its directive to II Corps and Alexander instructed Patton to launch an armoured thrust the following morning, March 30, and break through along the Gabès road.

Eager to succeed at last, Patton placed the 1st Armored Division's task force assembled for the mission under

British photographer Sergeant W. A. Jones featured pilots of No. 243 Squadron of No. 322 Wing, relaxing to the music from a wind-up gramophone. Their Spitfire Mark VBs are dispersed on the airfield at Souk el Khemis.

Colonel Clarence C. Benson, the commander of the 13th Armored Regiment, whose aggressiveness he respected. He also sent Brigadier General Hugh J. Gaffey, his own Chief-of-Staff, to 'keep an eye on the show'.

Task Force Benson was made up of the 2nd Battalion, 1st Armored Regiment; the 3rd Battalion, 13th Armored Regiment; the 81st Reconnaissance Battalion; the 899th Tank Destroyer Battalion; the 65th and 68th Field Artillery Battalions; and Company B of the 16th Engineer Combat Battalion. The 3rd Battalion, 39th Infantry, was attached from the 9th Infantry Division

on March 30 and the 2nd Battalion, 6th Armored Infantry, joined during the night of March 30/31.

After a morning of shelling by the massed artillery of both the 1st and 9th Infantry Divisions and the II Corps, and renewed attempts by the two infantry divisions on the hills on either side of the Gabès road, Task Force Benson moved out at noon of March 30. The armoured column did not get far however being stopped by a minefield that barred the pass between Djebel Mcheltat to the left of the road and Hill 369 on the right. Patton directed the attack to be renewed

On March 24, the B-26s from the 37th Bombardment Squadron, 17th Bombardment Group, were getting ready for the bomb run on the airfield north of Sfax when flak opened up. A shell struck the left wing and engine nacelle, riddling the plane from nose to tail. The pilot, Lieutenant Franklyn P. Bedford, released the bombs and then managed to limp back to his base at Telergma where he successfully belly-landed *Earthquake McGoon*.

Pictured over Djerba Island, off Gabès, this formation of Spitfire VBs were on an interception patrol to the Mareth Line area in early 1943. UF-V and UF-F belonged to No. 601 Squadron while IR-G in the foreground was the personal mount of Wing Commander Ian Gleed, the Wing Commander of No. 244 Wing.

at 4 p.m. in which infantry and armour would be co-ordinated with artillery and air support.

Without waiting for the scheduled afternoon attack, Benson launched a tank/infantry assault some time after midday. A lane was cleared through the minefield and the 2nd Battalion, 1st Armored Regiment, then pushed along and fanned out. The 3rd Battalion, 13th Armored Regiment, took over next afternoon but the Axis pressure on them increased and the two battalions had to give back some ground. In these two days of frustrating action, Task Force Benson had lost another 13 tanks and two tank destroyers.

That day, April 1, Montgomery signalled to Alexander his plans for an attack to break the Wadi Akarit position on the night of April 4/5. He again expressed his wish that II Corps press on, pointing that if they 'could come forward even a few miles it would make my task very simple'. However, Task Force Benson was still held up after three days so Alexander gave orders to return to the original plan of March 25 with infantry opening the way and the tanks in support.

Following these instructions, II Corps resumed its efforts, battling from April 2 to April 6 to occupy the hills and ridges along the Gumtree and Gabès roads. On the right, south of the Gabès road, the 9th Infantry Division suffered many casualties in unsuccessful struggles to conquer the rugged terrain of

Gleed was killed in action only a few days after the photo was taken. On April 16, he was leading a patrol over the Cap Bon area when German fighters of JG 77 covering the transport flights, shot down several of the RAF machines, including Gleed and his wingman. Gleed's Spitfire was later found on sand dunes near the sea on the western coast of Cap Bon. He was first buried at Tazoghrane but in April 1944 he was moved to the Military Cemetery at Enfidaville (Plot 5, Row E, Grave 22).

Time was short but Axis forces still succeeded in laying at least 4,000 mines along the Akarit position, mostly between the coastal road and Djebel Roumana, and in patches between

Roumana and Tebaga Fatnassa. *Left:* On April 6, Royal Engineers marked the gap they just cleared. *Right:* A nice comparison by Alan Waters with Djebel Roumana in background.

Djebel el Kheroua, and its renewed attacks to take Hill 772 were all repulsed. On the left, the 1st Infantry Division doggedly pressed on, the 18th Infantry taking the village of Sakket north of the Gumtree road on April 3 but it suffered painful losses in the process.

On April 4, German artillery harassed the American positions and, fearing an Axis counter-attack, II Corps called off the attack planned for the 5th. However, no counter-attack materialised and the two infantry divisions renewed their attack on April 6. Now, after ten days of gruelling combat, the 9th Infantry Division finally took Djebel Lettouchi and blood-soaked Hill 772. Only Hill 369 still held out. Task Force

Benson followed in the late afternoon, pushing down the Gabès highway beyond the road junction north-east of Hill 369.

The Allied command was much disappointed in II Corps operations to date and on April 5, following a suggestion from Alexander (which only confirmed his own inclination), Patton relieved the 1st Armored Division commander, General Ward, replacing him with Major General Ernest N. Harmon then commanding the 2nd Armored Division in Morocco.

On April 4, with II Corps unable to advance and threaten the rear of the Akarit Line, Alexander ordered the First Army to try farther north, using the newly-committed IX Corps to break

through the Fondouk Pass and push its armour to Kairouan.

Meanwhile, the Eighth Army shaped its plan to break the Akarit Line. The XXX Corps was to use three divisions to create a breach for the X Corps to follow through. Between them the two corps would have 462 tanks. The plan's first phase was for the 4th Indian Division to take the Fatnassa massif on the left during the night of April 5/6 and build a crossing over the anti-tank ditch. The following day the 50th Division was to breach the ditch and wadi in the centre, while on the right the 51st (Highland) Division was to take Djebel Roumana. All these attacks were west of the coastal road through Divisione Trieste, La Spezia and Pistoia sectors.

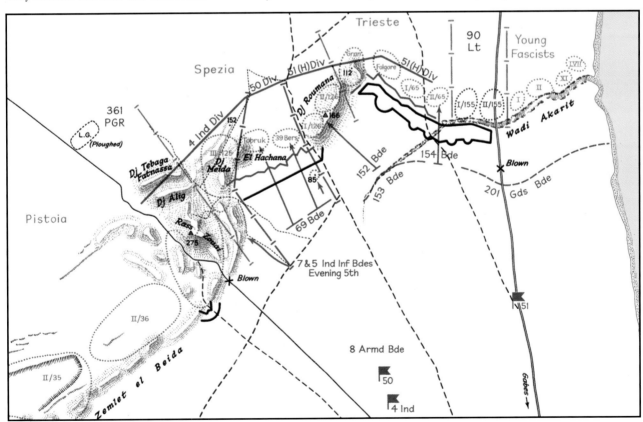

The battle of Wadi Akarit took place on April 6, 1943. The red lines show the XXX Corps plan of attack, with the start lines,

axis of advance and final objectives. Minefields are indicated with black lines and anti-tank ditches are in blue.

Left: **The western end of Djebel Roumana was captured on the morning of April 6 by the 5th Cameronians, at which point Captain Keating pictured the anti-tank ditch.** *Above:* **Alan Waters climbed to the same knoll to take this beautiful comparison, looking westwards with the line of the old anti-tank ditch still visible. In far background, from left to right, lie Rass Zouai, Djebel Meida and Djebel Tebaga Fatnassa.**

The attack began at 5 a.m. on April 6. By 8.30 a.m., the 4th Indian Division had taken most of the Fatnassa massif but in the centre the advance by the 50th Division was delayed at the anti-tank ditch and it was only by the middle of the day that the objective was reached. By that time, with many of the Italian defenders readily surrendering, the attack had spread west along the hills.

At 8 a.m. the two regiments of the 90. leichte Afrika-Division in reserve were ordered to counter-attack. Also, at Bayerlein's request, Heeresgruppe Afrika placed the tanks of the Afrikakorps which were still tied down in the battles at El Guettar, under the 1a Armata command. About 10 a.m. about half of the 80 panzers still running were on their way eastwards.

During the afternoon, the 15. Panzer-Division counter-attacked and managed to contain those elements of the X Corps that had penetrated into Divisione Trieste's sector. By then, the tanks from the Afrikakorps arrived and counter-attacked on the western side of Djebel Fatnassa. By now the Axis

British AFPU photographer Sergeant A. W. Ackland was present when the final, long-awaited link-up between US II Corps and Eighth Army occurred. He wrote that 'the first two men to meet and shake hands' were Sergeant Joseph A. Randall of State Centre, Iowa, and Lance-Sergeant William Brown of the Warrens, Holdsworthy, Devon.

It was at 3.25 p.m. on April 7 when Task Force Benson, comprising six scout cars and Jeeps, met a patrol of three armoured cars of the 12th Royal Lancers. The meeting took place 67 kilometres north-west of Gabès. Less than 50 men participated but, like so many other link-ups that took place during the war, the exact spot where it occurred is the subject of some confusion. The 1st Armored Division report recorded the map co-ordinates as Y-8869; the 2nd Armoured Brigade (the 12th Lancers' parent unit) reported it as Y-8367; Eighth Army as Y-8868; and the 18th Army Group as Y-9056! However, the latter being the only grid reference close to a tarmac road — a feature clearly visible in the photos — it would seem that map reference Y-9056 is the correct one. Nevertheless, to make matters even more complicated, where in 1943 the main road used to run south of the Sidi Mannsour salt lake, now lies to the north of it, along the remains of what was then a small track. So it is possible that the remains of the road marker on the abandoned section of the old main road south of the salt lake may still exist, lost and forgotten in the barren landscape.

The German rearguards moved out north of Sfax during the night of April 9/10 and the civilian population went mad with joy when the leaders of the Eighth Army entered the town next morning. *Left:* **This Valentine 'Buccaneer' belonged to the** 50th Royal Tank Regiment. *Right:* **The welcome was equally overwhelming when General Montgomery visited Sfax on April 11 in company with Major-General Erskine, the commander of the 7th Armoured Division.**

forces were totally exhausted and at 5 p.m. Messe and Bayerlein agreed that the game was up and orders to withdraw were issued during the night.

The Eighth Army renewed its attack on April 7 only to find that the Axis troops were pulling back. A large number of prisoners were taken, mostly Italians, and the figure of POWs counted on the 6th amounted to about 5,300, rising to a total of some 7,000 the following day.

On the night of April 6/7, reasoning that the battle for the Akarit position was reaching its critical stage, the 18th Army Group once again instructed II Corps to furnish maximum aid. Patton duly instructed his armour to push eastward next morning.

The Axis forces facing II Corps having pulled back during the night, abandoning their last positions on Djebel Berda, Hill 369 and in the pass down below, the morning attack on the 7th encountered no resistance. Task Force Benson soon rolled down along the Gabès road, Patton chasing by radio. He then followed in a Jeep, reaching the Kilometre 70 road marker (from Gabès). Reluctantly turning back, Patton told Benson to keep going 'for a fight or a bath' in the sea.

Task Force Benson pushed on eastward, soon crossing into the Eighth Army's zone and at 3.25 p.m., at the Kilometre 67 road marker south of the Sidi Mannsour salt lake, the leaders met up with an armoured car patrol of the 12th Royal Lancers, the reconnaissance regiment of the 1st Armoured Division. It was the first sizeable juncture of Allied forces from the eastern and western limits of the Mediterranean (reconnaissance parties had met well before).

Some 100 miles to the north, the attack of the IX Corps at the Fondouk Pass was launched on the 8th but the Axis defenders, mainly the Afrika-Schützen-Regiment 961, resisted tenaciously and the 6th Armoured Division did not manage to exit the gap until the morning of April 10, too late to interfere with the Axis retreat in any significant way.

The Eighth Army took Sfax on the morning of April 10. That night the German rearguards shifted north-west of Sousse and late on the 11th they were reaching positions at Enfidaville. Sousse was occupied on the morning of the 12th, and at the same time the X Corps of the Eighth Army was making contact with the IX Corps of First Army near Kairouan. By April 13, the two Allied armies squared up to the Axis forces trapped in north-eastern Tunisia.

The failure to penetrate the Fondouk passes expeditiously led to a great deal of recrimination between British and Americans. The IX Corps commander, Lieutenant-General John Crocker, blamed the failure upon the US 34th Infantry Division to get through the pass expeditiously. He recommended withdrawal of the division for retraining of junior officers at the rear under British guidance. American officers complained in turn about the poor corps' plan of attack on which General Crocker had insisted as being unnecessarily prodigal with American troops and matériel. The debate put the relationship between the Allies under considerable strain and Eisenhower and Alexander had to take swift action to try to halt the mounting tide of criticism. Yet, in spite of these efforts, these events had taken their toll, something that was to affect later British-American operations.

Jocks of the 51st (Highland) Division leave their calling card on the wall of a house in Sfax.

THE END OF THE WAR IN NORTH AFRICA

While operations in south and south-central Tunisia were still developing, General Alexander was considering plans for the final attack on the Axis bridgehead. He decided to follow Eisenhower's suggestion that the main effort should be made towards the east through First Army's sector. There, the concentration of forces could be completed sooner and subsequent maintenance would be easier. Alexander ordered Anderson to prepare to launch the main assault about April 22 and instructed Montgomery to release an armoured division and an armoured car brigade to strengthen First Army's attack.

Eisenhower was concerned about the disappointing results achieved by II Corps in southern Tunisia and, in a letter dated March 23, he insisted that the II Corps should be given a mission that would keep it committed aggressively. 'I desire that you make a real effort to use the II US Corps right up to the bitter end of the campaign, even if maintenance reasons compel it to be stripped down eventually to a total of two divisions and supporting Corps troops'.

Plans for the Finale

In conformity with these instructions, General Alexander's staff drafted plans which included provision for a II Corps zone at the northern flank of the Allied front where it was to capture Bizerte. Alexander's first thought had been to subordinate the II Corps to the First Army (since March 8 the corps was directly under 18th Army Group) and he discussed the idea with Patton on April 12. However, Patton strongly objected to the proposal, arguing that there was still a lot of ill will after IX Corps blamed the 34th Infantry Division for the failure at Fondouk, and also because of the dismissive attitude of the British staff towards the 1st Armored Division.

To try to smooth things over, on the 14th Eisenhower flew to Haïdra to confer with Generals Alexander, Anderson, Patton, and Bradley. As far as the arrangements involving II Corps were concerned, Alexander tactfully met American wishes and formally kept the II Corps under his own command, rather than under Anderson's First Army. However, he let Anderson give it its orders.

From April 10, units of II Corps started to move north to a new sector north-east of Béja. Five days later, Patton returned to planning the invasion of Sicily, and Bradley, his deputy commander for the past six weeks, took over.

On April 16, 18th Army Group issued the plan for the final offensive to be called Operation 'Vulcan'. The Allied operations were intended to tighten the cordon around the Axis bridgehead; then drive a wedge between Tunis and Bizerte, and finally overwhelm first the defenders of Tunis followed by those at Bizerte. The First Army was to capture Tunis and 'co-operate with II Corps in the capture of

Sergeant Elms of the 17th/21st Lancers and his crew, Trooper Bates, Signalman Bower, and Trooper Goddard, are pictured pulling through the barrel of their 6-pounder on their Crusader at El Aroussa while preparing for the drive on Tunis.

At the Casablanca conference, the Allied leaders impressed on General Alexander, the 18th Army Group commander, that the campaign in Tunisia must end by April 30 latest so that Operation 'Husky' — the invasion of Sicily — could be launched before August. Consequently, the plan for the final attack was issued on April 16. This Bofors anti-aircraft gun and crew with the First Army were pictured in action on the Goubellat Plain near Medjez el Bab.

General Alexander directed the First Army to make the main effort, first driving a wedge between Tunis and Bizerte; then clearing the Tunis sector and finally the Bizerte area. Operation 'Vulcan' was to commence on April 22.

General Anderson (left) visited Général Koeltz, the commander of the French XIXème Corps d'Armée, at his forward headquarters. The corps was positioned on the First Army's right flank with the task of pushing towards Zaghouan.

Bizerte', while the Eighth Army was to attack north from Enfidaville and 'prevent the enemy withdrawing into the Cap Bon Peninsula'. April 22 was fixed as the start date.

The First Army was to make the main effort with the V Corps. It was first to regain Longstop Hill (Djebel el Ahmera) and the road junction southeast of Medjez el Bab known as Peter's Corner, and then gain the high ground between El Bathan and Massicault. At the same time, IX Corps was to advance from an area south-west of Bou Arada, with its objective the high ground adjacent to the Sebkret el Kourzia, northwest of Pont du Fahs. From there it was to threaten the main highway north to Tunis. It was hoped that the Germans would then commit their armour giving IX Corps the chance to destroy it.

On the left flank, II Corps was first to take the high ground near Chouïgui on V Corps' left flank, and launch a second assault towards Bizerte via Sedjenane. On the First Army's right flank, the XIXème Corps d'Armée was directed to clear Djebel Chirich and Djebel Fkirine on the southern side of the road to Pont du Fahs and Djebel Mansour to the north of the road, but this attack was only to be started after those on each flank — V Corps on the left and the Eighth Army on the right — had reached a suitable stage. It was then to progress toward Zaghouan.

The Eighth Army was to attack first on the night of April 19-20, its attack on the Enfidaville line aimed at drawing Axis reinforcements to that portion of the front.

TO HOLD IN TUNISIA

On April 8 Hitler and Mussolini met at Klessheim Castle, near Salzburg, for the annual conference of the Axis partners. Deeply concerned that the Allies'

next step would be the invasion of Italy, Mussolini wanted the Germans to go on the defensive on the Eastern Front, even coming to terms with Stalin, in order to be able to meet the western threat with overwhelming power. His

plan to counter the Allied strategy in North Africa was to hold in Tunisia and fall on their forces from the rear by attacking through Spain and Spanish Morocco and seizing the Balearic Islands.

Meanwhile, Mussolini travelled to Austria on April 7 to discuss the on-going situation with Hitler. The Führer was waiting to greet the Duce at Puch railway station, south of Salzburg, both then moving on for discussions at Klessheim castle. The faltering Mussolini arrived with every intention of having his own way but, as Goebbels recorded in his diary, 'the Duce underwent a complete change' as Hitler 'succeeded in pushing Mussolini back on the rails'.

Rommel had to quit the North Africa battlefield through ill health and on March 10 he was succeeded as commander of Heeresgruppe Afrika by von Arnim (right). He, in turn, yielded command of the 5. Panzerarmee to General der Panzertruppen Gustav von Vaerst (left). This photo was taken by Kriegsberichter Hurtmanns in early May.

Hitler was also determined to hold on to Tunisia but the motive behind his decision was more political than strategic for the German High Command was convinced that a collapse in Tunisia would have dire consequences for Italy, possibly resulting in the overthrow of Mussolini. Hitler made clear to the Duce that there could be no compromise with the Soviets. Also, he argued that even if forces were available, the idea of moving through Spain, or a seizure of the Balearics, would arouse the Spaniards to stubborn resistance. He vowed that the Axis could hold Tunisia indefinitely and as long as the Allies were kept occupied there, they could not undertake any large-scale operation in Italy, Sicily or the French Mediterranean coast. In any case, the best Axis troops were in Tunisia and their evacuation was impossible.

In exchange for renewed promises of reinforcements, Hitler persuaded Mussolini to agree to allowing Italian cruisers and destroyers be used to transport men and materials to Tunisia. However, after he returned to the soberer atmosphere of his quarters in Rome, the Duce became as depressed as he was before the meeting with Hitler and he now endeavoured to back-track on his promises. By April 12, when he conferred with Kesselring, the Duce appeared in a somewhat upbeat mood and said that he was 'convinced that the Americans will do nothing before having settled the Tunisian problem. Only then will they eventually attack Sardinia, Sicily, Crete, etc.' Therefore, he stressed that Tunisia must be held until the autumn to rob the Allies of the favourable summer months. 'In the short time remaining before winter, they will do nothing.'

STRANGLED

In spite of increasing Italian doubts, the Germans continued to run supplies and reinforcements to Tunisia. The Axis supply ships now faced terrible odds. Since the beginning of the year, the Allied stranglehold on the Sicilian Channel had tightened, and almost every night destroyers and MTBs from Malta and Bône were on the lookout for Axis supply ships. From Malta, Beaufort torpedo-bombers daily attacked shipping while Beauforts and Albacores continued their minelaying operations in the approaches to harbours used by Axis. RAF and American bombers flying from Malta, Algerian and Cyrenaican airfields, raided harbours, attacking Naples, Messina, Palermo and Catania, and also the terminal airfields and harbours at Tunis, Bizerte, Sfax and Sousse.

High altitude formation bombing of shipping by B-17s also proved to be very effective, with a pattern of 28 tons of bombs having a good chance of sinking a medium-sized ship, when a normal formation of 18 B-17s carried double this load. On April 4, B-17s sunk the *Sicilia* (9,646 GRT) in Naples harbour, and on the 6th they sank the *Rovereto* (8,564 GRT) and the *San Diego* (6,013 GRT) off Bizerte.

In April 29 Axis ships were sent to the bottom with the loss of 15,500 tonnes of supplies, and two vessels were damaged. Supply by air still continued, bringing in 4,300 tons of supplies and 8,400 German soldiers, but at the horrendous cost of 117 transport aircraft. It was a heavy price to pay but even so 11,142 Germans (number of Italians is not recorded) were shipped to Tunisia in April along with 23,017 tonnes of supplies, 44 tanks, 277 vehicles and 47 guns.

In February the Allied air force command prepared a strong programme to choke off the Axis air supply line from Italy but the operation was repeatedly postponed for various reasons. Known

In March and April, the air forces were the main weapon in the Allied armoury against Axis shipping, and aircraft sank 33 Axis ships of over 500 GRT, compared to 26 by submarines and three by surface vessels. Ultra provided Allied commanders with accurate and timely information on the convoys to Tunisia and the timing of the Allied air forces interceptions was so perfect that Fliegerkorps Tunis concluded in mid-March 'that the course for Convoys D and C were betrayed to the enemy'. The original caption for this shot taken from a B-17 after just having scored a direct hit, is quite vague, but from the little information available it matches two successes by B-17s off Bizerte on April 6. The Italian cargo ship *Rovereto* (an ex-French ship of 8,564 GRT which had been seized by the Germans and then operated by the Italians), was hit and left on fire off Cape Zebib east of Bizerte to be finished off ten days later by the Royal Navy *MTB 634*. The second vessel sunk was the cargo ship *San Diego*, an ex-French ship of 6,013 GRT taken over by the Germans.

The harbour of Bizerte, which was the main port for the Axis naval supply effort, was the subject of a series of air raids by B-17s of the Northwest African Strategic Air Force between January and April. One particularly heavy raid was on January 23 when two waves, escorted by P-38s, hit the naval base. Much damage was done to the facilities with one vessel sunk in the harbour. Twenty Axis fighters which attacked the formations were claimed destroyed. The B-17s visited Bizerte again on January 29 and February 26 with RAF Wellingtons bombing during the night of the 25th and 27th. B-17s returned again on March 23 and April 12. The censored caption to this photo, date not specified, states that 'not only was shipping struck but great damage was done to shops and oil tanks along the coastline'.

as Operation 'Flax', it comprised fighter sweeps off the Sicilian narrows combined with bombing raids on the terminal and staging-post airfields. It finally began on April 5 when two formations struck Axis aircraft crossing the Sicilian straits early that morning, while a little later B-17s hit the Bizerte and Tunis airfields in an effort to catch on the ground those aircraft that might have got through. Other bombers went to Sicily to destroy any aircraft that might be staging there en route to Tunisia. Fighter sweeps contributed to the whole operation, which may have destroyed as many as 161 aircraft on the ground and 40 in the air.

On April 18, five squadrons intercepted a mixed formation of Junkers Ju 52s and Messerschmitt Me 323s flying at a very low altitude and 38 of them were claimed as destroyed. On April 22, as Operation 'Vulcan' began, 39 more Axis transports were intercepted and destroyed, some bursting into flames as if carrying supplies of fuel. Thereafter, the Axis were forced to fly at night, and in individual rather than formation flights, thus reducing deliveries by over 60 per cent.

Since those days Bizerte has been considerably expanded.

Apart from the 439 sorties carried out against the ports in Tunisia — Tunis, Bizerte, Ferryville, Sousse, Sfax — in March and April there were also 1,302 bombing sorties flown against the loading ports in Italy: Naples, Palermo, Messina and Catania. Office of War Information photographer Nick Parrino pictured this bomber crew being given a briefing on their Cyrenaican airfield before departure. The date is unknown but the sketch on the board shows that Palermo was their target so it could be either April 7 or 15 when B-24s raided the port. The marking partly visible identifies the aircraft as *The Vulgar Virgin*, 41-24198, of the 344th Squadron, 98th Bomb Group.

On April 26, Kesselring explained to Generale Ambrosio that 'the rate of transportation was too slow to bring the necessary reinforcements in time' to enable the exhausted troops to hold onto their present positions. He urged him to divert to Tunisia small vessels then being used to convoy matériel to Sardinia and he repeated his request that Italian destroyers should also be urgently employed since everything was needed at once in Tunisia: fuel, munitions, and men.

One of the most successful interceptions of Operation 'Flax' took place on April 18 when four squadrons of Curtis Warhawks — the 64th, 65th and 66th Fighter Squadrons of the 57th Fighter Group, and the attached 314th Fighter Squadron of the 324th Fighter Group — caught a scattered formation of Junkers Ju 52s heading back towards Sicily. The P-40s of the 64th Fighter Squadron, and the Spitfires of the RAF's No. 92 Squadron flying top cover, stayed high while the remaining three squadrons went in to attack the transports. Altogether, 24 of the Ju 52s, ten of the escorting Bf 109s, and an unknown number of Italian fighters were brought down. Nick Parrino took this photograph of members of the 64th Fighter Squadron.

On May 1, only four Siebel ferries and two small craft reached Tunisian ports, discharging 90 tons of fuel and 60 tons of ammunition. The last supply shipments reached Tunisia three days later, small vessels and ferries bringing in 1,100 tons of ammunition and 110 tons of fuel. Transport aircraft landed 70 tons of fuel and another 30 tons of ammunition.

Left: Lieutenant Robert J. Byrne of the 64th Fighter Squadron posed for Parrino after returning from the epic April mission having claimed to having destroyed three Bf 109s to add to his score of four Axis victories. The caption also says that Byrne was from Saint Louis, Missouri, and that before the war he was a pro-baseball player with Cincy farm system. *Right:* Lieutenant Richard E. Duffy of the 314th Fighter Squadron was pictured giving an account of the April 18 air battle in which he claimed five Ju 52s. He and two of other pilots — Second Lieutenants Arthur B. Cleaveland and MacArthur Powers — also shot down five Axis aircraft in this engagement to become the first American single-day aces of Second World War.

For the opening of Operation 'Flax' on April 5, 18 B-17s of the 97th Bomb Group escorted by American and British fighters attacked the main unloading airfields near Tunis at El Aouina and Sidi Ahmed, destroying several aircraft on the ground. Quite possibly this was the day when war photographer Seltsam from the Luftwaffe Kriegsberichter Kompanie 6 just happened to arrive as the raid was taking place. *Right:* Having stopped his car at a reasonable distance from one of the airfields, he took several shots of the huge pall of smoke drifting overhead. *Below:* After the attack was over, he toured the airfield to picture ground crews checking on the damage.

By the end of April, 105 Ju 52 transports are recorded as having been destroyed with a further 22 damaged in the effort to deliver supplies to Tunisia. Ground crews attempted to make airworthy those only lightly damaged.

The two Axis groupings, the 5. Panzerarmee and 1a Armata, were then holding a bridgehead running from the northern coast near Kef Abbed to the Gulf of Hammamet near Enfidaville. The 5. Panzerarmee were occupying the western portion with (from right to left) Division von Manteuffel, the 334. Infanterie-Division, and Division General Göring.

From the Miliane river to Saouaf, south of Zaghouan, the Afrikakorps assumed command of the zone between the 1a Armata and the 5. Panzerarmee using what remained of the 10. and 21. Panzer-Divisions, Divisione Superga, the 50a Brigada Speciale and some miscellaneous Italian units. Starting on April 21, the armoured and mobile elements of the two panzer divisions were gradually withdrawn from this mountainous sector, and tasked instead as a reserve force. The 10. Panzer-Division was then moved to the Medjerda plain, west of Tunis, to serve as mobile reserve against the expected Allied thrust against the city.

The Last Battles

In the coastal sector, the 1a Armata was holding the southern line with the XXI Corpo d'Armata on the right and the XX Corpo d'Armata on the left. The Divisione La Spezia was the furthest unit inland, then the 164. leichte Afrika-Division, and on hills to the east, the Divisione Pistoia, Giovani Fascisti, and Trieste. The 90. leichte Afrika-Division was on the coastal plain with the 15. Panzer-Division under Heeresgruppe Afrika's control in a second, supporting position south-east of Zaghouan. The remnants of the Fallschirmjäger-Brigade 1 and of Divisione Centauro, and the 19. Flak-Division, were also used to strengthen this sector of the bridgehead's defence.

One must remember that by now the strength of these units was greatly reduced, bearing little relationship to the normal composition of a division. The 10. and 15. Panzer-Divisions, each with a handful of tanks, were only equal to a single combat team, and the 90. and 164. leichte Afrika-Divisions together barely equalled one infantry division. Divisione Pistoia, Trieste and Giovani Fascisti together comprised less than a dozen battalions with about 90 guns, and as far as Divisione La Spezia was concerned, it was practically non-existent.

The 1a Armata had three-fifths of the Heeresgruppe artillery and two-thirds of the infantry and von Arnim warned Messe that he would hear no protests if he had to shift any units northwards, for example to meet the threat of an attack at Medjez el Bab or Bou Arada by the First Army.

The severe shortages of supplies and ammunition was clear to all and the general feeling was that the battle for the Tunisian bridgehead was approaching its terminal stage. To attempt to try and counter this mood, on April 12 and 14 von Arnim issued very stern

Sergeant Silverside took this shot of troops from 6th Armoured Division gathering round a road sign before the last battles began. Operation 'Vulcan' started early on April 22, the IX Corps opening the offensive, V Corps following on the 23rd.

For this last phase of the war in Africa, the air superiority of the Allies was overwhelming and their bombers struck endlessly at Axis forces and positions. In April, 30 Bostons from No. 114 Squadron, augmented by American aircraft from the 47th Bomb Group that was then attached to No. 326 Wing, attacked German positions that were holding up the advance of the 6th Armoured Division to Tunis.

In the Eighth Army sector, the X Corps closed up to the Axis positions established at Enfidaville where the hills jut eastwards at Takrouna, a precipitous rocky knoll with a village perched on top of it. This narrowed the coastal plain to a ribbon of flatland adjacent to the sea. The New Zealand Division attacked Takrouna on the night of April 19 but suffered heavy losses. Finally, at daybreak on the 20th, a small party from the 28th (Maori) Battalion managed to reach the top of the rock. The New Zealanders finally cleared the position on the 21st. Over on the western side, the 4th Indian Division also encountered strong resistance when they attacked Djebel Garci, and the fighting was so costly that Montgomery decided to suspend the attack for four days. *Above:* Artist Alex J. Ingram drew this dramatic painting of the Takrouna hill and landscape being peppered with exploding shells. *Right:* A nice comparison by Steve Hamilton.

The southernmost Axis positions were no more than screening defences held by light forces and they gave way at once. *Left:* On April 20, AFPU photographer Sergeant Fox pictured men of the 2nd/6th The Queen's Royal Regiment searching Enfidaville. *Above:* The particular combination of door, windows and roof enables the author to trace this obscure side street.

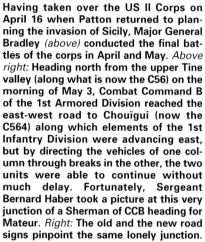

Having taken over the US II Corps on April 16 when Patton returned to planning the invasion of Sicily, Major General Bradley *(above)* conducted the final battles of the corps in April and May. *Above right:* Heading north from the upper Tine valley (along what is now the C56) on the morning of May 3, Combat Command B of the 1st Armored Division reached the east-west road to Chouïgui (now the C564) along which elements of the 1st Infantry Division were advancing east, but by directing the vehicles of one column through breaks in the other, the two units were able to continue without much delay. Fortunately, Sergeant Bernard Haber took a picture at this very junction of a Sherman of CCB heading for Mateur. *Right:* The old and the new road signs pinpoint the same lonely junction.

warnings against rumour-mongering and defeatist talk. On April 20, Kesselring echoed this and issued an Order of the Day in which he exhorted every German soldier to fight, in this historic hour, with bravery and unshakeable resolution, to 'destroy the enemy's hopes' to deliver a decisive blow in the Mediterranean.

With the intention of holding the Tunisian bridgehead for as long as possible, both German and Italian High Commands did not prepare any plans to evacuate troops from Tunisia. In any case, the means of transportation were so meagre that, in the words of Kesselring to Messe on April 16, 'there can no longer be any question of getting away 300,000 men'.

In any event, the Allies had plans of their own to forestall the evacuation of substantial forces to Italy, and their overwhelming naval and air superiority would have condemned any Axis attempt to evacuate troops. Perhaps with Dunkirk in mind, the elaborate naval and air plans designed to prevent an Axis withdrawal were known as Operation 'Retribution'.

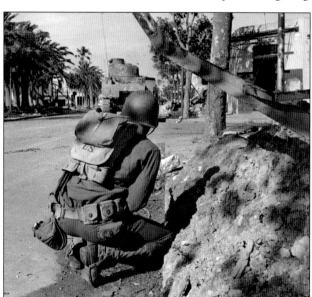

Left: The leaders of II Corps entered Bizerte during the afternoon of May 7. The main Axis forces had already evacuated the town and resistance was light. *Above:* The comparison was taken at the junction of Rue Habib Bourguiba and Rue Mongi Slim.

Above: In his caption, Sergeant Haber described the tactics to be used on May 7 as the tanks advanced. They were to 'locate the snipers and call the infantry to round them up from their hiding places'. Right: Then the street on the left was called the Boulevard de la République during the French protectorate but has now been renamed Rue Habib Bourguiba after the main figure leading Tunisia's struggle for independence. The former Avenue de France on the right is now Rue Taieb M'Hiri after another major player in the quest for independence. On May 8, the GIs stepped aside to allow the French Corps Franc d'Afrique to complete the mopping up of the town. This unit was raised in November 1942 comprising volunteers — non-French refugees, Moroccan and Algerian natives and Jews under restrictions — who could not readily be enrolled in the regular French Army.

Left: Another shot taken in the Boulevard de la République. The way that this patrol from the French Corps Franc d'Afrique was supposedly mopping up the town — outward from the centre — strongly suggests that this was a staged shot. Above: This is the junction with the old Rue de Savoie, now Rue Salah Ben Ali.

Sergeant Haber pictured this formation of the 15th Engineer Battalion, 9th Infantry Division, in Square Maréchal Foch shortly after the capture of Bizerte.

The distinctive building located across what is still known as Place Foch, was formerly the Grand Hôtel Europe, built in 1920, now a mix of shops and cafes.

On May 9, General Manton S. Eddy, the commander of the 9th Infantry Division, visited Bizerte in company with his assistant commander, Brigadier General Daniel A. Stroh.

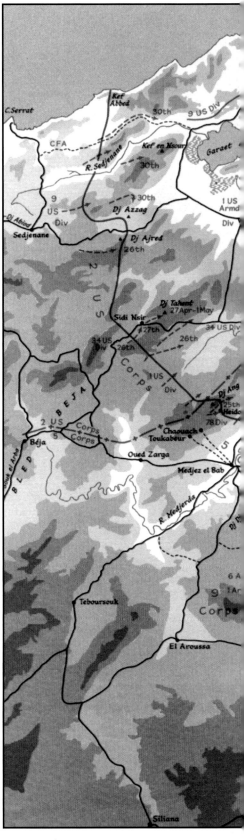

The clearing of the Axis bridgehead in Tunisia. The blue line shows the approximate Axis front line on April 22, the day when Operation 'Vulcan' began. Dashed red lines show the main Allied advances from April 22 onward, and the red lines those during the final Operation 'Strike' from May 6 through to May 11. In the south, from April 29 the Eighth Army's role was only that of holding the front.

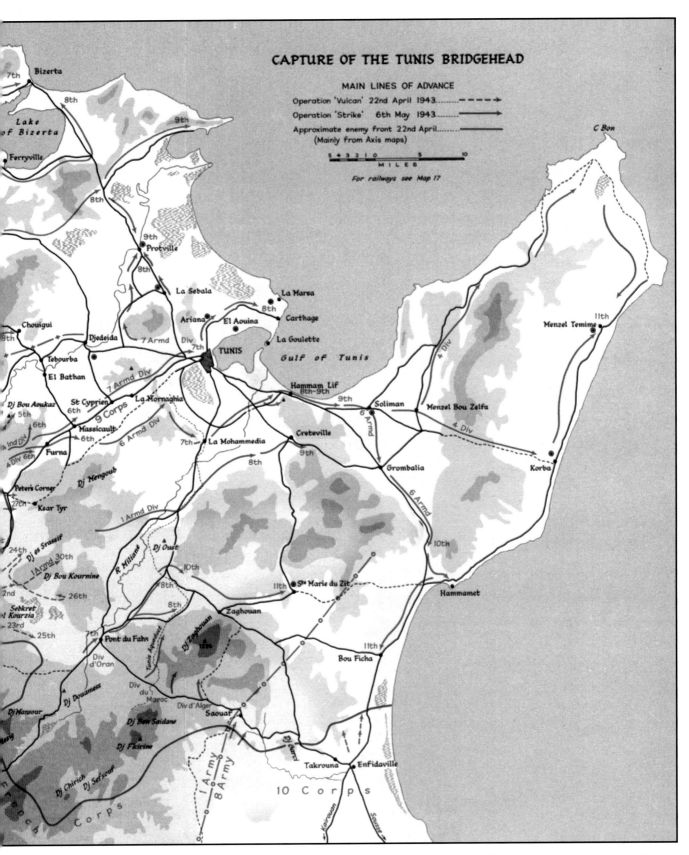

CAPTURE OF THE TUNIS BRIDGEHEAD

MAIN LINES OF ADVANCE

Operation 'Vulcan' 22nd April 1943.........----►
Operation 'Strike' 6th May 1943.........——►
Approximate enemy front 22nd April........——
(Mainly from Axis maps)

5 4 3 2 1 0   5   10
M I L E S

For railways see Map 17

On April 19, von Arnim approved a suggestion by Generalmajor Josef Schmid, the commander of Division General Göring, to mount a spoiling attack between Medjez el Bab and Goubellat. Just south of the main highway leading into Medjez el Bab, Group Audorff (Grenadier-Regiment 754 of the 334. Infanterie-Division) was to attack toward Djebel Bou Mouss.

In the centre, Group Schirmer (part of Jäger-Regiment Hermann Göring reinforced by elements of Panzer-Regiment 7) was to capture the strongholds on the hills north-west of Goubellat, while Group Funk (a battalion of the Grenadier-Regiment Hermann Göring) was to protect the southern flank by advancing against the northern foothills of Djebel Rihane.

The three battle groups attacked in the small hours of April 21. Achieving complete surprise, the assaults initially wrought some confusion among British troops and penetrated their lines along a 12-mile front to a depth of about five miles. British tanks and artillery moved in at daybreak and soon halted the attack, forcing the Germans to withdraw to their original lines by nightfall.

269

Left: **Operation 'Strike', the final blow, started early on May 6. On May 7 Churchill tanks of the North Irish Horse — Churchill Mark IIIs of the C Squadron — pushed through Tebourba in** support of the 3rd Brigade of the 1st (British) Division. *Right:* **Unfortunately, the characteristic house in background has gone to be replaced by a public swimming pool.**

The Germans claimed to have taken over 300 prisoners and to have destroyed five batteries of artillery, about 80 trucks and motor vehicles, and seven tanks, at a price of over 300 casualties, but their spoiling attack did not to delay the launch of the planned Allied offensive.

Operation 'Vulcan' begun at 3.40 a.m. on April 22 by IX Corps followed at intervals by the three other corps of First Army. On the right, the 128th Brigade was halted when it came up against dug-in defences but on the left the 138th Brigade had gained its objectives by noon. The 6th Armoured Division began later than had been hoped, and although it met with determined opposition from elements of Panzer-Regiment 7 and Panzer-Abteilung 501, it still managed to advance nearly ten miles before being brought to a standstill in front of resolute German defences.

The V Corps attack went in on the evening of April 22 on both sides of the Medjerda river with the 78th Infantry Division to the left of the river and the 1st Infantry Division on the right. The 4th Infantry entered the battle on the right wing on the 24th. Grim hand-to-hand fighting continued for several days, marked on the 26th by the capture of Djebel el Rhaa, the northern end of Longstop Hill. That day, seeing that V Corps was making progress while IX Corps was held up, Anderson directed the 6th Armoured Division into army reserve for the purpose of using it in the V Corps sector.

On the left flank, the US II Corps reached Sidi Nsir on the 27th while in the south the French XIXème Corps d'Armée closed on the road from Pont du Fahs to Enfidaville.

Above right: **Sergeant Lupson pictured men of the King's Shropshire Light Infantry chatting with locals beside an abandoned PzKpfw III at the level crossing at the northern entrance of the town. Stripped of its tracks and running gear, the tank has been cannibalised by German mechanics in a desperate quest for spare parts.** *Right:* **The railway crossing at Tebourba, then and now.**

270

Captain Keating caught up with the leading elements of the 11th Hussars — a Daimler armoured car leading, a White scout car, an Humber armoured car, a Jeep, another White scout car — entering Le Bardo, the western suburb of Tunis.

through and race to Tunis before the Axis had time to man the town defences. On the left wing, the II Corps was to take the river crossings at Tebourba and Djedeïda and finally make for Bizerte. On the right, V Corps was to take Djebel Bou Aoukaz on the southern side of the Medjerda river to cover the flank of IX Corps, while the XIXème Corps d'Armée was to take Zaghouan.

As General Crocker had been accidentally wounded on the 27th during a demonstration of the capricious PIAT weapon, Lieutenant-General Brian Horrocks was brought in from X Corps on April 30 to take over command of IX Corps while Freyberg replaced him at X Corps.

On May 5, knowing that the 334. Infanterie-Division and Division General Göring had been worn down by the fighting over the last ten days, von Arnim decided to move what remained of the 15. Panzer-Division into the sector in between them — the very sector that IX Corps was due to attack.

In the meantime, the Eighth Army had made half-hearted plans for an attack by X Corps. A local attack by the 169th Brigade of the newly-arrived 56th (London) Division during the night of April 28/29 resulted in the capture of Djebel Terhouna and Djebel es Srafi but an Axis counterattack next morning recaptured Srafi and caused the 169th Brigade to fall back into disorder. Acknowledging that the Eighth Army was not about to break through to Cap Bon, Montgomery asked Alexander to visit him. On the 30th Alexander then directed that the army was to take on a holding role, Montgomery having to transfer the 7th Armoured Division, the 4th Indian Division and the 201st Guards Brigade to First Army.

After visiting Montgomery, Alexander flew to see Anderson and run over the details for Operation 'Strike' — the final operation to end the campaign. The IX Corps was to break the Axis defences with the 4th British Division and the 4th Indian Division in the sector east of Medjez el Bab, and the initial artillery programme was to be huge. The 6th and 7th Armoured Divisions were quickly to follow

Keating then pictured French troops as they arrived at the city centre at 3.40 p.m. There were few Axis troops left and, apart from odd random shots which made them use this Bren Carrier for cover.

Left: These soldiers are passing Bab Bou Saadoun, the western gate to the old part of Tunis. *Above:* A famous landmark, the old gate is now in the centre of a roundabout.

A British Carrier and an American Jeep in Avenue de la Liberté as a French policeman directs the drivers of horse-drawn carts

On the evening of May 5, supported by over 600 guns, the 1st Infantry Division of V Corps captured the heights of Djebel Bou Aoukaz thus securing the IX Corps start line. Then opening at 3 a.m. on the 6th, massed artillery hammered the planned zone of advance of the IX Corps, a tremendous volume of fire with over 16,000 shells falling upon the Axis facing the 4th British Division in two hours. At first light, Allied air forces launched an intensive air attack, mounting nearly 2,000 sorties in 24 hours, something which had never been seen before in Africa in support of ground troops, so deepening and extending the area of bombardment as far as Massicault and Saint-Cyprien.

Crowds six deep line the street while others watch the arrival of Allied forces from the balconies. AFPU photographer

Sergeant Palmer took this photo of a Churchill driving down Avenue de Londres before turning left into Rue de la Liberté.

Another AFPU photographer, Sergeant Black, pictured enthusiastic civilians cheering the crew of a Bren Gun Carrier.

It was taken at the junction of the Avenue de Paris with what was then Avenue Jules Ferry, now Avenue Habib Bourguiba.

The 4th Indian Division then attacked on the left of the Medjez el Bab—Tunis road, while the 4th British Division went in on the right. This opened a channel for the armour and shortly after 11 a.m. the 6th and 7th Armoured Divisions began rolling toward Massicault. The attack overran two battalions of Panzergrenadier-Regiment 115 and pushed back the weak remnants of the 15. Panzer-Division although it still failed to make a decisive breakthrough. That evening the 7th Armoured Division settled into a position north of Massicault with the 6th Armoured to the east of it.

By May 6 von Arnim and his senior commanders — German and Italian — had practically lost overall control of their forces. That evening, he ordered a step-by-step retreat to the so-called 'fortress' area of Tunis—Bizerte. This meant that the 5. Panzerarmee was to pull its centre and left back to the line of Tebourba—Djebel Oust, and the Afrikakorps back to the area of Djebel Oust—Zaghouan. The 1a Armata was to hold its present positions and be responsible for the coastal defence of the Cap Bon peninsula.

The German plans however were hampered by the complete lack of fuel (by May 3 the Heeresgruppe Afrika as a whole was down to half a day's supply) and ammunition was extremely short. Indeed, it was only the providential discovery of a drum of aviation fuel among the flotsam on a nearby beach that enabled von Arnim to move his own headquarters from the northern side of the Cap Bon peninsula to the mountains between Zaghouan and Hammamet where it joined the Afrikakorps command post.

On the morning of May 7, the 6th and 7th Armoured Divisions moved forward from the Massicault area, meeting only scattered resistance, and just before 4 p.m. two patrols, one each from 1st Derbyshire Yeomanry and 11th Hussars, reached the centre of the city with crowds lining the street to welcome them in spite of the pouring rain. The 1st Derbyshire Yeomanry and 11th Hussars mopped up Tunis during the night where Axis troops were few.

Another convoy on the Avenue de Paris, this time being pictured by a Signal Corps photographer, Corporal Robert T. Cummins. These French troops are driving in the opposite direction to that of the Carrier at the top of the page.

Most of the buildings lining the street are unchanged.

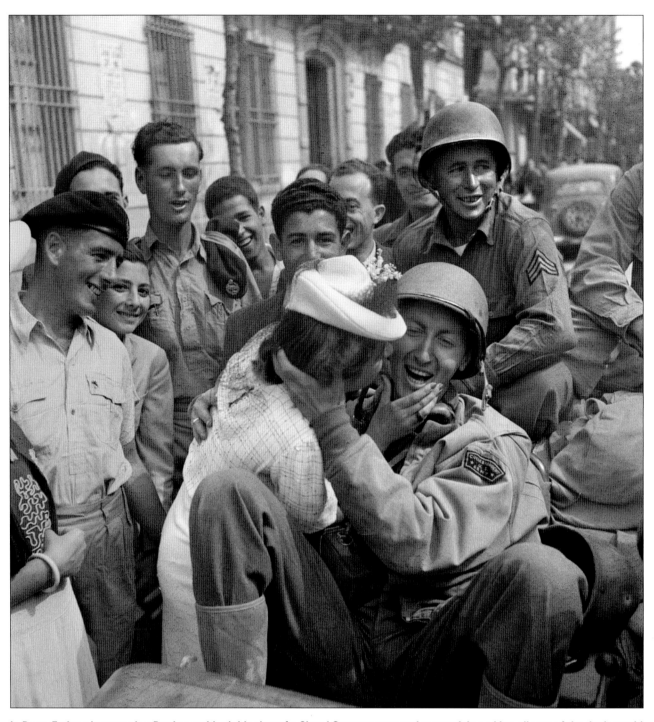

In Porto Farina photographer Parrino grabbed this shot of a Signal Corps correspondent receiving a kiss, all part of the day's work!

At the same time on the left wing, the 9th Reconnaissance Troop, US 9th Infantry Division, reached the outer limits of Bizerte at midday. Reconnaissance elements of the 894th Tank Destroyer Battalion reported their entry into the town at 4.15 p.m. and close behind them came the first two tanks of Company A, 751st Tank Battalion. It appeared that Axis troops had abandoned the town to deploy along the far side of the ship channel to Lac de Bizerte.

At 4.30 p.m., Anderson directed the 6th Armoured Division to turn southeast to stop Axis forces taking up positions to defend the Cap Bon peninsula. As the leading armour reached the Hammam Lif defile, a gap of 300 metres

between the cliff and the surf just east of Tunis, they found it strongly defended by Kampfgruppe Frantz armed with anti-tank guns and other artillery. For two days, the defenders led by Generalleutnant Gotthard Frantz of the 19. Flak-Division blocked the way forward.

The First Army drive to Tunis had split the Axis forces into two main parts with the much larger proportion south of the Allied corridor.

By the afternoon of May 8, the smaller northern forces were assembled in two major pockets. The northern group in the hills north of Garaet el Mabtouha and El Alia consisted mainly of the 5. Panzerarmee headquarters and the remainder of Division von

Manteuffel, with 15. Panzer-Division and some elements of the 10. Panzer-Division. To the south-west, beyond wide areas of Allied-held ground and impassable salt marshes, the remnants of the 334. Infanterie-Division and small groups of other units were encircled in the hills between Mateur and Tebourba. The hope that these troops could fight their way out of the pocket and join the main group to the northeast had been abandoned early on May 8. In the south, von Arnim attempted to build up a new defence line across the base of the Cap Bon peninsula from Hammam Lif through the mountains to Zaghouan and Enfidaville with what was left of the 1a Armata and the Afrikakorps.

Threatened with encirclement from the north, Division General Göring swiftly fell back to the Hammam Lif position. On its left, facing west, surviving elements of the 10. Panzer-Division were in the mountains east of Cheylus, next to Italian elements interspersed with what was left of the 90. and 164. leichte Afrika-Divisions. To the south, what remained of the 21. Panzer-Division and Divisione Superga had fought their way back to the area of Zaghouan. During the night of May 8-9, the two battalions of Panzergrenadier-Regiment Afrika and an artillery battalion were rushed to reinforce Kampfgruppe Frantz at Hammam Lif.

There were some inconclusive conferences in Rome about pulling out specialists and valuable officers and the Chief of the Army Personnel Office, Generalleutnant Rudolf Schmundt, raised the possibility with Jodl on April 20. Jodl consulted with Kesselring but rejected the idea because of the bad effect it would have on the morale of those left behind. Schmundt renewed his proposal on May 7 and, although the

On May 7, Admiral Cunningham launched Operation 'Retribution' with the colourful signal to 'Sink, burn and destroy. Let nothing pass'. As the Italian fleet was expected to intervene, so the battleships HMS *Nelson* and *Rodney* and the aircraft carrier HMS *Formidable* were moved to Algiers in readiness to counter any threat. In the event, the Italian navy did not leave port and there was no organised attempt to evacuate Axis forces by sea. Destroyers and flotillas of British MTBs and American PT boats patrolled the waters off Tunisia but only intercepted small craft. At sea, the Allies captured 897 of the Axis and over 650 men were thought to have escaped to Italy. An unknown number drowned. *Above:* A Royal Navy photographer pictured this fishing smack, crowded with 15 Italian officers and soldiers which was intercepted by the destroyer HMS *Lamberton* off Cape Bon. *Right:* Some Germans risked their lives in frighteningly small rubber dinghies to try to escape. Taking this shot from destroyer HMS *Jervis*, Lieutenant F. G. Roper commented that they had already paddled 15 miles out to sea before the Royal Navy caught up with them.

idea of withdrawing a specified list of individuals was accepted, it was by then too late for implementation. From his hospital in the Semmering, Rommel intervened, sending a message to ask 'that at least the irreplaceable people should be got out, people such as Gause, Bayerlein and Bülowius'.

At the end of April, certain senior officers were reported sick and were flown out to Italy. They included Generalmajor Weber (334. Infanterie-Division), Generalmajor von Manteuffel (Division von Manteuffel), and Generalmajor Bayerlein, Messe's Chief-of-Staff (Bayerlein was promoted Generalmajor on March 1).

On May 4, von Arnim sent Generalleutnant Alfred Gause, Chief-of-Staff of Heeresgruppe Afrika, to a conference in Italy, thus saving him from capture. Some days later Göring ordered Luftwaffe officers to leave and several from Division General Göring and of the Fallschirmjäger-Brigade 1 were airlifted out including Generalmajor Schmid, and Major Rudolf Witzig and Hauptmann Gerhart Schirmer, both famous from earlier paratrooper feats at Eben-Emael and in Holland in 1940, and Crete in 1941.

The day's catch, about to enter harbour. German prisoners picked up off Cape Bon by the destroyer HMS *Jervis* lined up on the deck ready to disembark.

Surrender

At 9.30 a.m. on May 9, General von Vaerst, who had moved his command post to El Alia, east of the Bizerte lake, sent the last situation report from the northern pocket: 'Our armour and artillery have been destroyed; without ammunition and fuel; we shall fight to the last'.

Half an hour later his emissaries reached Major General Harmon's headquarters. When General Bradley was told about this development, instructions were transmitted detailing the terms that had been agreed at the Casablanca Conference: simply unconditional surrender. At noon, von Vaerst accepted these terms, the 5. Panzerarmee achieving the sad accolade of becoming the second German army to capitulate in the war. (The first was the 6. Armee of Generalfeldmarschall Friedrich Paulus which had surrendered at Stalingrad on February 2.)

Eventually, the number of prisoners taken in this northern pocket reached a total of almost 40,000. Generals Gustav von Vaerst, Fritz Krause (334. Infanterie-Division), Karl Bülowius (Division von Manteuffel), Willibald Borowietz (15. Panzer-Division), Gerhard Bassenge (commander Fortress Area Tunis-Bizerte) and Georg Neuffer (20. Flak-Division), were all rounded up. They spent May 9/10 in custody at the headquarters of II Corps near Mateur before being transferred to First Army headquarters.

As the Allies entered the city Italian soldiers were herded out. The capture of Tunis had effectively split the Axis forces into two giving no possible option other than to surrender.

The northern group — the 5. Panzerarmee — was surrounded by the II Corps in the hills east and south of Bizerte and the army commander, General von Vaerst, surrendered at 9.30 a.m. on May 9. The number of prisoners taken in this northern pocket reached a total of nearly 40,000; here Signal Corps photographer Heuer pictured some of them.

Left: **These Italians are being loaded aboard wagons in the railway station at Grombalia to be taken to the larger POW compounds.** *Above:* **The railway line is still used by passenger and goods trains travelling south to Sousse and Sfax.**

A huge POW cage was hastily established just west of Mateur where approximately 38,000 prisoners were collected over the next three or four days. Sergeant Max Campbell hitched a ride in a light aircraft on May 9 to get a bird's eye view.

On the eastern half of the solitary peak of Djebel Ichkeul, making good use of caves dug into the mountainside, a group of about 300 men of Auf-klärungs-Abteilung General Göring held out until May 10.

During the afternoon of the 9th, the 6th Armoured Division finally forced the Hammam Lif defile in a co-ordinated attack, armoured elements driving along the beach over the firm wet sand at the very edge of the surf. This last battle was costly as it led to the loss of 22 Shermans. The 6th Armoured then pushed on towards Hammamet, gathering more and more prisoners as it went. The leaders reached

This comparison was taken from the side of the P7 road between Mateur and Sedjenane with the Djebel Ichkeul in the far distance.

The southern group surrounded east of Tunis was the largest part of the Axis force in Tunisia. On May 13 General von Arnim surrendered the two headquarters and staffs with him, i.e. Heeresgruppe Afrika and Afrikakorps. Their forces — various Italian units interspersed among remnants of the 90. and 164. leichte Afrika-Divisions, and what remained of the 21. Panzer-Division — soon came down from the hills. These Germans are surrendering to the crew of a Stuart.

Soliman on the morning of the 10th and by 5 p.m. they were at Grombalia, half way across the base of Cap Bon peninsula. Pushing on to the south-east, patrols of the 12th Royal Lancers soon linked up with the French XIXème Corps d'Armée in the vicinity of Zaghouan.

In the hills south-east of Zaghouan, the 1a Armata held out with its remaining Italian units interspersed among the Germans of the 90. and 164. leichte Afrika-Divisions, and what remained of the 21. Panzer-Division. General Freyberg had signalled Generalleutnant von Sponeck, commanding the 90. leichte Afrika-Division, to surrender but no reply was received.

On May 11, two brigades of the 4th Division made the circuit of the Cap Bon peninsula, the 10th Brigade driving along the coastal road to meet the 12th Brigade along the south-eastern side near Menzel Heurr. Meanwhile the leaders of the 6th Armoured Division drove south from Hammamet and reached Bou Ficha at 6 p.m. At the same time, just to the west, the French had received the surrender of a group of some 10,000 men under Oberst Pfeiffer.

Generals and high-ranking officers captured in the northern part of the final Axis bridgehead were taken to the headquarters of II Corps near Mateur where they spent May 9/10 before being transferred to First Army HQ. Among them were four generals from the Army, Generals Gustav von Vaerst (commanding 5. Panzerarmee), Fritz Krause (334. Infanterie-Division), Karl Bülowius (Division von Manteuffel) and Willibald Borowietz (15. Panzer-Division), and two from the Luftwaffe, Gerhard

Bassenge (commander Fortress Area Tunis-Bizerte) and Georg Neuffer (20. Flak-Division). Out of the 32 Axis generals — 16 of them German — who fell into Allied hands, Generalmajor Kurt von Liebenstein *(left)*, the commander of the 164. leichte Afrika-Division, appeared to raise particular attention. *Right:* General-leutnant Friedrich von Broich, commanding the 10. Panzer-Division, was wearing the Knight's Cross which had been awarded to him in August 1942.

On the morning of May 12, von Arnim ordered all the wireless equipment at his headquarters to be destroyed, thus cutting communications between himself and his superiors outside Africa. Just after midnight on the 12th/13th, the Afrikakorps sent its last operational signal: 'Ammunition shot off. Arms and equipment destroyed. In accordance with orders received Afrikakorps has fought itself to the condition where it can fight no more. The German Afrikakorps must rise again. Heia Safari. Cramer, General Commanding.'

At 1.15 p.m. on May 13 the Germans radio station in Rome reported to OKW: 'The last German radio station in Africa (Army Station XIII with AOK 1) closed down at 1312 hours. Radio Control Rome is no longer in radio communication with Africa.'

On May 13, in response to emissaries who had arrived from von Arnim's headquarters towards noon, Lieutenant-General Allfrey, commanding V Corps, and General Tuker, the CO of the 4th Indian Division, went to see the German commander at his HQ in the hills north of Sainte-Marie du Zit. Von Arnim insisted that he was not in communication with all his subordinates and that he could only surrender the two headquarters and staffs with him, i.e. Heeresgruppe Afrika and Afrikakorps. Von Arnim, Cramer, and their

Also raising much interest was Generalleutnant Theodor von Sponeck, who had commanded the 90. leichte Afrika-Division. This shot was taken on May 12 just after he alighted from his car after his arrival in New Zealand Division's lines near Bou Ficha. He is seen talking to Generals Keightley and Freyberg.

279

Above left: Surrendering on May 13, Maresciallo d'Italia Giovanni Messe, the C-in-C of the 1a Armata, was taken to Eighth Army headquarters where General Montgomery was waiting to meet him. No doubt Monty was looking forward to expropriating the Italian's caravan for his personal use. The officer holding the maps is General Freyberg. *Above right:* At Algiers, Sergeant Gunn photographed some of the generals leaving the coach that had acted as a prison bus to collect them from the aircraft that had brought them from Tunisia. Among the Germans were General Hans Cramer, commanding the Deutsches Afrikakorps, and Generalleutnant von Broich. The Italians included Generale Giuseppe Costa, second in command of Divisione Centauro, and Generale Alessandro Aporti, Chief of Military Justice with 1a Armata. In September 1943, when negotiating the armistice, the Italians were under the impression that all POWs would be released. Eisenhower also made a speech directed at the Italian government that intimated that Italians captured in Tunisia and thereafter would be repatriated once all the Allied prisoners in Italian hands were safely returned. At the same time, both London and Washington considered the Italian labour force far too important to help alleviate labour shortages. Also, bearing in mind that the Germans immediately took over Allied POW camps in Italy following the armistice, no exchange of prisoners ever took place. However, several of the Italian generals were released to join with the Esercito Cobelligerante Italiano (Italian Co-Belligerent Army) consisting of those units loyal to King Victor Emmanuel, many of which were reconstituted from POWs and armed by the Allies. Messe himself was made Chief-of-Staff of the Co-Belligerent Army.

Chiefs-of-Staff were then sent to General Anderson. Generalleutnant von Sponeck surrendered a few hours later.

Messe sent a signal on the evening of May 12 to the effect that he was ready to negotiate a surrender. He was told to send emissaries and the party, led by Generale Giuseppe Mancinelli, Chief-of-Staff of 1a Armata, arrived at the headquarters of X Corps the following morning. General Freyberg refused any discussion, stating that the terms were unconditional surrender. The emissaries returned, reaching Messe at 12.20 p.m. whereupon he agreed to surrender all his troops, German and Italian. Later on the 13th, Messe, with Generalmajor von Liebenstein, the commander of the 164. leichte Afrika-Division, surrendered to General Freyberg. Messe now holding the rank of Maresciallo, to which he had been promoted the day before. He was the last Marshal of Italy ever.

At 1.16 p.m. on May 13, General Alexander despatched this message to the Prime Minister: 'Sir, it is my duty to report that the Tunisian campaign is over. All enemy resistance has ceased. We are masters of the North African shores.'

In England, Major-General Ernest Gepp, Director of Prisoners of War at the War Office, welcomed Generale di Brigata Flavio Gioia (left), Chief engineer of the XXX Corpo d'Armata, and Generale di Divisione Pietro Belletti (centre), the Artillery Commander of the 1a Armata.

At Maison Blanche airfield in Algiers, Sergeant Gunn pictured Generaloberst von Arnim, the senior officer among the German generals captured in North Africa, as he stretched his legs while being flown to the UK for interrogation.

Following the Anglo-American arrangement regarding the German general officers, the British were to first take custody of all of them before they were transported to Britain. The British received the German generals with a great deal more cordiality than did the Americans. Breaking with customary protocol, Eisenhower simply refused to meet von Arnim while by contrast Alexander hosted him in his tent. On May 15, von Arnim was taken to Gibraltar before being flown to England the following day. Von Arnim ended up in Camp Clinton, Mississippi, but many of the German generals captured in Tunisia were sent to the camp at Cockfosters, north London, for interrogation. *Right:* This shot was taken in November 1943. Front row, sitting: Generalleutnant von Broich, Generalleutnant von Sponeck, Generalmajor von Liebenstein, and Generalmajor Bassenge. Standing, from left to right: Oberst Hans Reimann, Generalmajor Georg Neuffer, Generalmajor Krause, Oberst Otto Köhnke, and Oberstleutnant Ernst Wolters.

During its time as a special prisoner of war camp for high-ranking officers, Trent Park, known as 'The Cockfosters Cage', was home to over 80 generals and a number of lower-ranking staff.

In later years, the building became the campus of the Middlesex University, but since its closure the Grade II listed building has deteriorated, and is currently scheduled for redevelopment.

The air bridge to the Tunisian battlefield ended as a major disaster for the German transport fleet. Coming so soon after the slaughter suffered while trying to resupply the trapped 6. Armee at Stalingrad only five months previously, it left the Luftwaffe transport wings in an appalling situation with virtually no crews left. The repeated Allied bomber and fighter raids on the Tunisian airfields resulted in more losses in planes and personnel, leaving the damaged aircraft waiting for spare parts that proved impossible to obtain or facilities that were badly lacking. After the surrender, the Allies counted over 600 German and Italian aircraft in the areas of Tunis, Bizerte and Cap Bon. With wrecks sprawled all over the runways and tarmac, the airfield at El Aouina was a particularly impressive sight, attracting the attention of numerous photographers. *Right:* This Ju 52 of Kampfgruppe z.b.V. 172 in background appears in good shape. In the foreground, wrecked engines, including one Junkers Jumo 211 from a Ju 88 and one BMW 132 from a Ju 52.

Fruits of Victory

Though events had not worked out as planned — the rush to Tunisia ahead of the Axis back in December had led to failure — all the goals that General Eisenhower had been directed to gain with Operation 'Torch' were achieved by May 1943.

Not only had the Allies had won territory of strategic importance in conquering the whole Mediterranean coast of Africa, but so doing they had inflicted such losses on the Axis powers as to weaken their ability to fight, and, as far the Italians were concerned, undermine their will to fight. In addition, with the whole of North Africa now in their hands, the Allies were in position to intensify their air and sea operations in the Mediterranean and air operations deep into occupied Europe, while airfields in Morocco enabled long-range reconnaissance flights over the Atlantic in the search of U-Boats.

These curious GIs are inspecting the wreck of a six-engined Me 323 Gigant. The burned-out fabric shows the metal tube construction of the fuselage.

Left: A sorry sight at El Aouina airfield. Even so one must not forget what was achieved by the Axis transport squadrons in supporting North Africa: for the period from February 23 to

March 28 only, a total of 3,800 Ju 52s and 160 Me 323s landed at Tunis and Bizerte, and 100 Ju 52s at Sfax. *Right:* The same airfield is now the major Tunis-Carthage airport.

The Luftwaffe completed evacuation of all its serviceable aircraft from Tunisia on May 4 leaving behind wrecks in various stages of destruction. *Above left and right:* Some of the aircraft wrecks, like this FW 190A4, were of the latest type and their study was soon to provide the Allies much new technical information. This one appears to have been on the strength of III./Schnellkampfgeschwader 10, a unit that underwent a name change to III./Zerstörergeschwader 2 the month after it moved to Tunisia in November 1942. *Right:* Several of the wrecks pictured at El Aouina, like this Bf 109F4, were found minus engines, either waiting for a replacement or having been robbed to repair another aircraft. This one belonged to Jagdgeschwader 77, a fighter wing once supporting Rommel's army in Libya which then withdrew to Tunisia to operate there till the end in May. The markings on this particular machine identified it as having belonged to the Geschwader commander, Oberstleutnant Johannes Steinhoff, who took over the group late in March after its famous leader, Major Joachim Müncheberg, was killed in action on the 23rd.

One squadron of Henschel Hs 129s, ground attack aircraft, operated in Tunisia from the first days of December 1942. On the eve of the capitulation, the 8./Schlachtgeschwader 2 reported that it had six aircraft available at El Aouina, of which three were serviceable,

and nine pilots, three of them fit to carry out operations. *Left:* This Hs 129 appears to have force-landed, hence the bent propellers. *Right:* The GIs appear particularly interested in the tiny armoured cockpit and the angled bullet-proof glass of the windscreen.

Left: **At Porto Farina, a fishing village between Bizerte and Tunis, Nick Parrino pictured this SdKfz 7 half-track abandoned on the Sidi Ali El Mekki beach. Almost in a defiant gesture, it appears that this driver drove down into the sea as if to express his desire to cross to Italy.** *Above:* **The same beach today, the village having undergone a name change to Ghar El Melh.**

The defeat in Tunisia marked the end of the German strategic initiative in the West. Coming just after the loss of the 6. Armee at Stalingrad, it was a major blow to the Third Reich and the Axis partnership suffered a severe strain.

After the defeat in May, Hitler attempted to justify his costly and vain decision to hold Tunisia. An unsigned memo captured in Rommel's papers at the end of the war — *The Struggle for the African Outpost, the Balance Sheet of the Campaign in North Africa* — shows how in July 1943 Hitler declared to the principal commanders on the Eastern Front that he had prevented a loss of the war by defending the Tunisian bridgehead. He insisted that the Italians would otherwise have dropped out, allowing the Allies to march to the Brenner Pass unopposed at a time when the Germans were in no condition to stop them there. Hitler insisted that his decision had not only saved the war, but had cost the Allies dearly and had delayed a second front in Europe for six months.

Among the abandoned vehicles, this American M3 half-track has been commandeered by paratroopers who had added their own markings.

At Protville, some 30 kilometres north of Tunis, Axis engineers had blown the bridge over the Medjerda River. US and Royal Engineers quickly replaced it with a pontoon bridge.

After the war, the bridge was rebuilt in traditional French colonial style, but it has since been bypassed by a new bridge. Fortunately, the old stone structure was left in situ.

Whatever may be said against this claim, the fact is that Hitler's decision only gained him a few months, as the second front opened in July in Sicily, and it was only weeks until Italy dropped out of the war. The capture of Sicily in the summer, so soon after the Libyan and Tunisian defeats, was to lead directly to the Duce's downfall and Italy's withdrawal from the Axis in September.

LESSONS LEARNED

Lessons learned from the weeks of fighting in Tunisia were many and the green US Army was quick to learn from the setbacks it faced. Operations reports were reviewed and tactical lessons were extracted to be swiftly taught to troops in training.

Serious deficiencies appeared: in map reading; in the use of the compass and other methods of controlling direction; in movement by stealth and the in avoidance of ambush; in clarity of plans and instructions; in accuracy of reporting; in daylight reconnaissance to prepare for night patrolling, and in control over the members of a patrol. The campaign revealed repeatedly how deployment of infantry in depth and the mutual support of all heavy weapons from positions organised in depth were essential, particularly in resisting armoured attacks.

An impressive Victory Parade was held in Tunis on May 20 with detachments representative of the British, American, and French troops of the First Army. General Eisenhower and Général Giraud took the salute.

This photograph immediately brings to mind Kipling's immortal poem *Boots*, inspired by the sight of marching feet. In April 1885, when he was a 19-year-old correspondent for the *Civil and Military Gazette*, he wrote that 'Thousands of legs all moving together have stopped my sleep altogether'. We are told that if the first four words in each line are read at the rate of two words to a second, that will give the rate at which a foot soldier used to march. Now in another century, in the Victory Parade in Tunis, British army boots once again march across the sands of Africa.

We're foot—slog—slog—slog—sloggin' over Africa —
Foot—foot—foot—foot—sloggin' over Africa —
(Boots—boots—boots—boots—movin' up an' down again!)
There's no discharge in the war!
Seven—six—eleven—five—nine-an'-twenty mile to-day —
Four—eleven—seventeen—thirty-two the day before —
(Boots—boots—boots—boots—movin' up an' down again!)
There's no discharge in the war!

                        BOOTS, RUDYARD KIPLING

The major boulevard bordering the shore of the lake in Tunis, Avenue Gambetta, is now the Avenue Mohamed V.

As the French units began the parade, Cunningham admired the many different uniforms: 'the Foreign Legion, Chasseurs d'Afrique, Tirailleurs, Zouaves, and the Goums in their long, camel-hair robes and slapping sandals'. The march past had been timed to last 90 minutes but it took well over two hours to pass the saluting base, far too long for one of the British officers who was there. He said it was a disappointment as there were practically no bands. Admiral Cunningham explained later why it lasted so long. The French 'naturally wished to impress the Tunisian inhabitants, particularly the Arabs, so they had crowded in many more units than their proper allowance'. Also, the merger of the forces and administrations under Giraud and de Gaulle was still in the future so the Free French contingent refused to join Giraud's troops, preferring instead to march with the British units of the Eighth Army. The parade comprised a massive fly-past with over two hundred bombers and fighters taking part.

Over 50 high-ranking commanders and staff officers of all services stood on the large saluting base situated on Avenue Gambetta. Arrayed behind Eisenhower and Giraud were Generals Alexander and Anderson, Général Juin, Admiral Sir Andrew Cunningham, Naval C-in-C Mediterranean, Vice Admiral H. Kent Hewitt, C-in-C US Naval Forces, and Air Chief Marshal Sir Arthur Tedder, Air C-in-C Mediterranean. Harold Macmillan and Robert Murphy were present as political representatives for Churchill and Roosevelt. Bradley and Patton were relegated to another stand and Montgomery was absent. (He had departed four days earlier for London, claiming that he was in need of a thorough rest.) Altogether, 26,000 troops and tanks, armoured cars and guns took part, the order of precedence being French, American, then British. Admiral Cunningham described the parade as an 'impressive display' and that he was 'greatly struck by the fine appearance of the men of the British First Army.' They were in wonderful fettle, magnificent young men, fit, smart and in great spirits: toughened by their hard fighting and trying winter in the cold and mud.' Cunningham remarked to Macmillan 'that the very sight of them made one proud to be British'.

Left: **US photographer Parrino pictured troops of the 78th Infantry Division (identified by the battleaxe insignia) marching down Avenue Jules Ferry. Here, Général Giraud and other French brass hats take the salute while standing on the steps of the cathedral so, with a different saluting base, it is unlikely** that it shows the main parade on May 20. Although undated, most probably these shots were taken earlier on May 12 when Giraud arrived in Tunis to welcome the return of French authorities to the town. *Right:* **The cathedral still stands the same on the renamed Avenue Habib Bourguiba.**

As for the armoured units, the Tunisian battles had demonstrated that tactics then prevalent in the US Army, of speedy aggressive thrusts, were wrong. Instead, experience showed that tanks had to advance steadily and skilfully, while utilising every available means of reconnaissance and covering fire. Chance of success was greater by taking enough time to prepare an attack thoroughly and to disseminate the plans completely than by hurrying to the offensive in an attempt to get the jump on the enemy. Also, based on experience, the formula was laid down that three battalions of artillery should support one battalion of tanks in an attack.

The Tunisian experience left the air and ground commanders frustrated of the poor coordination that was achieved between air and ground units and in disagreement as to the degree of centralised control over air power that needed to be realised. The conflict remained to be worked out in subsequent months when Allied air resources were more plentiful.

This unidentified French unit has just passed the saluting stand. At the top of the street the parade made a U-turn to pass down the opposite carriageway.

The comparison was taken for us by Amine Bouattour, some distance further down the street so that it included the cathedral.

Spectators were massed at the vantage point of the junction of Avenue de France and Avenue Jules Ferry.

With the passing of the years the maturity of the trees forced Amine to take a position slightly off to the right.

The US Army was quick to learn from the problems it showed in Tunisia in organisation, combat leadership, and operations, and its performance in future operations would show marked improvement.

The Anglo-American coalition had lived through some hard tests during

campaign, with disappointments, frustrations, and recriminations, but General Eisenhower's integrated staff at Allied Force Headquarters proved highly effective and keen to take profit from the knowledge gained.

As far as the great strategy was concerned, as General Marshall had voiced

in the early planning of Operation 'Torch', the Mediterranean diversions were the major cause of the deferment of a cross-Channel attack until 1944. However, as pointed out by George F. Howe in the US official history (*Northwest Africa, Seizing the Initiative in the West*): 'Even if the Allies had succeeded

Understandably there was a huge frisson of excitement at the sign of French troops back in control.

Nevertheless, French colonial rule was finally ended in North Africa in March 1962.

Following the 'Trident' conference held in Washington from May 12-25, the Prime Minister flew to Algiers, via Gibraltar, to spend a week in North Africa. Discussions were held with General Eisenhower and General Marshall about the forthcoming invasion of Sicily with Churchill also spending time touring the battlefield and visiting British and American troops.

Left: On the first day, the Prime Minister was driven to the old Roman amphitheatre at Carthage where he was given a great reception by thousands of soldiers. AFPU photographer Sergeant Arthur Stubbs pictured him with General Anderson on their departure. *Right:* The amphitheatre remains as if time has stood still.

Churchill acknowledges the cheers and applause in his own inimitable style.

Left: **On June 2, the Prime Minister stopped to inspect a captured Tiger I on display in Tunis. This shot shows him acknowledging cheers from the people as he reached the tank.**

Escorting him is his bodyguard, Detective-Inspector Walter Thompson. *Right:* **Sergeant Stubbs pictured him being shown one of the huge 88mm shells.**

in establishing a bridgehead in Normandy in 1943, their experience in Tunisia demonstrated that they would have been unprepared for breaking out of this bridgehead and thrusting far toward the heart of Nazi Germany. This experience they gained by meeting the enemy at the outer periphery of the area to be liberated at a time when the Eastern Front continued to absorb the bulk of Axis military power. The triumph of Allied arms in Tunisia was achieved under conditions which taught them the way to win battles together, to meet and to recover from reverses, and to push on aggressively to the far harder struggle for final victory. For the US Army, the operations in Northwest Africa were of inestimable value in making it a far more efficient fighting force.'

On June 17, King George VI flew to North Africa to meet front line troops. In Algeria, he visited the V Corps, the 78th Infantry Division and the 6th Armoured Division. The following day he went to Tunisia where he inspected a Guard of Honour of the 24th Brigade drawn up on Tunis racecourse. The King was then driven along Avenue Gambetta lined with French troops to see the Tiger which was the first one to be captured intact by the Allies. Later, accompanied by Clark and Patton, the King reviewed American units, and later still with Eisenhower and Alexander, men of the 51st (Highland) Division. For decades it was believed that Tiger '131' was knocked out by Churchill tanks at Djebel Djafia, near Medjez el Bab, on April 21, but new research indicates that it was hit during an attack by 2nd Battalion The Sherwood Foresters on April 24 at Gueriat el Atach, some 15 miles away. The tank was moved to Tunis and shipped to the UK in October 1943. Handed over to the Tank Museum at Bovington in 1951, it underwent a major restoration in 2004, and today, in running condition, Tiger '131' is the most famous exhibit on show.

FRENCH REARMAMENT

Right from the beginning of his contacts with the Americans, Général Giraud made clear he was looking ahead to recreating the French Army which would not only take a hand in driving the Axis from Tunisia but would go on to participate in the liberation of France. The Allies, as stated earlier, promised Giraud, Mast, and the other Frenchmen who had dared work for unopposed Allied landings in North Africa, that they would rearm French troops with modern arms and equipment, promises that were reaffirmed to Darlan by Clark. In January 1943, at Casablanca, Roosevelt gave Giraud an 'Agreement in Principle' to deliver the matériel required for three armoured and eight infantry divisions, as well as 1,000 first-line aircraft, while French naval vessels were to be reconditioned in American shipyards.

The extent and timing of the delivery of arms and equipment was dependent upon events and conditions in the Mediterranean. One difficulty concerned cargo space, priority having to be given to supply Allied forces scheduled to land in Sicily and Italy. Also, the actual delivery of arms to the French was reduced for some months by shortages in armaments and ammunition and the preferential claims of the expanding American Army.

A special convoy of 15 ships loaded with matériel for the French was sent from the USA in March 1943 and ten more ships were planned to follow. The weapons and equipment arriving in April in North Africa were distributed to equip two infantry divisions, two armoured regiments, three tank destroyer battalions, three reconnaissance battalions, 12 anti-aircraft battalions, and ten truck companies. Training in the operation and maintenance of this matériel began even before the shipments arrived.

The aviation programme started a little later, American aircraft arriving at the rate of 60 per month until a total of 200 fighters, dive-bombers, and transports had been delivered. Training of aerial gunners commenced in April and of pilots in June at the rate of 100 for each of the first two months and 50 per month thereafter.

The task of uniting the two free and actively belligerent sections of the French nation — which had accepted leadership from Giraud and de Gaulle — into a single entity was to prove difficult. In spite of the swift victory in North Africa, and the rearmament of the French army successfully underway, the Gaullists vindictiveness to proscribe Frenchmen who had accepted the authority of the Vichy government still did not diminish.

On June 3, the Comité Français de Libération Nationale, CFLN (French Committee of National Liberation) was established in Algiers under the joint chairmanship of Giraud and de Gaulle. While Washington still refused to acknowledge that Giraud was not the right man to handle the hugely complex situation, Eisenhower knew it only too well and on June 22, in a report of the

Rearming the French Army with modern weaponry had been promised successively to Mast at Cherchell, Giraud at Gibraltar, and Darlan's group at Algiers, and was reinforced in January when Roosevelt gave Giraud a signed agreement for the schedule of supplies that he had submitted. Having now been recognised by Roosevelt as the French Commander-in-Chief, Giraud fully committed himself towards the conduct of military operations in Tunisia and in the rebuilding of the French Army. Here he is pictured in May 1943 visiting the front near Zaghouan where the 9ème Régiment de Tirailleurs Algériens had cleared the position on Djebel El Leri on the 10th.

Confident that Roosevelt's signed agreement was a binding contract, Giraud expected the Americans to immediately and vigorously carry out the re-equipping of his troops to reach the target of 11 divisions that had been set at Anfa. However, he was soon disappointed for on January 26, Eisenhower approved that 25,000 tons for each convoy from the United States was 'the maximum tonnage which could be spared for French military equipment' — far too insignificant to enable the Anfa programme to be fulfilled. This decision, and the small material assistance now offered, was totally inconsistent with his recent understanding with Roosevelt and Giraud, so he called on Eisenhower on February 16 to make strong representations as to the 25,000 tons limitations. In October 1943, these French and American soldiers were hard at work in Oran harbour assembling crated GMC trucks just arrived from the USA.

Général de Gaulle arrived in Algiers on May 30. Preliminary exchanges had cleared the way for the creation of the nucleus of an organisation which was eventually to become the Comité Français de Libération Nationale, CFLN (French Committee of National Liberation). *Right:* With supreme powers over the armed forces and civilian administration in North Africa, Général Giraud was in a strong position and could easily afford to extend an affable welcome to de Gaulle when his aircraft landed at Boufarik. De Gaulle, on the other hand, had little influence and his only friends in Algiers were those early associates who attempted to take over before the arrival of Allied forces (see pages 64 and 65). De Gaulle first set up his quarters in the Villa des Glycines, but he soon found the house too small and uncomfortable so in June he moved to the Villa des Oliviers, once occupied by Général Juin. The place was large enough to accommodate his close advisers and also his family so in July de Gaulle's wife Yvonne moved in with their daughter Anne.

Left: Above: The first meeting between the two belligerent sections of the French nation was held at the Palais d'Été on May 31. We were refused access to the building (now renamed the Palais du Peuple) but this postcard from the early 1960s offers a suitable comparison.

Left: This shot was possibly taken on June 1 when de Gaulle held a press conference at the Villa des Oliviers to announce the creation of the CFLN. *Above:* The Villa des Oliviers is now the residence of the French Ambassador to Algeria.

The programme to re-equip the French Army slowly increased, and in February and March some 256,000 tons of equipment were assigned to the French, of which 193,000 tons had reached North African ports by the end of April. This was sufficient to equip three infantry divisions, two armoured regiments, four tank destroyer battalions, five reconnaissance battalions, 14 anti-aircraft battalions, 12 truck companies, and three ordnance battalions. In the Algiers docks, Giraud inspected an M5 light tank that had just been delivered.

From November 1943, the first of the new French divisions joined the Corps Expéditionnaire Français (French Expeditionary Corps) in Italy, followed by a second division in December and two more in the early months of 1944. In January, the Corps took a decisive part in the first battle of Monte Cassino. Here the commander of the 3ème Division d'Infanterie Algérienne, Général Joseph de Monsabert, one of the leading pro-Allied patriots of November 1942, discusses the positions of his forces with Général de Gaulle.

situation to General Marshall, he insisted that Giraud was 'reactionary and old-fashioned' and had 'no, repeat no, political acumen whatsoever'.

In August Roosevelt finally recognised the CFLN as the de facto government of France, 'functioning within specific limitations during the war' after which 'the people of France will proceed in due course to select their own government and their own officials to administer it'.

In September, during the operations in Corsica, Giraud decided to send forces to support the resistance movement on the island, without informing the Committee. This drew more criticism from de Gaulle and other Allied leaders for arming Corsica's Front National, the Communist-dominated resistance group. Consequently, Giraud lost the co-presidency of the CFLN in November, and in April 1944 he finally chose to retire.

As soon as he was able to act, de Gaulle removed those generals and civilian officials who had too willingly followed Vichy's orders and actively opposed the Allied landings in November 1942. One was Général Noguès, who had no other choice but to resign in July 1943. (In 1947, while living in exile in Portugal, Noguès was put to trial in abstentia and found guilty of collaboration. The sentence was loss of civil rights and 20 years hard labour.)

Nevertheless, the swift rearmament of the French Army should be credited largely to Giraud's efforts. Though the rearmament programme was actually slower and smaller than the one Roosevelt had promised in January at Casablanca, results were nevertheless impressive. Units of the renewed French Army were assembled and trained during the summer and from November 1943 the Corps Expéditionnaire Français (French Expeditionary Corps) of four divisions was fighting on the Italian front under the US Fifth Army, soon taking part in the battles at Monte Cassino.

On May 8, an imposing ceremony was held in Algiers for the dual celebration of the fall of Tunisia, just wrested from Axis control, and for the formal handing over to Général Giraud of US matériel recently arrived in North African ports. The speech that General Eisenhower made on this occasion included a message from President Roosevelt: 'American workers,' said the message in part, 'are proud to deliver the goods and weapons to be used by French soldiers.' *Left:* On May 29, 1943, Giraud awarded Eisenhower with the Légion d'Honneur in a ceremony at the Palais d'Été. *Right:* Today, the Algerian Republic holds its own ceremonies in front of the same building, now named Palais du Peuple.

Casualties

As is so often the case, contemporary sources differ making it difficult to determine accurate casualty figures.

Allied casualties in the Tunisian campaign amounted to a total of 72,745: 10,053 killed, 38,583 wounded, and 24,109 missing or captured.

Top: **Chaplain Houle of the 316th Service Group officiated at the burial service for two American soldiers at the Pax Cemetery near Casablanca.** *Right:* **With 60 per cent of all American dead having been repatriated for burial in the United States at the request of the next of kin, the only American war cemetery in Tunisia is at Carthage where 2,841 casualties are interred. In addition, the Wall of the Missing commemorates 3,724 soldiers whose remains were never found.**

The Marine Corps colour party assigned to the American Embassy in Tunis marches past a Tunisian honour guard during a wreath-laying ceremony at the cemetery.

At the Ben M'Sick civilian cemetery at Casablanca, the Western Naval Task Force Marker commemorates the US Western Task Force which landed in Morocco in November 1942.

In eastern Algeria, the Annaba War Cemetery *(right)* contains 868 Commonwealth dead from the Second World War. There are also 14 non-war burials, mostly of merchant seamen whose deaths were not due to war operations, and one from the First World War. In Algeria, 2,260 Commonwealth military casualties now lie in five main cemeteries: three war cemeteries at Dely Ibrahim near Algiers; La Réunion near Béjaïa (Bougie) and Annaba (Bône), and two large Commonwealth sections within civilian cemeteries at Petit Lac near Oran and El Alia near Algiers. There are some 70 Commonwealth war graves in five cemeteries in Morocco but, for a few airmen killed in November 1942, these are casualties that were suffered later in 1943 and 1944. In Tunisia, which was the main battlefield against Axis forces, 10,490 Commonwealth casualties are buried in eight war cemeteries.

Some 30 kilometres south-west of Tunis, the Massicault War Cemetery contains the remains of 1,576 Commonwealth soldiers, 130 being unidentified. Many died in the final drive to Tunis in April and May 1943.

The Medjez el Bab War Cemetery lies 60 kilometres west of Tunis and contains the graves of 2,903 Commonwealth servicemen, 385 of the burials being unidentified. In addition, a memorial bears the names of almost 2,000 men who died during the operations in Algeria and Tunisia between November 1942 and May 1943 and who have no known graves. Trooper Jack Sumner of the 17th/21st Lancers was killed on January 18, 1943, near Bou Arada during the German offensive launched that day. He now lies in Plot 5, Row C, Grave 6.

The situation of the French war dead in North Africa is complex for the military cemeteries and plots also comprised graves of soldiers having lost their lives in the fighting against local tribes in the 18th century, in the First and Second World Wars and in latter periods. In Algeria, there are three French war cemeteries, at Mers el Kebir and Petit Lac, both near Oran, and Sidi Fredj near Algiers. In addition, there are military plots in three civilian cemeteries at Algiers, and one each at Annaba and Blida. A major concentration operation took place after independence and the Petit Lac cemetery now comprises 3,690 identified graves of military dead while the remains of 13,100 unidentified lie in an ossuary.

British losses (including Dominion troops serving with the Eighth Army) amounted to 38,360, broken down as 6,233 killed, 21,528 wounded, and 10,599 missing or captured. Of these, the First Army losses were 25,742: 4,094 killed, 12,566 wounded, and 9,082 missing or captured. These figures are for the period from November 8 hence they include casualties suffered in initial landings in Algeria. Those of the Eighth Army for its campaign in Tunisia (from February 9, 1943) were 12,618: 2,139 killed, 8,962 wounded, and 1,517 missing or captured.

American losses in the Tunisian campaign, November 12, 1942 to May 13, 1943, were 18,221, broken down as 2,715 killed, 8,978 wounded, and 6,528 missing or captured, these totals being taken from a report compiled in April 1945.

French losses in the renewed fight against the Axis, from November 20, 1942 through to the end in May 1943, amounted to 1,105 killed, 8,077 wounded and 6,982 missing, a total of 16,164.

North of Tunis, at Gammarth *(right)*, **the largest war cemetery in Tunisia comprises 1,871 individual graves, with another 2,318 in an ossuary. Another cemetery was established at Takrouna containing 235 French soldiers who died in the fighting in the winter of 1942 and spring of 1943. There are also two war cemeteries for Muslim soldiers from the French Army: at Tarf Ech Chena (442 burials) near Bou Arada, and at Haffouz (317 burials) just west of Kairouan.**

In Morocco, the French war grave commission now cares for seven cemeteries: at Rabat, Fès, Meknès, Marrakech, Agadir, Kénitra and Ben M'Sick. At Ben M'Sick near Casablanca, 111 French sailors killed in November 1942 were interred in Section 23.

Badly neglected since the independence of Algeria, the old French cemetries in the country, civilian and military, have been subjected to attacks by Islamist vandals for the last two decades. *Left:* **The worst incident took place in 2005 when nearly all of the 1,300 crosses in the Mers el Kebir cemetery** were smashed. *Right:* **Consequently, in 2006, the Direction de la Mémoire, du Patrimoine et des Archives of the defence ministry undertook a large programme for rebuilding the cemetery, the crosses now having been replaced by headstones flush with the ground.**

Axis casualties in the battles in Tunisia, other than the deaths of prisoners, numbered over 12,000 killed made up of 8,500 Germans and 3,700 Italians.

Axis casualties during the Tunisian campaign are uncertain but it is estimated that the Germans lost at least 8,500 men killed and the Italians 3,700. Over 40,000 Axis soldiers were wounded but as only a small proportion could be transferred to Italy before the surrender, a sizeable number are included in the figures given below for prisoners. The US Official History gives an estimated total of 275,000 Axis soldiers captured, and an 18th Army Group calculation of prisoners taken from March 20 to May 13 gives a grand total of about 245,000. Allied records covering unwounded prisoners held on May 25 give a total of 238,243: 101,784 Germans, 89,443 Italians, and 47,017 of nationality unspecified.

The German cemetery at Bordj Cedria *(below)* east of Tunis, was built between 1973 and 1975 to concentrate all the graves in Tunisia. The programme entailed the removal of the dead from six large field cemeteries at Bizerte, Sfax, Mateur, El M'Dou near Gabès, Naassen south of Tunis, and La Mornaghia, west of Tunis, and transferring them to Bordj Cedria, where there are now individual ossuaries, one for each of the initial field cemeteries. In the central courtyard, a memorial stone bears the inscription in Arabic, German and French: 'In this cemetery, 8,562 German soldiers rest from 1939 to 1945'.

There is no Italian military cemetery in Tunisia. The remains of those Italian soldiers killed (or who died in captivity) in Morocco, Algeria and Tunisia were removed to the Sacrario dei Caduti Oltremare (War Memorial of the Fallen Overseas) established at Bari *(below left)*, in the Apulia region of southern Italy. The burials there are divided into ten sectors, each corresponding to a different theatre and/or time period, of which four comprise remains of soldiers who died in the three countries where Operation 'Torch' and the ensuing battles took place. The Bari Military Cemetery contains the remains of 75,098 Italian soldiers, of whom 29,051 are known, 5,675 known but not identified, and 40,372 unknown. *Below right:* A memorial at Takrouna (see page 265) commemorates the soldiers of the Divisione Folgore killed in Tunisia at Mareth, Wadi Akarit and Takrouna. The Italian Ambassador at Tunis holds an annual ceremony there in April, the anniversary of the Takrouna battle, attended by an honour guard of the Tunisian army and the military attachés of the embassies accredited in Tunisia.

In January 1943, Hollywood stars Martha Ray, Carol Landis and Kay Francis chatted with a local at a crossroads west of Algiers.

Photograph Credits

Copyright is indicated for all original illustrations where known. Unless otherwise stated, the present-day comparisons are the copyright of the author and/or After the Battle.

Tatar Adlene: 236 centre right.
Ad'O: 49 top, 49 centre right, 50 top right, 50 bottom right, 51 centre right, 52 bottom, 53 top right, 53 bottom right.
After the Battle Archives: 10 top, 11 top, 12 top, 12 centre, 36 top, 36 bottom, 37 top right, 37 bottom, 39 top, 47 bottom, 48 top, 77 top left, 78 bottom left, 79 top left, 114 top, 114 bottom, 115 top, 115 bottom left, 116 bottom, 117 top, 117 centre left, 117 centre right, 117 bottom left, 118 top left, 118 centre, 118 bottom left, 119 centre left, 119 bottom, 120 top left, 120 centre, 121 top, 121 centre, 121 bottom, 156 bottom left, 157 top, 171 top, 172 top, 176 bottom left, 178 top left, 178 centre, 178 bottom left, 179 top left, 179 centre, 179 bottom left, 180 top, 181 top left, 181 centre, 184 centre, 184 bottom left, 187 top left, 187 top right, 187 bottom, 194 centre, 195 bottom left, 195 bottom right, 197 top, 197 bottom right, 200 bottom, 202 bottom, 208 top left, 208 top right, 208 bottom left, 226 top left, 229 bottom, 230 top, 238 top left, 240 bottom left, 241 bottom left, 242 top left, 243 top, 243 centre left, 244 top right, 246 bottom, 249 centre, 251 top, 253 top left, 254 top left, 254 centre, 254 bottom, 255 top left, 259 top left, 259 bottom, 260 top, 260 bottom, 265 bottom left, 266 top left, 266 bottom left, 267 bottom left, 268 bottom, 270 top left, 270 centre, 271 top, 271 centre, 271 bottom left, 273 top left, 277 top left, 279 top left, 279 top right, 279 bottom, 280 top left, 280 top right, 280 bottom, 283 top right, 283 bottom left, 283 bottom right, 284 bottom, 292 bottom left, 294 centre, 294 bottom left.
El Akramine: 135 bottom.
AlgeriArt: 293 bottom right.
Andalucia.com: 46 bottom.
Mohamed Riadh Benbouali: 64 bottom right, 68 top right, 70 bottom, 76 bottom, 78 centre right, 292 bottom right.
Tiziana Bianchi: 297 bottom right.
Amine Bouattour: 157 bottom, 161 centre right, 161 bottom right, 162 bottom, 163 centre right, 273 bottom, 287 top right, 287 bottom right, 288 top right, 288 bottom right.
Samir Bouzidi: 148 bottom.
Bundesarchiv: The name of the photographer is given where known. 168 top (Bild 101I-549-0742-22, Arppe), 174 top left (Bild 101I-049-0008-32, Fenske), 174 centre right (Bild 101I-049-0008-30, Fenske), 174 bottom left (Bild 101I-049-0008-34, Fenske), 175 top left (Bild 101I-788-0006A-25A, Wörner), 175 centre right (Bild 101I-788-0006A-28A), 175 bottom left (Bild 101I-788-0006A-27A, Wörner), 230 bottom (Bild 101I-557-1018-26A, Arppe), 231 top (Bild 101I-557-1020-33A, Arppe), 231 bottom left (Bild 101I-557-1020-27A, Arppe), 232 top left (Bild 101I-557-1020-18A, Arppe), 232 bottom left (Bild 101I-557-1023-30A, Arppe), 232 bottom right (Bild 101I-557-1020-05A, Arppe), 233 top (Bild 101I-557-1020-26A, Arppe), 233 centre left (Bild 101I-557-1023-26A, Arppe), 233 bottom (Bild 101I-557 1022-26A, Arppe), 234 top left (Bild 101I-557-1022-02A, Arppe), 234 top right (Bild 101I-557-1022-05A, Arppe), 238 bottom left (Bild 146-1978-118-27A), 263 centre right (Bild 101I-419-1878-10, Seltsam), 263 bottom (Bild 101I-419-1878-36, Seltsam), 281 centre right (MSg 2 Bild-14835-006).
Cegesoma: 11 centre right, 11 bottom left.
Charles: 271 bottom right.
US Consulate, Casablanca: 191 bottom right.
Continent 8 Technologies Ltd: 56 bottom.
François Denis: 113 bottom, 115 bottom right.
Abdelatif Djerboua: 77 top right, 78 bottom right, 79 top right, 81 bottom, 166 bottom right, 167 top right, 182 centre right, 186 centre right, 196 top right.
Établissement de Communication et de Production Audiovisuelle de la Défense (ECPAD): The name of the photographer is given where known. 10 bottom left (DAT 57 L05), 13 top (Vichy 100-1798, Pierre Potentier), 40 top (Terre 7-84), 40 bottom (Terre 6-59, Marcel Viard), 41 top left (Vichy 100-1817, Pierre Potentier), 41 bottom left (Marine 352-3498), 41 bottom right (Terre 152-3375, Jacques Belin), 42 top (Vichy 254-4563, Crespi), 42 bottom

(Terre 40-779), 43 top (Vichy 256-4577, Crespi), 43 bottom (Vichy 256-4578, Crespi), 44 top (Air 9-300, A. Rolando), 44 centre right (Air 9-297, A. Rolando), 44 bottom (Air 9-294, A. Rolando), 45 top (Air 42-7-R110), 45 bottom left (Air 9-283, A. Rolando), 45 bottom right (Air 9-273, A. Rolando), 52 top (ALG 57-233 R27, Jacques Bouchenoire), 53 top left (ALG 57 233 R01, Jacques Bouchenoire), 53 bottom left (ALG 57-233 R33, Jacques Bouchenoire), 54 top (ALG 57-233 R21, Jacques Bouchenoire), 54 bottom left (ALG 57-233 R20, Jacques Bouchenoire), 64 top (Vichy 150-3135), 64 bottom left (Vichy 150-3138, Crespi), 65 top (Terre 120-2457), 152-153 (DAK 265 L21), 154 top (DAA 2580 L07), 155 top (DAA 2580 L10), 155 bottom (DAK 289 L01), 156 top (DAA 2580 L12), 156 bottom right (DAK 265 L08), 158 top left (DAK 269 L09), 158 top right (DAK 271 L02), 158 bottom left (DAT 1744 L09), 159 top left (DAT 1744 L01), 159 top right (DAA 2580 L04), 159 bottom (DAK 273 L02), 160 top (DAK 268 L04), 160 bottom (DAK 265 L02), 161 top (DAK 267 L12), 161 bottom left (DAK 267 L13), 162 top (DAK 267 L15), 163 top (DAK 267 L18), 163 bottom left (DAK 268 L19), 167 bottom left (Terre 3-34), 167 bottom right (Terre 6-66), 168 centre left (DAK 271 L10), 170 top (DAT 579 L01bis, Friedrich), 170 bottom (DAT 1751 L06, Friedrich), 171 bottom (DAK 275 L14), 172 bottom (DAT 596 L02, Dullin), 173 top (DAT 596 L07, Dullin), 173 bottom (DAT 595 L07, Dullin), 182 top (Terre 8-90), 182 bottom left (Terre 5-54), 185 bottom right (Terre 42-815), 196 top left (Terre 3-28), 196 bottom (Terre 3-23), 197 bottom left (Terre 9-112), 202 top (DAK 157 L30), 202 centre right (DAA 3184 L15, Helmuth Pirath), 203 top (DAT 1742 L25), 203 bottom left (DAT 1742 L09), 203 bottom right (DAT 1742 L26), 204 top left (DAT 1743 L05), 204 top right (DAT 1743 L08), 204 centre right (DAA 3184 L31, Helmuth Pirath), 204 bottom (DAT 1743 L23), 210 bottom (DAK 145 L01), 213 bottom (DAK 151 L21), 214 top left (DAK 156 L26), 214 bottom (DAK 156 L09), 215 top (DAK 156 L29), 215 bottom (DAK 145 L07), 216 top (DAK 282 L10), 216 bottom left (DAK 282 L02), 217 top (DAK 282 L22), 217 centre (DAK 282 L28), 219 top (DAK 152 L22), 219 bottom (DAK 146 L33), 220 top left (DAK 154 L02), 220 top right (DAK 154 L01), 220 centre right (DAK 146 L07), 220 bottom left (DAK 146 L03), 221 top left (DAK 146 L26), 221 centre right (DAK 145 L21), 221 bottom left (DAK 154 L20), 222 top left (DAK 153 L22), 222 centre right (DAK 154 L10), 223 top (DAK 154 L25), 223 bottom left (DAK 154 L30), 224 top (DAK 152 L28), 228 bottom (Terre 27-487, Rolando Lévêque), 259 top right (Terre 50-978), 285 bottom (Terre 61-1144), 290 centre right (Terre 73-L12276), 291 top (Terre 59-1083), 291 bottom (Terre 115-L2366), 292 top (Terre 65-1191), 292 centre left (Terre 65-1199), 293 top left (Terre 34-625), 293 top right (Terre 223-4927), 293 bottom left (Terre 63-1164), 303 (DAK 153 L34).

Eisenhower Library: 18 top.
Saidou Ellul: 99 top right, 99 bottom right.
Tony Evans: 38 top right.
Frédéric Gaillot: 296 bottom right.
Daniel Gonzalvez: 87 bottom right.
Google (reproduced under licence): 69 centre right, 91 top right, 116 top, 116 centre right, 194 top, 213 top right, 250 bottom, 261 bottom, 266 bottom right, 267 centre right, 267 bottom right, 268 centre right.
Jean Goubet: 282 bottom right.
Steve Hamilton: 265 centre right.
Hanane el Hamrani: 123 bottom.
Nathan Harig: 57 bottom.
Kevin Hymel: 136 bottom right.
Institut National de l'Audiovisuel: 49 centre left, 50 top left, 50 centre right, 50 bottom left, 51 top left, 51 top right.
Imperial War Museum: 150 top left (NA 238).
Dennis Jarvis: 163 bottom right.
Philippe Landru: 183 bottom right.
Mario Leddo: 92 bottom.
Library of Congress: 15 bottom, 22 top, 22 bottom left, 23 top, 23 bottom, 28 bottom, 29 top, 29 bottom, 30 bottom, 31 bottom left, 31 bottom right, 32 top, 32 bottom, 33 top, 33 bottom, 34 top, 35 centre, 35 bottom, 41 top right, 76 top, 89 top, 89 bottom left, 138 top left, 138 bottom, 169 centre left, 169 bottom, 177 bottom, 188 top, 190 top, 190 centre left, 191 top right, 191 bottom left, 192 centre, 195 top left, 205 top left, 212 bottom, 237 top, 250 top, 251 bottom, 252 top, 261 centre, 262 top, 262 bottom right, 263 top left, 263 top right, 274 top, 276 top, 278 bottom, 282 top, 282 centre, 282 bottom left, 283 centre, 284 top left, 286 top left, 286 bottom, 287 top left, 287 bottom left, 288 top left, 288 bottom left, 297 top, 305, 307, 308.
Majid Majid: 95 bottom, 101 bottom.
El Maroqui: 122 bottom.
Omar Mecheri: 185 centre right.
Jalel Hadj Moussa: 150 top right.
Muszka: 89 bottom right.
Naval History and Heritage Command: 8-9, 14 top left, 14 top right, 14 bottom, 28 top, 71 bottom left, 102 top, 103 bottom, 104 top, 105 top, 105 bottom, 106 top, 106 bottom, 107 top, 108 top, 108 bottom, 110 bottom, 113 top, 119 top, 126 top, 129 top, 130 top, 132 top, 132 centre, 132 bottom, 133 top, 133 bottom, 134 top right, 139 top, 140 top, 140 bottom, 141 top, 141 centre, 141 bottom, 143 top, 144 centre.
Nikitsonev: 154 bottom.
NIOD: 168 bottom, 195 top right.
Norfolk Navy Yards: 22 bottom right.
OT-Adda: 100 bottom.
Ouest France: 296 bottom left.
Matthew P: 150 bottom.
The War Graves Photographic Project: 295 centre.
Sacrario dei Caduti Oltremare: 297 bottom left.
Nacer Sandjak: 72 bottom.
Society for the Studies of the ETO: 12 bottom left, 15 top left, 17 top left, 18 bottom, 19 top, 24 top, 27 top, 38 top left, 58-59, 60 top, 60 bottom, 61 top, 66 top, 66 bottom, 67 top, 67 centre right, 68 top, 68 bottom, 69 top, 69 bottom left, 70 top, 72 top, 73 top, 74 top, 75 centre right, 80 top, 82 top, 82 bottom, 83 top, 83 bottom, 84 top, 85 top,

86 top left, 86 centre right, 86 bottom left, 86 bottom right, 90 top, 92 top, 93 bottom right, 94 bottom, 95 top, 101 top left, 148 top, 149 bottom, 150 centre right, 151 top, 164 top, 165 top left, 165 bottom left, 165 bottom right, 169 top left, 169 top right, 176 top, 185 top, 188 bottom left, 189 top, 191 centre left, 200 top left, 200 top right, 205 top right, 205 centre right, 208 centre right, 226 centre right, 226 bottom left, 226 bottom right, 239 top, 243 bottom, 252 bottom, 255 bottom, 255 top right, 258 top, 258 bottom, 264 top, 264 bottom, 265 top, 272 bottom, 275 top, 275 centre right, 275 bottom, 278 top, 281 top left, 281 top right, 283 top left, 285 top, 289 top left, 289 bottom, 290 top left, 290 top right, 290 bottom.
Summer's Adventure: 39 bottom.
Adel el Touati: 71 bottom right.
US National Archives: Front cover, front endpaper, 2-3, 13 bottom, 16 top, 16 bottom, 19 bottom, 26 bottom, 31 top, 35 top left, 35 top right, 38 bottom, 46 top, 47 top, 55 bottom, 56 top, 57 top, 63 top, 63 bottom, 71 top, 74 bottom, 75 top, 75 bottom, 77 bottom, 78 top, 79 bottom, 80 bottom, 81 top, 87 top, 87 bottom left, 88 top, 88 bottom, 90 bottom left, 91 top left, 91 bottom, 92 centre, 93 top, 93 bottom left, 96 top, 96 bottom, 97 top, 97 bottom, 98 top, 98 bottom, 99 top left, 99 centre, 99 bottom left, 100 top, 101 centre, 102 bottom, 103 top, 104 bottom left, 104 bottom right, 109 top, 111 bottom, 112 top, 112 bottom left, 122 top, 123 top, 125 top left, 125 centre, 127 top, 127 bottom left, 127 bottom right, 128 top, 130 bottom, 131 bottom, 134 top left, 134 bottom, 135 top, 136 top, 136 bottom left, 137 top, 137 centre, 139 bottom, 142 top, 142 bottom, 144 top left, 144 bottom left, 145 top left, 145 centre, 146 top left, 146 centre, 146 bottom left, 147 top left, 147 centre, 147 bottom left, 151 bottom, 165 top right, 166 top, 166 bottom left, 167 top left, 183 top left, 183 top right, 183 centre, 183 bottom left, 184 top left, 185 bottom left, 186 top, 186 centre left, 186 bottom left, 189 bottom left, 190 bottom, 192 top left, 193 top, 193 bottom left, 198-199, 205 bottom left, 206 top, 207 top left, 207 centre, 209 top, 210 top, 212 centre, 213 top left, 218 bottom, 227 top left, 227 bottom left, 228 top left, 229 top left, 229 top right, 229 centre, 234 bottom, 235 top left, 235 bottom, 236 top, 236 centre left, 236 centre, 236 bottom, 237 bottom, 244 top left, 245 top, 245 centre, 246 top, 247 top, 247 bottom, 248, 249 top left, 249 bottom left, 256-257, 266 top right, 267 top, 268 top, 272 top left, 273 centre, 276 bottom, 277 centre, 284 bottom left, 286 centre, 294 top, 298, 300, rear endpaper.
US National Archives (maps): 84-85, 110, 111, 124, 131, 218, 224-225.
Dirk Verwimp: 88 centre right.
Abdul Wadud: 101 top right.
Alan Waters: 176 bottom right, 222 top right, 240 top, 241 bottom right, 242 top right, 253 top right, 254 top right, 295 bottom left, 295 bottom right.
Bruce White: 15 top right.
Arif Yelles: 54 bottom right, 86 top right.
Mohamed Zidi: 169 centre right.

The green American troops had received a rough baptism of fire in their first encounter with German forces in southern Tunisia in February 1943. The Kasserine setback was a blessing in disguise for it occurred over a year before the main campaign in Western Europe, and the US Army was quick to learn and rewrite army doctrines, particularly for the armour.

Index

COMPILED BY PETER B. GUNN

Note: Page numbers in *italics* refer to illustrations. There may also be textual references on these pages.

Marjory Collins, Office of War Information photographer pictured wrecked Axis aircraft at El Aouiana airfield near Tunis. **Amongst the wrecks were several Henschel Hs 129s and the burned-out remains of a six-engined Messerschmitt Me 323.**